PENNY STALLINGS

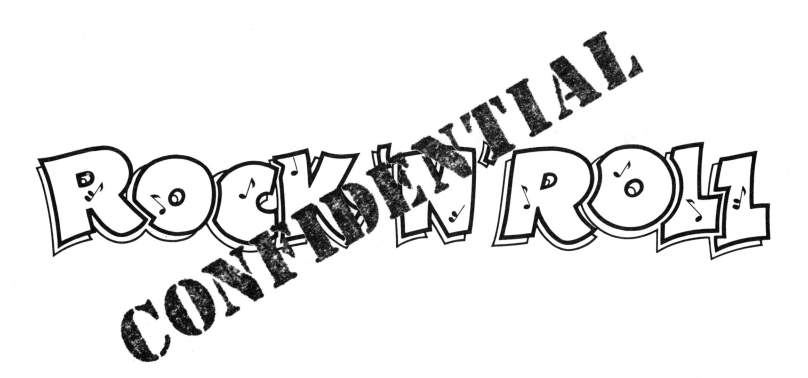

VERMILION
London Melbourne Sydney Auckland Johannesburg

The author gratefully acknowledges the following for permission to reprint:
"Our Last Show" by Sonny Bono, copyright © Chris Marc Music 1974; "Your Own Back Yard" by Dion DiMucci and Tony Fasce, copyright © 1970 Wedge Music, Inc./Aliben Music;

Vermilion & Company
An imprint of the Hutchinson Publishing Group
17–21 Conway Street, London WIP 6JD

Hutchinson Publishing Group (Australia) Pty Ltd
PO Box 496, 16–22 Church Street, Hawthorne, Melbourne, Victoria 3122
PO Box 151, Broadway, New South Wales 2007

Hutchinson Group (NZ) Ltd
32–34 View Road, PO Box 40-086, Glenfield, Auckland 10

Hutchinson Group (SA) Pty Ltd
PO Box 337, Bergvlei 2012, South Africa

First published in the USA by Little, Brown and Company 1984
First published in Great Britain 1985

PRINTED AND BOUND IN THE UNITED STATES OF AMERICA

BRITISH LIBRARY CATALOGUING IN PUBLICATION DATA

Stallings, Penny
    Rock 'n' roll confidential.
    1. Rock music — Pictorial works
    I. Title
    784.5'4'00222   ML3534
    ISBN 0-09-153811-4

CONTENTS

INTRODUCTION 6

BORN TO BE WILD 8

THERE BUT FOR FORTUNE 18

LOOK SHARP 42

FIRST I LOOK AT THE PURSE 68

AIN'T NOTHIN' LIKE THE REAL THING 80

LOOK WHAT THEY DONE TO MY SONG, MA 108

CAN'T STOP THE MOVIES 132

YOU CAN'T DO THAT 148

THE GREAT ROCK 'N' ROLL RUMORS 160

ONLY YOU KNOW AND I KNOW 166

WHO'S MAKIN' LOVE WITH YOUR OLD LADY
(WHILE YOU WAS OUT MAKIN' LOVE) 186

ROCK 'N' ROLL HEAVEN 188

LIFE IN THE FAST LANE 224

SO YOU WANT TO BE A ROCK 'N' ROLL STAR? . . . 242

INDEX 255

ACKNOWLEDGMENTS 256

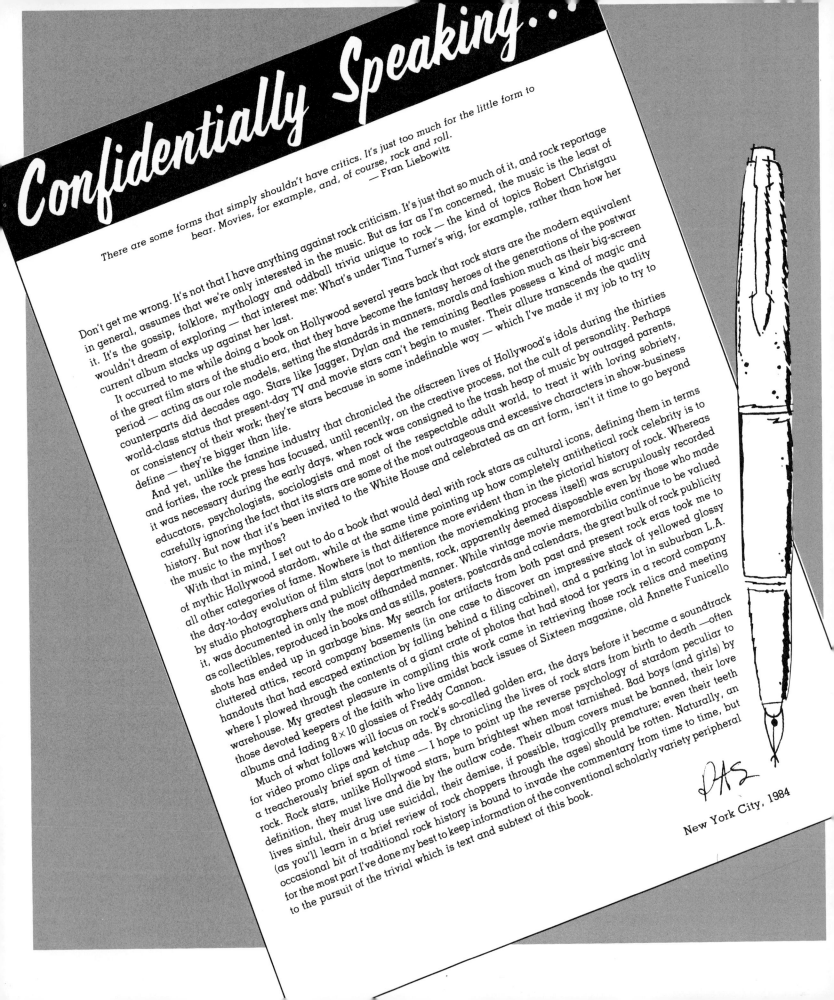

Confidentially Speaking...

There are some forms that simply shouldn't have critics. It's just too much for the little form to bear. Movies, for example, and, of course, rock and roll.
— Fran Liebowitz

Don't get me wrong. It's not that I have anything against rock criticism. It's just that so much of it, and rock reportage in general, assumes that we're only interested in the music. But as far as I'm concerned, the music is the least of it. It's the gossip, folklore, mythology and oddball trivia unique to rock — the kind of topics Robert Christgau wouldn't dream of exploring — that interest me: What's under Tina Turner's wig, for example, rather than how her current album stacks up against her last.

It occurred to me while doing a book on Hollywood several years back that rock stars are the modern equivalent of the great film stars of the studio era, that they have become the fantasy heroes of the generations of the postwar period — acting as our role models, setting the standards in manners, morals and fashion much as their big-screen counterparts did decades ago. Stars like Jagger, Dylan and the remaining Beatles possess a kind of magic and world-class status that present-day TV and movie stars can't begin to muster. Their allure transcends the quality or consistency of their work; they're stars because in some indefinable way — which I've made it my job to try to define — they're bigger than life.

And yet, unlike the fanzine industry that chronicled the offscreen lives of Hollywood's idols during the thirties and forties, the rock press has focused, until recently, on the creative process, not the cult of personality. Perhaps it was necessary during the early days, when rock was consigned to the trash heap of music by outraged parents, educators, psychologists, sociologists and most of the respectable adult world, to treat it with loving sobriety, carefully ignoring the fact that its stars are some of the most outrageous and excessive characters in show-business history. But now that it's been invited to the White House and celebrated as an art form, isn't it time to go beyond the music to the mythos?

With that in mind, I set out to do a book that would deal with rock stars as cultural icons, defining them in terms of mythic Hollywood stardom, while at the same time pointing up how completely antithetical rock celebrity is to all other categories of fame. Nowhere is this difference more evident than in the pictorial history of rock. Whereas the day-to-day evolution of film stars (not to mention the moviemaking process itself) was scrupulously recorded by studio photographers and publicity departments, rock, apparently deemed disposable even by those who made it, was documented in only the most offhanded manner. While vintage movie memorabilia continue to be valued as collectibles, reproduced in books and as stills, posters, postcards and calendars, the great bulk of rock publicity shots has ended up in garbage bins. My search for artifacts from both past and present rock eras took me to cluttered attics, record company basements (in one case to discover an impressive stack of yellowed glossy handouts that had escaped extinction by falling behind a filing cabinet), and a parking lot in suburban L.A. where I plowed through the contents of a giant crate of photos that had stood for years in a record company warehouse. My greatest pleasure in compiling this work came in retrieving those rock relics and meeting those devoted keepers of the faith who live amidst back issues of Sixteen magazine, old Annette Funicello albums and fading 8 × 10 glossies of Freddy Cannon.

Much of what follows will focus on rock's so-called golden era, the days before it became a soundtrack for video promo clips and ketchup ads. By chronicling the lives of rock stars from birth to death —often a treacherously brief span of time — I hope to point up the reverse psychology of stardom peculiar to rock. Rock stars, unlike Hollywood stars, burn brightest when most tarnished. Bad boys (and girls) by definition, they must live and die by the outlaw code. Their album covers must be banned, their love lives sinful, their drug use suicidal, their demise, if possible, tragically premature; even their teeth (as you'll learn in a brief review of rock choppers through the ages) should be rotten. Naturally, an occasional bit of traditional rock history is bound to invade the commentary from time to time, but for the most part I've done my best to keep information of the conventional scholarly variety peripheral to the pursuit of the trivial which is text and subtext of this book.

New York City, 1984

ROCK 'N' ROLL CONFIDENTIAL

BORN TO BE

Would it surprise you to know that Debbie Harry grew up in suburban New Jersey and Bruce Springsteen pumped gas after school? That Jimi Hendrix was a Boy Scout back in Seattle and Patti Smith was voted Senior Class Clown? Sounds normal enough, doesn't it? Well, don't kid yourself. Rock stars are different from you and me.

That difference usually starts to manifest itself in high school, where members of the Future Rock Stars Club tend to be outsiders — if not full-fledged rejects. Debbie Harry probably seemed normal enough back at Hawthorne High School if you ignored the fact that her French twist was a different color every week. "I must have had ten or twelve different colors of hair," she recalls. "There was no color I didn't try, including green, even if it was a mistake."

Bruce Springsteen? Well, apparently The Boss was your classic pizza-faced nonentity in high school — one who is remembered only as a pimply youngster with a Beatle haircut who liked to play the guitar. By the time he got to Ocean County Community College, however, Bruce had managed to make a very distinct impression upon faculty and fellow students — it seems he was resoundingly disliked, so much so that a student ad hoc committee once petitioned to have him thrown out.

At sixteen, Jimi Hendrix dropped out of high school to join the army, but was back on the street in a matter of months — after his penchant for simulating electronic sound effects and sleeping with his guitar convinced the base psychiatrist that Jimi himself was a few strings short.

On the reverse side of the coin was the teenaged Patti Smith, who won all sorts of popularity contests for being true to her school. The only problem was that she never had any dates: "I was horny, but I was innocent 'cause I was a real late bloomer. At dances in South Jersey, I'd lurk about in my limp taffeta and fantasize about Dylan. My James Dean, my knight. He'd walk across the dance floor, cold and alone, take me in his arms and we'd do the strand to 'A Million to One.' "

Most likely, Debbie and Bruce and Jimi and Patti — like everyone else — wanted desperately to be accepted when they were growing up. But there was something different about them, something that held them apart, even then. For Frank Zappa, it was his Leo Carrillo mustache and Elvis Presley pompadour. ("I was always old," he once observed. "I had a mustache when I was twelve.") For the young Pete Townshend it was his nose. "It was huge," he says. "It was the reason I did everything. It's the reason I played the guitar . . . the reason I wrote songs. When I was in school the geezers that were snappy dressers and got chicks would always talk about my nose. This seemed to be the biggest thing in my life; my fucking nose."

Like a lot of other artistic types and belated high achievers, most rock stars tend to be loners during their Wonder Years. In the long run, though, they are well served by the peer rejection they endure since the resentment, eccentricity and ambition it

triggers help to make for a first-class rebel hero. Once sprung from the hell of high school, they soon discover that the very qualities that kept them out of the In Crowd as kids are what qualify them for rock stardom.

Still, it's a long way from class reject to pop idol. There was a time when an aspiring star's public persona was manufactured by the studio publicity department; names were changed, personalities redrawn, and personal histories were laundered and puffed up like fairy tales. But today we like our pop heroes to have colorful backgrounds — the raunchier the better. A rags-to-riches saga, a stretch in the funny farm or the pen, can be the hook on which a career is hung. Of course, not everyone is lucky enough to be born in a cross-fire hurricane — to have started life in a backwoods shanty, like Elvis, or to grow up poor and blind like Ray Charles. So most would-be rock stars are obliged to invent their own legends. Ex–navy brat Jim Morrison spiced up an otherwise undistinguished past by killing off his middle-class parents in early record company bios. Vincent Furnier overcame the shame of being a minister's son by putting on a dress and calling himself Alice. For Perry Miller, do-it-yourself mystique was a simple matter of changing his white-bread moniker to the more romantic-sounding Jesse Colin Young. The same would be true for Ronald Crosby (Jerry Jeff Walker), Henry John Deutschendorf (John Denver), Martin Buchwald (Marty Balin), Pauline Matthews (Kiki Dee), John Simon Ritchie (Sid Vicious), and Louis "Butch" Firbank (Lou Reed). There are more, of course, but these are some of the best.

Some ordinary kids have gone to extremes to cultivate an aura of misanthropy and the semblance of Funk that are so necessary to rock star mystique. Eric Clapton once admitted to an interviewer that the reason he'd first started using heroin was because he'd heard it was junk that made Ray Charles sound so soulful. Whatever his secret, it worked. Clapton came across as the very embodiment of the blues. He may have been a regular Joe, but his audiences were convinced his melancholy was for real; that he'd Paid His Dues.

Rock's roots lie in the rural South and urban ghettos, but for nearly two decades now, most of the reigning crop of popsters have been spawned by the great American and British middle class — as you will see when you look at the sprouts pictured in the vintage photographs in this rock family album. Consider the sad-eyed Elvis Presley posed in front of a cheap painted backdrop in a Tupelo photographer's studio versus the young John Lennon in his smart grammar-school duds; and the eight-year-old Grace Slick as a little princess perched regally in front of the family piano versus Brenda Lee, not much older, as a hard working hillbilly trouper. For the most part, these pictures won't look a lot different from the family portraits that hang on your mother's bedroom wall. Yet, if you study their subjects closely, you'll notice that while most still bear the bloom of innocence, some — though still children — are already stars.

WILD

ROCK and ROLL

PHOTO ALBUM

THEY ONLY LOOK NORMAL...

Elvis Aron Presley
Tupelo, Miss 1947

Brenda Lee
1956

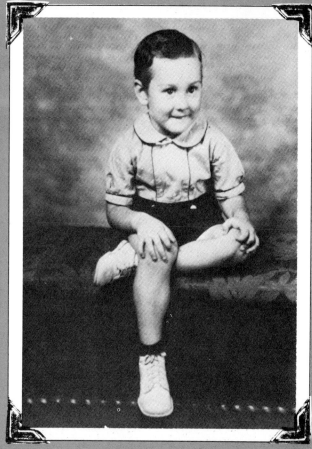

Charles Hardin Holley
Lubbock, Texas 1940

Charles Edward
Anderson Berry
St. Louis, Mo. 1939

Riley B. King, age 16

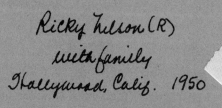

Ricky Nelson (R)
with family
Hollywood, Calif. 1950

Carol Klein
James Madison High
Brooklyn, N.Y.
Class of '58

Neil Sedaka with his mother
Brooklyn, N.Y. 1949

Paul Anka
with sister
Ottawa, Canada 1948

Joan Baez
age 10

Gordon Lightfoot
Orillia, Ontario 1950

Robert Allen Zimmerman & friend
Hibbing, Minnesota 1955

Tommy Roe
Age 1

Brian Wilson
Hawthorne, Calif. 1951

Steveland Judkins Morris
Detroit, Michigan 1960

Gladys Maria Knight
Age 8
Winner Original Amateur Hour
National Championship
1952

Aaron Neville
Age 7
New Orleans, La.

Nona Hendryx
age 15

Donovan Phillip Leitch
Hatfield, England 1961

John Winston Lennon
Liverpool, England 1948

George Harrison
Liverpool, England 1947

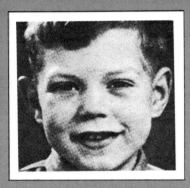

Michael Philip Jagger
Dartford, Kent, England
1951

Keith Richards
Dartford, Kent, England
1952

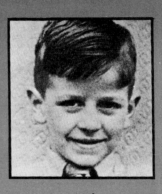

Richard Starkey
Liverpool, England
1949

James Paul McCartney
Liverpool, England 1950

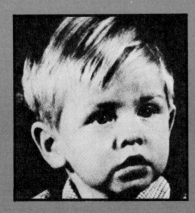

Brian Jones,
6 yrs.
England 1946

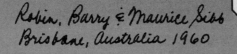

Robin, Barry & Maurice Gibb
Brisbane, Australia 1960

13

Janis Joplin
Port Arthur, Texas
1951

Grace Barnett Wing
San Francisco, Calif.
1947

Diane Ross
Cass Technical School
Detroit, Michigan

Francis Vincent Zappa
Antelope Valley High
Lancaster, California
Class of 1958

Henry John Deutschendorf, Jr.
Arlington Heights High
Fort Worth, Texas
Class of 1961

Reginald Kenneth Dwight
Pinner, Middlesex, England
1957

14

Martin
Buchwald
San Francisco,
Calif.

Kris Kristofferson
San Mateo High
San Mateo, Calif.
Class of 1954

Linda Ronstadt
Catalina High
Tucson, Arizona
Class of 1963

Stephen Demetri Georgiou
London, England 1962

Howard Duane Allman
Seabreeze Senior High
Daytona Beach, Fla
Class of 1964

Gregory Lenoir Allman
Seabreeze Senior High
Daytona Beach, Fla
Class of 1965

Rod Stewart with father
North London 1946

Lowell George
Hollywood High
Class of 1968

Bruce Springsteen
Freehold High
Freehold, N.J.
Class of 1967

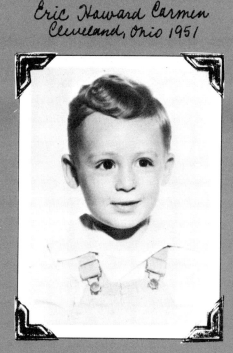

Eric Howard Carmen
Cleveland, Ohio 1951

Roger Daltrey
Age 2

Barry Manilow
Eastern Dist. H.S.
Class of 1964
Brooklyn, N.Y.

David Cassidy
Rexford High School
Beverly Hills, Calif.
Class of 1967

Peter Frampton
Beckenham, Kent.
England 1952

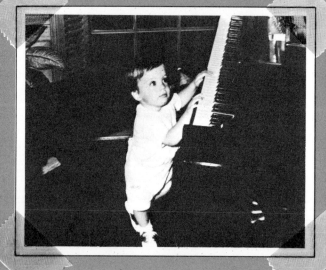

Shaun Cassidy
Beverly Hills, Calif.
1960

Peter Townshend
Age 10
London, Eng.

Keith Moon
Age 2

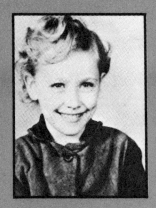

Dolly Parton
Sevierville, Tenn.
1954

Vincent Furnier
Detroit, Michigan 1957

John Beverly
1968

Patti Lee Smith
Woodbury Gardens, N.J.
1954

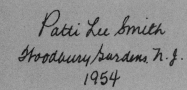

Gene Klein
Newton High Queens, N.Y.
Class of 1968

Michael Jackson Age 7
Detroit, Mich

Yoko Ono
Tokyo, Japan
1939

Nicolette Larson
8 years

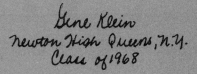

17

THERE BUT FOR FORTUNE

Tommy Chong in Bobby Taylor and the Vancouvers

Dozens of makeshift rock groups scored regional and national hits during rock's golden era, but for most, the first hit would be the last. . . .

"Look, anybody can be a rock star if they put their mind to it. That's what makes rock'n'roll so great is that somebody like me can actually be a star."
— ELTON JOHN

Used to be, if you wanted to get real famous real fast in the entertainment biz, you headed for Hollywood. Breaking into films was just about the best way going to become a household word overnight. For one thing, being a movie star didn't mean you had to have artistic pretensions or that you actually had to act. All it took was a touch of charisma and the ability to play oneself.

The requisites for stardom remain pretty much the same today; the only difference is that for some time now, the road to instant fame and fortune has been paved with Top Ten gold. Instead of imagining themselves up there on the Big Screen, most starstruck kids dream of black leather, stacks of amps and basketball arenas full of screaming fans. In other words, if Bogart or Dean were starting out tomorrow, he'd join a rock'n'roll band.

Why spend your time parking cars and pumping gas till someone notices you in that bit part on *Love Boat* when a hit record can catapult you to full-blown celebrity overnight? Consider how many stage, screen and TV notables have parlayed success in the pop marketplace into a "legit" show-biz career. It seems rather improbable, for example, that Hollywood would've tapped *meeskites* like Bette Midler, Ringo Starr and Willie Nelson for sought-after starring roles had they not already proven their pop appeal. And cute as he is, Kris Kristofferson would likely never have gypsied his rangy hips onto the silver screen without all those crossover country hits. David Bowie, Al Green, Linda Ronstadt and Cher all used their home-run hit records as springboards to featured roles on Broadway. Even Tommy Chong, movie star, film director and one half of the world's preeminent hippie comedy team, began his illustrious career as a pompadoured guitarist with a bad-ass rock group called Bobby Taylor and the Vancouvers. (He penned their first and only hit, "Does Your Mama Know About Me?") Not surprisingly, pop has also found its way into the political arena of late. Although he'd probably just as soon you forgot it, the honorable Mike Curb sashayed himself into the 1976 California lieutenant governor's seat by way of countless sappy pop hits and the soundtracks of such screen favorites as *Mondo Teeno.*

In the primordial days of rock when Elvis, Jerry Lee, Little Richard and Chuck Berry were first getting up in front of people to perform, no one set out to use his pop status as a launching pad to mainstream show-biz standing — mainly because back then, rock'n'roll stars didn't exist. By the mid-fifties, of course, these men had defined rock stardom simply by being; rock'n'roll was who they were and what they did. Before long, almost every kid in the country wanted to do it too.

This meant that for a while during the fifties, rock'n'roll existed as an authentic form of youthful expression — teen music played with unbridled glee by teenage performers. Talent scouts and small-time producers began to scour big-city street corners and neighborhood talent shows in search of kids to record. By the sixties, the craze for do-it-yourself rock spread from urban centers to suburban America. With the onset of the British Invasion a few years later, almost any amateur musician with a souped-up guitar, a few friends of like-minded persuasion and a place to rehearse out of parental hearing could transform himself into a neighborhood rock celeb. Once a group had mastered three or four Top Ten hits, they were ready to test their performing prowess at countless low-paying gigs. (Bruce Springsteen and Billy Joel are two of many who got their start playing Beatle tunes at Piggly Wiggly openings and VFW halls.) Dozens of amateur rock groups scored regional and even national hits during this period. Some kept at it for many years afterward, but for most, the first hit would be the last. Those few who did manage to stick it out found that staying in The Business usually meant backing Helen Reddy or working in a record store.

Of course, for every kid who played on a hit record, there were thousands more who nurtured dreams of rock stardom on through high school and sometimes well into college — only to kiss them good-bye on graduation day. Some hung in a few more years — crashing at friends' apartments and selling nickel bags to get by. Sometimes it seemed as if it wasn't talent that separated rock royalty from the peasants so much as the ability to subsist on a brown rice diet and sleep on the floor.

Billy Joel camped out in Long Island laundromats rather than return home in disgrace following the breakup of his high-school band, the Hassles. And at fifteen, Chaka Khan had already left home to share a railroad flat on Chicago's tough North Side with her group, the Shades of Black. "There were eight or nine of us living together as a family," she recalls, "doing four sets a night, living on welfare and stealing money."

The training ground for rock stars is no bed of roses;

19

The Band as the Hawks

those ambitious enough to stick it out
have a tendency to grow up fast. While playing
in a psychedelic-style band called Hourglass,
Duane and Gregg Allman lived in a run-down
Sunset Strip motel until they collided head on
with stark reality one morning in 1967. "I happened
to look in the next room," recalls Gregg, "and there's this
cat lying on the floor covered with a blanket. Cop standing
there. The cat had left a note and downed 95 Seconals. That was
the first dead body I ever saw." Taking this ugly episode to be an omen,
brother Duane decided to chuck his dreams of Beatlesque stardom and return
to honest work as a sessionman in Muscle Schoals. "Fuck this whole thing," he
told his little brother. "Fuck wearing these weird clothes and playing this 'In a
Gadda da Vida' shit." It was there in Muscle Shoals, of course, that he would
finally begin to acquire the recognition he'd been seeking so long.

Bonnie Bramlett headlined parking lots and bowling alleys as Marion of Marion
and the Riots before teaming up with Delaney Bramlett. Leon Russell backed
Frank Sinatra and put in time with the Shin-Dogs (as did Billy Preston), the house
band for the sixties TV show. Delbert McLinton spend twenty-five years ducking
beer bottles in Texas honky-tonks before waxing his first hit record. And these
were the lucky ones.

Most aspiring rock stars have to pursue a nine-to-five grind to subsidize their
passion. Elvis Costello was a computer programmer, Chuck Berry a hairdresser,
Chubby Checker a part-time chicken plucker; Rod Stewart was a gravedigger
and Bill Withers installed toilets on 747s until he finally hit with "Ain't No Sun-
shine" at the age of thirty-seven. Pat Benatar spent years studying to be an opera
singer, but for a time, she earned her living as a singing waitress in a Virginia
diner. "It was horrible," she recalls. "I used to sing Diana Ross songs with blue
cheese dressing on the front of my uniform."

After being rejected by every record company in L.A., Frank Zappa opened
a porno-to-go business in Cucamonga, California, which specialized in
custom-made skin flicks with "the fetish-of-your-choice" for 300 bucks.
Zappa's Studio Z flourished until the local vice squad raided it,
resulting in the arrests of both Zappa and his associate, a
certain Miss Belcher. Soon after, Zappa split for Hollywood
with a band he'd put together at Studio Z, which would
come to be known as the Mothers of Invention.
Others who used their sexual savvy to pay the
rent while struggling to establish them-

Cass Elliot in the Mugwumps

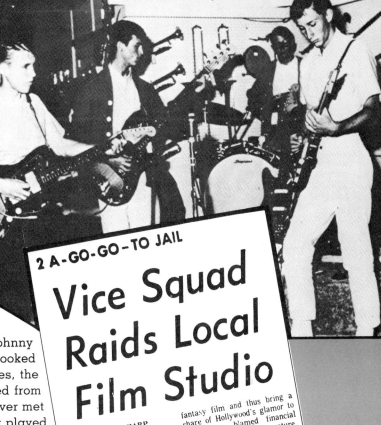

selves in pop include Debbie Harry, who did time as a Playboy bunny following the breakup of her folk group, the Wind in the Willows, and disco queen Sylvester who starred in the Cockette review, the celebrated transvestite burlesque troupe. (Of whom literary gadfly Gore Vidal once observed, "It's simply not enough just to be untalented.") One of the Village People made ends meet as a male escort with a New York "dating service," and before being tapped to head up the Plasmatics, Wendy O. Williams acted the part of a dominatrix in a live sex act on New York's fabled Forty-second Street.

Speaking of which, the unlikely rise to stardom of the Mohawk-fringed Wendy demonstrates that, though rare, there are a few Cinderella stories in rock — for like Fabian, Marianne Faithfull and Johnny Rotten, Wendy was recruited to be a rock star primarily because she looked the part. This was likewise the case with the members of the Monkees, the Runaways, the Village People and the Sex Pistols, who were plucked from obscurity and packaged to cash in on an ongoing craze. Most had never met before they were first brought together to perform, and few had ever played or sung before they met. Some — like Rick Nelson, David and Shaun Cassidy and Natalie Cole — sailed into pop stardom on their famous names; others — like Cilla Black and Mary Hopkin — were virtually handed hit records by illustrious friends. A few pop success stories read like the script of a Busby Berkeley movie — such as the one in which Evelyn "Champagne" King was discovered by a record producer as she hummed a Sam Cooke tune while scrubbing the floor in a Philadelphia office building. On the other hand, the tale that has Diana Ross discovering the Jackson Five at a Gary, Indiana talent show is about as factual as the one starring Lana Turner on a stool at Schwab's.

For most, making the climb to rock stardom has meant bouncing from one dinky group to another and taking any gig, no matter how meager the pay, until that first breakthrough hit. So let us return then to those thrilling days of yesteryear for a look at some of rock's greatest names as journeymen musicians and struggling unknowns.

Dusty Springfield in the Springfields.

2 A-GO-GO-TO JAIL

Vice Squad Raids Local Film Studio

By TED HARP

CUCAMONGA — Vice Squad investigators stilled the tape recorders of a free - swinging, a-go-go film and recording studio here Friday and arrested a self - styled movie producer and his buxom, red - haired companion.

Booked on suspicion of conspiracy to manufacture pornographic materials and suspicion of sex perversion, both felonies, at county jail were:

Frank Vincent Zappa, 24, and Lorraine Belcher, 19, both of the studio address, 8040 N. Archibald Ave.

Rent Movie

The surprise raid came after an undercover officer, following a tip from the Ontario Police Department, entered the rambling, three-room studio on the pretext of wanting to rent a stag movie.

Sgt. Jim Willis, vice investigator of the San Bernardino County Sheriff's Office, said the suspect, Zappa, offered to do even better — he would film the movie for $300, according to Willis.

When Zappa became convinced the detective was "allright," he played a tape recording for him. The recording was for sale and it featured, according to police, Zappa and Miss Belcher in a somewhat "blue" dialogue.

More Enter

Shortly after the sneak sound preview, the suspect's hopes for a sale were shattered when two more sheriff's detectives and one from the Ontario Police Department entered and placed the couple under arrest.

Zappa, who recently was the subject of a news story on his hopes to produce a low - budget fantasy film and thus bring a share of Hollywood's glamor to Cucamonga, blamed financial woes for his latest venture.

Inside his studio when the raid came was recording and sound equipment valued at more than $22,000, according to Zappa.

Musical Instruments

Also, a piano, trap drums, vibraphones and several electric guitars were stored among the Dalhian litter of the main studio. On the walls, Zappa had hung such varied memorabilia as divorce papers, a picture of himself on the Steve Allen television show, a threat from the Department of Motor Vehicles to revoke his driver's license, several song publishers' rejection letters and works of "pop" art.

Among Zappa's completed musical scores were such titles as "Memories of El Monte" and "Streets of Fontana."

The latter, written before several utility companies had forsaken the budding composer, opens:

'Sweeping Streets'

"As I was out sweeping the streets of Fontana.

As I was out sweeping Fontana one day,

I spied in the gutter a moldy banana.

And with the peeling I started to play . . .''

Assisting Sgt. Willis in the raid were sheriff's vice investigators Jim Mayfield and Phillip Ponders, and Ontario detective Stan McCloskey.

Arraignment for Zappa and Miss Belcher next week will bring them close to home. Cucamonga Justice Court is right across the street from the studio.

Elvis Presley in the Blue Moon Boys

Roy Orbison and the Teen-Kings

Waylon Jennings and the Crickets at their last date with **Buddy Holly** in Clear Lake, Iowa, February 2, 1959

Jim Seals and **Dash Crofts** in the Champs   **Levon Helm** in the Hawks

Sam Cooke in the Soul-Stirrers

James Brown and his Famous Flames

Jackie Wilson in the Dominoes

Chuck Berry and the Chuck Berry Combo

Clyde McPhatter in the Dominoes

25

Little Anthony Gourdine in the Duponts

Wilson Pickett in the Falcons

Phil Spector in the Teddy Bears

Al Kooper in the Royal Teens

Gene Chandler in the Du-Kays

Bert Convy in the Cheers

Art Garfunkel as Artie Garr

ARTIE GARR

Ben E. King in the Drifters

Curtis Mayfield in the Impressions

Nona Hendryx, Patti LaBelle
and **Sarah Dash** as the Blue Bells

Minnie Riperton in the Gems

Smokey Robinson in the Miracles

Teddy Pendergrass in the Blue Notes

Jimi Hendrix as Jimmy of Jimmy James and the Blue Flames

Lamonte McLemore, Ron Townson, Marilyn McCoo, Billy Davis and **Florence Gordon** of the Fifth Dimension as the Versatiles

THE TARRIERS

Including:
MY NAME IS MORGAN
BUT IT AIN'T J. P.
LITTLE BOXES
CRAWDAD SONG
GUANTANAMERA
SAN FRANCISCO BAY BLUES
COME ON IN THIS HOUSE
QUINTO

Alan Arkin in the Tarriers

John Phillips and **Scott McKenzie**
in the Wayfarers

Cass Elliot in the Big 3

STEREO

The BIG 3

FM

John Denver in the Chad Mitchell Trio

THE CHUCK BARRIS SYNDICATE

SINGING 'BAJA CALIFORNIA'
A DOT RECORD RELEASE

Chuck Barris in the Chuck Barris Syndicate

Kenny Rogers in the First Edition

Paul Williams in the Holy Mackerel

Stephen Stills in the Au Go-Go Singers

Eric Clapton in the Yardbirds

Ringo Starr in Rory Storme and the Hurricanes

Van Morrison in Them

Jimmy Page in the Yardbirds

Bev Bevan and Jeff Lynne in the Move

Graham Nash in the Hollies   Steve Marriott, Kenny Jones and Ronnie Lane in the Small Faces

Bob Seger in the Decibels

Daryl Hall in Gulliver

Rick Derringer in the McCoys

34

Gram Parsons in the International Submarine Band

David Crosby and **Roger McGuinn** in the Byrds

Carl and **Brian Wilson** performing at a Hawthorne High School assembly

David Bowie as Davy Jones, with the Lower 3rd

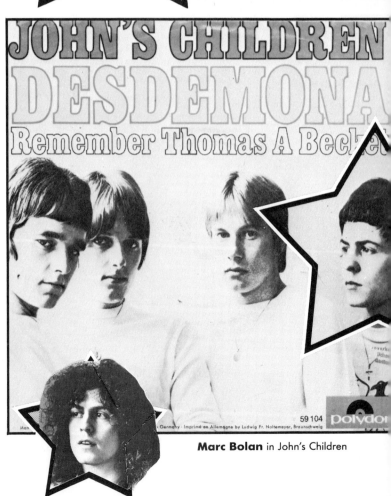

Marc Bolan in John's Children

Jeff Beck, Rod Stewart and **Ron Wood** in the Jeff Beck Group

Ron Wood in the Birds

Peter Frampton in the Herd

Mark Farner and **Terry Knight** in the Pack

Iggy Pop in the Iguanas

na33
NOT WRONG LONG b/v ⎯⎯ THE ICE

Todd Rundgren in the Nazz

Leslie West in the Vagrants

Steve Tyler in the Chain Reaction

DO NOT CROSS DEPT.

Eric Carmen in Cyrus Erie

Billy Joel in the Hassles

CARP

Produced by Dan Moore and Buzz Clifford
Arranged by Carp

EPIC
E 30212

Side 1
DRINK TO THE QUEEN OF THE MAY (2:15)
Words: G. Busey
Music: R. Getman
CIRCUIT PREACHER BROWN (2:30)
Words: G. Busey
Music: R. Getman and G. Busey
HE'S COMIN' BACK TO CHECK ON
    WHAT YOU'VE DONE (3:10)
Words: G. Busey
Music: R. Getman and G. Mitchell
PINE CREEK BRIDGE (3:10)
Words: G. Busey
Music: R. Getman and J. Crowder
ROSABELLE BOVINE (2:00)
Words: G. Busey
Music: R. Getman and G. Mitchell

Side 2
JOTHAM CLAY, MISSISSIPPI (2:46)
Words: G. Busey
Music: R. Getman
THE GREAT KANSAS HYMN (4:10)
Words and Music: Michael McGinnis
MAMMOTH MOUNTAIN BLUES (2:50)
Words: G. Busey
Music: R. Getman, J. Crowder, G. Mitchell
    and G. Busey
THERE GOES THE BAND (2:00)
Words: G. Busey
Music: J. Crowder, G. Busey and R. Getman
JESUS IS THE MOUNTAIN (4:45)
Words: G. Busey
Music: R. Getman and G. Busey
THE FIREHOUSE DOG (2:00)
Words and Harmonica: G. Busey
Mouth Percussion and Strings: R. Getman
    and J. Crowder

Carp was formed in the spring of 1966 by four
Oklahoma State University students looking
to pick up some extra money. Gary Busey on
drums, guitarist Ron Getman, John Crowder
on bass and Glen Mitchell playing honky-tonk
piano make up the group.
    Carp is one of the few groups that doesn't
sound like somebody else. While every other
group is imitating the Airplane and sixteen
girls sound like Bessie Smith, Carp cuts
through the chocolate-pudding texture of rock
to come up with an open, easy sound.
Carp doesn't knock you over with a wall of
sound; these are basic harmonies and simple,
solid rhythms.
    The lyrics aren't a series of disconnected
images strung together or a ponderous account
of how hard life is; they tell a story of life
in the early West and South. Some deal with
Jesus. And there are a couple of blues thrown in.
This is Carp's first album. Listen.

CARP is THANKF...
"Bouncin'" "Bo...
GOES THE BAND...
Sneaky Pete—Steel...
BROWN and THERE G...
THANX to:
Don "Tazmanian Devil" Mo...
for their vocal inspiration in...
HE'S COMIN' BACK TO CHECK...
ON WHAT YOU'VE DONE, PAGE 2...
PINE CREEK BRI...
Also, Gordon Shryock: PINE CREEK BR...
    We thank our Mammoth Mountain Friend,
one and all.

Publishing Company on all songs except: T...
Great Kansas Hymn is TRASHFISH TUNE...
Publishing on The Great Kansas Hymn:
SPEED MUSIC, BMI.

Thanks to our "stylish" engineer:
Alex Kazenegras.

Gary Busey in Carp

Bruce Springsteen in the Castiles

Deborah Harry in the Wind in the Willows

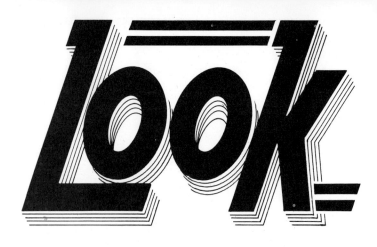

"People are more interested in what Boy George's socks are like than in what his voice is like: they understand he has a good voice — but what about his socks?"
— MALCOLM MCLAREN

"Basically rock stardom comes down to the cut of your trousers."
— DAVID BOWIE

So you want to be a rock'n'roll star? Well, if you aim to catch the public's fancy, you'd better Look Sharp. A flashy exterior does more than make the world glance in your direction; it suggests that a unique sensibility dwells within. Although official party line has sometimes required that rock musicians dismiss fashion as frivolity, the real heavies are well aware of its impact and they cultivate it accordingly. The many faces of Bob Dylan (world-weary bard, mod hipster, heavy-metal mime) point up just how hard even the most reluctant pop idols work on their images. In the long run, the stars with the greatest staying power are those with the ability to negotiate radical stylistic transition gracefully and inspire others to follow suit. Mick Jagger, David Bowie, Dylan, Cher — these are the special few who redefine pop chic every time they appear in a new guise.

Once society swells and movie stars inaugurated the clothing trends that Seventh Avenue knocked off and the hoi polloi rushed to imitate. But from the moment kids got their first look at Elvis Presley, the standards of populist chic would be set by rock's dedicated followers of fashion. Their affectations and adornments — Elvis's sideburns, Cher's bell-bottoms, Janis's see-through blouses —turned the fashion world inside out. Style became the province of the young as more and more fans proclaimed their undying devotion to their Fave Raves by aping the way they looked. Eventually even haute couture's *ancien régime* would come to worship at the altar of youth.

Pop chic has become a commodity unto itself — one that sometimes survives the music craze or star that first brought it to life. In a sense that's what happened with punk. While punk music itself (whatever *that* was) has long since been coopted by mainstream pop, the costume and cosmetic vogues it introduced continue to flourish among rock stars and civilians alike. The punk movement was barely a year old when the garment industry flooded department stores with mass-produced imitations of the calculated disarray affected by groups like the

1956   1957   1962   1964   1967   1969

SHARP!

Sex Pistols, the Dead Boys, the Damned, Blondie and the Ramones. And though those groups are now defunct or faltering, the pastel-colored hair and biker fashions they pioneered can still be seen everywhere from suburban malls to the pages of trendy fashion slicks like *Bazaar* and *Vogue* (which christened the spiky punk hairdo that is all the rage this season "the windblown look"). Punk has become a fashion staple — a standard embellishment for designer collections and a sartorial rite of passage through which millions of teenagers here and abroad now pass on their way to more grown-up concerns. (The look has become so accessible that "punk day" has replaced "tacky day" as the traditional year-end costume party at hundreds of American high schools.) Thus what started out as an angry antiestablishment statement born of the anger and frustration of down-and-out Britishers has ended up being appropriated by the very people it was meant to offend — straights and fashion hounds. By rushing to cash in on this, the latest Youth Craze, commercial profiteers make a mockery of the mockery, thereby providing the impetus for their youthful antagonists to come up with the next style sensation.

In the last few years fashion tie-ins have become so heavy-handed that you sometimes see a pop clothing fad being marketed right along with records. (Devo's recent albums carry a printed order form for Club Devo, the group's accessory house, which markets a wide variety of futuristic fashion products that include the official Devo jumpsuit at $13.50, red plastic "energy dome" hats at $6.00, and Devovision 3-D sunglasses at a very reasonable $1.25.) But that may be because today's bands know that eventually everything ends up being converted into consumer artifacts anyway. By seizing control of that process, they mean to make pop fashion merchandising itself an art form — or at least eliminate the middleman.

Granted, this kind of approach is relatively new. Up until around the mid-sixties, teen fashion crazes, not to mention the stars who launched them, had a tendency to catch the world of commerce with its pants down. No one could predict when the Next Big Thing would hit, least of all teenagers themselves. They were at a loss to explain why they wanted to look like Elvis one minute and Dylan the next. One thing was certain though: if you had to ask, you'd never know.

But if we're going to talk about rock'n'roll fashion, why don't we start at the beginning — back when Pop Chic was more a state-of-mind than a mass-produced item that could be bought off the rack . . .

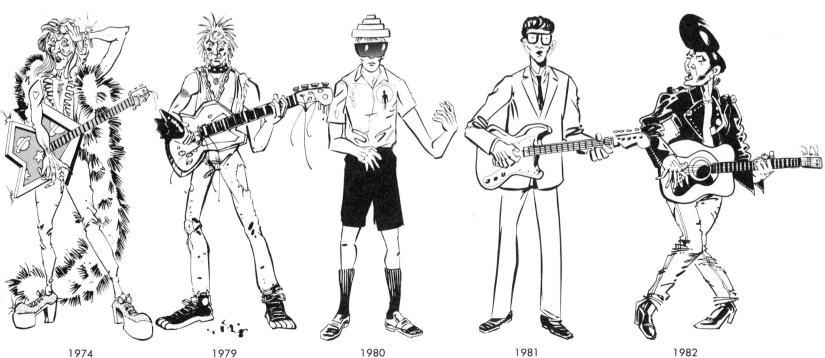

1974   1979   1980   1981   1982

A white sportscoat and a pink carnation; in the fifties members of rock'n'roll groups dressed alike — usually in a zooted-up version of typical Big Band wear.

Bill Haley and the Comets

Johnny and the Hurricanes

Little Richard

The Isley Brothers

Damita Jo

Jerry Butler

Just as R&B was more up front with regard to language and sexual imagery than white pop music of the day, so were its stars more flamboyant in their approach to fashion. The exaggerated cut and bawdy spirit of the stagewear worn by the likes of Chuck Berry, Little Richard, and Solomon Burke were a reflection of that worn by the hipsters, flipsters and finger poppin' daddies who made the black club scene during the forties and fifties. It was the provocative touches — Damita Jo's cleavage, the cartoon-like shape and drape of the Isleys' zoot suits — that transported early R&B fashion into an entirely different realm.

Black musicians may have been looser and more lavish in their sartorial approach, but it was Elvis Presley who first disseminated the Cool Cat look to the masses. His unblushing narcissism launched the Peacock Revolution in male clothing, simply by making it acceptable for men to exhibit an interest in fashion, something that had been considered unmanly in the uptight fifties.

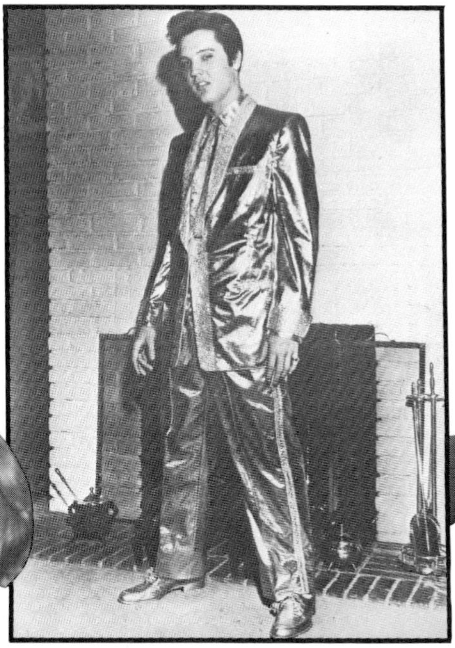

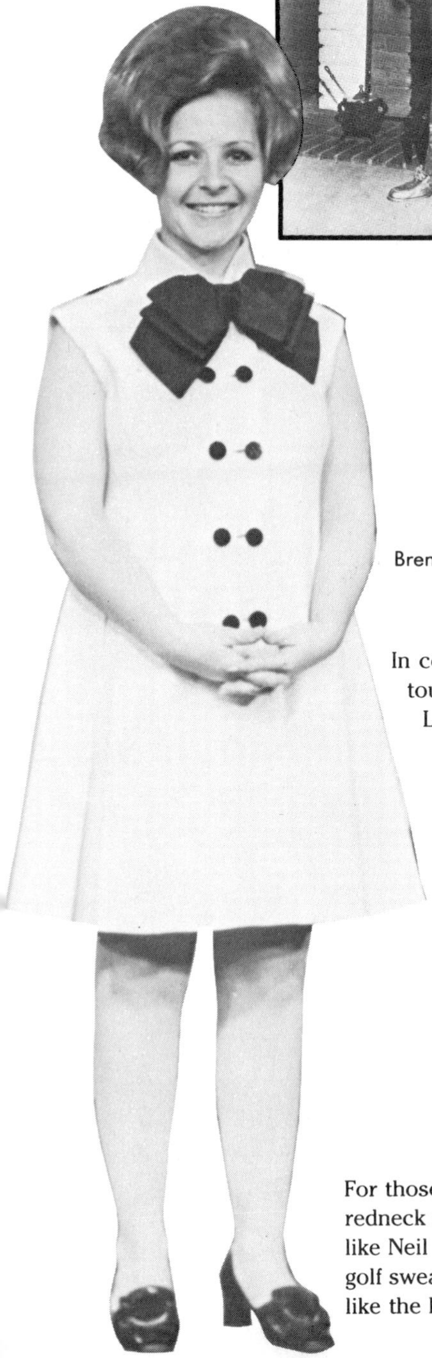

Brenda Lee

Right: Neil Sedaka; *below:* Johnny Tillotson, and Frankie Avalon

In contrast to primal rockers like Elvis, Vincent, Jerry Lee et al., who looked as tough as their music sounded, the handful of girl-next-door types like Brenda Lee, Connie Francis and Annette Funicello, who scored hits during rock's early years, dressed for photos and public appearances as if they were going to a church social or out on a date. Their junior deb shirtwaists, petticoats, hair ribbons and French heels were meant to make them look Cute, and to emphasize femininity rather than sex.

For those who liked rock'n'roll but were turned off by its early redneck fashion aesthetic, there were wash'n'wear alternatives like Neil Sedaka, Frankie Avalon, and Johnny Tillotson, whose golf sweaters, white bucks and Sunday suits made them look like the kind of boy a girl could take home to mother.

45

The Shangri-Las

The Dixie Cups   The Ronettes

The stiletto heels, plastic go-go boots and skintight cha-cha pants worn by members of sixties girl groups like the Ronettes and the Shangri-Las introduced a car hop's sense of glamour to rock fashion. Okay, so they weren't exactly liberated, but they were the first mainstream women rockers to confront both their own sexuality and that of their music.

Like Motown's juke-box spirituals, the Motown Look (ball gowns for the women, gussied-up tuxedos for the men) was an outgrowth of Berry Gordy's desire to broaden the appeal of his product so as to attract mainstream white audiences. Created by in-house dressmakers often according to Gordy's own specifications, Motown stagewear was sassy, flashy and opulent, expressly designed to lend a touch of class to the talented ghetto kids who wore it. Here three girls from Detroit's Brewster Projects model vintage Motown chic.

The Supremes

Bob Dylan

David Bromberg

Melanie

By dressing the same way offstage as on, the folkies of the early sixties became the first pop clique to use fashion as a means of extending their public image into real life. The tattered jeans and weather-beaten work clothes affected by Dylan, Tom Rush, David Bromberg, et al. were meant to suggest the footloose existence of the wandering troubadour while at the same time mirroring the working-class heroes their music extolled. Likewise, the standard-issue boho wear (black turtlenecks, tights, leotards) and gypsylike getups favored by Joan Baez and others of her ilk during this period were at once earnest and contrived, a look meant to convince audiences, as well as themselves, of their lofty intentions and disdain for convention.

Tom Rush

The Hollies

Patti Boyd

The Beatles (ca. 1964)

The next major fashion shakeup that grew out of the pop music scene was initiated by the Beatles and in time the various other groups of the British Invasion. It was those first photos of the Fab Four in their lapel-less suits and pointy Beatle boots (an Anglicized version of Cuban roach killers) that detonated the mod explosion of the mid-sixties. Although its heyday was brief, Carnaby Street reigned as the fashion capital of the world, and mod designers like Mary Quant and Ossie Clark emerged as international stars. Thanks to the healthy consumer economy of the period, mod became the first pop fashion to be fully exploited by Seventh Avenue (personalized Elvis products notwithstanding) as affluent young consumers bought mass-produced miniskirts, bell-bottoms and Beatle boots by the millions. While the mod uniform (Continental suits, porkpie hats, parkas and desert boots) never became the rage in the States that it was in England, many a high-school boy attempted a variation on the theme. Girlchiks copied the high gear worn by Marianne Faithfull, Patti Boyd and most especially Cher, who along with husband Sonny was mod's most prominent proponent on these American shores.

Sonny and Cher

The Beatles (ca. 1967)

Gary Puckett and the Union Gap

Paul Revere and the Raiders

The psychedelic era that dawned with the Summer of Love in 1967 brought with it a whole new kind of sartorial whimsy — one which, like the mod movement before it, was ushered in by the Beatles. The Fab Four's fanciful self-transformation into Sgt. Pepper's Lonely Hearts Club Band earlier that year inspired countless self-styled psychedelic groups to don uniforms, love beads and Nehru jackets in Day-Glo prints.
This look was taken several steps further by the impoverished yet resourceful street people of San Francisco's Haight-Ashbury district, who created a whole new kind of Costume Ball Chic from the odds and ends they found while rummaging through secondhand stores. During the next few years, period clothes, romance and fantasy all came out of the closet and a do-your-own-thing approach to fashion was born.

The Byrds

The Stones (ca. 1971)

The Rolling Stones (ca. 1965)

Jimmy Page

The Stones (ca. 1969)

Rod Stewart

The Stones were the first influential rock group to dispense with matching or themed costumes. They wore whatever they bloody well felt like for both publicity photographs and public appearances — be it a ruffled blouse and Edwardian waistcoat or the things they'd slept in the night before. This individualistic approach eventually evolved into two very different schools of rock fashion —

the proletarian chic of anonymous jeans and T-shirts . . .

and classic wrecked rock star elegance: velvet jackets, platform boots, top hats and long flowered scarves.

The Guess Who

Country Joe and the Fish

Though Bowie, Bolan, Reed and Cooper are most often credited with popularizing androgynous glamrock drag, the movement's roots lay in the New York underground scene where drag queens and Off-Off-Broadway actors in avant garde companies like Café La Mama had been affecting a version of the look for years. Glamrock came and went quickly, but not before seducing such dyed-in-the-wool heteros as Ian Hunter, Todd Rundgren, Daryl Hall and John Cougar Mellencamp into its ranks. Even Bob Dylan attempted a variation on the theme with white greasepaint, kohl-lined eyes and a Bedouin-style babushka.

Marc Bolan

Alice Cooper

David Bowie

Photos left: Ann and Nancy Wilson, Stevie Nicks

Glamrock proved to be more a fashion fad than a school of musical thought. And since glitter and spandex made front-page fashion news only when worn by men, women were somewhat redundant to that particular scene. A few female performers like Buffy Sainte-Marie tried to keep pace with the craze by pinning on extra feathers and raising their skirts and platforms. Joan Baez responded to the craze by donning a gold lamé jacket and an old aviator cap. But only Labelle succeeded in pulling off anything close to a fashion coup with their space-age foundation garments by New York designer Larry Le Gaspi.

Buffy Sainte-Marie

Labelle

The Ritchie Family

Parlet

Grace Jones

David Bowie

Bob Welch

Billy Preston

Starguard

Glamrock chic slid into the "disco look" which mixed a gay fashion sensibility with Frederick's of Hollywood glitz. For men, this movement signaled a "return to elegance" on the order of the fancy bib and tucker affected by Roxy Music's Bryan Ferry and David Bowie in his guise as the Thin White Duke. For women, it meant décolleté, hooker shoes, spandex and, for some, getups so campy that they came off looking like female impersonators. (See Grace Jones.) As usual, soul groups like the Isleys and Earth, Wind and Fire proved to be the fad's most uninhibited interpreters, taking it to the limit with outrageous S&M and sci-fi creations.

By the mid-seventies, the "disco look" had filtered down to the masses as Seventh Avenue flooded the market with bell-bottomed polyester suits *à la* John Travolta in *Saturday Night Fever* and gaudy, form-fitting "bodywear." There was even a book that provided instruction in the esoteric art of "disco makeup."

The Isley Brothers

Legend has it that John Lydon was the first to slash his clothes and patch them back together with safety pins. True or not, Lydon was certainly one of the earliest icons of the punk scene, a movement that called for its disciples to show their disdain for the strictures of fashion by mutilating their clothes. It seems somehow fitting that this antifashion protest should be launched from a clothing boutique and masterminded by a former tailor and fashion maven, Malcolm McLaren. At Sex, his Chelsea boutique, he and his erstwhile lover and protégée, the brilliant designer Vivienne Westwood, sold stylized rage to alienated youth, drawing the inspiration for bondage trousers, rubberwear, and ripped T-shirts from bikers, gays and out-of-work rock'n'rollers. The look they created — so provocative it was regularly confiscated by the police — was later exported to America by groups like the Clash and McLaren's very own brainchild, the Sex Pistols. Since then punk has become a staple of pop culture and a common denominator for several diverse modes of youthful fashion expression.

Johnny Rotten

Too clean to be mean? Debbie Harry in suburban punk

There was a time when all rock aficionados, stars and fans alike, dressed the same. But now that rock has splintered into myriad factions, it boasts as many schools of sartorial style as it does of musicianship. As a rule, most old-timers cling to the various looks with which they became identified during their heyday, while aspiring rockers approach fashion with a sense of history on the order of the Stray Cats' redneck revivalism or the B-52's high sixties camp. Rock fashion statements vary not just among groups but within them as well, as with the members of the original Pretenders who evoked no fewer than four distinct rock epochs among them. By lifting familiar images from the past and juxtaposing them in a droll, sardonic way, these performers are not only creating a new rock'n'roll style, but commenting on a fragmented and self-conscious society.

London's Blitz movement has hatched what may be rock's most imaginative fashion advance to date. The so-called New Romanticism of wigged-out mannequins like Steve Strange and Boy George replaces punk's S&M fashions and cancer ward cosmetics with an updated Hollywood-style glamour, with the point being to create a beautiful or at least entertaining facade.

Boy George

Now that TV has replaced radio as the font of rock music and culture, the visual impact of such sartorially *outré* groups as Culture Club and Eurythmics has become more important than ever. Probably the last word on the current state of rock and fashion was had by a member of the Blitz group Spandau Ballet, who recently told a reporter from *Rolling Stone*, "Music is irrelevant. It's just an excuse to dress up."

The Clash

Far left: Robert Gordon

Below right: The B-52's

Suzi Quatro: you're never wrong when you're wearing black leather.

The Split Enz

Of all the trends taken up by rock musicians over the years, only one has survived the test of time. Dark glasses, or shades, as an all-purpose fashion accessory were first popularized during the forties and fifties by stoned-out beats and jazzbos who wore them round the clock — daytime, nighttime, indoors and out — to disguise the fact that their eyes were "pinned" and to filter out annoying sunlight. Since then, shades have come to hold a very special glamour for rock scene-makers. Not only do they evoke that cool jazz era, but by suggesting that the wearer is just too wasted to look the world straight in the eye, they provide the perfect hip cover for prescription specs.

Because there was a concerted effort on the part of fifties imagemakers to keep rockers from looking any more sinister to parents than they already did, you rarely saw Presley (who would later become a familiar sight in his gradient density 007's), Vincent, Lewis, et al., let alone any R&B stars, hiding behind their Foster Grants: you didn't see them wearing cheaters either — but not because they had 20/20 vision. Of the big-name rock pioneers, only Buddy Holly went public with his specs. But even he traded his nerdy Cuban half-rims for bop glasses shortly after scoring his first few hits. Chances are he'd have switched to contacts or shades (aviators? granny glasses?) had he lived.

Roy Orbison

The first rocker to become synonymous with his shades was Roy Orbison. He wore his Bausch and Lomb Wayfarers for both public appearances and photographs because he was painfully shy and didn't want to see or be seen too closely by his audiences. Dark glasses also helped disguise the fact that the Big O was (and is) slightly crosseyed. Within a short time, such diverse performers as Link Ray, Question Mark and, of course, Stevie Wonder would all become famous for their shades. (Stevie and Bob Dylan wore matching Porsche shades when they presented the award for Top Single on the 1984 Grammy Show.)

Came the sixties and shades became fashionable with the zonked-out acid rockers of the drug era. The nearsighted Bob Dylan, who had worn the Wayfarer during the early sixties, switched to aviators toward the end of the decade. John Lennon also wore bop shades (offstage) during the first

flurry of Beatlemania; in 1966 he switched to the National Health–style eyeglasses (later nicknamed Ben Franklin or granny glasses) that had helped to facilitate his transformation into Private Gripwood for the film *How I Won the War*. Variations on this owl-eyed style, such as rimless lenses or old-fashioned wire-rim frames in offbeat shapes and colors were later popularized by Roger McQuinn. Before long, granny glasses could be seen on such stars as John Sebastian, Paul Kantner and John Denver. As stylish as this new look became, dark glasses were still regarded as cooler. Even Lennon himself came to prefer an inky "bottle glass" tint for his "John Lennon glasses."

Although a few stars get away with wearing specs onstage nowadays (Elton John, for instance, but then he always was a nerd), shades continue to be *de rigueur* for the current crop of punk and New Wave rock musicians. Debbie Harry's famous sunglass wardrobe boasts oversized celebrity goggles, hitter wraparounds, aviators and cat-eye Harlequins. Johnny Rotten favors updated granny glasses with dark lenses. And though Peter Wolfe recently abandoned his ubiquitous Wayfarers for mascara and contacts, there are still dozens of rockers like Ian Hunter, Joey Ramone and Graham Parker who wouldn't be caught dead in public without their shades.

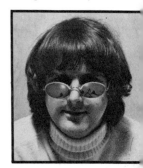

Photos clockwise from above left: John Sebastian, Roger McGuinn, Stevie Wonder, Ian Hunter, Graham Parker, Bob Dylan, Link Ray.

Director Richard Lester oversees the creation of John Lennon's new look for *How I Won the War*.

When the Pretenders first began attracting wide-scale public attention, leader Chrissie Hynde wondered aloud to a reporter how long it would take before she'd start seeing the group's female fans dressed in go-go boots and fingerless black lace gloves like hers. Then she'd know she'd really made it. And she was right. For one of the truest measures of pop celebrity is the lengths fans will go to to emulate their idols.

In addition to the major fashion trends spawned by sundry pop music movements, countless self-contained fads — usually inexpensive little embellishments like Chrissie's gloves or go-go boots — have become the rage simply because a particular pop luminary wore them. In fact, some stars are remembered more for these than for their music.

1956

Elvis Presley: turned-up collars

1958

Pat Boone: white bucks

American Bandstand: lace collars, sweater sets, rolled socks, and saddle oxfords with a belt in the back

Roger Daltrey: fringed everything

1969

Janis Joplin: tie-dye, bangles, spangles and feathers

Jimi Hendrix: headbands and single ear studs for men

The Beatles: Nehru jackets, love beads, uniforms, costume ball chic

Sly Stone: pimp hats and knit caps

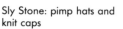

1970

Cher and Rita Coolidge: Indian jewelry

1973

Rod Stewart: dollybird hats

Elton John: platforms

1960

Elvis Presley:
the shirt jac

1962

Bob Dylan: tattered jeans,
work shirts, the Dylan cap

Sonny and Cher: pop tops,
bell-bottoms, hip huggers, and
fur vests

1967

Roger McGuinn and
John Lennon: granny
glasses

1964

The Beatles: lapel-less
suits, Beatle boots

The Who: Mod

Spring ahead in shoe fashion
with the NEW

DENSON
Springers

The elastic-sided fashion
shoes in the latest styles

DENSON — LEADERS OF FASHION IN SHOES FOR MEN

John Lennon: the Beatle
cap

David Bowie:
football
shoulders and
pleated pants

1977

The Sex Pistols: torn
clothes, safety pins,
punk

1979

Debbie Harry: miniskirts

Olivia Newton-John:
headbands (again)

1982

53

Nobody knows why exactly, but hair has always played a significant part in the rock mystique. From the elaborate processed "do's" worn by R&B stars to David Bowie's Space Oddity fringe, rock'n'roll hair has helped to create some of the most indelible images in pop. (Remember Jerry Lee Lewis flinging loose his wavy blond mane and then languorously combing it back in place? And the Beatles shaking their shaggy Mop Tops in unison?) In the years since Elvis first made the sideburn a national issue, the hairdos affected by rock musicians — as exaggerated and impertinent as they usually are — have set the style for countless imitators and millions of fans. Here then is a brief history of two and a half decades of rock'n'roll hair . . .

When the young Elvis Presley first piled his hair into what *Time* magazine would later describe as "five inches of hot buttered yak wool," he was imitating good-old-Memphis-boys, truck drivers and movie star Tony Curtis, whose glamour pix hung on his bedroom wall. His sideburns and greaser pomp soon became the standard look for aspiring male rockers and scores of teenaged boys. It separated hep cats from the older crew-cut generation that had won the war, and provided a figurative rallying point for the newly emerging teen culture of the fifties. The youthful obsession with hair that has flourished ever since — from the long-hair rebellion of the sixties to the short-hair rebellion of the punk era — all started here.

Marvin Gaye   Wilson Pickett   Major Lance

In the fifties, most black rock'n'rollers (and Wayne Cochran) wore their hair in a processed "do," a look favored by American blacks since the twenties. Acquiring it required endless hours with a specialist who straightened naturally nappy locks with relaxing solution and flattened the hair with hot irons (hence the aptly graphic expression "fried, dried and laid on the side"), after which it was glossed with pomade and sculpted into a glistening version of the prevailing white style. In the twenties and thirties, patent leather hair *à la* Cab Calloway was the desired result, but at the beginning of rock's golden era, the style shifted to "conks" — pompadours with marcelled sides and a towering cascade of waves and curls. Because humidity sent these extravagant creations back into their natural state, off-duty conks were kept in place with "do-rags" — a kerchief or stockinglike turban. Many stars abandoned their processed "do's" with the utmost reluctance. Some, like Chuck Berry, still wear them today.

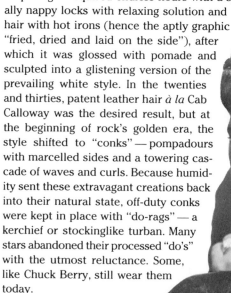

Percy Sledge

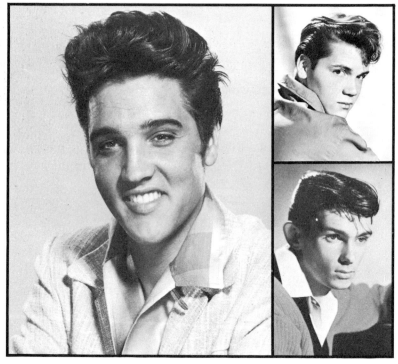

Photos clockwise from left: Elvis Presley, Brian Hyland, Gene Pitney

As a young performer, Ike Turner wore his hair in a conk and later in a processed version of the Beatle cut. His Ex, the glorious Tina Turner, also processed her hair into a conventional bob in the fifties. Now she is said to favor a hair weaving technique in which individual strands of synthetic or natural hair are tied to existing hair and then styled. However, it has also been rumored that the luxuriant mane Tina tosses around with such abandon is actually a wig. One reporter who claims to have seen her without it reports that Tina's real hair is plaited into tiny "corn-row" braids.

Ike and Tina

Dodie Stevens

Annette

Connie Stevens

D. D. Phillips

Letting their hair down in public was what it was all about for rockers like Elvis and Jerry Lee, but their female counterparts — Brenda Lee, Connie Francis, Annette, et al. — were expected to be ladylike and demure, and that went for their hairdos as well. For this reason, the girl rockers of the fifties didn't really pioneer any new hairstyles — although Annette can be credited with introducing pincushion bangs (which sat atop a pageboy and usually had a bow in the center) and Connie Stevens's Daisy Mae do's provided a transition from pin curl bobs to the bouffants of the sixties.

Jackie Kennedy should probably be credited with popularizing the bouffant, but it was the Ronettes who had the last word on the subject. Their awesome beehives looked as if they'd been spun out of industrial-grade nylon and appeared to stand at least two feet high. For millions of middle-class women with the time and money to invest in marathon stretches at the beauty parlor, these elaborate coifs were a status symbol of sorts. Consequently, it took courage to be the first on your block to deflate your "bubble" and let it grow into the peasant look worn by folkies like Joan Baez and Buffy Sainte-Marie.

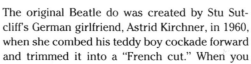

The Ronettes

Dionne Warwick

The Beatles

This Minnesota boy wore his hair in a pompadour like Elvis's in high school. When he arrived in New York, he let it grow long into what writer Janet Maslin once described as a "fabulous corona of unkempt hair." Eric Clapton says he permed his hair in imitation of Dylan's Jewish natural. Others would too.

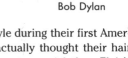

Bob Dylan

The original Beatle do was created by Stu Sutcliff's German girlfriend, Astrid Kirchner, in 1960, when she combed his teddy boy cockade forward and trimmed it into a "French cut." When you look at photographs of the Beatles wearing this style during their first American tour, it's hard to believe now that anyone actually thought their hair was long. But their mop tops were even more controversial than Elvis's sideburns. For some reason, the idea that any red-blooded male would want to comb his hair down over his forehead and ears seemed downright wicked back in 1964.

No one was impartial on the issue of Beatle hair. Sociologists, pop observers, TV news correspondents, men of the cloth and Dr. Joyce Brothers all had their say on the subject. Even President Lyndon Johnson took a break from his busy schedule to inform the British prime minister that the Beatles needed a trim. Thanks to all the commotion, Beatle wigs — which could be purchased at most neighborhood dime stores — became a popular party gag, the hottest-selling novelty item since the yo-yo. For a time, there was even a rumor that the Beatles themselves wore them.

George Harrison   Ringo Starr   Paul McCartney   John Lennon

But to teenage boys all over America, the Beatles' mop tops were no joke. They copied the look by the millions, thereby delighting their girlfriends and horrifying their elders. (Even Elvis attempted a version of the look. See his Beatle bangs in *Change of Habit*.) It was not until years later that high-school administrators would stop suspending schoolboys who refused to give up their Beatle do's.

With the mod explosion came guiche curls, geometric cuts and long straight bobs with shaggy bangs of the kind worn by Patti Boyd, Marianne Faithfull and, of course, Cher. By this point some women had already switched to folkie hair or toned down their bouffants *à la* Petula Clark, but it wasn't until the latter part of the sixties and the unrestricted hairstyles of the counter-culture movement that teenaged girls (and boys) would stop ironing and straightening their hair in imitation of Limey rock stars and trendy British birds.

Petula Clark   Lulu   Cher

Jimi Hendrix rendered the processed "do" obsolete with his glorious mushroom cloud Afro, and in so doing became a major symbol (for a time) of the burgeoning Black Power movement. Ironically, Hendrix first frizzled his hair to its most outrageous dimensions at the behest of his white managers who wanted him and his group the Experience to appear as outlandish as possible when they made their debut in England. The strategy worked; all London was agog over Hendrix in the summer of 1967 — over his talent, his onstage theatrics and, most of all, the way he looked.

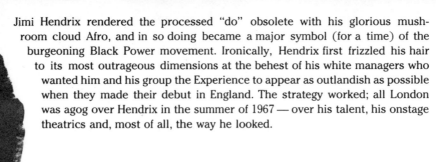

Jimi Hendrix

Still caught up in the standard conventions of Barbie Doll prettiness, Grace Slick and Carly Simon corralled their frizzy tresses into long, sleek hairstyles well into the seventies. It took Janis Joplin, whose shoulder-length hair hung loose in a tangled mane, to give women the courage to throw out their spray net, styling gel and chemical curl relaxers.

There was a time, back in the days when he wasn't nearly as famous as his billing boasted, when James Brown's conk soared higher even than Little Richard's. "I used to wear my hair real high," he says. "And people would ask, 'Why you wear your hair so high?' I tell 'em so people don't say, '*Where* he is, but *there* he is.'" But then came success and the Black Power movement and suddenly it was no longer cool for a black public figure to wear a hairdo created for blacks who wanted to look white. The problem was that the Afro was just a mite too funky for Soul Brother Number One. So James Brown compromised with a processed natural — hair straightened with relaxers, set on rollers and styled into a smoother, more genteel version of the natural look. When Brown is on the road, his hair is washed and set as many as four times a day, either by his personal stylist of twenty-six years or one of a team of hairdressers he keeps on retainer in Augusta, New York and L.A. Between coiffeurs and Luster Silk, he currently drops about $500 to $700 a week to maintain his modified 'fro. "It was like givin' up something for Lent," Brown told journalist Gerri Hirshey, speaking of his now defunct conk. "I want people to know that one of the most prized things I let go of was my hair. It was a real attraction to my business, but I would cut it off for the Movement."

Below left: Bob Marley
Stevie Wonder

An increased ethnic awareness on the part of American blacks helped to bring about a new interest in African clothing and hairstyles in the sixties and seventies. Leading the way, as always, were pop music figures. Reggae stars like Bob Marley and Peter Tosh were known for the size of their splifs and the length of their dreadlocks. But it was Stevie Wonder who made the greatest impact on black hairstyles of the last decade with his Masai warrior braids. Today the look has become standard for stars like Rick James, Sister Sledge, Valerie Simpson and, of course, Bo Derek and Cher.

Peaches of Peaches and Herb   Sister Sledge   Cher

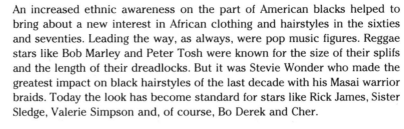

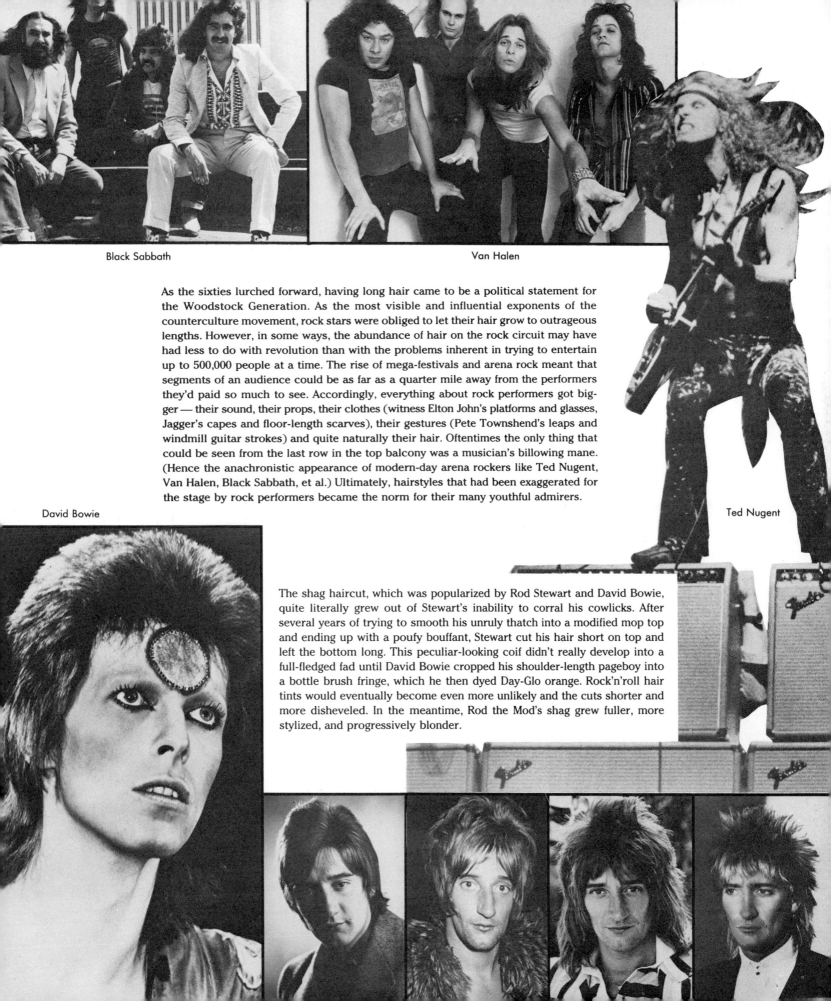

Black Sabbath

Van Halen

David Bowie

Ted Nugent

As the sixties lurched forward, having long hair came to be a political statement for the Woodstock Generation. As the most visible and influential exponents of the counterculture movement, rock stars were obliged to let their hair grow to outrageous lengths. However, in some ways, the abundance of hair on the rock circuit may have had less to do with revolution than with the problems inherent in trying to entertain up to 500,000 people at a time. The rise of mega-festivals and arena rock meant that segments of an audience could be as far as a quarter mile away from the performers they'd paid so much to see. Accordingly, everything about rock performers got bigger — their sound, their props, their clothes (witness Elton John's platforms and glasses, Jagger's capes and floor-length scarves), their gestures (Pete Townshend's leaps and windmill guitar strokes) and quite naturally their hair. Oftentimes the only thing that could be seen from the last row in the top balcony was a musician's billowing mane. (Hence the anachronistic appearance of modern-day arena rockers like Ted Nugent, Van Halen, Black Sabbath, et al.) Ultimately, hairstyles that had been exaggerated for the stage by rock performers became the norm for their many youthful admirers.

The shag haircut, which was popularized by Rod Stewart and David Bowie, quite literally grew out of Stewart's inability to corral his cowlicks. After several years of trying to smooth his unruly thatch into a modified mop top and ending up with a poufy bouffant, Stewart cut his hair short on top and left the bottom long. This peculiar-looking coif didn't really develop into a full-fledged fad until David Bowie cropped his shoulder-length pageboy into a bottle brush fringe, which he then dyed Day-Glo orange. Rock'n'roll hair tints would eventually become even more unlikely and the cuts shorter and more disheveled. In the meantime, Rod the Mod's shag grew fuller, more stylized, and progressively blonder.

Punk chic may have originated in London, but philosophically speaking it grew out of the boredom felt by kids everywhere with the mellowed-out smugness of the Woodstock generation and the studied sleaziness of the Euro-disco scene. Its primary goal was to express contempt for wealthy rock stars and aging hippies who, like their parents before them, were fast becoming boring old farts. Because that crowd wore their shoulder-length hair as a badge of honor, the first thing the punks did was to chop theirs off. This alone wasn't enough to get anyone uptight. But, dying the mangled fringe in Easter Egg colors was another story entirely. Add to this a Chuck-Berry-Is-Dead T-shirt and bondage pants and you could usually get a rise out of even the most laid-back peace freak.

Note: Despite its chaotic appearance, punk hair requires tremendous maintenance. First there is the jagged haircut, then color and teasing (or a body perm) to get it to stand on end. Next come vaselined roots and a spritz of Aquanet to keep the whole thing looking suitably disheveled. And now word comes from California that serious hair mavens like Rod Stewart are achieving the look by hanging from gravity boots while they blow-dry their hair.

Richard Hell

Siouxsie Sioux

Wendy O. Williams

Hope I Die Before I Go Bald Dept.: Unlike the old days when pop singers all conformed to a single hair fashion, rock hairstyles are a mixed bag at the moment. It no longer matters how a rocker wears his hair, just so long as it's there. Yes, there is no fate more dire for a rock star than going bald. Jimi Hendrix actually used to have nightmares about losing his hair. In fact, he was so nervous about the well-being of his celebrated Afro that he wore a hat to bed the last several years of his life.

And pity poor Elton John; just as it seemed he'd finally gotten his weight under control, his hair abandoned ship. (Elton attributes his baldness to overbleaching.) Unfortunately, the transplants he underwent in 1980 didn't "take" and he was forced to reactivate his extensive wardrobe of hats in order to camouflage his chrome dome.

Because the counterculture movement of the sixties rendered such cosmetic pretenses as trick hairdos and toupees déclassé, most rockers, like Elton, disguise their receding hairlines with hats — the rock'n'roll toupee. Mike Love, Mick Fleetwood and Dash Crofts have worn them since the sixties. Sting, Adam Ant and Phil Collins will be wearing them soon. Every once in a while, however, a pop star will resort to a transplant (Paul Anka) or glue on a little store-bought hair when his own gets thin. Bobby Goldsboro has been known to sport a full wig and Del Shannon and Jim Stafford wear hairpieces, as did Clyde McPhatter, Bobby Darin, and Michael Jackson after his hair pomade caught fire during the filming of a TV commercial in early 1984. And last but not least, there's Carl Perkins, whose rug would look phony on a department store dummy. But the ultimate in scalp camouflage is the sci-fi bouffant A Flock of Seagull's Mike Score uses to disguise his balding pate.

The Stray Cats

The Romantics

Mick Fleetwood   Mike Love   Dash Crofts   Elton John   Carl Perkins

In addition to the many clothing and hair styles popularized by rock stars, countless cosmetic vogues of the last twenty-five years have had their origins in the rock scene. Sometimes fads were created by a performer's reluctance to make the usual cosmetic concessions to stardom — like nose jobs and capped teeth. However, this phenomenon didn't develop until rock's second decade. In the fifties, singing idols like Elvis, Anka, etc. were still trying their best to look like the reigning Hollywood heartthrobs.

A basic part of the enduring Elvis Presley image is the King's shiny black hair. However, when Elvis made his first appearance on the screen in *Love Me Tender*, his pompadour was a light sandy brown color. Upon his return to the screen after four years of army duty, his hair had been dyed a bluish black. His bodyguard Red West says that the change was inspired by Roy Orbison, whose talent — and hair — Elvis had always envied. (Orbison dyed his hair too.) Later Elvis ordered his ward, the future Priscilla Presley, to darken her hair to the same shade — in imitation, West speculates, of either Elvis's first Hollywood crush, Debra Paget, or his beloved mother, Gladys.

Elvis, who is said to have regarded himself as no less than a Greek god, wasn't above using an earthly trick or two to embellish his divine good looks. He wore heavy makeup for stage and screen performances, body girdles, and lifts in his shoes (including the slippers he wore around the house). Toward the end of his life, when drug use and massive weight fluctuations had ravaged his appearance, he resorted to plastic surgery — specifically an eye job and a "mini" lift. By then, dye jobs covered hair that had gone almost completely white.

Like aspiring Hollywood starlets during the studio era, teen singing idols in the fifties were sometimes required to reduce their noses a notch or two. Although Phil Ochs, Eric Carmen and Andy Kim remodeled theirs while still teenagers, most underwent this cosmetic rite of passage after they'd scored with one or two hits. Annette Funicello had her nose reshaped around the time she made the transition from Mouseketeer to movie and recording star. Paul Anka did his shortly after meeting Annette. Connie Francis had already made several top-selling records by the time she got around to having her nose overhauled. In the late seventies, however, Connie discovered that a subsequent operation to widen her nasal passages had left her unable to sing. It was four years, several operations and two or three major traumas

Anka before   and after

before Connie would return to performing. Tom Jones revamped his nose around the time he arrived in America. At first, he claimed that his new nose was "an accident," that he'd noticed it was "shorter" after a sinus operation. "They must have cut something out of it," he said then, "though I must say I like it better than the old one...it was in the beer before I'd taken a sip." However, Tom later admitted to a reporter from the *Evening Standard* that he'd undergone the operation because his old nose was ugly, and he just couldn't stand having anything ugly on his otherwise perfect self.

Tom — perfect

It was during the counterculture revolution of the mid-sixties, when standards of beauty flipflopped, that large bumpy noses with "character" suddenly became all the rage. Fashion slicks like *Vogue* and *Harper's* gushed over them, mounting glorious pictorial tributes to Streisand's and Cher's ample honkers. And the well-endowed schnozzolas of such rock greats as Ringo Starr and Pete Townshend became almost as famous as Durante's. However, in what may signal a return to old-time glamour, there is the new, streamlined smeller Michael Jackson presented to the world after setting sail as a solo. And now comes word that Rod Stewart's potato-shaped proboscis, long a rock landmark, has recently undergone a slight cosmetic renovation.

Speaking of Cher, there was talk a few years back when the glorious one dropped into New York to have her breasts surgically uplifted that she also intended to submit her famous beak to a slight cosmetic bobbing. Conjecture on the subject made headlines in several of the New York dailies. However, some Cher watchers claim that she actually had her nose tipped at Sonny's insistence years ago when the duo was billed as Caesar and Cleo. (Sonny had his own nose remodeled around that time.) To give you a chance to make up your own mind on the matter, here's a nineteen-year retrospective of Cher's celebrated smeller. And remember, while Cher may not actually have altered her nose surgically, that doesn't mean that the various photogs who've snapped it over the years haven't utilized a little lighting and retouching magic to minimize her natural assets.

1963   1968   1974   1982

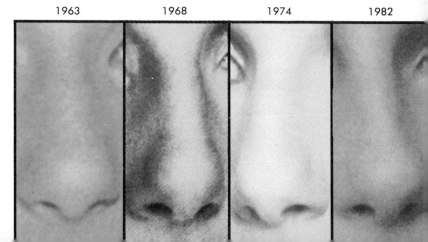

Their stardom is based upon the way they look as much as their talent, but unlike movie stars, politicos and other public figures, rock musicians have always manifested a spectacular lack of regard for their choppers. If anything, bad teeth are something of a status symbol in rock, even a fetish of sorts.

Maybe it started with impoverished black musicians or the anemic-looking Limeys who invaded these shores in the mid-sixties. (A passion for sweets, socialized dentistry and malnourishment during the war years are primarily to blame for the notoriously lousy condition of British teeth.) But whatever the reason, decayed molars and rotting bicuspids have become a sign of toughness for rockers. They signify a devil-may-care approach to life, a disregard for health and convention. While it's true that such famous snaggle-tooths as Keith Richards, Peter Asher and David Bowie have renovated their mouths and Diana Ross recently underwent orthodontia, crumbling teeth continue to be a rock tradition. In fact, onetime punk rave Johnny Rotten is named for his teeth and not, as everyone supposes, his manners and morals.

"You've only got to have one broken tooth for everyone to think you're an outlaw," Keith Richards mused as he contemplated a large piece of rotting molar that dropped out of his mouth while he was giving an interview in 1979. "Actually, I've always grooved on it myself, but just recently I lost another chunk of my front tooth and you might say that since then my teeth have fallen out of favor with me." (Richards has since remodeled his mouth with extensive dental work.)

Remember when George Harrison was the Quiet One, the serious Beatle who rarely, if ever, smiled? Well, it turns out that George wasn't really all *that* serious. He was just self-conscious about the overcrowded condition of his mouth. Nowadays, however, his smile's just beaming thanks to the glistening Hollywood cap job he got following the Beatles' split and his subsequent move to L.A.

After sitting through three and a half hours of Bob Dylan's jumbled docu-drama, *Renaldo and Clara*, one dazed critic from the *Village Voice* wrote that the only revelation the film had to offer was that Dylan undoubtedly had the worst teeth in rock'n'roll. That's no small claim, given that at the time (1978) the competition included Keith Richards, Keith Moon and all four of the Clash.

Keith Moon lost his front tooth on that famous night in 1965 when he drove a Lincoln Continental into the swimming pool of a Flint, Michigan, Holiday Inn during the course of a postconcert bash. After executing a Houdini-like escape from the car, Moon — clad only in his soaking wet underpants — strolled back into the hotel to continue celebrating, only to run into the town sheriff. Positive he was going to be shot on the spot, he made a dash for the door — at which point he slipped on a stray piece of marzipan and fell on his face. Moon spent the rest of the night in jail with a local dentist who repaired the damage with a removable false front tooth, which he wore on and off, depending on his mood, for the rest of his life.

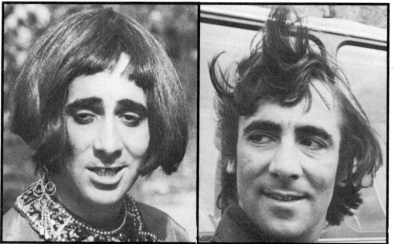

The ultimate in rock'n'roll teeth chic is having no teeth at all. Take Richie Havens and Dr. John. Their careers flourished during the years they let their gums go *au naturel*, but neither has had any luck on the charts since being outfitted with new store-bought choppers. About the only time you hear Dr. John on the airwaves any more is when he sings the jingle for Tic Tac, the breath deodorizer.

Male genitalia, or "baskets" as they're known in gay parlance, have played a big part in rock'n'roll mystique and fashion ever since Elvis first patented his crowd-pleasing pelvic thrust. And while there are some teen heartthrobs who shy away from calling attention to their crotches (Donny Osmond's mother makes sure that all unsightly bulges are cropped or airbrushed out of his publicity photos), male rock stars are usually expected to display a healthy bulge below the belt.

"Some of my lady fans have accused me of putting bananas or socks down my pants to fill them up, so naturally I have to let 'em come up for a feel to show them they're wrong," Black Oak Arkansas's Jim Dandy Mangrum has been quoted as saying. Dandy's stage costumes usually consist of little more than tight-fitting breeches and thigh-high boots.

Mick Jagger is another who dresses in formfitting fashions designed to display his family jewels to their best advantage. However, like a lot of other pinup stars past and present, Jagger may not be all he would have us believe. At least not according to Etta James. She discovered the secret of Mick's charm during a Stones' performance in the mid-seventies when what she calls "that little package he wears in his pants" slipped down over his knees during a particularly vigorous *tour jeté* and ended up protruding from his tights. Etta, who was standing backstage after opening for the group, discovered Mick crouched sheepishly behind a speaker, hurriedly trying to reposition his macho image.

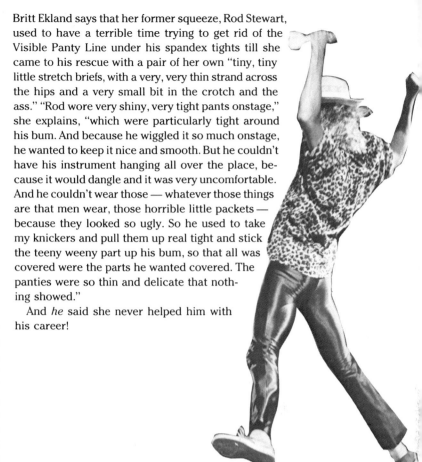

Britt Ekland says that her former squeeze, Rod Stewart, used to have a terrible time trying to get rid of the Visible Panty Line under his spandex tights till she came to his rescue with a pair of her own "tiny, tiny little stretch briefs, with a very, very thin strand across the hips and a very small bit in the crotch and the ass." "Rod wore very shiny, very tight pants onstage," she explains, "which were particularly tight around his bum. And because he wiggled it so much onstage, he wanted to keep it nice and smooth. But he couldn't have his instrument hanging all over the place, because it would dangle and it was very uncomfortable. And he couldn't wear those — whatever those things are that men wear, those horrible little packets — because they looked so ugly. So he used to take my knickers and pull them up real tight and stick the teeny weeny part up his bum, so that all was covered were the parts he wanted covered. The panties were so thin and delicate that nothing showed."

And *he* said she never helped him with his career!

In the early seventies, a new kind of heavy-metal star emerged on the rock scene: pretty boys with long, tousled blond manes and smooth, hairless chests which were almost always on display. These basic components were rounded off with formfitting ballet tights, all the better to show off genital endowment as they stalked the stage. Beginning with Roger Daltrey and Robert Plant, proponents of this new male esthetic include Mark Farner, Jim Dandy Mangrum, David Lee Roth and of course Ted Nugent, who stripped the look down to basics by wearing only Roman sandals and a fur loincloth.

While all the macho rockers worry about filling out their crotches, it appears that Barry Manilow has the flip side of that problem. About a year ago, *Creem* magazine reported that Manilow had engaged an exclusive Hollywood corsetier to create a padded underpant to go under those skintight bellbottoms he wears on stage in order to round out his derrière *à la* Rod Stewart.

I Dreamt I Was On Stage In Front Of 10,000 People In A Codpiece Dept.: Not every fashion fancy favored by a rock star becomes a national craze. A while back, for example, Jethro Tull's Ian Anderson tried to launch a codpiece revival, but for some reason the look never quite caught on. After years of what he once described as "waggling my codpiece and masturbating with my flute" before millions of fans, Anderson finally decided he'd outgrown his crotch cover and abandoned it for good in 1976. "The codpiece business was all very amusing," he said later with some embarrassment, "but when your private parts are wrapped with several layers of felt, nylon and cotton for two hours at a stretch, it's not the best thing for your virility. Seriously, the very year I gave up my codpiece was the year I begat a son."

As much as their clothes, hairstyles and cosmetic affectations, the pose and attitude rock stars assume in photographs define their public personae. You may not recognize a particular star or group in an 8×10 glossy, but you can peg their era and their trip by the way they relate to the camera.

After Elvis went to Hollywood to start work on his first film, *Love Me Tender*, he told the picture's screenwriter, Hal Kanter, "I've been studying the people in the movies that have made some kind of impression on me — Humphrey Bogart, James Dean and Marlon Brando — and there's one thing about all of them, they never smile."

With Bogart, the tough guy image was mostly a pose, but there was a very real reason why Elvis never saw Brando or Dean smiling in their films or photos. As serious *artistes*, both men sat for publicity portraits with the utmost reluctance. Dean in particular hated posing for photo sessions. The sullen way he stared into the camera, his usual unkempt appearance and slouchy posture were meant to express his contempt for Hollywood, the star system and the cynical way young actors were packaged and sold.

Elvis had no such qualms. On the contrary, he wanted most of all to become a movie star. He simply admired the charisma of Bogart, Dean and Brando and wanted to project a similar aura. To that end, he consciously cultivated a petulant expression when posing for photographs. On the rare occasions that he did smile, his upper lip tended to curl back, thus turning what should have been a friendly expression into something of a sneer. A shot of Elvis with an unqualified grin was rare and, as such, highly prized. Variations on Presley's surly image — the pouty, almost resentful way he looked out from his photographs, would become the standard for two generations of rock stars to follow.

Teen idols of the fifties were often presented in such a way as to counter Presley's surly allure while at the same time exploiting his basic physical components. The publicity pics that hyped heartthrobs like Frankie and Fabe in pube pulps were either photos of the star at home with Mom, contrived theme shots or glamour portraits that made their subjects look friendly and cuddly cute.

Photos this page: Tommy Roe, Buddy Knox, Frankie Avalon, Pat Boone, Fabian, Neil Sedaka, Tony Orlando, Bobby Rydell.

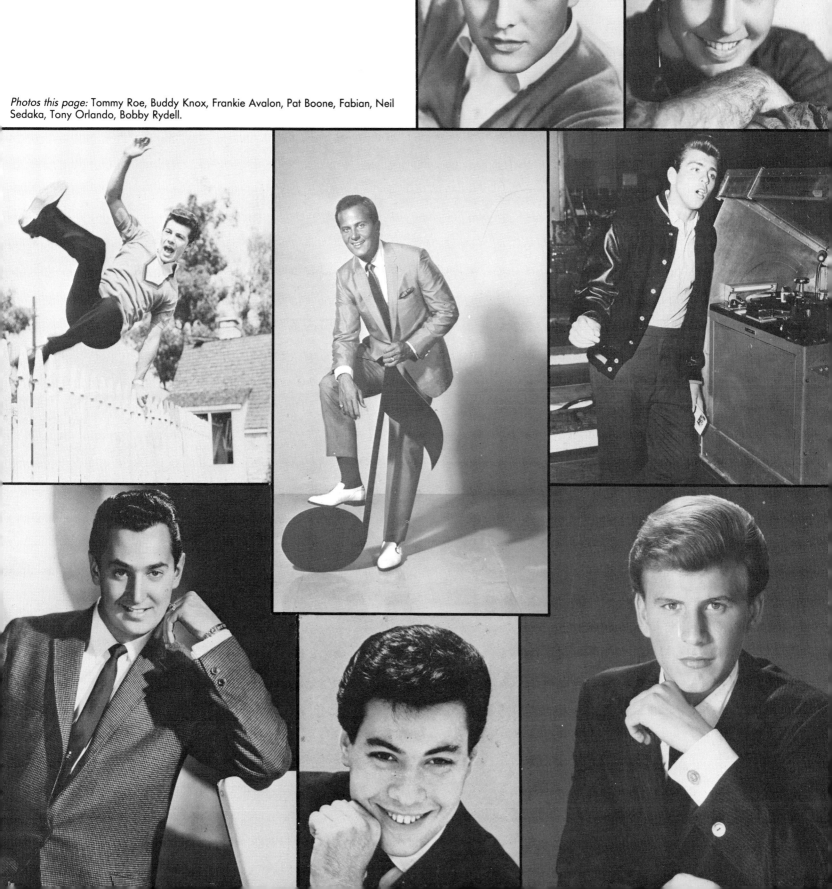

Photos clockwise from left: Gary (U.S.) Bonds, the Marvelettes, Shirley and Lee, Danny and the Juniors, the Four Tops, the Temptations, the Contours, Gladys Knight and the Pips.

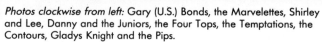

During the fifties and early sixties, publicity photographs for rock'n'roll performers were usually elaborately staged affairs of the kind created for record companies and sometimes the stars themselves by rock's status portraitmaker, James J. Kriegsmann. Like the Hollywood lensmen of the old studio era, Kriegsmann utilized complex lighting and retouching techniques to make the most of his subjects. He and his colleagues — Maurice Seymour and Bruno of Hollywood (who was based in New York) — posed pop personalities in the act of making a typical stage gesture. When you look at Kriegsmann's photograph of the Marvelettes, for example, you can almost hear them intoning, "Don't Mess with Bill."

The Nashville Teens

The Kinks

We Five

The Beatles

The Beatles had a special knack for presenting themselves as lighthearted — almost comical — figures in their early photographs. Somehow able to mug and cavort without losing their cool, the Fab Four were absolutely inspired when it came to improvising in front of the camera. They grinned, waved, jumped, saluted, stood stiffly with their arms outstretched and fingers parted wide.

Their insouciance was imitated by countless other British Invasion bands and even such unlikely American groups as Sly and the Family Stone and the Grateful Dead.

The Grateful Dead

The Zombies

Sly and the Family Stone

Having shed their Beatlesque pretensions once and for all in the late sixties, the Rolling Stones and members of the various San Francisco acid bands wouldn't have been caught dead hamming it up in front of the camera. They resurrected Presley's glower by staring contemptuously into the camera.

Sly and the Family Stone

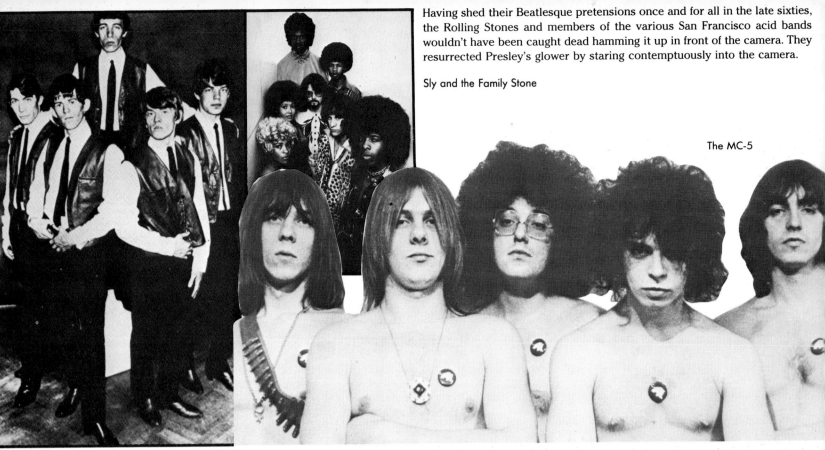

The MC-5

The Rolling Stones

Bryan Ferry

During the glamrock period, stars like David Bowie and Bryan Ferry attempted to revive the old-fashioned glamour photography of the Hollywood studio years. The publicity stills that resulted were sometimes theme shots, which created an aura of mystery and melancholy or evoked a bygone cinematic era. But for the most part, their subjects just posed languorously and peered enticingly into the camera.

Lou Reed

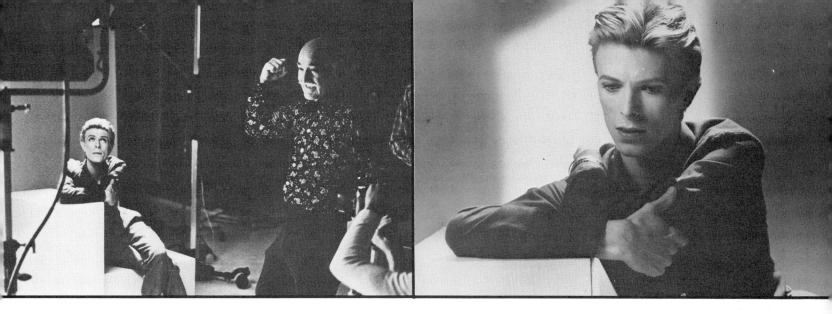

Here, Tom Kelley, the forties photog who took the famous Monroe calendar shot, prepares to capture a new kind of sex symbol on celluloid. "David Bowie took me back to the golden era of movie stars," Kelley said. "He's a visionary who looks into the camera as though he can see the finished pictures."

The rock'n'roll scowl has been updated by a wide variety of punks and New Wavers into an amazing array of snarls and grimaces. The old thumbs up and peace signs of the sixties have been replaced with more dramatic forms of body language — single and double finger salutes, crotch clutching and various tongue tricks.

As with all things extreme, the punk pose has a certain built-in obsolescence. Its outlandishness portends a radical shift in attitude for rockers — most likely a return to (or parody of) the genteel approach of the forties and fifties, as with Linda Ronstadt's pinup photo on the cover of *What's New?*

Photos from left: the Lost Kids, the Dead Boys, Ted Nugent

First

I LOOK AT THE

Purse!

"Record companies are being taken over by accountants. Puds outta college that get certified as economically smart. If ever there was such a thing as an aesthetic decision at the executive level, there's no sign of it now."

— FRANK ZAPPA

In the old days a rock mogul was either a small-time hustler who trafficked in "nigger music" — which he recorded in his bathroom and dispensed from the trunk of his car — or one of those proverbial cigar chompers who hawked rock singers like sideshow freaks. This is not to say that there weren't a few genuine enthusiasts in this crowd, but for the most part the hucksters who were first drawn to this uncharted entertainment frontier were like the pioneers of the movie business — men of modest artistic ambition and nearly imperceptible ethics.

And like those early film barons, the men who sold rock'n'roll in the beginning depended on the naïveté of the artists whose talents they exploited. The late Leonard Chess was one of dozens of small-time entrepreneurs who amassed a fortune by recording authentic blues and R&B while many of his artists struggled to keep their heads above water. Etta James said of her former mentor, "I didn't know nothing about business and business was his thing, so he screwed me. But he screwed me in a teachin' way. So I finally learned how not to get screwed, which is a lesson I'll remember the rest of my life. . . . Yeah, Leonard Chess was like a father to me."

You can imagine the esteem in which men like Chess were held by decent folk at the time; they ranked right up there with used-car salesmen and sex deviates. But the main complaint wasn't the fact that they sometimes bilked their artists, coopted their music and pocketed the profits, but rather that they sold black music to white kids. To parents who considered rock's "jungle rhythms" to be a clarion call to perdition, this amounted

to villainy of the highest order. (Of course, today we know that their fears were well founded.) Even so, the relationship of sin to rock music ceased to be a burning issue once big business figured out a way to harness the demon and make it pay. In the quarter-century since its emergence, rock's remarkable selling power has made it a cornerstone of our consumer-oriented society. As a result, rock and the people who peddle it couldn't be more respectable today. Yes, if there's anything we Americans R-E-S-P-E-C-T, it's a four-billion-dollar annual take. And that, give or take a few billion, is what rock grosses every year.

Today's new model rock moguls can be found snugly sequestered in the oak-paneled boardrooms of the giant corporate monoliths. For as rock has grown richer, its center of finance has moved from garages and converted houses to Wall Street. There, awesome powers like CBS and Warner Communications compute artistry in terms of dollars and cents. So it is that the new rock moguls are successful company men with one eye on the stock market and the other on the Top Ten. However, that doesn't necessarily mean that they're any more charitable toward rock and the people who make it than their less-distinguished predecessors. They may have traded their stogies and Panama hats for Lacoste shirts and Gucci loafers, but their heads are still in the same place. Then, now and forevermore, rock'n'roll's livelihood rests on the bottom line.

Still, if enterprising hustlers like Leonard Chess hadn't recognized the commercial potential in the music of the rural South and urban ghettos when they did, it might have died with the humble people who made it — unheard and unpreserved. The same holds true for the music of today's reigning pop auteurs. Like it or not, the story of rock is as much the story of the men who sell it as of its artists and fans. So, let us now pause to pay tribute to a few of the colorful personalities who inadvertently shaped pop culture while trying to make a fast buck.

It was P. T. Barnum who said, "There's a sucker born every minute." By landing the biggest sucker of them all, a naïve starstruck hillbilly named Elvis Aron Presley, Colonel Tom Parker proved that one is really all you need.

The man who calls himself Colonel Tom Parker is actually Andreas Cornelius van Kuijk, a wily Dutchman born on June 26, 1909, in Breda, Holland. First surfacing in this country in Uncle Sam's army twenty-one years later, Parker soon hit the carnival trail, where his bag of tricks reportedly included trained chickens that "danced" on an electric hot plate and sparrows that he painted yellow and sold as canaries. As a personal manager, Parker sold Elvis Presley like a sideshow attraction, promoting him with a mixture of media hype, big top hoopla and backroom politicking. On his first headlining tour, for example, Elvis appeared with a motley collection of old vaudeville comics, mom'n'pop singers and circus acrobats — each one carefully selected by the Colonel to ensure that Elvis came off as the star. Towns that hosted this troupe were inundated with posters and flyers for weeks in advance, plus a parade on the day of the Big Event. Years later, after Elvis had become the world's top-drawing solo attraction, Parker still employed the same kind of splashy ad campaigns and merchandising schemes to publicize his Las Vegas stints, despite the fact that they were already sold out and could have been many more times over.

How much of this overkill was for Elvis's good and how much for the good of the Colonel is still being debated — and up until recently investigated and litigated. Almost four years to the day following Presley's death, Blanchard E. Tual, a Memphis attorney representing Elvis's daughter, Lisa Marie, charged that in the late sixties, Parker contracted Presley to play Vegas's International Hotel for what he characterized as the "surprisingly low figure of $100,000 to $130,000 a week, a price that was soon surpassed by acts of far less commercial value." Tual's report quoted Alex Shoofey, International's general manager, as saying that the Presley contract was "the best deal ever made in this town." Shoofey also said that Parker, who had developed a passion for the Vegas casino action, "was one of the best customers we ever had. He was good for a million dollars a year." "The impropriety of a manager losing such sums in the same hotel with which he has to negotiate on behalf of his client goes without saying," observed Tual. "He sold Elvis short."

In addition, Parker also negotiated a seven-year contract with RCA, which gave Elvis a royalty one-half that of the other major artists of the day. A separate agreement between Parker and the same company gave him upward of $1.75 million in return for his promotional expertise. Of this arrangement, Tual noted: "Col. Parker could not possibly deal with RCA at arm's length on Elvis's behalf when he was receiving that much money from RCA."

In 1973 Parker sold all of Elvis's masters to RCA for $5 million, split 50–50 between himself and his client. Tual comments: "Elvis was only 37 years old (at the time), and it was illogical for him to consider selling an almost certain lifetime annuity from his catalogue for over 700 chart songs. The tax implications alone should have prohibited such an agreement. . . ." And in fact, of his $2.5 million share of the sale, Elvis realized only $1.25 million after taxes.

Tual's allegations fit in neatly with Presley biographer Albert Goldman's observation that the Colonel "enjoys a reputation as one of the Internal Revenue Service's very best customers. Where other men go to great lengths to avoid paying taxes, the Colonel is so eager to pay his tax bill and so careless of opportunities to dodge behind shelters that it is said that he *overpays* the taxmen."

The lifelong air of secrecy that has surrounded both Parker's private life and financial intriguing have caused some to suggest that he is a man with something to hide. Because he has no credit cards, no passport, no certificate of birth, Parker's true history is a virtual blank — leading to speculation that it may have been purposely obscured to conceal possible criminal activity, or more likely, the fact that he is an illegal alien.

Why else would a man who was known to personally hawk programs for quarters at Elvis concerts refrain from accepting million-dollar offers for Elvis to perform abroad, if not to avoid the attendant governmental scrutiny that would inevitably result? Indeed, why would a man with Parker's connections and financial resources have allowed his boy to be drafted and sent overseas at the height of his career without attempting to pull a few strings to get him (even temporarily) off the hook?

Not only have Parker's business methods been questioned of late, but also his putative father-son relationship with Elvis. Goldman claims, for example, that in all their years together, Presley never once socialized with his mentor. And Larry Geller, a longtime Presley friend, said recently, "Elvis respected the Colonel for his ability to manipulate lawyers, companies and situations, but he felt very uncomfortable around him." It has been widely reported that one of the talents Parker picked up during his carny days was the art of mesmerism. Phil Spector is one of many who believes to this day that the Colonel maintained his control over Presley not through business acumen or goodwill, but by hypnotizing him.

Toward the end of the summer of 1983 came word that the Presley estate had reached a settlement with Parker and RCA (which was accused of conspiring with Parker to defraud Presley of recording royalties). Parker, who continued to collect millions in royalties after Presley's death, was ordered to sever his relationship with the estate and to turn over his collection of Presley memorabilia to Graceland for public display. In return, it is believed that he received a sizable cash settlement.

Tote that barge, lift that bale: the Colonel hitches Elvis up for another shift on the *Love Me Tender* set.

In the meantime, the IRS and lawyers for the estate continue to haggle over just how much Presley was worth at the time of his death and who's entitled to what's left. Speculation has it that Lisa Marie, Presley's only heir, may stand to inherit substantially less than the many millions originally estimated. One investigator remarked that she may discover that her only inheritance is her father's famous name.

Now that the ghastly story of Elvis's final years has been made public, it has to make you wonder whether the Colonel wasn't fully aware of his client's massive drug abuse and shocking physical deterioration all along. And if so, whether Elvis's condition disturbed him or in fact suited his purposes. Regardless, Presley's death certainly had a curious effect on Parker. At the funeral, he conspicuously avoided looking at Elvis in the coffin. And yet, Elvis's body wasn't even cold before he was on the phone feverishly cutting merchandising deals to beat out the swarms of bootleggers trying to capitalize on the death of the King.

They didn't even have a name for it when Alan Freed, a former classical trombonist from Salem, Ohio, first broadcast his Moon Dog House Rock'n'Roll Party over Cleveland's WJW in June of 1951. What Freed was playing — and blacks and whites alike were buying by the truckload — was Rhythm and Blues, or in pejorative industry lingo, "race records." He's been called the "father of rock'n'roll," but — although he may have been the first to give it a name (borrowing the term from R&B lyrics), he wasn't the first to play it. There was nineteen-year-old Huggie Boy on KRKD in Los Angeles, Hunter Hancock also in L.A., and a Shreveport, Louisiana, jock named Bob Smith whose howl would eventually be worth millions under the name Wolfman Jack.

Nevertheless, Alan Freed has earned a place in rock'n'roll history as its great popularizer. Pounding out the beat with his fist on a telephone book, Freed enthusiastically promoted the music not just on the air, but on stage, television and the big screen. And like any good show-biz sharpie, he got his piece of the action too.

To his credit, though Freed was a profiteer, he had the good taste to match his dollars-and-sense. Despite constant complaints, he vigorously plugged black artists and independent labels at a time when major record companies were pressing up lame whitebread derivatives of popular R&B platters.

Of course, his enthusiasm tended to be even greater if he happened to have a share of the songwriting royalties — as he did on "Maybellene," the Chuck Berry record he helped make such a massive hit. In all, Freed was given co-writing credit on fifteen rock'n'roll hits, even though it's unlikely that he did anything more than promote them.

As rock'n'roll became *the* sound of teenage America, Alan Freed became its patron saint. When a New York paper attacked the new music as a major cause of juvenile delinquency, it was Freed (by then the star of New York's WINS) who responded to the charges both on the air and on a CBS-TV news panel. He appeared in a number of popular rock flicks like *Mr. Rock'n'Roll*, *Don't Knock the Rock* and *Rock Around the Clock*, and his Brooklyn Paramount revues were like weekly Who's Whos of classic rock and R&B talent. However, along with his growing prestige came accusations that Freed made a practice of overselling his concerts, not to mention "mixing the races." A frenzied 1958 Jerry Lee Lewis concert in Boston — where Freed as promoter and emcee was arrested on charges of anarchy and inciting to riot — marked the beginning of an early end.

Sobbing audibly as he took to the air one November afternoon in 1959, Freed announced that he was resigning his post as top disc jockey dog at New York's WABC. Later it was revealed that he'd been asked to leave after refusing "on principle" to sign a statement swearing that he had never taken money or gifts in exchange for playing records. Within two days, he'd also been bounced from his popular TV dance party, *The Big Beat*. (A shot of black teen singing star Frankie Lymon dancing with a white girl on the program also helped to hasten its demise.) Upon hearing the news, his

ROCK 'N ROLL with ALAN FREED

The Story of "ROCK 'n ROLL"

A LETTER FROM ALAN FREED

Dear Gang:
Well, the big fight is over and you and I have won . . . if there was really any fight at all. It seems to me, as I am sure it does to you, that Rock and Roll music is here to stay. A year ago, the skeptics and critics were hollering loud and long that Rock and Roll music would never last. But you and I knew better. This is the exciting dance music of today's teenage generation. I brought it to you and it belongs to you.
I am deeply grateful for the success that you have made possible and I hope and pray that we will be Rocking and Rolling together for a long time to come.
Sincerely,
Alan Freed

Alan Freed pens a premature letter of triumph in a 1957 concert booklet.

youthful studio audience was reduced to tears. "Now they've taken away our father!"one girl cried into the camera.

Freed was, in effect, the payola squad's sacrificial lamb. The altogether more wholesome Dick Clark of *American Bandstand* got off with hardly a slap on the wrist in spite of allegations of millions of dollars' worth of conflicting interests, while Freed took the fall for an alleged $30,650.

His $400 fine and suspended jail term were nothing compared to the public humiliation he would suffer. Then in 1964, the IRS nailed him for income tax evasion. Broke, unemployable and sinking deeper into an alcoholic abyss, he died in a Florida hospital a year later at the age of forty-three. One of rock'n'roll's earliest heroes, he ended up as one of its first casualties.

Photos from left: Freed . . . while still top deejay dog at New York's WINS   With wife Jackie   Counseling the Everlys backstage at one of his Brooklyn bashes   Making his film debut in *Rock Around the Clock*

"I don't make culture — I just sell it. I'm the storekeeper. The shelves are empty. I put the stock on. I make no comment pro or con."

— DICK CLARK

Depending on whom you talk to, Dick Clark represents everything that's right *and* wrong with rock'n'roll commerce. He has spent a quarter of a century as the host of rock TV's make-believe ballroom, *American Bandstand*, spreading the gospel from within the system. But behind that public picture of the sensible but fun-loving chaperon of teendom's ongoing party, the ageless Clark is, like some Top 40 Dorian Gray, a cool and crafty powerbroker who has consciously or otherwise come very close to killing the revolutionary spirit of the music he professes to love so dearly.

In his 1976 collection of somewhat self-serving true confessions, *Rock, Roll, and Remember*, Clark admits rather sheepishly that when he first became the host of the Philadelphia *Bandstand* in 1956, he was familiar with only one or two songs on the show's Top Ten — a list which included such all-time greats as Elvis Presley's "Hound Dog," Little Richard's "Ready Teddy," and "Be-Bop-A-Lula" by Gene Vincent. (Years later when talk show host Merv Griffin asked him what kind of music he listened to, a straight-faced Clark would say that his favorite record was a collection of discount classics he'd ordered from TV — the one with the commercial that begins, "You know this familiar melody as 'Stranger in Paradise,' but its real title is the 'Polovetsian Dances' by Borodin.")

Clark's indifference to rock is telling, given his casual approach to broadcasting it. Denying the spontaneity at the heart of the music, Clark insisted on a lip-sync policy (that is, mouthing the words to a pre-recorded track) for all his musical guests. And then there was the cold shoulder he gave some of the giants of the era. Among the first to get this treatment was Jerry Lee Lewis following his marriage to his thirteen-year-old cousin. Clark also turned his back on Chuck Berry after his arrest for violating the Mann Act. To fill the gap left by the genuine rock pioneers, Clark and his associates offered less menacing substitutes on the order of Frankie Avalon, Fabian and Bobby Rydell — neighborhood "faces" who'd been expressly packaged to meet the taste of *Bandstand's* afterschool audience (as well as that of their folks).

Clark's interest in these vacuous dreamboats may have been directed by more than just casual appreciation. During the 1959–60 payola furor, it was revealed that he held whole or part interest in thirty-three rock'n'roll-related businesses, including record and publishing companies, a management concern and a record pressing plant. He also promoted cross-country tours of one-nighters under the banner of Dick Clark's Caravan of Stars (although most of the principals were paid like anything but stars).

These sins aside, there are any number of reasons for Dick Clark's longevity. His Young Republican good looks and earnest boy-next-door demeanor (not to mention his agreement in 1960 to divest himself of what has since been estimated as $8 million worth of outside business interests) helped to get him off the Senate subcommittee's hit list. And although he has been married three times, his private life has never been besmirched by scandal — a fact he credits primarily to a fortuitous lack of interest in the winsome jailbait that has surrounded him for the last thirty years. In addition, he has made sure that Dick Clark is the *only* star of *American Bandstand*. (Rumor has it he instigated a non-repeater policy for his dancers when he moved the show to California so he wouldn't have any "regulars" stealing his thunder as they did back in Philly.)

In the seventies, Clark managed to make the transition from TV teen idol to prime-time TV star without missing a beat by hosting *Bandstand* anniversary shows, blooper specials and *The Twenty-five Thousand Dollar Pyramid*. He has scant trouble landing these lucrative gigs since most of them are packaged by his own Dick Clark Productions which produces movies, radio shows, concerts and up to two hundred TV shows a year. Even Jerry Lee Lewis and Chuck Berry have managed to forget the old hurts in order to get next to Dick again. (Indeed Jerry Lee was an honoree on Clark's syndie *Tribute* show last year.)

But then Dick Clark is an extremely ingratiating fellow and a very rich and powerful one to boot. Even though his influence in the current pop music marketplace is marginal, no one wants to be on his bad side. So what if he played Bobby Rydell instead of Jerry Lee Lewis and made Chuck Berry lip-sync "Maybellene." He'll always have a place in the hearts of TV executives and the generation who grew up watching him after school.

Albert Grossman was a starmaker for the sixties, one who took great pains to distinguish himself from the music-business establishment by styling himself after his artists — affecting the jeans, long hair and mercurial manner of the counterculture heroes (Bob Dylan, Peter, Paul and Mary, Janis Joplin, The Band, et al.) whose fortunes he charted. He cut an odd figure in those days — this middle-aged man with the granny glasses, ponytail and round amiable face of a kosher Ben Franklin. Everything about the way he presented himself was meant to intimidate — his looks, his sparse conversation, his unblinking stare. Industry people dreaded the thought of negotiating with him, employees trembled in his presence, and world-famous pop stars competed for his love and attention. In *Buried Alive*, Myra Friedman, his former publicity director, wrote that "his office in the rock hierarchy was like the Vatican, just as powerful and shrouded in just as much mystery. And in the same sense, Albert Grossman was its Pope."

But although Grossman radiated a sinister presence, his integrity has never really been an issue. Of course, he wasn't shy about taking a healthy (25 percent) cut of his acts' earnings, nor did he hesitate to go for the jugular when doing his thing. (See him bring the BBC to its knees in a bidding war for a Dylan appearance, in *Don't Look Back*.) No, the biggest complaint about Grossman was his tendency to disappear for weeks at a time — retreating to the solitude of his Woodstock sanctum.

If anything, Grossman was a father figure to his rambunctious pups — trying his best to keep pace with what Friedman has described as Janis Joplin's endless efforts to "outrage him, unnerve him, seduce him, drive him half crazy if she could." And it was Grossman who propped Dylan up following his split with Suze Rotollo and again, after his traumatic motorcycle accident — as well as introducing him to Sara Lowndes, the woman who would become his wife. Like all fathers, however, Grossman has watched his children grow up and move on — some have passed on to their final reward, while others have rebelled for reasons that remain unclear.

In 1969, Bob Dylan let his contract with Grossman lapse, thus bringing to an end one of the most symbiotic artist-manager collaborations in pop. (Apparently when Dylan said good-bye to Grossman, he didn't look back; Grossman was forced to sue his former client for $600,000 in uncollected managerial commissions in 1981.)

By the early seventies, some people were saying that Grossman had lost his touch. Whether by design or default, he has since stepped out of the music business mainstream, choosing instead to tend to his real estate investments in upstate New York. He still oversees the Bearsville management operation, but for the time being, the nearest thing he's got to a star is Todd Rundgren. (Close, but no cigar.) But who needs the high-pressure show-biz grind when you can live the life of a country squire? On his Woodstock estate, Grossman has fashioned what must surely be an aging music mogul's idea of heaven — a country retreat, a recording studio and his very own Chinese restaurant.

Janis and her band were awed when Albert agreed to take them on. "Don't ever trust me," he warned them on the day they finalized the deal.

Allen Klein . . . his very name struck terror in the hearts of record company execs.

Allen Klein had an affinity for fine print, ledger sheets and the bottom line, and a driving ambition to control the top-selling rock groups of all time. Simply put, he was an accountant who wanted to rule the world.

Klein got his start in 1958 when he cornered Bobby Vinton at a mutual friend's wedding and asked him if he'd like to make $100,000. "Sure," replied the startled singer. "What would I have to do?" "Nothing," replied Klein. "Just leave it to me." A few months later, Vinton received a check for $100,000 for previously overlooked fees and recording royalties ferreted out by Klein. From there, Klein went on to perform comparable feats of accounting wizardry for everyone from Sam Cooke to Steve and Edie. To them, he was a financial miracle worker, a dragonslayer who brought the giant record companies to their knees. But to the industry, he was a posturing blowhard — one who would sooner shatter an artist's career than walk away from a negotiation empty-handed.

In 1964, Klein quite naturally set his sights on the Beatles. But instead of pursuing them directly, he applied his considerable energies to acquiring other eminent British Invaders like the Kinks, Donovan, the Dave Clark Five, Jeff Beck, the Animals, the Yardbirds, Marianne Faithfull, Terry Reid and most notably the Fab Four's bad boy rivals, the Rolling Stones. It was on the recommendation of record producer Mickey Most that Andrew Oldham signed Klein to advise the group and look after his own personal business affairs. Several months later, in what was a tremendous personal coup, Klein, acting on behalf of the Stones, extracted from Decca Records what was then the highest advance (variously reported at somewhere between $1.25 million and $7 million) ever paid a music act. Jagger and Oldham were ecstatic, but it was not long afterward that a dispute erupted between Klein and Oldham as to exactly where and how that money had been disbursed. (Oldham claimed that the advance should have been paid to Nanker Phelge Music Ltd., a British company owned and operated by him and the Stones, but instead, it had been paid to a different Nanker Phelge — this one a recently formed American subsidiary of Allen Klein and Company that claimed Klein as its president and sole stockholder.) Klein eventually settled a $1.5 million suit brought by Oldham claiming that the company had been used as a "vehicle for the diversion of assets and income" from him and the Stones by offering Oldham a million-dollar buyout of his residual interests in the Stones.* Within the next few years, Klein also suceeded in adding Herman's Hermits, Donovan, the Animals and the Dave Clark Five to his stable. Still, the one group he coveted most lay beyond his reach. Then, in 1967, Brian Epstein died, leaving the Beatles to fend for themselves. For many close to the group, this signaled the beginning of the end.

Keith Richards recently observed, "We knew it was all over for the Beatles once Epstein died and Klein took over. The Stones could survive by themselves as always, but Epstein was the glue that held the Beatles together. We were trying to get rid of Klein as manager when they were just about to sign on with him and we said, 'No, no. Don't. Why do you think we're getting out?' " But Richards's account fails to mention one pertinent fact: although the Stones would eventually mount a multimillion-dollar lawsuit against Klein, Mick Jagger was the one who touted Klein to John Lennon in the first place.

Still, it was Klein's fancy dancing — his vast knowledge of Lennon's personal contribution to the Beatles' musical treasure trove and his tales of childhood hardship (like Lennon, he'd been farmed out to relatives as a kid) — that convinced the head Beatle that he was the one man who could fill Epstein's shoes. But instead of saving the group, Klein's involvement only aggravated an already sensitive situation. It is here, amidst the disintegration of the Beatles and their utopian vision of self-sustaining artistic community, that most pop fans first became familiar with Allen Klein's name, and got their first look at the tubby little man with the greasy hair, checkered pants and meatball visage who presumed to take Brian Epstein's place. To them, as well as to most British record industry insiders, Klein looked like he'd stepped out of a gangster movie. (The Beatlemaniacs who camped outside the Apple offices during this period were known to shout "Mafia! Mafia!" at him as he came and went.) They still blame him for bleeding Apple dry, for killing the dream. Fair or not, Klein remains, for many, the prototype of the money-grubbing parasite who feeds off the naïveté of rock'n'roll stars.

In fact, Klein has been accused of an amazing variety of financial swindles over the years — everything from skimming money off the sale of albums to benefit George Harrison's Pakistan relief fund to failure to report revenues from the illegal sale of Beatles promotional albums. In 1971, Klein was a leading character in Paul McCartney's suit to terminate the Beatles' affiliation when the presiding judge in the case accused his company, ABKCO, of receiving "commissions grossly in excess of that specified" (20 percent of all Beatles' incomes) in their original agreement. Finally, in 1979, Klein was convicted and sentenced to five years and a $10,000 fine for filing a false tax return after a federal judge concluded that he had lied during an earlier tax fraud trial. The following year he was sent up the (East) river to do a greatly reduced stretch of two months at the Manhattan Correctional Center.

Since his release, Klein has busied himself by bankrolling movies (*The Greek Tycoon, Personal Best*) and Broadway shows (most notably a failed Renée Taylor–Joseph Bologna comedy collaboration, *It Had to Be You*, and Edward Albee's *Man with Three Arms*). However, his most interesting business transaction of late involved the purchase of the rights to "He's So Fine" following a lawsuit accusing George Harrison of borrowing heavily from that song's melody line in "My Sweet Lord." But although Harrison was later found to have committed unconscious plagiarism, the court, noting Klein's recent acquisition of the song, assigned a fine of $500,000 — exactly the same amount Klein had paid for the rights.

---

* The terms of a 1984 settlement allowed Klein to maintain control of the enormously valuable copyrights to the Stones classics he acquired in this coup.

Berry Gordy has come in for his share of accusations over the years. He has been called everything from an Uncle Tom to a Mafia front. Still, his ambitions didn't land him in the Big House; but in a breathtaking Bel Air estate with free-roaming peacocks, hilltop tennis courts and a stone-inlaid pool. His story was good enough to inspire a Broadway musical (*Dreamgirls*), and while his power may not be quite as potent today as it was in the sixties, Berry Gordy is still very much the mogul of Motown, the only black-owned record company to make it in the world of white-dominated pop.

It was, just like the record label said, "The Sound of Young America." The sound of young American dollars, black and white, rolling into Berry Gordy, Jr.'s coffers. The Motown legacy on record was one of a world united by soul, teens of all creeds and colors dancing in the streets to a black beat embellished with uptown schmaltz. But as high-minded as that Motor City sound and vision was, and in some ways still is, it was nevertheless the direct product of founder and chief Gordy's passionate thirst for power, prestige and the good old dough-re-mi that can buy them.

The stories of Berry Gordy's poverty-filled upbringing that circulated during Motown's early years are mostly his own invention. In reality, he came from a family of self-starters who ran several small businesses in the black section of Detroit. Not rich, but not ghetto poor either, the Gordys were comfortably well off. In the late forties, at the age of twenty-five, Gordy opened his first self-owned business — a record store. After it went bankrupt in 1955, he put in two years on a Ford assembly line before striking out again as a small-time record producer and songwriter. By 1959, Gordy had family financing, family labor and a new name — Motown Records. Most of all, he had, in Detroit alone, a wealth of talent on which to build his company.

Actually, "empire" is more like it. In his old Detroit mansion, there used to hang a portrait of Gordy dressed like Napoleon Bonaparte. And in fact, the diminutive Gordy is said to have presided over Motown like a power-mad tyrant, a despot as charming as he was cantankerous. He put his artists through a rigorous in-house charm school — not unlike those of the old Hollywood star factories — where former ghetto kids learned everything from dining etiquette to slicked-up Apollo Theater–style choreography. At times, Gordy's dictums seemed arbitrary, almost perverse in a way — like his habit of changing intricately synchronized dance routines just minutes before showtime. And when he instigated a "Hits Only" policy at Motown, he wasn't kidding. He often sent Smokey Robinson and writer-producers like Holland, Dozier and Holland back into the studio over and over again to correct flaws he alone could hear.

Sometimes it seemed as if Gordy didn't want any of his people getting too comfortable, thinking they'd mastered the rules of his game. He could humiliate a staff member one minute, then tuck a hundred-dollar bill in his pocket the next. Perks for top-selling artists might take the form of fur coats and Cadillacs. However, they came at a time when those same artists were pulling little more than $200 a week in salaries while the company itself was grossing $30 million a year (with Gordy as sole stockholder).

Gordy's erratic behavior and frugal — some say devious — financial dealings ultimately cost him most of his original stars. In 1968, Holland, Dozier and Holland sued the company for $22 million in unpaid royalties. The Temptations, the first Motown stars to order an audit, finally abandoned the label in the late seventies. Stevie Wonder stayed with Motown, but only after winning a bigger piece of the action, and total artistic autonomy. And in what must have been a tremendous blow to his ego, Diana Ross, the object of Gordy's romantic and professional obsessions for more than fifteen years, defected to RCA (and New York) in 1981. Ross had been Gordy's Galatea. He'd molded her into a superstar and, in return, she had provided him with entrée into the world of white-ruled show business — starting with the Supremes' minstrel shows in Las Vegas and culminating with movies and Hollywood. "I wanted it that way," Ross says now. "It was safe. Berry did it all for me. He was father, mother, brother, sister, lover." Diana Ross was nurtured and protected as no other Motown artist would be again, but sometimes at the expense of her personal relationships. Shortly before his divorce from Ross in 1977, Robert Silberstein, her husband of six years, complained bitterly, "She's totally dominated by a man who never read a book in his life. I just

can't stand it anymore to hear them calling Stevie Wonder a genius. Whatever happened to Freud?"

For a multitude of reasons — from the defections of Marvin Gaye and Diana Ross, to the company's diminished clout in the marketplace — the giddy high of Motown's Detroit "family" era is no more. Despite the ongoing success of relative newcomers like the Commodores, Rockwell and Rick James and the return of the Temptations, that old black magic has been sadly depleted. Today the corridors of the company's Hollywood headquarters are a subdued place. The recent industry slump hit Motown particularly hard, the staff has been pruned back judiciously, and intrigue runs high among those who remain. Gordy himself rarely comes into the offices, preferring to conduct his business Hollywood style, from his lavish hilltop estate.

Yet thanks to its hit-filled back catalogues, Motown is still a very viable operation — so much so that although Gordy is only in his fifties, the right to inherit his throne is already shaping up to be a battle royal among the executives currently at the helm and the boss's children. And to complicate matters, there has been some speculation that Gordy might bypass all likely contenders to name Jermaine Jackson, former Jackson 5 brother and husband of his beloved daughter, Hazel, as his successor (although that would seem unlikely now that Jermaine has patched things up with his brothers and switched to another label).

When all the uproar has died down, what will be Berry Gordy's legacy? Gordy has often been accused of watering down black R&B for white consumption, and to some degree, that charge is true. He openly catered to white tastes with the bright pop flourishes on his records and the clean-cut Motown family image of his acts and supperclub-style stage shows. But in spite of this, as much as because of

it, Berry Gordy, Jr., created a brilliant new sound of soul. It is a testament to his instincts and his artists that "You Really Got a Hold on Me," "My Girl," "I Want You Back" and "What's Goin' On" — to name four out of hundreds of Motown classics — will last a lot longer than the fantastic riches they begat.

By the industry standards of his day, Brian Epstein didn't exactly fit the part of rock tycoon. Neither a natural-born promoter like Colonel Tom Parker nor a financial wizard like Allen Klein, too personable to be a corporate stiff, Epstein was simply an astute middle-class businessman with a passion for the theater and the manners of a veddy proper British gent. That he made his millions by guiding the Beatles to world-class celebrity is at once a tribute to his singular devotion to the group and a remarkable quirk of fate.

A product of private school (with a brief unsuccessful fling at the Royal Academy of Dramatic Art), he was already a local Liverpool success as the head of the record department of his family's thriving retail business by the time he signed the Beatles in 1961. Though he undoubtedly sensed their commercial potential, his commitment to the group had a religious fervor that transcended monetary lust. During their early years together, he not only booked their gigs, but postered, publicized and promoted them like royal command performances — even though his net profit was sometimes as low as one pound. He also instructed the band on the fine art of professionalism. No more showing up late for shows (much less not at all); no more playing just any old song in just any old order; and no more ratty black leather jackets. Epstein dressed The Boys in natty gray suits with velvet collars and thin lapels. He even made them switch from Woodbines, the workingman's cigarette, to a classier smoke called Senior Service. The one thing he never did was to tell them what or how to play.

In return, the Beatles got him into show business. Ironically, that's when Epstein's troubles began; for what worked on a neighborhood scale in Liverpool did not work in the big-money circles in which he soon found himself. When producer Walter Shenson first began drawing up a Beatle film deal for *A Hard Day's Night*, for example, Brian thought a 7½-percent piece of the action was called for, whereas Shenson had intended to offer him 25. Further, his inability to cope with bootleggers of Beatle merchandise resulted in a disastrous contract with a British company to control the sale of authorized Beatle gear — one which provided the Beatles themselves with only a paltry 10-percent cut of the action.

There were personal problems as well, including the fact that Epstein was gay. The prejudice and leftover Victorian morals of preswinging Britain had forced Epstein to lead a double life as a teenager. The international attention focused on him as a result of his fantastic success with the Beatles and other pop acts as well — Cilla Black, Gerry and the Pacemakers, etc. — only served to intensify the dilemma. His melancholy is also said to have been exacerbated by his unrequited (or was it?) passion for John Lennon. As time wore on, Epstein began to suffer from fears that the Beatles and the business were slipping away from him. Apple Press liaison Derek Taylor has said, "He sought an exclusivity in his relationships; he didn't like sharing too much. He was the following things: very funny, very romantic, very sensitive to beautiful things. Still, he had other areas in his life which caused him some pain. We never knew where he went at night and he was often depressed and lonely. And like a lot of people who seem to have a full address book, there were times when he couldn't reach people. If no one answered the phone on a particular night, he would get very upset, very paranoid. It was during one of those weekends that he died." Brian Epstein's death on August 27, 1967, of a barbiturate overdose — while the Beatles were off searching for inner peace with a publicity-hungry Indian guru — was a tragic accident. It may also have been a merciful end.

Though he is often dismissed today as a naïve businessman of vastly overrated promotional talent, there is still no question that it was Brian Epstein who was largely responsible for transforming the Beatles from an exceptionally talented group of working-class punks into the most beloved pop group in history. "No one could possibly replace Brian," was Paul's eulogy. And no one ever did.

Only nineteen himself when he first signed the Stones, Oldham understood intuitively what his peers wanted and, more importantly, how to get them to go out and buy it. All it took was a highly combustible mixture of mod flamboyance, Artful Dodger chicanery and zealous generation-gap marketing — in short, nothing more than the natural components of Oldham's own personality. At right he encourages the group to sneer for the birdie.

Christopher "Kit" Lambert has been described as the kind of spacey upper-class eccentric who thinks nothing of wearing a pajama top with a $1,000 Savile Row suit. The son of Constant Lambert, an acclaimed classical composer and conductor who died of alcoholism at the age of forty, Lambert originally entertained notions of becoming a filmmaker, first as a student at Cambridge, and later as an assistant director at England's Shepperton Studios, until stumbling upon a fledgling group called the High Numbers — later to become the Who. Lambert's friend, Simon Napier-Bell, himself a celebrated rock manager, says, "When Kit met the Who, he found in Peter Townshend an undirected intelligence that fed hungrily on his own anarchistic self-destructive ideas. Most critics saw this as an incitement to violence, but they were wrong. It was symbolic suicide — Kit Lambert's glamorized version of his father's drunken self-destruction."

Easily as neurotic, high-strung and megalomaniacal as any of the Who's celebrated loons, Lambert was anything but a savvy business mind or hard-nosed deal-maker. Theatrics, packaging and hype — these were his strengths. It was Lambert who first suggested that Townshend convert a tantrum over a piece of malfunctioning equipment, which had resulted in his bashing his guitar to bits during a performance, into a piece of ongoing shtick in the Who's stage act. ("Auto-destruction" he called it.) And it was Lambert who provided the group with their infamous mod jacket made from the Union Jack. More to the point, he groomed Pete Townshend into the ultimate rock star savant — providing him with the pop art philosophy on which the Who was mounted, praising and believing in his schemes and blowing them up to even grander proportions. In the years that he and Chris Stamp (the street-smart brother of actor Terence Stamp) managed the Who, Lambert handled production duties on some of the group's most popular LPs. He also founded the pioneering Track Records label and was the first to sign Jimi Hendrix.

As for the man himself, Napier-Bell remembers Lambert as always being "totally up or totally down, depressed or wickedly witty, desolate or ecstatic. He had an underlying distrust of life, hated its boredom, its slowness, its conventions, and yet, he was continually amused and amazed by every second of it. He was delighted by failures. He collected them. His stories were of things gone wrong, and the bigger the disaster, the better the story."

Lambert got a tragedy of epic proportions in his break with the Who, a break ostensibly precipitated by missing sums of money and a casual kind of bookkeeping that led to monumental tax problems. But at the heart of the split was Lambert's collaboration with Townshend. Roger Daltrey had always resented the exclusivity of their conspiratorial relationship, feeling that it gave Townshend the power base from which to dominate the group. Not surprisingly, it was Daltrey who initiated an audit of Lambert and Stamp's books and who lobbied incessantly to sever the group from their control. For his part, Lambert harbored deep resentment at not having his role as one of the creators of *Tommy* acknowledged. Further, he was appalled by Townshend's swearing off drugs and other recreational excess in the early seventies, deeming it priggish and unsuitable behavior for a rock star. More damaging, though, was the fact that by this point Lambert was almost completely deranged owing to full-scale drugging and debauchery. Finally, in mid-1973, Daltrey told the Who it would have to choose between Lambert and him. Faced with losing the group's very popular lead singer, Townshend finally agreed to his former mentor's ouster.

Finding no other outlet worthy of his interest, Lambert decamped to Venice where he bought a decrepit *palazzo* and plunged headlong into showy self-abuse. In 1978, the man who had parlayed a modest inheritance into a fortune by packaging the Who declared himself unfit to handle his own finances and was made a ward of the court. Broke and homeless, he spent the last years of his life chasing comely young Italian men and moving from one small hotel to another. In 1981, he suffered a severe head injury during what was either a mugging assault or a beating supposedly administered at a gay club. The next day his skull was fractured in a fall down the stairs at his mother's house. He died in the hospital three days later after his family agreed to switch off his life-support system.

★

Andrew Loog Oldham is generally regarded as the original brains behind the Rolling Stones — the Svengali who both plucked the group from obscurity and was responsible for packaging their image. Yet in the long run, Oldham didn't fare much better with the boys than their ubiquitous ladyfriends; his collaboration with Mick Jagger and Keith Richards sailed along for a few exuberant years and then suddenly he was gone. Whatever his contributions to the group's success, ultimately Oldham proved to be expendable. Today Jagger ranks him as little more than a dilettante. "Andrew really didn't have any original ideas at all," he has observed. "Basically, he just nicked." Of course, so did the Stones just nick. It's just that they did it so much better.

Before discovering the Stones on the London pub circuit, Oldham had already launched two wildly unsuccessful singing careers under the dubious names of Chancery Lane and Sandy Beach. He had also done promotion and publicity for fashion queen Mary Quant, operated his own booking agency, and even worked briefly as a record plugger for Beatles manager Brian Epstein. Hip and brilliant, with a flair for images, ideas and putting the right people together, Oldham proved himself to be a precocious media manipulator during those early years. Still a teenager himself when he first signed the Stones, he understood intuitively what his peers wanted and, more importantly, how to get them to go out and buy it.

Interestingly, the one innovation with which Oldham is most widely credited — the Stones' renegade image — was not his invention. On the contrary, he fought it in the beginning, trying to transform the scruffy punks into ersatz Mop Tops. It was only after Oldham realized that the press was far more interested in playing up the differences between the two groups that he began to capitalize on the Stones' coarse looks and loutish behavior, encouraging them to come on surly with interviewers and creating slogans ("Would you want your sister to marry a Rolling Stone?") that playfully pointed up their antisocial stance.

In *A Clockwork Orange*, Anthony Burgess's novel of future gang terrorism, Oldham found a virtual textbook of embellishment for the Stones' hype. He imitated Burgess's brutal artificial language in his liner notes for *The Rolling Stones Now* and encouraged Jagger to acquire the rights to the novel (which he held on to for years) in the hope that he and Keith would play the star droogies on screen. "There was a time when Mick and I got on really well with Andrew," Richards remembers. "We went through that whole *Clockwork Orange* thing. Very butch sort of number."

Oldham's unrelentingly trendy image — his malchick get-ups, campy behavior, and fondness for mascara and pancake makeup together with his very chummy relationship with Jagger (they shared an apartment for a while) — ultimately led to talk that he harbored a romantic fixation on the nubile lead Stone. Even so, by 1967 and the super-spaced-out *Satanic Majesties* sessions, Oldham and the Stones had unceremoniously parted company. In a 1978 interview, he chalked up the split to diverging attitudes and life-styles. What is more likely is that the Stones, now famous beyond their wildest dreams, were no longer in need of a pitchman/mentor — especially not one as heavy-handed as Oldham. Besides which, they shared a belief that Oldham had been entirely too generous to himself with their money. In a 1971 legal action, the group charged that in addition to his 25-percent cut off the top of the Stones' pie, Oldham and Eric Easton had made a "secret" deal with Decca in 1963 to give them an 8-percent share of Stones' recording royalties over and above theirs. In any case, Allen Klein, who had originally been brought in by Oldham to act as his personal financial manager, eventually bought him out of his share. By that time, however, Oldham had already launched his own record label, Immediate. The roster of acts — the Nice, Humble Pie, Small Faces and, briefly, Fleetwood Mac — was impressive. And yet, within three years the company had folded. Soon after, Oldham went into what appeared to be a semiretirement with the exception of a brief and disastrous liaison with Motown as a staff producer in 1969, and an unsuccessful attempt to revive the Immediate label by recording Marianne Faithfull in 1976. When last heard from the erstwhile boy genius, who now lives in New York with his beautiful South American wife and baby son, was touting a band called the Werewolves (whose lead singer was the spitting image of Keith Richards) and freelancing special projects for none other than Allen Klein.

In today's world of corporate-ruled rock perhaps the only self-owned tycoon who functions for the most part outside the mainstream is Bill Graham. As father of modern rock concert promotion in the sixties at the Fillmores East and West, Graham (born Wolfgang Grajanca in Berlin in 1931) showed the world how to present maverick talent like the Jefferson Airplane, Lenny Bruce, the Mothers of Invention, Miles Davis and B.B. King on a weekly basis and still turn a profit — both spiritually and otherwise. Considered a major villain during the flower power era, owing primarily to his gruff exterior and refusal to apologize for making tons of money from the flourishing music scene, Graham was constantly assailed by members of the counterculture movement as a dirty, no-good Capitalist (a bad word in those days). They demanded free concerts for The People, a share of his take, and in some cases, the Fillmore itself. Nasty confrontations between him and local longhairs were daily occurrences in the streets of San Francisco and the Lower East Side. Growing more embittered and hostile, Graham began admonishing fifteen-year-olds to "go out and earn a living," and throwing overzealous fans off his stage with a maniacal glee.

His relationship with performers, not to mention managers and agents, was no less volatile; a masterful negotiator, he could scream, threaten and cajole in the same breath. (As a young man, Graham wanted to be an actor, and there was nothing he loved more than an opportunity to emote. Myra Friedman once described one of his backstage performances as "Rasputin trying out for the Moscow Art Theater.") The only time anyone got the better of him in an argument occurred many years ago when he sat bound and gagged on the New York Fillmore stage while Abbie Hoffman told him off.

When Graham closed the Fillmore East in 1971, he predicted that the greed of rock artists, whose astronomical fees had forced rock concerts into racetracks and football stadiums with mushy acoustics and limited visibility, would ultimately be its death. Today, of course, Graham is *the* status promoter of rock stadium shows — having produced the Dylan/Band tour of 1974, the Watkins Glen superfestival in 1973, the Band's Thanksgiving extravaganza and their Last Waltz at Winterland, and the Rolling Stones' 1981 Sherman-like march through the States, to name just a few. He's the person you call to make a megaconcert, if not exactly intimate, at least flashy and well-tuned. And now, Bill Graham's a movie star, having played himself in *A Star Is Born* and (more or less himself) in *Apocalypse Now*. There are fewer fights, fewer hysterical outbursts; he seems mellower, not to mention richer, than ever before. Of course, every so often that old spark is ignited and the legendary Graham vitriol starts to flow — as it did a few years back when Graham reportedly tried to kick down the door of his then-client Van Morrison in order to gain an audience with the reclusive singer, and more recently, when an unlucky group of aisle-blocking concertgoers at the New York City, Graham-produced ARMS benefit had the misfortune of getting in his way.

The 1980s version of the precocious young starmakers of the sixties are baby record moguls like David Geffen and big deal managers like Irving Azoff and Elliot Roberts. Not that they make any pretense of being selflessly devoted to their pop star clientele. On the contrary, power is their game, money their motivation. The resemblance is more a matter of personal style. To the industry, they're talented whiz kids — as volatile and erratic as the people they front. To their clients, they're big brothers — who come on with a you-and-me-against-the-world approach. As personal manager (Joni Mitchell, Jackson Browne, etc.) Elliot Roberts says, "People see now that they can become millionaires by doing it right. They used to think that you had to beat someone for all their publishing to hit the jackpot. We showed them that it was the other way around."

But then, these new-style tycoons better play it straight. After all, they're no longer dealing with backwoods pickers who wouldn't know a copyright from a hole in the ground. Today's rocker makes it a point to stay on top of his financial affairs. "Sure, we have regular meetings on merchandising," says Gene Simmons of Kiss. "I'm a good Jewish boy from Brooklyn and all four of us are members of the board. I don't have any respect for bands who get ripped off. Christianity and Disney have nothing on us."

At thirty-eight, poor Elvis Presley was well on his way to Rock'n'Roll Heaven, his talent and vitality severely undermined by the machinations of a ruthless powerbroker. But some eight years later at the same age, Mick Jagger was not only fronting the most durable rock group of all time, but commanding its financial affairs as well. Underneath Jagger's tights and carefully torn shirts lurks a closet businessman in a pin-striped suit. After years of getting burned by marauding money changers, the head Stone finally took over the reins of the group's business management in the late sixties. Today he oversees the day-to-day details of the Stones' empire — everything from tax shelters to album packaging. Thanks largely to his efforts, the Stones' 1981 tour is estimated to have grossed somewhere in the neighborhood of $50 million — not including the income generated from the airplay and sales of *Tattoo You*, the top-selling album the group toured to promote. Not bad for ten weeks' work.

As a rock entrepreneur, Jagger has proven himself to be as mercenary and manipulative as any of the old-time wheeler-dealers. In a move unsurpassed in its commercial inventiveness, for example, he got a perfume company to underwrite the extravagant travel, lodging and trucking expenses for the '81 tour in exchange for exclusive sponsorship rights. And if performing before a million people at around $40 a pop wasn't enough, Jagger also engineered a scheme whereby the group's final concert date would be televised via closed circuit to every major city in the country. However, his demand that independent theater owners cough up a hefty $40,000 advance for the honor of hosting the show ended up boondoggling the project altogether. Further evidence of Jagger's money-mindedness came to light when it was revealed that the Stones had declined to meet James Brown's asking price as an opening act for the tour. In the past, the Stones had insisted on using black performers as opening acts, but that may be because somebody else (namely local promoters) was footing the bill.

Of course, nobody ever said the Rolling Stones were running a charity. On the contrary, it's that very sense of survival that has allowed the group to endure all these years. Mick Jagger understands that the Rolling Stones are first and foremost a business enterprise. He knows that with a little luck, any idiot can stumble his way into a Top Twenty Hit, but it takes financial horse sense to parlay it into a twenty-year career and an income higher than the gross national product of Peru.

Underneath Jagger's tights lurks a closet businessman in a pin-striped suit.

Lest you think that the old-fashioned rock mastermind is entirely a thing of the past, consider Malcolm McLaren — the man who brought you Johnny Rotten and the Sex Pistols. A former tailor with an art school education, McLaren's involvement with rock management grew out of an infatuation with the New York Dolls born during their ill-starred European tour of 1975. He followed the group back to New York where he used his wages as a window dresser to revamp their fading glitter tramp image. Drawing his inspiration from a group of self-styled French intellectuals with Marxist/Dadaist leanings, he adorned the group in leather jumpsuits and placed them in front of a giant hammer-and-sickle backdrop. But despite his efforts, apathy and heroin eventually consumed the band, and McLaren headed back to London.

The Sex Pistols, McLaren's next foray into rock, grew out of the scene at Sex, the anti-fashion boutique he opened with his then-consort, Vivienne Westwood. The group whose first incarnation combined the remnants of two amateurish bands called the Swankers and the Moors Murderers (named after a pair of sadistic child killers who terrorized Manchester in the early sixties) was born in earnest on the fateful day that John Lydon walked into the store. His body stooped from a childhood bout with meningitis, his hair orange and spiky and his lips curled back over rotting teeth in a crazed snarl, Lydon was anything but a pinup boy. Nevertheless, McLaren knew he had something. Prevailing over Lydon's naturally suspicious nature, he induced him to audition for the group using the store's juke box as accompaniment. Lydon made no attempt whatever to sing, choosing instead to shout what he knew of the lyrics to an Alice Cooper song at the top of his lungs. Brimming over with rage and frustration, he stopped in the middle and screamed, "I can't sing this shit." It was an hysterical and altogether frightening performance — one that convinced McLaren that he had stumbled upon some sort of genius.

Under McLaren's tutelage, the Sex Pistols found their first audiences by pulling into local concerts and posing as the backup band. In 1976, the group gained widespread attention when it pelted a British TV interviewer with four-letter words. The episode got the group banned from practically every venue in the country. In a televised press conference a few days later, McLaren shrugged, "What can I say? Boys will be boys." At the few gigs that remained open to the group, Lydon managed to taunt audiences into a violent frenzy, provoking free-for-alls that left a slew of broken furniture, equipment and heads in their wake. Upon returning home, the group again caused a national incident by engaging in what spectators later described as a spitting contest at Heathrow Airport. After hurling epithets at airline employees and luckless passersby, Sid Vicious capped off the evening's festivities by throwing up in an airport elevator. This display got the group unceremoniously bounced from their label, EMI, but not before McLaren had extracted a hefty settlement to ease the pain of their public disgrace.

A subsequent alliance, with A&M Records, also went up in a blaze of publicity after Rotten was arrested for amphetamine possession, and several of the group were accused of assaulting a local deejay because he refused to play their new single. Once again, McLaren won a cash settlement — this one almost twice as large as the last. Barred from virtually every record label as well as most clubs and theaters, the Sex Pistols were nevertheless growing richer by the minute. Finally, the group was picked up by Virgin Records, which released their single "God Save the Queen," wherein Rotten called the monarch a moron in honor of her Silver Jubilee celebration.

McLaren then announced that they would tour America in conjunction with the release of their debut album, *Never Mind the Bollocks, Here's the Sex Pistols.* Hoping to provoke continued headline-making confrontations with their audiences, McLaren booked the group into small clubs and redneck honky-tonks. Unfortunately, however, the Pistols' dates were attended mostly by well-behaved middle-class kids. Even the Pistols seemed curiously tame. Later, it was revealed that Rotten's subdued behavior was the result of his exasperation with acting out McLaren's finely tuned shock rock tactics. (McLaren had been known to stand in the wings and conduct the lead Pistol's onstage theatrics and violent outbursts.)

McLaren tried to get control of his boy by turning the other members of the group against him. Rotten retaliated by abandoning ship — thereby pushing the group into a void and McLaren into a corner. McLaren fled to Paris and withdrew into what one observer described as a state of "catatonic" depression.

The subsequent announcement of the group's split was upstaged by the news of Sid Vicious's near fatal OD during a cross-country plane trip, and subsequent arrest for the murder of his girlfriend, Nancy Spungen. McLaren immediately came to Sid's aid. But a short time later Sid was dead — along with any hopes McLaren might have had for reviving the band.

In 1979, Lydon and McLaren squared off in court when Lydon sought to be released from his management contract, and to block the distribution of the film *The Great Rock'n'Roll Swindle* — claiming that its lurid scenes of group sex, incest and necrophilia were too horrific even for him. In the end, the film was temporarily shelved, and an executor was appointed to sort out the Pistols' tangled financial affairs. While the court battle raged, the soundtrack album for *The Great Rock'n'Roll Swindle* hit the streets. Designed as an epitaph for the group, its message seemed to be "The joke's on you if you thought we were for real."

While in seclusion following the trial, the ever-alert McLaren focused on the prevailing obsession of the music industry — home taping — and composed a paean to the new tape piracy, which he bestowed on three former Ants (of Adam and) and an exotic-looking nymphet named Annabella Lwin whom he'd discovered working in a dry cleaner's. He christened the group Bow Wow Wow and the girl Lolita.

McLaren decided to market his new group's first effort with a children's magazine, a "junior *Playboy*" called *Chicken.* "Vulgarity was a necessity, of course, absolutely vital to sell the magazine," he said. "We needed [Lolita] nude on the cover." Lolita's mother quickly pulled the plug on that idea but not before McLaren used it to reap reams of sleazy publicity. Nevertheless, the public outcry promptly killed his deal with EMI, leaving McLaren to move on to the greener pastures of RCA. "Of course, I've heard the horror stories," said a label exec, "but we can't let the history of the manager stand in the way of artistry. We made it clear that the deal was for the music, not for McLaren."

But of course, when you get a McLaren group, what you're mostly getting is McLaren himself — his music, his hype, his particular brand of anything-for-a-buck anarchy. Just look at the Sex Pistols. It seems like only yesterday that they were being hailed as the Saviors of Rock. Now where are they? McLaren, on the other hand, has never been more visible. In the short time since the Pistols' demise, he has not only launched Bow Wow Wow, but in a roundabout manner, Adam Ant and the ubiquitous Boy George. A 1982 appearance at a national convention of record retailers was followed by a chichi fashion spread in *Vogue* featuring him and Westwood. And then, last year, McLaren finally stepped out from behind the curtain to perform a square dance rap on "Buffalo Gal." *Rolling Stone* gave his first album effort (*Duck Rock*) three and a half stars, *Time* magazine hailed his *Duck Rock* videos as some of the year's best, and *Newsweek* called him the "most brilliant, outrageous, and controversial Svengali on the British music scene today." And so, when all is said and done, it just may turn out that McLaren's most cunning piece of media manipulation is the public image he has conjured up for himself.

Malcolm McLaren: Buck Rock

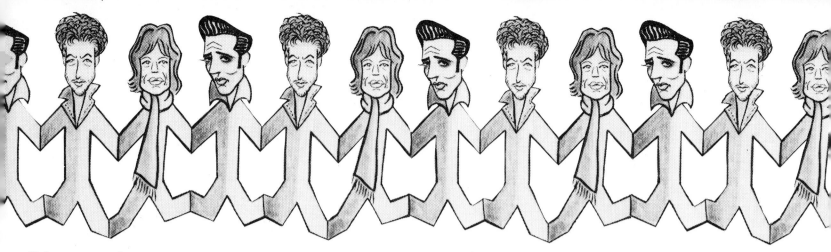

Take one stand-up comic, one folksinger and one blond musical comedy actress fresh from an Off-Broadway flop; dress them in coffeehouse chic and have them sing the usual folk favorites, along with a few trendy protest anthems, in a brassy, upbeat style. Put them together and what have you got? The Kingston Trio with sex appeal. At least, that's what Albert Grossman had in mind back in 1961 when he cast Paul Stookey, Peter Yarrow and Mary Travers to play the issue-conscious, protest-minded singing group Peter, Paul and Mary. And who can blame Grossman for wanting a folk trio of his very own? Groups like the Limelighters, the Chad Mitchell Trio and the aforementioned Kingston Trio were cleaning up with the button-down college crowd at the time. By creating a streamlined version of the Latest Rage, Grossman was simply upholding the time-honored American credo that you can't have too much of a good thing. In that, he was no different from the old Hollywood studio barons who'd utilized an assembly-line approach to crank out countless reasonable facsimiles of their big-name stars and successful screen formats during the thirties and forties, just as the television industry would do in decades to come. But even before the folk boom took the pop world by storm, rock'n'roll had fallen prey to this exploitative mentality.

Gene Vincent, Jerry Lee Lewis and Carl Perkins were just a few of the rockabilly cats who hitched a ride into the pop arena on Elvis Presley's coattails in 1957. A year later, when Elvis went off to the army, second-stringers like Ricky Nelson and Conway Twitty did their best to fill his shoes. Both Little Anthony and Ronnie Spector got the nod from their record-producer mentors thanks to the resemblance their singing styles bore to that of the late Frankie Lymon. Tommy Roe and Bobby Vee likewise parlayed a talent for mimicking the late Buddy Holly's hiccup into countless hit records. (Vee quite literally stepped into the dead singer's place by subbing for him at the Moorhead, North Dakota, date to which he was headed on the night he was killed.) In the early sixties, the Beach Boys spawned all sorts of nasal-sounding surf rockers, and the cloning of the Beatles had practically become an industry unto itself by the

latter part of the decade.

Even today, with the growing sophistication of pop audiences, there continue to be scads of carbon-copy rockers and formula records that replicate time-tested grooves. To the uninitiated, heavy-metal groups like AC/DC, Foreigner, Toto and Journey that attempt to fill the void created by the demise of Led Zeppelin seem more or less interchangeable. And almost two decades after Dylan's emergence as the pop messiah, rockers like Tom Petty, Ian Hunter and Mark Knophler continue to make a handsome living by braying out songs like the Master.

Sometimes the striking resemblance between an era's hot pop attractions reflects the public's ongoing passion for a particular personality or musical style, but more often than not, it's a direct result of well-plotted industry hype. Countless pop phenoms — Frankie Avalon, Fabian, Engelbert Humperdinck and even the Rolling Stones — were born of a super-manager's ambition to have his very own version of a big-name star, just as Jennifer Warnes's restyled image and sound on *Shot Through the Heart* had everything to do with the Arista label's desire to have its own Linda Ronstadt.

On the other hand, the similarities between pop attractions may be a simple matter of an up-and-comer's blatant imitation of another, bigger star. Until he developed his own fervent style, Otis Redding spent years trying to sing like Sam Cooke; after Otis's death, his protégé, Arthur Conley, resurrected Otis's gut bucket vocals and syncopated stutter. Etta James and Esther Phillips patterned their singing styles after that of the late Dinah Washington, just as Janis Joplin would pattern hers after theirs more than a decade later. And Dee Clark, Jackie Wilson and Smokey Robinson are just a few who were profoundly "influenced" by the late Clyde McPhatter.

Imitation is not only the sincerest form of flattery, it's an excellent way for a rookie to get a foot in the door. All it takes is the success of one self-styled Space Oddity or one platinum-haired *femme fatale* backed by a group of leather-clad New Wavers to convince all the record company honchos that they ought to have one of their own. Should a newcomer happen to

Millions of fans have settled for second best when their Fave Raves were otherwise engaged, but still . . .

bear some sort of likeness to the latest pop frontrunner, he or she is obviously ahead of the game. Still, this approach does have its liabilities.

Karla Bonoff and Nicolette Larson are two raven-haired songstresses who've suffered as much as they've gained from the comparisons drawn between them and Linda Ronstadt. But then, who could live up to being called the New Ronstadt? Or the New Dylan? Or Jagger? And besides, who needs a new or second-best version of a big-name attraction when they've got the Real Thing?

By allowing themselves to become identified with a particular pop star, newcomers also run the risk of passing from vogue along with the original model. Buffy Sainte-Marie is one of many who presented herself as a Baez-style protest singer in the sixties; but though she later attempted to make the transition to pop — and even to glitter rock — her popularity eventually capsized along with Baez's.

Rock's unique contribution to the field of copycat stardom is the rock star impersonator. Aided by elaborate costumes, wigs, makeup and sometimes even plastic surgery, these professional *poseurs* play the part of Late Great rock legends for thousands of fans who missed the originals during their heyday — as well as for those who just can't get enough of a particular Fave Rave, dead or alive. Not surprisingly, the focal point of this eerie phenomenon is Elvis Presley. At last count, there were an estimated 10,000 ersatz Elvises out there in the field. Many play Las Vegas on a regular basis and one (Rick Sorcedo) has even had his own one-man show on Broadway. As you probably know, the various Elvis androids represent practically every stage of the King's life and career — from young rockabilly buck to broken-down wreck. Old El has even been played by a woman in the *Rock'n'Roll Heaven Revue* — a now defunct road show troupe which also featured surgically altered lookalikes of Jim Croce, Jim Morrison and Janis Joplin. Also big on the rock clone circuit for a time was Randy Hansen — who didn't let being white keep him from posing as Jimi Hendrix. But, of all the contenders in the rock impersonation racket, top honors must go to Bob Gill

and Robert Rabinowitz, the folks who gave us the unbelievably tacky *Beatlemania* along with the more recent *Rock'n'Roll: The First 5,000 Years* — 69 "authentically reproduced" rock hits embellished with an elaborate multimedia assault. (Sample: A medley consisting of "Sh-Boom," "Will You Still Love Me Tomorrow?" and "Da Doo Ron Ron" was mounted against newsreel footage showing a Ku Klux Klan cross burning, which dissolved into a giant painting of the Crucifixion.)

Yet another innovation in the field of rock clonedom has been spawned by the hard-sell marketing companies that hawk soundalike albums on late-night TV. Born of financial necessity when the royalties for the real greatest hits compilations became too expensive, these packages proffer pseudonymous singers and studio musicians doing what are often remarkably on-target vocal impersonations of big-name stars performing their latest hit singles. Still, it's doubtful that you'd ever mistake them for the originals. But apparently, fidelity is not a big issue since most of the audience for this sort of thing falls in the eight- to ten-year age bracket and consequently aren't nearly as interested in listening to the Real Barry Manilow or the Real Rod Stewart as in copping twenty hit songs for half the price of an ordinary LP.

Add to this development the emergence of bogus "ghost groups" which crisscross the country pretending to be well-known (but rarely seen) bands from the fifties and sixties, plus soundalike groups which perform "tributes" to heavyweights like the Stones, the Dead, and the Doors by rendering verbatim versions of their hit record repertoires at local nightspots — and you've got what amounts to an epidemic.

The funny thing is that many of the various and sundry rock star clones have ended up becoming as firmly entrenched in the pop scene as their more admired (and better paid) counterparts. A good-sized number have built solid reputations around their ability to imitate others, and some have gone on to make their own unique contribution to rock music and culture. So, with that in mind, why not send in the clones?

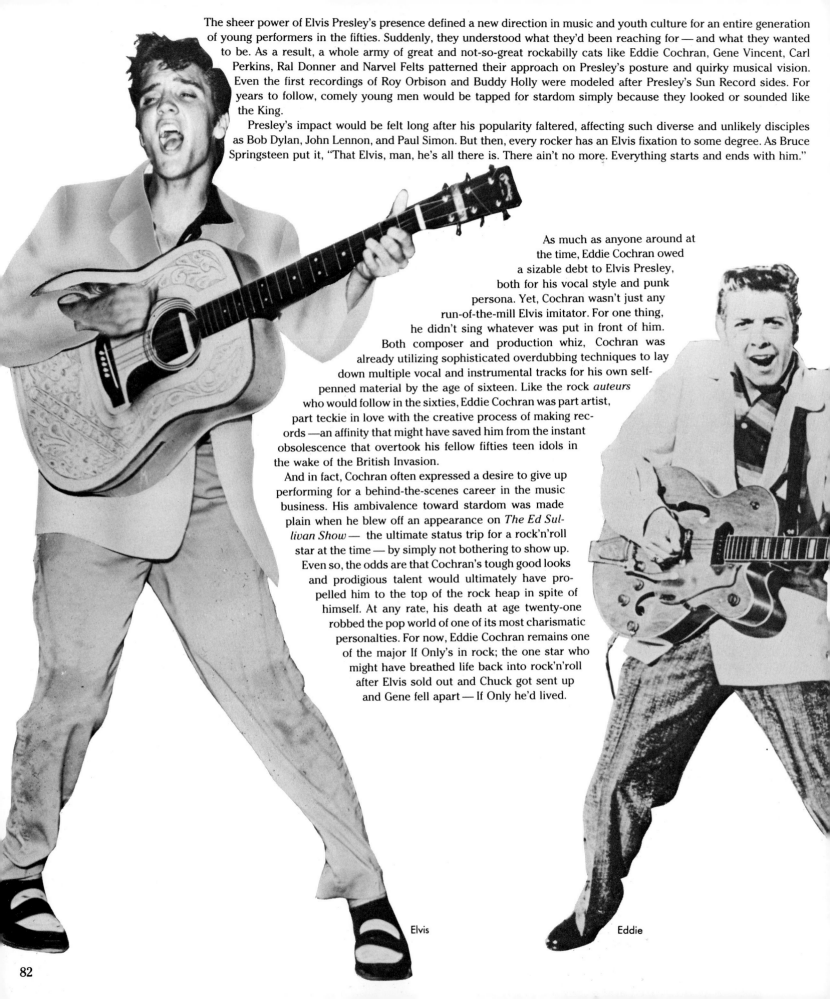

The sheer power of Elvis Presley's presence defined a new direction in music and youth culture for an entire generation of young performers in the fifties. Suddenly, they understood what they'd been reaching for — and what they wanted to be. As a result, a whole army of great and not-so-great rockabilly cats like Eddie Cochran, Gene Vincent, Carl Perkins, Ral Donner and Narvel Felts patterned their approach on Presley's posture and quirky musical vision. Even the first recordings of Roy Orbison and Buddy Holly were modeled after Presley's Sun Record sides. For years to follow, comely young men would be tapped for stardom simply because they looked or sounded like the King.

Presley's impact would be felt long after his popularity faltered, affecting such diverse and unlikely disciples as Bob Dylan, John Lennon, and Paul Simon. But then, every rocker has an Elvis fixation to some degree. As Bruce Springsteen put it, "That Elvis, man, he's all there is. There ain't no more. Everything starts and ends with him."

As much as anyone around at the time, Eddie Cochran owed a sizable debt to Elvis Presley, both for his vocal style and punk persona. Yet, Cochran wasn't just any run-of-the-mill Elvis imitator. For one thing, he didn't sing whatever was put in front of him. Both composer and production whiz, Cochran was already utilizing sophisticated overdubbing techniques to lay down multiple vocal and instrumental tracks for his own self-penned material by the age of sixteen. Like the rock *auteurs* who would follow in the sixties, Eddie Cochran was part artist, part teckie in love with the creative process of making records —an affinity that might have saved him from the instant obsolescence that overtook his fellow fifties teen idols in the wake of the British Invasion.

And in fact, Cochran often expressed a desire to give up performing for a behind-the-scenes career in the music business. His ambivalence toward stardom was made plain when he blew off an appearance on *The Ed Sullivan Show* — the ultimate status trip for a rock'n'roll star at the time — by simply not bothering to show up. Even so, the odds are that Cochran's tough good looks and prodigious talent would ultimately have propelled him to the top of the rock heap in spite of himself. At any rate, his death at age twenty-one robbed the pop world of one of its most charismatic personalities. For now, Eddie Cochran remains one of the major If Only's in rock; the one star who might have breathed life back into rock'n'roll after Elvis sold out and Chuck got sent up and Gene fell apart — If Only he'd lived.

Elvis

Eddie

In 1957, Capitol Records, a longtime holdout in the rock'n'roll sweepstakes, launched a talent search for "the New Elvis." That contest resulted in the discovery of an unassuming country boy by the name of Gene Vincent. His rise to the top of the charts was swift and stunning, and yet, his career would be in eclipse just a few short years later — owing partly to Capitol's reluctance to get fully behind him and partly to his own tendency to muck things up.

Because Vincent had first come to prominence as the "New Elvis," it figured that he would draw heavily on Presley's style. But sadly, the inevitable comparisons that resulted only served to point up his shortcomings. For one thing, Vincent simply wasn't blessed with Presley's winsomeness and personal style; his pale craggy face and poor-boy clothes made him look more like a duded-up grease monkey than a teen dream. Further, his raw sexual energy and impassioned style caused adults to view him as even more depraved, and therefore more dangerous, than Elvis.

While Presley rode out the radical shifts in music and fashion that swept the sixties by making the switchover to Vegas-style schmaltz, Vincent held fast to his black leather and rockabilly roots. Idolized by second-generation British and American pop stars, he nonetheless became a glaring anachronism during the Flower Power Era, an aging cool cat frozen in a bygone age. And yet, for many young fans today, Gene Vincent remains the original punk — a wild-eyed crazy kid who actually delivered what Elvis only promised.

You might remember that Tommy Sands got his big break by playing a thinly disguised Elvis Presley character in a TV drama back in the fifties. But here's a twist: he says that *he* was responsible for giving Elvis *his* big break. It seems that Sands was managed by Colonel Tom Parker several years before the Colonel hooked up with Elvis. Dubious about Tommy's star potential, Parker eventually cut him loose, but not before Sands had launched a sales pitch on behalf of a new kid named Presley. "I kept telling Colonel Parker about Elvis. Finally, I guess I whetted his appetite and he went and saw him and signed him up. I didn't see Parker until a couple of years after Elvis had become a big star. NBC had a deal with Parker to do a story that would parallel Elvis's life (and star him as well) but by the time the script was completed, he was too hot. So they went through a lot of auditions, but it was pretty hard to find anybody like Elvis at the time. He was so unique. But Colonel Parker remembered me and sent me the money to fly to New York to audition for *The Singing Idol*." That TV appearance and the subsequent movie adaptation quite literally made Sands an overnight sensation. "Teenage Crush," one of the show's featured songs, became Tommy's first record hit.

Because the Colonel had already begun his strategy of limiting Elvis's exposure by this point — holding out for Hollywood and a few choice concert and TV appearances — the fans were starved for the sight of their beloved. Tommy Sands was one of the many Next Best Things they embraced to compensate for the King's absence. Unfortunately, Capitol, his record label, failed to realize that Sands's popularity rested primarily on his Presleyish stance. Instead, they dressed him in tuxes and stuck him with Big Band–style standards in an attempt to turn him into a pretty-boy crooner. Guest appearances on hokey TV shows didn't help matters either.

Sands's career was languishing by the time his much-publicized five-year marriage to Nancy Sinatra ended in divorce in the mid-sixties. Fed up and exhausted,

Gene

Tommy

he chucked everything and headed for Hawaii to roam the Islands. When last heard from, Tommy Sands was a package tour conductor in Honolulu. "I quit singing in 1969," he says now, "and I haven't sung a note since — and that includes in the shower."

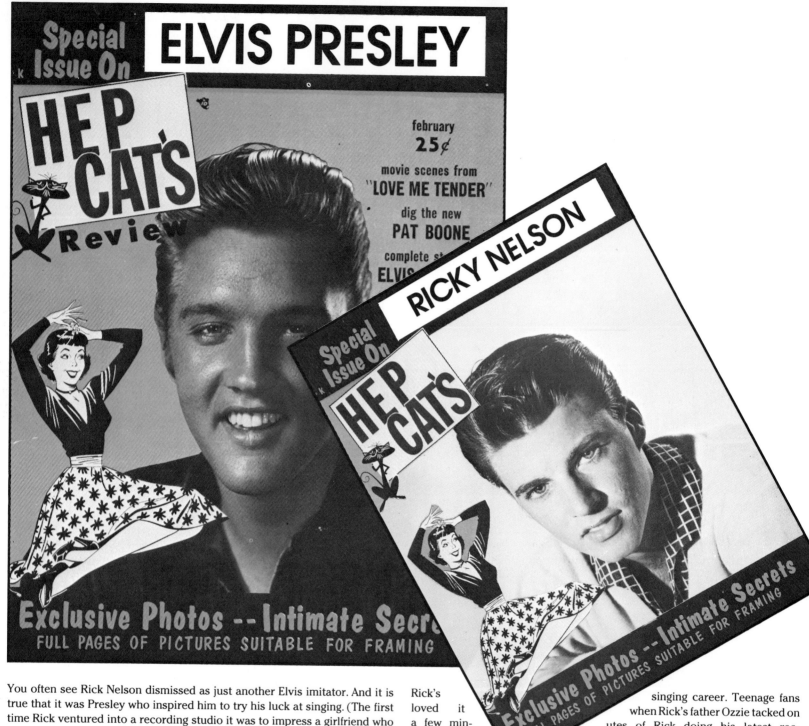

You often see Rick Nelson dismissed as just another Elvis imitator. And it is true that it was Presley who inspired him to try his luck at singing. (The first time Rick ventured into a recording studio it was to impress a girlfriend who was impressed with Elvis.) And both singers did have the same sleepy eyes, lopsided grin, and vaselined hair. But there's one major difference between Nelson and the horde of self-styled Presleys that invaded the pop scene in the fifties — Rick Nelson's sound was distinctly his own. His choice of material and backup musicians may have leaned toward early Elvis-style rockabilly, but his voice was teenagey sweet, his delivery devoid of raunch. Sneer and turned-up collars notwithstanding, Rick Nelson reeked of suburbs and station wagons and dances at the gym. He offered a full-blooded clean-cut alternative to Elvis for those who couldn't quite stomach Pat Boone. And unlike dozens of Elvis also-rans, Nelson enjoyed a prolific recording career. In fact, his homerun hit average almost eclipsed that of his rival; he scored just under 50 chart singles during his heyday, including 26 that made the Top Twenty.

It was television that converted "the irrepressible Ricky" into Rick Nelson, Teen Idol. And alas, it was television that eventually sapped the life out of Rick's singing career. Teenage fans loved it when Rick's father Ozzie tacked on a few minutes of Rick doing his latest record at the end of each *Ozzie and Harriet* episode. Even parents didn't seem to mind — after all, they'd known him and his folks for years. However, Rick's gee-Mom-gee-Dad image proved to be a liability as the years wore on. By the dawning of the psychedelic era the Nelsons had become something of national joke. Rick's record sales had plummeted, along with the Nelsons' ratings.

There was talk after Presley's death that Colonel Parker had decided to take over Rick Nelson's management, but it turned out to be just that — talk. (Possibly the Colonel backed out after discovering that Elvis was bigger business in death than he'd been for years in life.) And maybe that's just as well. More than likely an association with Elvis's former mentor would only have given new life to the comparisons between the two singers. And whether it's fair or not, that's one department in which Rick Nelson tends to come up short.

They didn't sound all that much alike and they didn't particularly look alike, and yet, more than any other contender, it was Jerry Lee Lewis who came closest to deposing Elvis as the King of Rock'n'Roll. In fact, for a while there in '57 and '58, when radio stations pitted the two against each other in call-in polls, it was Jerry Lee who most often came out on top. Lewis told Tom Snyder recently that during a farewell visit to the Sun studios before leaving for his two-year tour of army duty overseas, Elvis suddenly collapsed over his piano, sobbing, "Well, it's over for me now — I've had it now. It's all yours, buddy. All you have to do is reach out and take it." But that was 1958, the same year that Lewis married his thirteen-year-old cousin, creating a scandal that rocked the rock world and KO'd his career. Of course, Elvis would import his own teenage cutie to Memphis just a few years later, but Colonel Parker saw to it that the presence of the once and future Priscilla Presley at Graceland was kept tightly under wraps until the couple's marriage in 1967.

This chain of events points up one of the most telling distinctions between the fates and fortunes of Elvis and Jerry Lee. Elvis could always look to the Colonel to keep his image clean — so long as he played the game according to Parker's rules. But Lewis, being the contrary kind of person he is, would never have stood still for anyone — let alone someone like the Colonel — telling him how to run his life. But, of course, therein lies his charm.

Even today, after more than twenty-five years of bankruptcy, busts, three messy divorces and the deaths of two sons and two wives, Jerry Lee is just as ornery as ever. Unchastened by his own close scrape with death following surgery for a perforated ulcer in 1981 and a brief period of repentance instigated by his cousin, the fire-and-brimstone preacher Jimmy Lee Swaggert, the Killer continues to do it his way — missing concert dates, insulting audiences and occasionally refusing to perform when he does deign to show up.

The one subject he seems to have mellowed on is his long-standing rivalry with Elvis. There was a time when Lewis left the impression that he believed Presley's success had been carved out of his own bad luck. But now that old El has passed on to his final reward, Jerry Lee insists that he always liked him well enough and never resented his success either then or now. That's a far cry from the Jerry Lee who was arrested on a summer's night in 1976 for using a .38 derringer to convince a guard at Graceland that he should be granted an audience with the lord of the manor. "You all treat Elvis like he was some sort of god," he had admonished a reporter earlier that same evening, "and me like I was some kind of white trash. I'll admit I'm no angel, but I'm a pretty nice guy."

The first thing Harold Jenkins heard on the radio when he got home in 1955 from an overseas tour of army duty was a record called "Mystery Train" by Elvis Presley. Jenkins, an Arkansas boy who'd been drafted just as he was about to sign a contract with the Philadelphia Phillies, changed his mind about baseball after hearing Elvis. As a kid, he'd wanted to be a hillbilly singer but he'd never really thought he was good enough to sing Country. This rock'n'roll stuff, though, now *that* was different. Anybody could sing that.

Jenkins changed his name to Conway Twitty ("'cause it sounded more like show business"), got himself some black leather get-ups, and practiced his sneer and, sure enough, it wasn't long before he was snapped up by Mercury in yet another record company attempt to cash in on RCA's success with Presley. Twitty did his best Elvis imitation on "I Need Your Lovin'," his first single on the Mercury label, but the record just lay there and died. From there, he eventually moved to MGM where he had better luck with "It's Only Make Believe" — which just happened to be released around the time Elvis left for the army; not surprisingly, it was a smash. Twitty's career flourished during Presley's absence, but it skidded dramatically when the King came marching home. In 1964, bitter and depressed, Twitty walked out on a poorly attended concert date and went back to the hillbilly haunts of his native Arkansas to sing Country songs. At first, the Southern jocks were skeptical about his defection from pop to Country. It wasn't until the release of "Next in Line" in 1968 and "To See My Angel Cry" and "I Love You More Today" in 1969 that his switchover was secured. Today, Twitty is one of C&W's biggest stars; he sells millions of records, sponsors a celebrity golf tournament, and owns a tourist complex outside of Nashville called Twitty City and a baronial estate that looks a lot like Graceland.

Carl Perkins

Carl Perkins was on his way to New York to perform "Blue Suede Shoes" on the Ed Sullivan and Perry Como shows on a March night in 1956 when his car smashed into a bridge abutment outside Dover, Delaware. Up until that moment, Perkins had been on top of the world; "Blue Suede Shoes," his first release for Sun Records, was the country's fourth highest selling record, and his guest shots on the Sullivan and Como shows were to be his first network TV appearances. Instead, he woke up three days later in a traction sling with four broken ribs, a broken shoulder and numerous internal injuries. One night during his long and painful recuperation, he happened to switch on his TV set to find his buddy Elvis Presley doing a guest shot on *Stage Show*, the old Dorsey Brothers show. The moment remains vivid in his memory: "Elvis came on TV and said, 'And now ladies and gentlemen, I'd like to do my new record for you,' and the next thing I knew, he was singing, 'Well, it's-a one for the money, two for the show, three to get ready, now go cat go.' Well, I like to have fell out of bed. I guess a lot of people probably forgot Carl Perkins had ever sung that song after that."

Like Elvis and Jerry Lee Lewis, Carl Perkins had been one of Sam Phillips's Great White Hopes. A poor country boy who'd headed to Memphis after hearing one of Elvis's records on the radio, he'd landed an audition with Phillips by singing him one of his compositions from a pay phone. After Phillips sold Elvis to RCA, he put Perkins in the studio to record "Blue Suede Shoes," the song Perkins had sung to him over the telephone.

About a year after the accident, Perkins, along with Jerry Lee Lewis and Johnny Cash, was in the middle of cutting a follow-up to his first hit at Sun's Memphis studios when a very cocky Elvis Presley — Vegas showgirl in tow — barged into the session unannounced. Carl remembers: "We was so glad to see him . . . well, everything just sort of fell apart. We all just started singin'. I think I woulda had another 'Blue Suede Shoes' that day if Elvis hadn't interrupted me. Up to then, we was really honkin'. But instead, what came out of it was a lot of talkin' and snatches of songs." (Otherwise known as the Million Dollar Quartet.)

Carl Perkins never entirely rallied from that tragic accident in 1956. Not only had his first (and only) hit become solidly identified with Elvis and his career put on hold, but worst of all, his brother Jay never recovered from injuries sustained in that same collision; he died two years later. Disconsolate over his brother's death, Perkins began to drink heavily and lapsed into a deep depression that lasted for several years. He laments, "You can't take the strain without a crutch. For me it was booze — I've seen the bottom of a lot of bottles."

With the help of his family and friends, Johnny Cash in particular, Perkins eventually got back into performing. Today, he continues to record and tour occasionally. As for his feelings about Elvis and his encroachment upon his own career — well, he doesn't hold a grudge. He figures that the way things happen are the way they're meant to be. He once reflected, "You'd have to say Elvis did have the looks on me. The girls were going for him for more reasons than the music. I mean even then, I was a grown-up man with three kids and all. Still, in the old days we was so good that Elvis wouldn't let the Colonel book us together — even after he started to make it big. But I've never been bitter. Most kids from my background never even drive a new car."

86

In the years that preceded the beat explosion of the sixties, the British rock scene consisted mostly of Elvis imitators — pretty boys like Adam Faith, Tommy Steele and Billy Fury, with vaselined pomps, pink socks and guitars they couldn't play. Of this group, it was Cliff Richard who emerged as the Top of the Pops, England's answer to Elvis. But unfortunately for Cliff, no one in the States asked the question. And America was where you made it — then as now. Although he enjoyed solid popularity in Britain and Australia throughout the fifties and sixties, Cliff Richard never gave up his dream of conquering America.

Miraculously, he managed to do just that almost two decades later with "Devil Woman," the first of several MOR hits he would wax for Rocket Records, Elton John's label. One dream he never realized, however, was that of meeting his idol, Elvis Presley. Though Richard tried for years to wangle an audience with the King, the closest he ever came was touring Graceland as the guest of Vernon Presley while Elvis was out of town.

Ral Donner's Chicago home was an Elvis Presley shrine. "He was the King," Ral Donner said as he sat in his living room amid by photographs of the dead singer. Like so many others who modeled themselves after Elvis, Donner never made any secret as to the source of his inspiration. "It goes all the way back to 1961," he recalled. A song called "The Girl of My Best Friend" had been a hit for Presley in Europe, but had not been released as a single in the States, an oversight that prompted an A&R man at Gone Records to cut the song with Donner. Though Ral's specialty was singing like Elvis in local bars and such, the idea of doing it on record made him feel a little funny. But, as he told it many years later, "It worked. After that, I had four or five chart records in a row. I even got to meet Elvis. Some friends of his took me up to his house in California. He came walking downstairs with Connie Stevens. He didn't show one iota of 'Hey, what do you think you're doing trying to sound like me!' In fact, he told me, 'If anyone gives you any problems, let me know and I'll back you up!'" From that time on, Donner continued to draw his creative impetus from Presley; it was as if his entire career was mounted as some kind of homage to his idol.

After several good years, the hits stopped coming for Donner, and before long, Gone Records had made good on its name. Donner married and moved into the home of his wife's parents where he lived with his wife and son, Ral junior. For three years, he drove a truck and tried to make the transition to civilian life. Not surprisingly, it was Elvis Presley who once again provided the incentive that got Donner back into performing; he was so broken up over Presley's death that he composed a musical tribute to him entitled "The Day the Beat Stopped." He said of that record, "If you listen closely to that song [you hear that] a couple of times I nearly break down crying. We did the track in one take, I couldn't have done it another time."

Donner's periodic attempts over the years to establish himself as something other than an Elvis imitator were unsuccessful. Although bootleggers had a field day with an unauthorized album entitled *Ral Donner's Elvis Presley Scrapbook* (Ral on wax — Elvis on the cover), his legitimate releases have created scarcely a ripple of interest. Likewise, his narration (as the voice of Elvis) for *This is Elvis!* won him only passing notice. Finally, in the spring of 1984, Donner died after a long bout with cancer. He was forty-one — two years younger than Presley at the time of his death.

Cliff Richard

ELVIS PRESLEY You Don't Know What You've Got

RAL DONNER You Don't Know What You've Got

Not everyone had Sam Phillips's flair for unearthing backwoods pickers and rockabilly cats. Finding it difficult to come up with their own authentic rock'n'roll talents, industry hustlers in New York, L.A. and Philly sometimes attempted to mold their own from callow local kids. These homemade heartthrobs were created to cash in on the King's following but they were groomed as junior-league Sinatras.

Sinatra himself had been America's first singing teen idol — the first to be denounced by parents and politicos (from the floor of the Senate, no less) and the first to graduate from public menace to elder statesman. It was his career, his easy mastery of every facet of performing, that set the standard for the old-line music-biz manipulators. Besides which, he'd sung the music they'd loved when they were kids. Teen idols like Frankie Avalon, Bobby Rydell, Fabian, and Tommy Sands may have been styled after Elvis in the beginning, but their mentors believed that their longevity rested on their ability to make the transition to movies and the supperclub circuit — as Sinatra had done before them. Ultimately, however, their ring-a-ding approach to rock'n'roll proved disastrous to their careers, not to mention rock itself.

Ol' Blue Eyes

Some early teen idols didn't need to be prodded to follow in Ol' Blue Eyes' direction. From the start, it was obvious that Bobby Darin was no hayseed rocker with a guitar. Even when he sang about the "Queen of the Hop," his finger-popping delivery was pure Sinatra. In fact, Darin had originally kicked off his recording career not with rock'n'roll but with standards like "Million Dollar Baby," which he rendered in a jazzy hup-hup style. With the success of "Splish Splash," a novelty tune he'd thrown together (with Murray the K) as something of a joke, Darin suddenly found himself a teen idol, but even during those early years, he kept his sights firmly set on Hollywood and Las Vegas — a fact that was written all over his sharkskin suits. Darin eventually made the transition from the Clearasil Set to the double-knit crowd with his version of "Mack the Knife" (the phrasing and lyric changes of which he lifted verbatim from the old Louis Armstrong classic). Its phenomenal success allowed him to go "legit." The kids bought "Mack" because it was by Bobby Darin, but their parents bought it because it sounded like a Sinatra record.

Bobby

Not everyone who made the jump from teen idol to adult entertainer took the change in stride, however. Paul Anka may come across as just another poor man's Sinatra, but as a plump lonely kid growing up in Ottawa, Canada, his early musical ambitions sprang from a passion for R&B and Chuck Berry–style rock'n'roll. While it's true that even as a young performer Anka sometimes came on as a Sinatra-style crooner, he nevertheless relished his status as a teen idol. That's one of the reasons he took it so hard when he was deposed by the new wave of British rockers in the mid-sixties: "I didn't accept the turnaround easily and I was a bit defiant," he says now. "It was the closest I've ever come to being really distraught. I began to question if it was all over for me. All of a sudden, I wasn't working and I had some heavy thinking to do. I was still performing, but I was living on my past success. Nobody really cares if your chips are down. You either become obstinate or change with the times. I changed." Yes, Paul changed from dippy teen anthems to dippy grown-up anthems like "My Way" and "You're Havin' My Baby." And in the end, his genius for fashioning relentlessly catchy pop hooks would earn him top billing in Vegas instead of guest shots on the *Sha Na Na* show.

Paul

When Philadelphia became the center of the pop music universe in the fifties, local talent was mined the way Liverpool's would be in the sixties. The most successful of the lot were Philadelphia's Big Three — Frankie Avalon, Bobby Rydell and Fabian — all well-mannered Italian boys who were handsome in a Ken Doll sort of way. While Avalon and Rydell could each play a few instruments and sing a little, Fabe — well, Fabe was hunky and had a nice smile. All three were owned by local labels in which Dick Clark was rumored to be a *sotto voce* partner. But after the payola scandal of early 1960, Clark was no longer in a position to give their careers the friendly boost he had in the past. By 1961, the *Bandstand* star-making apparatus virtually ground to a halt, ultimately taking with it the hit-making careers of these three young singers.

Rydell and Avalon managed to avoid going the rock'n'roll revival route by parlaying their modest musical talents and teen fame into an occasional acting job and a perennial gig on the nightclub and dinner theater circuit. Like Darin before them, they had reached for the grown-up sophistication of intimate smoke-filled rooms right from the beginning. Maybe that's why it doesn't hurt to see them today.

Frankie

Bobby

Fabe

Poor Fabe is another story. His career went steadily downhill after he became the brunt of a lengthy tirade by one of the interrogators at the payola hearings, who called him a no-talent "hunk" among other things. Thrust into the limelight as a sixteen-year-old kid, manipulated in a heavy-handed manner for years, he suddenly found himself cast adrift at the age of twenty-one after splitting with his mentor, Bob Marcucci. "I felt controlled. I felt plastic," Fabian has been quoted as saying. "I felt like a puppet. How would you feel if you were put in a little black box and taken out like an animal and told to go and sing and then were put back in that box again? My managers were awful. I hated them. All they wanted was money. They were always pushing and pushing me to go out and make money. I reached a point where I couldn't face it any more. I was in bad shape mentally then. I decided to quit singing. I got a lawyer and bought out my contract. After that, I could breathe. I vowed then that no one was going to put me on a string again."

By 1975, Fabian had blown most of the money he'd made during those early years and suffered the breakup of his eight-year marriage. Although his primary claim to fame rests more on good looks than talent, he continues to try to make it as a singer/actor in Hollywood. Twenty years wiser, with several botched comeback attempts and a notorious *Playgirl* centerfold behind him, he avows, "I wouldn't wish my career on a friend. I'll tell you, there's been a lot of pain involved."

Larry Williams was still in his teens when he parlayed a job as R&B star Lloyd Price's valet into a gig with his band and later into a contract with Specialty Records, Price's onetime label. But although it seemed that he was being groomed as his former boss's successor (his first release was a cover of the Price hit "Just Because"), Specialty had signed him with another of its artists in mind — the one and only Little Richard. The self-proclaimed black King of Rock'n'Roll had sold millions of records for Specialty, and they were in the market for a few more like him. Williams was expressly recruited to come up with Little Richard–type ditties. Which he did — with style. Thus when Little Richard proffered "Long Tall Sally," Williams rejoined with "Short Fat Fanny"; Richard's "Good Golly, Miss Molly" begat Larry's "Dizzy Miss Lizzy." And so it went. A simple case of a record company knocking off its own product before someone else got the chance.

With the onset of the sixties, Williams grew tired of dishing up reheated servings of Little Richard hits. He wanted to experiment with ballads and jazz, but what with Richard temporarily retired from rock and out preaching the Gospel, the folks at Specialty wouldn't hear of it. Their unyielding attitude ultimately forced Williams to quit the label. Like many other fifties rock greats, he did some touring abroad during the following years, but his career was spotty from then on out. Though his old hits had become solidly entrenched in rock vernacular, Williams himself faded quickly from public memory. (He wasn't even included among the thousand or so musicians listed in *Rolling Stone*'s *History of Rock and Roll*.) It was several years before he resurfaced again in the States for a stint as an A&R man for Epic-Columbia-OKeh. Ironically, one of the first acts he signed during his short-lived tenure there was Little Richard, who was by then attempting a comeback.

Richard eventually returned to preaching, while Williams, who'd always been something of a maverick, remained a free-agent for most of his life. The last time the two men's paths would cross was in 1980, when the Reverend Richard Penniman wailed a mournful a cappella version of "Precious Lord" at Larry Williams's funeral.

Larry Williams

Little Richard

They'd cut a couple of records, and even made an appearance at one of Alan Freed's Brooklyn bashes, yet no one seemed particularly interested in a group of do-wopping high-school boys called the Duponts until 1956, when Frankie Lymon and the Teenagers broke nationally.

It wasn't long afterward that the Duponts were signed by George Goldner, the president of the record stable that also owned Lymon. At their first session, Goldner coached backup singer Anthony Gourdine to duplicate Lymon's little-boy style, telling him, "You have a very childlike voice. Lighten it up, get it higher." The result was "Tears on My Pillow," one of the classic teen laments of the fifties.

By the time "Tears" was released, an ill-advised split had doomed the fortunes of both Lymon and the Teenagers, leaving the newly christened Little Anthony and the Imperials to take their place. Although they scored another moderate-sized hit with "Shimmy, Shimmy, Ko-ko Bop," the Imperials simply couldn't fill the Teenagers' shoes. To make matters worse, Little Anthony, like Lymon, was also encouraged to launch a solo career. "My head was big," he says today. "I wanted to be a big star. . . . People were filling my head with garbage, so I broke away from the group and for two years, I did nothing, absolutely nothing." As it turned out, Little Anthony's greatest success would come when he teamed up again with the Imperials to record the songs of singer/songwriter Teddy Randazzo ("Goin' Out of My Head," "I'm on the Outside Looking In," "Make It Easy on Yourself," "Hurt So Bad," etc.).

Like Frankie Lymon, Little Anthony did not come away from his years of stardom a rich man, despite the many millions of records he sold. When the hits stopped coming for him and the Imperials, they relied on periodic appearances with rock'n'roll revivals to pay the rent. "I never finished high school," he says. "I really didn't know where I was goin', all I could do was sing."

In 1977, he dropped out of the pop scene to move to L.A. in an attempt to launch a career as a movie and TV actor. After three frustrating years, Little Anthony returned to the nostalgia circuit. Today, he records occasionally and tours the country singing his old hits.

With his mile-high conk and maniacal smile, Esquerita could easily be mistaken for Little Richard circa 1956. As a matter of fact, Esquerita even sounds like Little Richard. Little Richard sideways, that is. But that's no mere coincidence, because Esquerita was Capital Records' "answer" to that chart-topping Specialty star back in the fifties.

From his high-pitched yelps to his knuckle-pounding piano style, Esquerita matched his idol riff for riff on such crowd-pleasers as "Batty Over Hattie" and "Good Golly, Annie May." And yet, his was not exactly a literal duplication. Actually, most of Esquerita's old Capitol sides sound as if someone had dismantled all of Little Richard's classic hits and pieced them together at random. The overall effect is something like what you'd get if you left "Good Golly, Miss Molly" out in the sun too long. Still, Esquerita did have an occasional burst of originality. On "The Voola," for example, he executes ten minutes of an off-key Latin-flavored piano concerto accompanied by his own hysterical screams that sound like nothing you've ever heard. It's hard to believe that anyone from his label listened to this number either during the time it was being recorded or after. As rock scholar Charlie Gillett put it, "If there was ever a producer or arranger deputed to these sessions, he must have been bound and gagged in the corner."

Unfortunately, not much is known about Esquerita aside from the fact that he is the composer (under the name of S.Q. Reeder) of "Green Door," the old Jim Lowe hit. The only sample of his work that survives today is a double album reissue of his vintage Capitol sides. Pressed in France, where Esquerita is something of a cult figure (of course), it's a collector's item over here. But even if you do get hold of one, don't expect to come away with much in the way of Esquerita data. Its silly liner notes appear to be purposely vague (example: "For the most stompin' all out rock'n'roller, Esquerita takes a back seat to no one, in fact he takes no seat at all"). Although Esquerita has recently materialized at a rock club in Manhattan (playing airport lounge music much to the chagrin of his fans), he remains a mystery man. No, we'll probably never know who Esquerita really is, where he came from and, more important, whether or not he's for real.

LITTLE RICHARD

BELIEVE ME WHEN I SAY ROCK'N'ROLL IS HERE TO STAY

ESQUERITA!

12 UNRELEASED WILD ROCKIN' SONGS!

CAPITOL

Round Robin

Chubby Checker managed to convert "The Twist" into a couple of other hit single variations ("Let's Twist Again," "Slow Twistin' ") as well as launching several other moderately successful dance crazes (the Fly, the Limbo and the Hucklebuck, etc.), but the best his disciple Round Robin could come up with was "The Slauson." It was his first and only "hit," and at that, it just barely slausoned onto the charts.

Chubby

Just as most would-be rock stars wanted to be Elvis in the fifties, so did most up-and-coming folkies aspire to be Dylan in the sixties. And for a while there, it seemed like almost all of them were.

Donovan started out as England's answer to Bob Dylan before cranking up his own cosmic wheels. Some considered Phil Ochs to be Dylan had Dylan not "sold out." (Of course, Ochs would've sold out in a minute, if only he'd known how.) The late David Blue (né Cohen) was an actor who became a folksinger after Ochs convinced him that "if Zimmerman could do it, anybody could." Joan Baez was tagged the "female Dylan," even though her celebrity had preceded his. Kris Kristofferson was the "hillbilly Dylan" and Bob Neuwirth, Dylan's crony of many years, was rumored to be the "real Dylan." Genuine talents like Tim Hardin, Tim Buckley, Eric Andersen and David Ackles were routinely dismissed as Dylan imitators or, at the very least, his "spiritual disciples." When Dylan dropped from sight following his harrowing motorcycle accident, Arlo Guthrie was one of the many dubbed "heir apparent." But then, that was natural since Arlo had been so candid about citing Dylan as his idol and inspiration (an irony in itself seeing as how Dylan got his

start imitating Arlo's dad). With the dawning of the seventies, Bruce Springsteen was hailed as the New Dylan by no less an authority than *Time* magazine. In the meantime, several groups scored hits by waxing shameless Dylan imitations. Mott the Hoople intentionally styled themselves to sound like Dylan backed by the Stones, and sometimes it seemed as if the reclusive minstrel was recording under the names Dire Straits and Stealers Wheel. As the decade wore on, Bob Marley was hailed as the Rasta Dylan, Tom Petty the New Wave Dylan and Jim Carroll the street-wise Dylan. John Prine represented for many the last vestige of vintage Dylan. So where does that leave the object of all this sincere flattery? After experimenting with a new, throatier singing style in the early seventies, the original Dylan has since gone back to imitating himself.

Photos clockwise from left: Bob Dylan; Eric Andersen; David Blue; Arlo Guthrie; Pete Seeger; Woody Guthrie; Joan Baez; Joni Mitchell; Buffy Sainte-Marie; Joanie Phoanie; Melanie; Jim Carroll; Bob Dylan; Bruce Springsteen; Tim Buckley; Phil Ochs and Donovan

She was an original — the prototype for what would become the serious girl folkie with long, lank hair, dowdy clothes and a face conspicuously free of makeup. Accompanied only by her guitar, she stood alone on the stage, mournfully wailing ancient labor organizing songs that all sounded alike. No, there was no one like Joan Baez when she first appeared on the pop scene, but within several years, every coffeehouse and college dorm in the country would have a few of their own — well-meaning girls who wore black tights and turtlenecks and sat in the corner playing the guitar.

Baez may have been called the "female Dylan," but in reality, she was as much a trendsetter as he — one who inspired her own line of "spiritual disciples." There were so many similarities between the young Joan Baez and Judy Collins, for example, that people confuse them to this day. Both are brunettes who have worn their hair long and straight, and both are quavery sopranos who started out singing dour folk ballads and whose song choices still tend to be a touch on the downbeat side — a quality which they share with Collins's friend and one-time protégée, Joni Mitchell, herself another Baez-style folkie until she settled into her current jazz-pop groove. Mimi (Baez) Fariña, Buffy Sainte-Marie and Mirabai are just a few more of the many girl folkies cast in the Baez mold. Even Melanie, who was more Piaf-style chanteuse than folksinger, felt obliged to dress in muumuus and play a guitar during the sixties. But more than being a musical trendsetter, Baez represented a certain moral stance, an earth-mother style — one that would strongly influence not only other female singers of the era but also the blossoming girl children of the burgeoning Woodstock Generation.

MY FIRST SONG WILL BE THE ONE THAT WON THE "BROTHER-HOOD AWARD" — "BAGELS AND BACON"!!

The Liverpool Five

The British Walkers

In the sixties, the public's hunger for all things Beatle sent music industry bigwigs both here and abroad scurrying in search of anything remotely like them. Even Brian Epstein recruited a few of his own makeshift Mop Tops (Gerry and the Pacemakers and Billy J. Kramer and the Dakotas) to cash in on the Beatle explosion. When groups couldn't be found, they were often manufactured to order. (And a few previously unknown American rockers, like "Sir" Douglas Sahm, managed to get hits by masquerading as Britishers.) For every second-string group like Herman's Hermits, the Merseybeats and Freddie and the Dreamers who placed a few singles in the upper reaches of the charts, there were dozens more, like the British Walkers and the Liverpool Five, who never even got to first base — despite the fact that many of them looked and sounded more like the Beatles than the Beatles themselves.

Beatlemania sparked a pop revolution that turned America and its recording industry upside down — opening the door for countless British groups who played Mersey-style music and wore shaggy hair and pointy boots. Within two years of the Fab Four's arrival, there were no fewer than twenty Limey invaders on the American charts, where before there were none. Of course, most turned out to be little more than limp imitations, with the exception of a few like the Stones, the Kinks and the Who. (And even they resorted to a good deal of Beatle-inspired shtick when they were first starting out.)

Oddly enough, it wasn't these supergroups that posed the most serious competition to the Beatles in the beginning, but rather an outfit called the Dave Clark Five, whose coming-out festivities (a tumultuous Kennedy Airport welcome and a guest shot on *The Ed Sullivan Show*) looked like an instant replay of the Beatles' arrival a few months earlier. Yet despite their obvious similarities, their aggressive and crude hard rock sound was a far cry from that of their rivals. Fortunately for them, the DC5 boasted a savvy business mind and major dreamboat in the person of Dave Clark, their leader and co-manager. But in retrospect, it's plain to see that no group could hope to have rivaled the fecundity of the Beatles during this period. Within a few years of the initial British Invasion, the Dave Clark Five's popularity, like that of so many others, was eclipsed by the success of their predecessors. And yet, unlike most other Mersey-style also-rans, the group's records hold up remarkably well today.

Even the Stones did their share of head shaking in the beginning.

The Monkees were the ultimate in synthetic pop, the last word in media hype. Never before (and probably never since) have teenaged fans been conned on such a monumental scale. Which is not to say that the Monkees' weekly TV shows weren't fun to watch; on the contrary, considering that they were little more than an abbreviated rehash of *A Hard Day's Night*, most were remarkably well crafted by such then-fledgling talents as Bob Rafelson and Paul Mazursky.

In creating *The Monkees*, Colgems auditioned hundreds of young actors and musicians (including such unlikely candidates as Stephen Stills and John Sebastian) until they arrived at the proper mix of personalities to effectively mirror the real-life Beatles. Mike Nesmith was the "intellectual" Monkee — the Lennonish leader; Peter Tork the shy Ringo type; Davy Jones and Mickey Dolenz a combination of Paul and George, with Jones initially slated to be the group's McCartneyish heartthrob.

Beginning with their first broadcast in 1966, the Monkees became a major attraction both in the ratings and on the charts, scoring two or three hits a year through 1968 and performing in concert before hundreds of thousands of fans. But by their second season together, the press had blown the whistle on the pre-fab Fab Four by pointing out that the group, which didn't write or play any of their hit record material, wasn't really a group at all, just four actors playing parts. At first, the boys responded to the criticism by demanding more creative control over their music and actually trying to shape themselves into a serviceable band. Their failure to do so eventually led to friction with their Colgems mentors, and ended with the group's demise.

Peter Tork was the first to break away from the show. After an attempt to start up his own legitimate rock group fizzled, he disappeared for a while, only to surface in 1972 in federal prison after being convicted of hashish possession. He has since done time as a teacher, a singing waiter and most recently as the star of a group called Peter Tork and the New Monks. Dolenz and Jones also made a stab at a comeback in 1975 when they teamed up with Boyce and Hart, the two songwriters who'd provided many of the Monkees' early hits. But their reunion proved to be something of an embarrassment.

Mike Nesmith now runs his own small but influential record label, Pacific Arts, in Carmel, California. You might see him in the video rock and comedy pieces he produces for cable TV and network variety shows. When asked about the Monkees, he likes to say, "The Monkees were a television show first, last and always. We were no more a rock band than Marcus Welby was a real doctor."

Peter   Davy   Michael   Mickey

And then there were the inevitable "popular priced" record rip-offs of the Beatle craze which featured Merseyish songs performed by Beatle sound-alikes. Because their covers were usually adorned with caricatures or half-lit photos of mop-top types, these inferior-grade swindles could easily be confused with tacky compilations of the Beatles' early British and European singles, if not with their current record releases. Sometimes the only outwardly discernible difference between these "bargain" Beatles and the genuine article was the fact that they cost 69¢. Indeed, over sixty small-time promoters were hauled into court on charges of misleading or unauthorized exploitation of the word "Beatle" during the first flush of Beatlemania. Even so, you'd have to have been a little thick (or very young) not to have noticed that these "Beatles" spelled their names with two t's or two e's.

Shown here are some of the silliest of the counterfeit Beatles. Of all, the prize must surely go to *Beattle Mash*, which featured three middle-aged musicians in Beatle wigs who called themselves the Liverpool Lads.

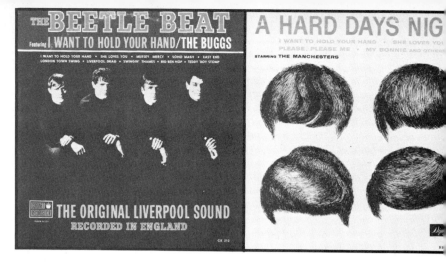

A tribute, a send-up or a cheap rip-off? Liverpool didn't care what you thought of their approach so long as they got your attention. Like a lot of other dimestore-style Beatles, Liverpool wasn't from Liverpool — or even from England for that matter. In fact, they weren't even a group — just some sessionmen brought into the studio for a day to jam on some Mersey-style numbers.

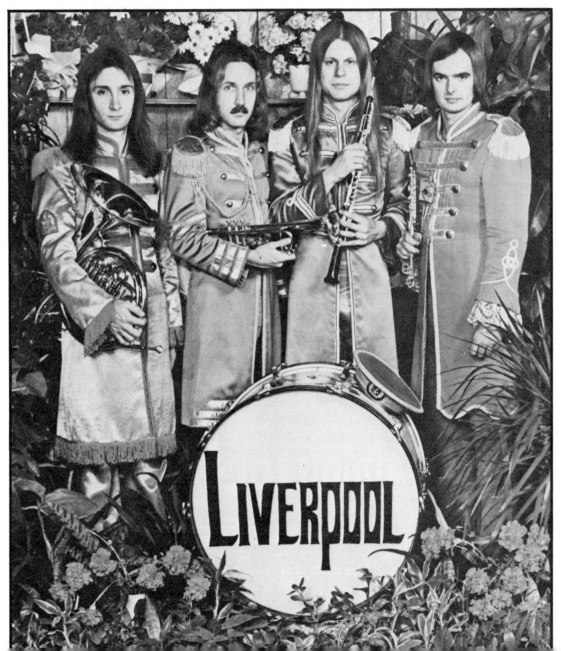

The Bay City Rollers were a group of Scottish lads who were marketed as the "New Beatles" in 1975 — complete with a frantic New York airport arrival scene and a whirlwind concert tour. But while plenty of preteeners took the bait, Rollermania came to a standstill after only a year. No doubt the group would've stood a better chance if Ed Sullivan had still been alive.

The Bay City Rollers

A few weeks after the Knack blasted out of nowhere with their smash single, "My Sharona," the group's leader, Doug Fieger, gushed to a reporter that the Knack had "the craft, the excitement, feeling and love that the Beatles brought to rock'n'roll." But Fieger would live to regret those words once the rock press began to lambast the group for its casual appropriation of the Beatle myth and iconography, pointing to the blatant similarities between its sound, album cover graphics, wardrobe and even its choice of record labels to those of the Beatles. The media backlash became so fierce that Knack guitarist Berton Averre was moved to protest, "Asking a new band if they're trying to copy the Beatles is like asking a rookie outfielder if he's trying to be Babe Ruth. Obviously, the answer's gonna be yes."

The group's second album, . . . *But the Little Girls Understand* (a reference to a *Creem* article, which maintained that the critics may despise the Knack, "but the little girls understand"), outraged everyone from feminists to child welfare groups, who decried its pedophilic fixation. With that, the Knack imposed a strict moratorium on interviews, apparently feeling that anything they said would only make matters worse. The press responded to their silence with the fury of a lynch mob. Clearly, the Knack had a lot to answer for — their Beatlesque pretensions, their smug misogyny, their arrogance and, most of all, their easy success. But instead of confronting their detractors in print, they attempted to make amends on their third album, *Round Trip*, wherein they confessed their sins and pleaded for a second chance. Both the press and the public remained unmoved. By 1982, the group had officially called it quits, just a scant three years after their smashing "Sharona" success.

Above: the Beatles on *The Ed Sullivan Show;* on screen: the Knack in a staged publicity shot

Louis and Keely

In the beginning, they played the part of social outcasts, hippie rebels whose clothes were loud and whose hair too long, but by the time Sonny and Cher had moved on to the greener pastures of Las Vegas and prime time, they had developed an act that portrayed Sonny as a dim-witted court jester and Cher as a smart, tough-talking doll who belted ballads and cut Sonny down to size with carefully scripted ad libs. In real life, however, Sonny was the brains behind the operation, and Cher, his beautiful and talented drawing card. What their millions of fans didn't know was that their act had actually been originated over a decade earlier by another pizza-faced hipster and his raven-haired wife.

Louis Prima created the character of the gumbah stooge who played it for laughs while his droll ladyfriend sang pretty and cracked wise back in 1948. Like Bono, Prima was a musician and songwriter of Italian extraction who had enjoyed only modest success until teaming up with his wife, Keely Smith, for a reverse take on the old George and Gracie routine. Like Cher, Keely Smith was an exotic beauty, part Native American, who wore her hair in a straight bob with bangs, and sang in a husky contralto. And also like Cher, Keely jumped when her old man pulled the strings. For years, she performed the thankless task of delivering staid renditions of this song and that while Prima, whose stage persona was a cross between Jake La Motta and Chico Marx, mugged unmercifully behind her back. They made an unlikely combo and yet they became one of the most popular and highest paid acts ever to play the supperclub circuit; their collaboration resulted in several hit singles and the starring roles in a movie musical loosely based on their lives (*Hey Boy, Hey Girl*). The Primas were a hardy Las Vegas perennial until 1961, when Keely finally got fed up with playing it straight and filed for divorce.

In 1971, the Louis-Keely formula was dusted off for Sonny and Cher when they launched the *Sonny and Cher Good Time Hour*, their weekly comedy/variety series on CBS. Their revamped image brought them millions of new grown-up fans. But in 1974 Cher abandoned both Sonny and the show to strike out on her own. Three years later, the cool public response to the newly liberated Cher forced her back into a professional reconciliation with Sonny on a revival of their old TV format. But this time around, the formula that had originally made the show such a big winner proved to be its downfall: Sonny and Cher's invented personae had been undermined by real life. It was common knowledge that the couple had been embroiled in a messy divorce (made messier by Sonny's claim that he'd been shafted to the tune of $14 million by Cher's then-boyfriend David Geffen). During that time, Cher had also entered into a controversial marriage to rock star ne'er-do-well Gregg Allman and given birth to his child. Consequently, Cher's standard put-downs of Sonny came across as downright cruel.

But just because the Louis-Keely formula has outlived its usefulness for Sonny and Cher doesn't mean that it's been permanently retired. Even as the Bonos were calling it quits for the second — and presumably last — time, the formula was already being recycled for the toothsome duo of Donny and Marie Osmond (along with a sexy new image for the virginal Marie, courtesy of Cher's costumier, Bob Mackie) and shortly thereafter for the husband-and-wife team of the Captain and Tennille and the brother-sister act of Jimmy and Kristy McNichol.

Sonny and Cher

Donny and Marie

The Captain and Tennille

Kristy and Jimmy

The Mamas and the Papas

Although the hype that sold Spanky and Our Gang as the "East Coast's answer to the Mamas and the Papas" represents a prime example of a record company (in this case Mercury) packaging a pop act to capitalize on the success of a pre-existing one, Elaine "Spanky" McFarlane freely admits to having been influenced by the Mamas and the Papas—especially by Cass Elliot, her counterpart in that singing ensemble. Echoing their "good time music" sound, Spanky and friends earned a handful of hits ("Sunday Will Never Be the Same," "Lazy Day," "Like to Get to Know You") in rapid succession.

The group's momentum came to an abrupt halt in 1968 when Malcolm Hale, singer and vocal arranger for the group, died in his sleep from complications arising from bronchial pneumonia. "I knew then that if Malcolm was dead, I must be tired," Spanky said many years later. "His death kind of turned everything sour for me in my head. I could've replaced him, but I just didn't want to. It made me too sad." This tragedy, coupled with a longtime desire to settle down and start a family, convinced Spanky to retire. Five years and two children later, after an unsuccessful attempt to revive the group, she began taking acting lessons with the hope of playing her friend and idol, the late Cass Elliot, in a screen bio. But rather than playing Cass on screen, Spanky ended up taking her place with the real-life Mamas and Papas when John Phillips overhauled his old group for a comeback in 1982.

The Fifth Dimension

Spanky and Our Gang

The Friends of Distinction

When pop mastermind Gordon Mills signed up an undistinguished singer by the name of Arnold Dorsey back in 1966, it was with the belief that he saw in Dorsey's slightly wolfish-looking face a smoldering intensity that is irresistible to certain women—the kind who read pocket romances and cream for Tom Jones, the Welsh dreamboat whose career Mills had steered toward stardom a couple of years prior. Dorsey's mentor dressed his new singing Heathcliff in Edwardian velvets and Tom Jones shirts, dyed his hair black, and rechristened him Engelbert Humperdinck after the nineteenth-century composer. Not long after, Eng got his first hit record and was shipped in tandem with Jones to the United States.

But what might at first have seemed like a dream come true ultimately turned out to be a nightmare for Eng. "I was just a puppet," he says. "They'd wind me up, put me on a plane, stand me up in front of an audience and keep me from talking to the press." The situation got so bad that Eng finally felt compelled to break with Mills. Today, the Hump (as he is affectionately known to his fans) calls the shots in his career. Although he is no longer the sensation he was in the sixties, he can boast of healthy album sales and as many paternity suits (fourteen) as any star in the business.

Despite his status, Eng is still bitter about the price he had to pay to get there. "I was a slave," he laments. "A total creation of my management. Or rather, my *ex*-management. And let's get another thing straight. I'm *not* Tom Jones. Nor is he my best friend. In fact, I hardly know the man."

Tom

The Fifth Dimension were often called the "black Mamas and Papas" during their heyday. Though attacked by some for their white-bread song-styling, the group racked up hit after hit during the late sixties and early seventies with their distinctive brand of champagne soul. Originally consisting of Marilyn McCoo, LaMonte McLemore, Floyd Butler and Harry Elston, the group was shattered by internal dissension before it got off the ground, resulting in Butler and Elston's formation of the Friends of Distinction. As the poor man's Fifth Dimension, the Friends scored a couple of respectable singles before breaking up in 1971.

Eng

101

In defending the Osmond Brothers against the charge that they're nothing more than honky rip-offs of the black Jackson 5, their fans point to the fact that the Osmonds' show-biz debut actually predates that of the Jacksons by some five years. But don't let that fool you — when the Osmonds started out, they were very far removed indeed from the rhinestone jumpsuits and mechanized choreography that would characterize their hit-making days. Back then, their tastes ran to candy-striped blazers and barbershop renditions of "My Gal Sal." No, the Osmonds didn't start out imitating the Jacksons — they wouldn't get around to that for years. They were imitating the Williams Brothers, the slick family act that had launched Andy Williams. As a matter of fact, the Osmonds were discovered by Andy's dad.

The idea of grooming the Osmonds as a rock attraction didn't occur to anyone until the Jackson 5 scored their first R&B bubblegum hit in 1970. A few months later, the Osmonds released "One Bad Apple," which sounded so much like the Jacksons that it fooled a lot of folks. Despite (or because of) the confusion, the song was a hit and the Osmonds became rock stars overnight. Their candy-striped blazers were replaced with matching fringed jackets, and Little Donny was sent forth to shuck and jive *à la* Michael Jackson while the rest of the group provided nerdy backup.

The Osmond appeal, then as now, was mostly to preteens and grandmas. Teeny-bopper fanzines like *Sixteen*, knowing a movement when they saw one, were quick to take them under their wing as they had the Jacksons. To older rock audiences, the Osmonds were something of an embarrassment, unlike the Jacksons, whose associations with Motown established their soul brother credentials. As *Creem* put it: "The Osmonds are to the Jacksons what a nickel bag of oregano is to a palmful of Panama red."

The Osmond clan has always rankled at being compared with the Jackson brothers. When an interviewer asked them outright if they hadn't in fact "borrowed" heavily from the Jacksons, a group spokesman allowed as how, "Well, we might have — in the beginning. But," he added, "the group feels that if they sound like anyone, it's Crosby, Stills, Nash and Young."

Strictly speaking, family rock actually originated with a group called the Cowsills. One of the many American bands that rode into the pop scene on the Beatles' coattails, the Cowsills racked up several Merseyish-sounding hits before the media began to focus on their real-life identities as sibling rockers. That was the beginning of the end. The problem was that they were so relentlessly wholesome — an attribute that is anathema to rock'n'roll. Worse yet, their *mother* played with them. And as if that wasn't enough, at the height of their popularity, they became the official spokesmen for *milk*.

For a while there, the Cowsills seemed to be everywhere — billboards, radio and TV. There was even a sitcom (*The Partridge Family*) loosely based on their lives. Ironically, however, while the Partridges blossomed as a record

act, placing one song after another on the charts, their real-life prototypes began to flounder. Eventually, the bubble burst and the Partridges went the way of the Cowsills. David Cassidy renounced his teen idol status and suffered a period of emotional letdown that led to a drinking problem. Although that was a long time ago, he hasn't particularly mellowed in his feelings toward the people who engineered the Partridge hype.

While the Osmonds' success proved that the Jackson 5 formula could be adapted for a white group, the emergence of the Sylvers showed that it could work for another black group as well. In fact, by this time the approach had almost become a cliché — one that gave birth not only to the Sylvers, but also to the DeFrancos and the 5 Stairsteps: family groups that were marketed like breakfast food, complete with posters, premiums and send-aways.

Of all the family rockers, only the Sylvers exhibited any potential for longevity. For a while, during the mid-seventies, it looked as if they might step into the void created when the Jacksons split from Motown. Unfortunately, however, they got their start with MGM — a label that had no feel whatsoever for black music. A move to Capitol got them back on the track — but only for a moment.

When the Jacksons had first signed with Gordy, Motown had been at the peak of its power, having just undergone a decade of tremendous growth. The Jacksons became the in-house favorites, the last to receive the full-blown Motown star treatment. Of course, no one can deny their superior talents, but one wonders if the Jacksons would have ended up like the Sylvers without the Motown writing and producing talents that guided them during their early years.

For the most part, family rock has gone the way of surf music and glitter rock. The Osmonds have officially broken up, the Cowsills are currently an L.A. punk band, the Partridges were canceled, and the rest continue to bounce from label to label in search of the direction that will give their careers a second wind. Even the Jacksons, the group that started it all, have been eclipsed by brother Michael's stunning solo success — although all that may change now that boxing entrepreneur Don King has entered the picture. But, chances are that the Jacksons, like so many other artists who have fled the comfort and tyranny of Berry Gordy's kingdom, may never again recapture the glory of their Motown days.

Photos clockwise from left: The Osmonds, the Cowsills, the Sylvers, the 5 Stairsteps, the Brady Bunch, the DeFrancos, the Partridge Family, the Jackson 5, the Jackson Sisters.

When the Rolling Stones first began to attract attention, they were considered downright Neanderthal in appearance, even by their most ardent fans. It was a toss-up as to which one — Keith Richards, who looked dead even then, basset hound Bill Wyman, pointy-headed Charlie Watts or main man Mick Jagger, with his craggy face and dimestore wax lips — looked the worst. Only blond, puffy-eyed Brian Jones came anywhere close to conforming to the ongoing vogue for mop tops and golden-haired surfers. (And he looked pretty wasted himself.) Moreover, it turned out that they behaved as badly as they looked. They weren't cuddly or funny like the Beatles, Hermits, et al. They were surly and intentionally rude.

Nor did their rough exteriors hide hearts of gold; they were evidently as cold and mean-spirited as their pose implied. The emergence of the Stones as the second most powerful attraction in rock, the darkly sinister alter egos of pop's reigning Sun Kings, meant that two vastly differing sensibilities prevailed in rock fashion in the late sixties — the genial row-diness of the Beatles and the studied hostility of the Stones. Just as there were countless numbers of surrogate Beatles around at the time, so there began to be any number of second-string Stones. As the decade wore on, you began to see more and more groups — especially those of the garage band variety — affecting Stones-inspired glowers and mismatched finery. Suddenly, oaf-ishness was in and any unsightly bruiser who played an instrument could become a hot property overnight. Some groups, like the Pretty Things, were intentionally conceived, as one critic put it, to "out-gross grossed-out Stones fans." Even the Beatles themselves showed signs of having been in-fluenced by the Stones' outlaw aesthetic toward the end of their collaboration.

Now that Jagger and company have come to epit-omize the ultimate in rock stardom, it's more important than ever for aspiring rockers to look and act like the Stones. Jagger, in par-ticular, has fathered an entire face of rock androgynes (Bob Geldof, David Johan-sen, Carly Simon, Cindy Bullens, etc.) with gaunt visages and protruding lips.

Maybe what we're seeing here is a subtle evolutionary force at work. Who knows, what with the world so smitten with Jag-ger, Richards, et al., maybe some day the whole world will look like the Rolling Stones.

Aerosmith

David Johansen

The early seventies brought new refine-ments to the art of imitating the Stones. It was no longer enough simply to ape their antisocial stance and repertoire; by then the members of such groups such as Aerosmith and the New York Dolls also bore startling resemblances to Jagger and his crew — both in look and sound. (There was even a rumor at the time that Aerosmith's lead singer, Steven Tyler, had submitted to plastic surgery in the form of a sil-icone implant — to give his lips a more Jaggeresque pout.)

But while Aerosmith did man-age for a while to fill the de-mand for arena rock created by the Stones' absence, they never won over the critics. After several wildly suc-cessful years on the concert circuit, Aerosmith's blues-based heavy-metal ulti-mately wilted under the resurgence of the Stones originals.

While fronting the Dolls, David Johansen (the pretty one) patterned himself after the '69 model Jagger via top hats, tight pants, floor-length feather boas and a tantalizing bisexual swagger. Johansen threw away his top hats and boas when the band broke up in 1975, but the specter of Jagger continues to haunt him. Like others who have come to prominence by virtue of their resemblance to another, bigger, star, he's had a real struggle gaining acceptance on his own merits — despite con-siderable MTV exposure and a modest-sized hit with an Animals' medley in 1982. Still, he and the Dolls are credited with inspiring much of the late seventies onslaught of punk and New Wave — setting an example that would influence no less a personage than Jagger himself, who responded to the trend by laying on his own mascara and bad boy burlesque extra thick.

The New York Dolls, unlike Aerosmith, did have the critics on their side. It was the public that never got behind them — perhaps because of their early glamrock image with its unsubtle hint of transvestism. Forgetting that the Stones, too, had been blatantly derivative during their days as a struggling blues band, Jagger scornfully observed, "The Dolls are awright if you want a good laugh, but they're so very camp and silly. I mean one of them is quite pretty [the one who looked like him, naturally] but he can't sing."

Mick and the gang: Joan Rivers says Mick's lips are so big he could give Ohio a hickey.

The Dolls

Bob Geldof of the Boomtown Rats is another prominent rock front man who suffers from constant comparisons with Jagger. "I've got a big mouth. There the similarity ends," he insists. "I'm not coordinated. Jagger is balletic. I'm gangling, apelike. He's smaller than me. There's a chasm of difference between us." However, Geldof has conceded that when he was younger, "Jagger *was* my savior. I found it hard to talk to girls in school. I was called rubber lips. It got on my fucking nerves. Then the Stones appeared and suddenly it was hip to have big lips."

Bob Geldof

Tim Curry makes no bones about his resemblance to Mick Jagger. In fact, he spent the early part of his career openly lampooning it — first in the London stage production of *The Rocky Horror Show* and later in the film version. The multitalented Curry had since become a pop singer in his own right (with the Stonesified "I Do the Rock"), a hit on Broadway in *Amadeus* and a full-fledged movie star, in *Times Square* and *Annie* (in a part originally tailored, believe it or not, for Mick Jagger).

Tim Curry

105

No one could blame you if you haven't gotten choked up over the various Chipmunk rip-offs that have been perpetrated over the years. After all, the Chipmunks themselves are just electronic gimmickry in the first place. Their "creator," Ross Bagdasarian, first devised their cloyingly cute sound by layering accelerated versions of his own vocal tracks in 1958. While this effect was considered a major innovation at the time, reproducing it was child's play for anyone with access to the proper facilities. Not surprisingly, a counterfeit chipmunk act — the Nutty Squirrels — made its debut less than a year later. "Uh Oh," their first record, was a winner but all that changed once people realized that the Squirrels were only Chipmunk impersonators. Clearly, the public wasn't in the market for just *any* electronic gimmickry — they wanted the real thing.

Although Ross Bagdasarian is no longer with us (he died in California in 1972 at the Chipmunk Ranch), the group continues to carry on his legacy. Indeed, with the possible exception of Gladys Knight and the Pips, they've exhibited the most amazing versatility and staying power of any group in pop history (this despite Alvin's brief defection from the group in 1976 to join a fundamentalist Christian sect). In their twenty-five years together, they've sold over 25 million records — encompassing such diverse musical fads as the Twist, the cha-cha, punk and Country — as well as outlasting their upstart competition (including the most recent, Shirley and Squirrely). Their current credits include a Saturday morning TV show and a tremendously popular touring company starring midgets in Chipmunk suits who lip-sync the group's greatest hits.

Clothes, pose, style — they're all part of the packaging that goes into the marketing of a pop star. Take the cover photo of Rickie Lee Jones's debut album, for example. The fact that Rickie Lee happened to be dressed in Joni Mitchell drag wasn't necessarily meant to suggest that she sounded like Joni (though there are certain stylistic similarities between the two — such as their affection for Lambert, Hendricks and Ross–style vocalese) but rather that Rickie Lee was one of those sensitive singer-songwriter types as opposed to, say, Cher or Grace Jones. Still, with her berets and long blond hair, Rickie could easily have passed for Joni on a bad day — or maybe her little sister. Even so, the rock cognoscenti have known from the beginning that Rickie Lee is really Tom Waits.

Alice

Joni, Rickie Lee and Tom

Speaking of gimmicks — remember Alice Cooper? That guy who used to wear dresses, torture chickens and guillotine himself onstage? Of course, that was a long time ago. Nowadays, you're more likely to see Alice teeing off at a celebrity golf tournament or hanging out in an X on *The Hollywood Squares*. Yes, time and rock'n'roll wait for no man — not even a man like Alice. The sad fact is that it's not nearly so easy to offend straights as it used to be — what with so many of today's young moms and dads having been raised on Hendrix and Morrison. For them, S&M-laced theatrics are just so much show biz. And besides, how could Alice hope to keep 'em down on the farm after they'd gotten a load of Kiss?

The four high-heeled monsters of Kiss stripped Alice Cooper's Grand Guignol down to its most puerile elements, them pumped it up with Barnum and Bailey schmaltz. Everything Alice did, Kiss did bigger, with all the subtlety of a blow to the head with a sledgehammer. Of course, lots of groups borrowed heavily from Alice's shtick during the seventies, but none quite so brazenly.*

Alice bristles at the suggestion that Kiss has usurped his title as the King of Schlock Rock, but there's no denying that the group has milked his brand of hokum dry. His scaled-down nightmares look pretty tired by comparison. One recent concert review even went so far as to compare him to an old stripper who'd lost her looks and whose "mincing desperation" was little more than "pathetically endearing."

And what about Kiss? For eight years, the group's saturation marketing techniques — lunchboxes, comic books, records, etc. — have made it a veritable money machine. But now, like Alice, its popularity is decidedly on the wane, with the prospects for spin-off and solo acts equally dim. But that's not really so surprising. From the beginning, the group's individual members have existed as little more than ciphers — devoid of identity outside their greasepaint and Japanese sci-fi getups. (Their decision to go public with their own gruesome faces last year pointed up the necessity of that initial strategy.) More than likely, the anonymity Kiss courted so avidly in the beginning will soon be theirs whether they want it or not.

* It should be noted that Alice's shtick owes a major debt to Frank Zappa's special brand of theatrical *misha gass*.

Jobriath looked like your average rock singer when he first commenced his pursuit of fame. Jeans, beads, shoulder-length hair — you know the type. But that approach got him nowhere fast. Then one day David Bowie fell to earth and suddenly Jobriath saw the light. He traded his jeans for intergalactic jumpsuits, plucked his brows, and cut his hair in a Space Oddity fringe. He announced that he was God and he was gay. He voiced a desire to be kidnapped by extraterrestrial invaders. Then he sat back and waited for the world to catch up.

Sure enough, it wasn't long before music-biz wiz David Geffen took the bait. Geffen gave Jobriath a buildup fit for a queen — including block-long billboards on Broadway and star-studded coming-out parties at which Jobriath regaled the press with such pronouncements as: "It's gay time and I think the world is ready for a true fairy." But if the world *was* ready for a true fairy, Jobriath wasn't the one. It was clear he was just recycled Ziggy — and who needed that when the original was still around.

That's the way it was back in 1973. Poor Jobriath has been lost in the stars ever since. He did surface long enough to audition for the part of Al Pacino's lover in *Dog Day Afternoon*, but alas, he didn't get the role. (It can't be easy to gain acceptance as a serious actor when you were last seen on *The Midnight Special* wearing a giant vacuum cleaner nozzle.)

Ziggy

Kiss

Jobriath

Who needs soul to rock and roll? Certainly not Walter Brennan, Annette Funicello, Everett Dirksen or John Travolta. These are just a few of the big-name celebs who have proved that you don't need talent to break into the Top Ten. Yes, when prime time TV stars, silver haired politicos, prizefighters and popes get hep to the jive, it means money in the bank for the music biz. But . . .

LOOK WHAT THEY'VE DONE

"When you're on television and thirty million people watch you every week, you can sell a lot of records. Of course, that doesn't mean that they're good records."

— PAUL PETERSEN, former star of *The Donna Reed Show*

"Extraordinary how potent cheap music is."

— NOEL COWARD

Do you remember when Tiny Tim was a rock star? Sure, *YOU* never took him seriously, but somebody out there must have, because he sold over a million records during his heyday. Capacity crowds flocked to the Fillmores East and West to see him perform, and his marriage to Miss Vicky was one of the major media events of 1969. But look beyond the hoopla and what did you find? An aging weirdo who sounded like an old Victrola record and looked like Margaret Hamilton in drag. What was it that made millions of fans fall in love with Tiny Tim? What secret power transformed this pathetic creature into a full-blown superstar? The power of television, that's what.

Tiny Tim became an overnight sensation following his debut on *The Tonight Show* in 1966. From there, he went on to preside as the resident freak on NBC's *Laugh-In*, the most celebrated comedy show of its day. Frequent appearances on these two popular programs supplied him with a forum for his quirky musical repertoire — a collection of antique ditties, which he rendered in a rickety high-pitched falsetto. Hardly the stuff hits are made of, yet they ended up providing him with a best-selling album and a Top Twenty hit ("Tiptoe Through the Tulips").

Tiny Tim was just one of countless oddball personalities to attain pop idol status as a result of massive media exposure — only to fade into oblivion once the novelty wore thin. His success as a hit-maker confirmed what the record industry had learned earlier from the spin-off recording careers of TV stars like Ricky Nelson, Edd "Kookie" Byrnes and Annette Funicello: if only a tiny fraction of a TV star's weekly viewing audience went out

and bought him on record, he was virtually guaranteed a hit.

Taking this idea a step farther, a number of enterprising waxstax barons foraged through other categories of celebrity in search of likely recording talent. Ultimately, they managed to talk a multitude of screen stars, pro athletes, politicians and stand-up comics into making a bid for pop stardom. This gimmick reached its quintessence during the late fifties and early sixties, when the music industry was still controlled by the Old Guard — middle-aged grads of the Big Band era who longed for a return to the "good music" of their youth. They didn't have a clue as to what made rock'n'roll what it was, let alone why anyone would want to listen to it. But that didn't prevent them from trying to manufacture their own. Not surprisingly, most of the stuff they foisted off on the public under the guise of teen music was intentionally moronic. This customized schlock ran the gamut from novelty numbers like child actor Jimmy Boyd singing "I Saw Mommy Kissing Santa Claus" to cloying schmaltz like "Teen Age Meeting" by former **Big Band** singer Don Cornell.

Although you may not have noticed it, this particular brand of pop exploitation is still very much with us. It's just more subtle, that's all. Just because many of the big wheels who currently head up the record biz are young enough to have grown up listening to Elvis and Little Richard, or even the Beatles and the Stones, doesn't mean that their approach to packaging pop is any less condescending or crass than that of their industry elders.

Take the late merchandising mastermind Neil Bogart, for example — himself once an aspiring teen idol in the fifties who went by the name of Neil Scott. After years of struggle and only one pint-sized hit ("Bobby") to show for his trouble, he ended up trading his dreams of rock'n'roll glory for a desk job at Cameo Records. During his subsequent tenure as president of the Buddah label, Bogart was largely responsible for detonating the simpy bubblegum explosion of the sixties, which featured anonymous studio groups like the Ohio Express and the 1910 Fruitgum Company doing sanitized formula rock with relentlessly catchy hooks. Later, he set up shop at Casablanca Rec-

TO MY Song, MA

Mae West Sez:
I've Got the Music in Me

ords, where he was instrumental in introducing Kiss and the Village People to the world. At one point, Bogart got so carried away that he actually tried to talk Bianca Jagger into cutting a disco record. He even signed sitcom star Louise Lasser (*Mary Hartman, Mary Hartman*) to a recording contract — pronouncing her "a cross between Barbra Streisand and Olivia Newton-John." But who can blame him for latching on to any available gimmick that stacked up as a shortcut to a sure thing? Artistic integrity is for Sunday painters — not record execs. Let us not forget that pop music is a business — first, last and always.

The glory days when an independent producer could take a local act and turn it into a nationally known name are no more. Now that popular music has been devoured by giant holding companies like MCA, EMI, Kinney, et al., even the most avid music mavens are obliged to spend most of their time playing corporate chess. Once they actually manage to maneuver their way into a position of power, they're usually too tired or too jaded to relate to the music of the streets. And anyway, who wants to brave the front lines in search of talent when you can sweet-talk the latest media sensation into waxing a platter? There's nothing that says it'll make the top of the charts, but given the massive hype that inevitably accompanies this sort of coup, a healthy amount of sales is bound to result. Whatever the outcome, it beats baby-sitting for Johnny Rotten or trying to make a household name out of Iggy Pop.

Over the years, this particular marketing approach has given birth to a unique brand of musical schlock; one that encompasses an oddly varied string of hits (and misses) by everyone from Muhammad Ali to Mae West. You probably won't see this kind of thing anthologized in hard-sell K-Tell compilations, and yet, it's as solid a tradition as any in the history of pop. These records may sound silly today, but they still rate a special place in our hearts. Like it or not, they're a part of our shared cultural consciousness. Our memories will forever be littered with the sounds of "Tall Paul," "Tammy," and "Kookie, Kookie (Lend Me Your Comb)."

When the movie business began to slump during the postwar era, Warner Brothers became one of the first of the old-line studios to size up the situation and move with the times. Rather than try to squeeze more mileage out of its aging screen stars, it tackled TV — signing a bevy of fresh young faces (mostly male) in the hope of reaping their fair share of teen coin. One thing didn't change at Warners, however, and that was the painstaking process it utilized to groom its contract players before putting them on public display. New initiates were stripped of their pasts, and rebuilt in the image of stars. Those who survived were featured in the studio's lavishly produced dramatic series, *Warner Brothers Presents*. If they clicked within a particular format, it was quickly spun off into a weekly show. Before long, the studs in the Warners TV stable had become veritable household words.

Warners eventually realized that the next logical step in its campaign to corner the kiddie market was to recycle its younger stars into singing sensations — whether they could carry a tune or not. And that's how the Warner Brothers record label made the transition from being a run-of-the-mill movie soundtrack distributor to the colossal industry power it is today — by providing an outlet for such stellar singing talents as Will Hutchins of *Sugarfoot* and Clint Walker of *Cheyenne*. Both of these stars stuck primarily to Bobby Vinton–style ballads, with just a touch of clink-clink jazz, while Roger Smith of *77 Sunset Strip* made a more blatant play for teen affections with the wimpy "Beach Romance." His co-star, Efrem Zimbalist, Jr., who inherited his musical know-how from his father, concert violinist Efrem Zimbalist, Sr., and his mother, opera singer Alma Gluck, contributed a rousing version of "Adeste Fideles" (in English and Latin, yet).

These Warners heartthrobs sold truckloads of records during the years their shows reigned in the ratings, but no one really came close to attracting large enough followings to qualify as a bona fide singing star. No one, that is, until Edd Byrnes came along.

Byrnes played the part of Kookie, the jive-talking car jockey on *77 Sunset Strip*. Despite the brevity of his early appearances on the show, it wasn't long before the letters from his fans outnumbered not only those received by the rest of the cast combined but also by any Warners star before or since.

Byrnes himself was well into his twenties when he hit as Kookie, but his pseudo-hipster shtick was too corny for older teens and people his own age. Instead, his following derived from their younger brothers and sisters — the up-and-coming Woodstock Generation. Of course, when this group pooled its allowances, it manifested awesome buying power — a fact not lost on the folks at Warners. They wasted no time in putting Byrnes into the studio to cut the immortal "Kookie, Kookie," which was then incorporated into the action on one of *Strip*'s weekly episodes. Backed by Don Ralke's Big Sound,

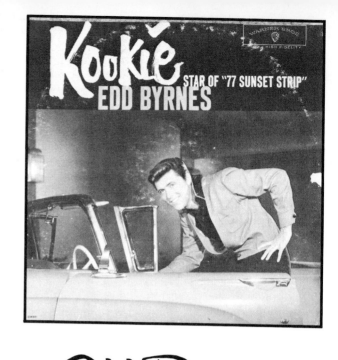

Edd Byrnes:

Is He a TRICK or TREAT?

"Kookie" consists of Byrnes reciting a string of Kookieisms while another Warners starlet, Connie Stevens, intoned the chorus, "Kookie, Kookie, lend me your comb."

As rock'n'roll goes, "Kookie" was strictly from Hungersville. The Chipmunks had more soul. Nevertheless, his fans bought it by the millions in the spring of 1959. Warners continued to pump steam into Kookiemania by releasing "Like I Love You" followed by "Yulesville" (Kookie's answer to "White Christmas") that same year. Byrnes also cut an album that boasted such bizarre bits of business as "Kookie's Mad Pad," in which he took his listeners on an imaginary tour of his room, describing all the Far Out things contained therein. (When asked about this album today, Byrnes often claims not to remember it.)

Although his reign was brief, Edd Byrnes scaled the heights of Teen Idoldom as few have before or since. In a very short period of time, he became *Strip*'s feature attraction, as well as the star of several Warners films. He also sold over a million records and became a "Rock and Roll" star in the process, despite the fact that he made no attempt whatsoever to sing. The curious part about this whole story is that it was Kookie who became the star, while Byrnes himself remained an anonymous figure trapped inside Kookie's fame.

By 1963, Kookie's novelty had worn thin and the show was in decline. Following *Sunset Strip*'s subsequent demise, Byrnes discovered that he'd become typecast as a character that was now hopelessly passé. Finding it next to impossible to land work in Hollywood, he became the first ex–Teen Idol to join the ranks of movie stars and expatriates who had forsaken Hollywood for Rome. He lived there and in England for most of what was left of the sixties, returning to this country for an occasional summer stock appearance or a guest shot on TV. For many years, he refused to talk about his Kookie period, saying only "Yesterday is forgotten — it's gone — it's dead — it's over. What's happening now is the thing that counts." It was only when times got rough that he consented to capitalize on his Kookie guise by doing commercials for men's hot-air styling combs.

It would be nice to think that Byrnes's stint with Warners had left him a wealthy man, especially in light of the negative effect the whole Kookie business had on his career, but that doesn't seem to be the case. As a Warners contract player, Byrnes was basically just a salaried employee with no significant share in the profits, from either the series or his own record hits. Not long ago, he told an interviewer, "I made more money in one year making [low-budget] European films than I did the entire time I was with Warners."

Still, Byrnes's feelings about the old days appear to have mellowed over the years — so much so that he's come to regard the whole experience as more or less a fluke. Hopefully, he can now afford to be philosophical, what with landing a featured role in the hit movie *Grease*, numerous TV guest shots (*Love Boat*, etc.) and his own (albeit short-lived) series, *Sweepstakes*, in 1979.

KNOW YOUR KOOKIE TALK?

	Translation
Mushroom people	Live it up at nite
A Washington	The dollar
It's real nervous	It's good
Antsville	A place full of people
Chick in the skins	Girl in fur coat
Smog in the noggin	Lost her memory
Lid of your cave	Door to an office
Long Green	Money
The long and airy	An airplane ride
Blue boys	Police
No tilt	No fooling
Take a yellow jet	Take a cab
Cool it	Simmer down
Roost	Sit

Connie Stevens was just another Monroe-style starlet with platinum hair and a little-girl voice when she first hit Hollywood in the late fifties. Had she appeared on the scene just a trifle earlier, that image probably would have stuck. However, by the time Connie started making the rounds, the Era of the Teenager was in full flower, so Warners decided to turn her into a girl-next-door type — sort of a singing Sandra Dee.

During her first year with the studio, Connie appeared to be one of those stars who exists only in the pages of *Photoplay* magazine. Even with no TV or screen credits to speak of, she was nonetheless all over the movie and teen monthlies, dispensing dating tips, makeup tricks and her recipe for spaghetti sauce. When the time seemed right, Warners paired her with Edd Byrnes on the aforementioned "Kookie, Kookie (Lend Me Your Comb)." She couldn't miss, and she didn't.

For Connie's first solo release, Warners provided her with "Sixteen Reasons," a formula ballad, which had Connie Pledging her Ten Commandments of Love. The lyrics were corny, but it was a passable slow dance tune and, as such, hung around the top of the charts for twenty-four weeks. The only problem was that Warners couldn't come up with comparable material for Connie's subsequent releases. Her follow-up, "Too Young to Go Steady," was a dud.

Although Connie's recording career faded quickly, the studio continued to exploit her squeaky-clean image on TV in *Hawaiian Eye* and on the screen with roles that were even dumber than her records. (In *Susan Slade*, for example, Connie played an unwed mother who eludes public disgrace by pretending that her illegitimate son is her brother.)

All things considered, Connie Stevens was one of the few studio-manufactured teen stars of the fifties who managed to hold on to lasting stardom. She continues to show up in things like *The Hollywood Squares* and *Grease 2*, and of course, her celebrity hasn't been hurt by her much-publicized marriages to actor James Stacy and the inimitable Eddie Fisher.

Despite the unprecedented response to TV theme songs like "Let Me Go Lover" and "Davy Crockett" in 1954, the money-changers in the record industry didn't really make the connection between TV exposure and record sales until Rick Nelson parlayed his sitcom status into an astounding string of hits four years later. The only hitch was that very few performers were able to withstand prolonged TV exposure. And when a TV teen's career petered out, his recording career almost always went with it, thereby making him doubly passé.

Darlene had the talent, and Sharon had the smile, but Annette had — well, you know what Annette had. For almost five years, her T-shirt was the major attraction on Walt Disney's *Mickey Mouse Club*. Not that anybody planned it that way; it was just one of those lucky twists of fate. You see, puberty worked a stunning change on little Annette Funicello, the sweet-faced Italian kid from Utica, New York. One day she was just another moppet in the Mouseketeer lineup, the next, she practically formed her own row. Largely as a result of her stunning metamorphosis, she was catapulted from Mouseketeer to movie star. Somewhere along the way, she even became a Teen Singing Sensation, thus providing what must surely be one of the more unusual chapters in the history of rock.

At first, the Disney people were blind to Annette's burgeoning potential. In fact, they were downright dismayed at the way she was growing up and out — until somebody happened to notice that her fan mail had accelerated to a startling 1,000 letters a week. Not surprisingly, her newfound following was composed primarily of teenaged boys. Annette was plucked from the Mouska-ranks and given her own mini-series, as well as several starring roles in Disney feature films. Before long, her name and face graced all sorts of products, ranging from paper dolls to "Rock and Roll," and she became an industry unto herself.

This kind of thing was nothing new for Uncle Walt, who virtually invented the spin-off merchandising techniques for movies and TV that have become standard today. Actually, for an organization primarily accustomed to marketing lunchboxes and ceramic ducks, the people at Disney were remarkably astute in packaging Annette's modest singing talents for the pop marketplace. First she was provided with catchy, up-beat ditties ("Tall Paul," "First Name Initial") with a five-note range, and then her sweet but shallow singing voice was pumped up by means of multitracking techniques. Of course, all the fairy dust in Fantasy Land couldn't transform Annette into a singer, but that didn't matter to her fans.

The crazy thing is that Annette ended up making a real mark on Rock and Roll. In her brief singing career, she racked up a track record many a more talented and enduring star would envy. She sang with the Beach Boys, sold millions of records, and got two singles in the Top Ten. Today, in fact, her discs are listed right alongside those of the legendary Ronettes and Shangri-Las in many of those serious Girl Group discographies, and her old albums fetch as much as fifty bucks on the current collector's circuit.

Until the release of her Country album early in 1984, Annette's public appearances had been pretty much limited to Dick Clark oldie shows and peanut butter ads. In the eighteen years since her last album, she's seemed more interested in staying at home and looking after her three kids than in a show-biz career. But America never forgot her. Even today, some twenty years after she turned in her Mouska-ears, Johnny Carson can still get a laugh by describing something as "bigger than Annette Funicello's training bra."

Annette wasn't the only kiddie star on the lot whom Disney attempted to transform into a teen idol. He also gave the big push to Mouseketeers Darlene Gillespie and Tommy Kirk — but with little success. The only other Disney star who managed to score a Top Ten single was Hayley Mills, whose hit recording of "Let's Get Together" came on the heels of her triumph as the screen *Pollyanna*. Like Annette's, Hayley's records were pleasant enough. Still, it was always a little disconcerting to hear her enunciating the lyrics of things like "Johnny Jingo" in that veddy British accent of hers.

Here Hayley teams up with another perennial teen favorite, Maurice Chevalier.

In 1962, Paul Petersen, better known as Donna Reed's TV son, Jeff, was handed a recording career by Colpix, the same folks who had masterminded his sitcom stardom. During the show's eight-year run, both he and his TV sister, Shelley Fabares, ended up with best-selling hits. He says of his recording career today, "I had no control over it whatsoever. It was just a part of being on the show."

Paul's first hit single, "She Can't Find Her Keys," was introduced on a January telecast as part of a fantasy sequence in which Jeff dreams that he's a teenaged recording star. By the time Paul's fourth single was released eight months later, Jeff's dream had come true. "My Dad" was a saccharine tearjerker created especially for Paul to do on the show by the prolific songwriting team of Barry Mann and Cynthia Weil. Colpix knew they had a hit when Paul's rendition of the song reduced the cast and crew to tears.

Incidentally, Shelley and Paul are still very active today. Shelley has appeared in several TV series over the last few years (*Mary Hartman, Mary Hartman, Hello Larry, One Day at a Time*, etc.), and Paul supplements his rerun residuals with the profits from his successful L.A. limo service.

Paul Petersen pens a letter to you-know-who.

With her grown-up pantsuits and lacquered flip, Patty Duke made an unlikely candidate for pop stardom back in the Beatle-crazy days of the mid-sixties. But thanks to the millions of kids who watched her play identical cousins ("they laugh alike, they walk alike, at times they even talk alike") on her weekly TV show, Patty ended up putting a gold record (for the Lesley Gore-ish "Don't Just Stand There") next to the Oscar back in 1965.

The producers of *The Rifleman* had ratings on their mind when they talked Johnny Crawford's father into letting him cut a Rock and Roll record in 1961. Although Johnny had a tendency to whine instead of sing, he scored several hits, the biggest being "Your Nose Is Gonna Grow." His newfound teen following helped keep *The Rifleman* on the air another couple of years.

113

Although record sales weren't always an automatic by-product of series and sitcom sinecure, a record company really had to fumble the ball in order not to score. The rare flops include the abbreviated singing careers of Jerry (Beaver Cleaver) Mathers, Noreen (*Bachelor Father*) Corcoran and George "Goober" Lindsey of *The Andy Griffith Show*.

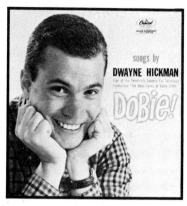

Dwayne Hickman's success as a recording star should've been a sure thing, given the millions of fans who tuned in to watch him every week as TV's Dobie Gillis. Hickman might have had a chance if only he'd been allowed to perform as himself. Unfortunately, like Edd Byrnes before him, he was required to hide behind his TV persona on songs like "Who Needs Elvis" and "I'm a Lover Not a Fighter." Even his most ardent fans couldn't swallow the idea of the nebbishy Dobie as a Rock and Roll star.

(By the way, you'll be happy to know that Dwayne Hickman is nebbishy no more; he's currently a highly placed executive in the TV industry.)

With one home out of three tuning it in weekly, *Batman* was one of the biggest things to hit TV in 1966. It was so popular that when ABC broke into a *Batman* telecast to announce the safe return of Gemini 8 astronauts Neil Armstrong and David Scott, who had earlier suffered a close scrape with death when a malfunction sent their craft tumbling through space, network switchboards were lit up with irate calls protesting the interruption. The merchandise boom that accompanied *Batman*'s rise in the ratings (along with the network's desire to squelch the rumor that the Caped Crusader and his hunky young ward were more than Just Friends) ultimately led to Adam West's spin-off career as a romantic balladeer.

As Sister Bertrille, a perky young novice who happens to be able to fly, Sally Field soared high above the competition as *The Flying Nun*. But despite the show's loyal following and the blessings of the Catholic Church (which commended it for "humanizing" nuns), Sally's singing career never took wing.

"The Lurch" was one of those self-appointed dance crazes that never quite got off the ground — despite the popularity of its originator, the late Ted Cassidy, otherwise known as Lurch, the hulking, zombielike butler on *The Addams Family*. You rang?

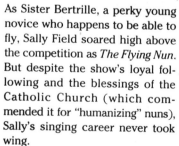

Barbara (*I Dream of Jeannie*) Eden played it safe by sticking to Fats Domino and Everly Brothers tunes on her album debut, but her recording career lasted little more than the blink of an eye.

114

All the members of the Cartwright clan waxed albums during the early sixties when *Bonanza*'s popularity was at its height. As you would expect, each of the Cartwright men was given musical material that conformed to his image on the show. Pernell Roberts murmured thoughtful ballads and Hoss sang cutesy country tales, while Michael Landon did "Linda Is Lonesome," a typical teen-type lament. But it took Pa Cartwright (Lorne Greene) to come up with the bona fide hit. His rousing recitation of the saga of "Ringo" made it to Number One in 1964.

In the sixties, millions of Americans happily kept an appointment each week with two young medical men — Ben Casey (Vince Edwards in real life), and NBC's Dr. Kildare (Richard Chamberlain). During their respective five-year runs, *Ben Casey* became ABC's number one show, and Chamberlain received more fan mail than Gable at his peak. Naturally, it wasn't long before someone hit on the idea of steering the good doctors into recording careers.

Of the two, Chamberlain was by far the more successful, actually managing to score three major hits ("Love Me Tender," "The Theme from Dr. Kildare" and "All I Have to Do Is Dream") before being stripped of his whites. Vince Edwards, on the other hand, looked completely unconvincing with a microphone in his hand. This was due primarily to his stern TV image; Ben Casey was much too uptight to get down and boogie.

Hugh (*Wyatt Earp*) O'Brian and George (*Route 66*) Maharis were two of the many stars hustled into cutting albums as a result of their TV clout. Although Maharis had a moderate-sized hit with "Teach Me Tonight," no one really took his recording career seriously — least of all Maharis himself. Neither he nor Hugh ever attempted to sing again — except for an occasional telethon. Today, their albums are big items in Oldie shops, pricing out at anywhere from twenty-five to fifty bucks, and at garage sales, where they usually go for around twenty-five to fifty cents.

116

Michael Parks was well on his way to cult stardom when his series, *Then Came Bronson*, was canceled out from under him in 1970. One of the few TV actors with the mystery and charisma to become a genuine pop idol, Parks blew his chance at the big time by trying to live up to his rebel image on the set. As a result, MGM sent him packing despite his enormous popularity and the Top Twenty single ("Long Lonesome Highway") he'd scored off the show.

Parks dropped from sight following *Bronson*'s demise, only to resurface again in the mid-seventies. Today he can be seen in made-for-TV movies and action dramas, usually playing psychotics and wayward cops.

David McCallum covered the Beatles, the Monkees and Simon and Garfunkel on this, one of the many albums he recorded at the height of his fame as Illya Kuryakin, the Russian spy on *The Man from U.N.C.L.E.*

Soupy Sales cut his album back when all of America was tuning in his TV show to see celebs like Frank Sinatra and Tony Bennett get a pie in the face. Some of its stand-out selections include "Your Brains Fall Out" and of course "The Mouse," the dance craze that Soupy always insisted was sweeping the nation.

Shortly after recording "The Mouse," Soupy was lured back to Hollywood to film *Birds Do It* — a dreary low-budget comedy with Buddy Hackett, which brought his career to a screaming halt. While he remains a familiar face on quiz shows, Soupy never again regained his footing in the ratings or the charts.

On *Love Songs from a Cop*, Joe E. Ross (Officer Gunther Toody of *Car 54, Where Are You?*) spiced up teen favorites and ballads like "Are You Lonesome Tonight?" with a few of his patented "ooh, ooh!" 's.

STEREO

DEL·FI
with delphonic sound

The Many Sides of Pepino

THE REAL McCOY THEME

BALLADS

CALYPSO

NOVELTY TUNES

POPULAR

CHA CHA CHA

JAZZ

COMEDY   MAMBO

MERENGUE

Yep, it's Pepino, the Mexican farmhand who "came with the house" on TV's *The Real McCoys*. But did you know that in real life that "little bundle of dynamite" was actually Tony Martinez, the "multitalented show-business vet"? On *The McCoys*, all Tony was required to do was mug and shrug his shoulders while Grandpappy Amos (Walter Brennan) jumped up and down and called him a ninny, but on his album, Tony got a chance to show off his versatility by performing such favorites as "La Bamba" and "I Dig You the Most." Someday maybe you too will discover the many sides of Pepino.

Hugh Downs waxed this one back in 1959 in between his duties as Jack Paar's head flunky on the old *Tonight Show* and host of the original *Concentration*.

Jack Narz was no stranger to celebrity when he cut *Sing the Folk Hits* in 1960. Not only was he the announcer for the radio version of *Queen for a Day* in 1949, he was also the first TV game show host to become embroiled in the quiz show scandals after it was revealed that *Dotto* (which he had hosted for a month in 1958) was rigged. And what does all this have to do with folksinging, you say? Well, as orchestra leader Bob Crosby noted in the liner commentary for the album, "Not only is Jack a top flight announcer, but he plays a hell of a game of golf."

And now when you least expect it...*It's Time for Regis!* Regis Philbin, that is — the nerdy announcer and now local talk show host whose main claim to fame was the time he tearfully walked off his post as announcer on the old *Joey Bishop Show* because he felt he wasn't properly appreciated. One spin of Regis's album and you'll soon agree that all that abuse Bishop used to heap on him was more than deserved.

When Ed McMahon first announced his plans to cut an album on *The Tonight Show*, Johnny Carson threatened to make a citizen's arrest on his tonsils.

Trying to parlay prime-time clout into pop stardom may seem as dated as Shelley Fabares's ponytail, and yet you still see it attempted today. Of course, that's only because every so often it works.

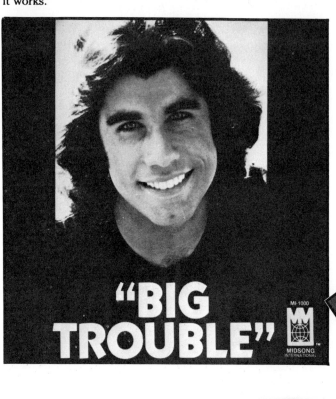

"BIG TROUBLE"

It came as something of a surprise when John Travolta's first release, "Let Her In," made it to the Top Ten; he'd been just another Sweathog in the *Welcome Back, Kotter* meatrack when he was signed to a recording contract with a small but aggressive independent company called Midland International. However, once Travolta clicked with *Saturday Night Fever*, he began to get antsy about being tied down to such a modest little label — especially since he was getting the big rush from *Fever*'s powerful producer, Robert Stigwood.

Travolta eventually switched to RSO, where he landed on the charts again in 1978 with "You're the One That I Want," his duet from *Grease* with Olivia Newton-John. In the meantime, Midland continued to release material he'd recorded for them earlier as if nothing had changed. In 1972, they put out a rerelease of "Big Trouble," the original flip side of "Let Her In." But unlike Travolta's earlier musical efforts, this one didn't have a movie or TV hit to coast on. By then, Travolta's career was in (temporary) Big Trouble — owing to his disastrous screen rendezvous with Lily Tomlin in *Moment by Moment*.

All of which brings to mind David Naughton, the engagingly boyish actor who played Billy Manero, brother of the Travolta character in *Makin' It*, the TV spin-off of *Saturday Night Fever*. Naughton's singing career was carefully patterned after Travolta's, complete with a record release timed to coincide with his sitcom debut. Oddly enough, his first effort, the theme from *Makin' It*, made it big, but the series itself was a bomb. Once the show was canceled, Naughton went back to being a Pepper in the soft drink ads — a cushy gig that eventually led to a starring role in *An American Werewolf in London* among others.

In search of a hit, Dot Records gave us the song stylings of Mr. Spock.

In 1973, *Midnight Special* emcee Wolfman Jack, who had become an underground phenomenon during the sixties by imitating black deejays on pirate radio stations, howled his way through "I Ain't Never Seen a White Man."

ALL Roads [Lead Back To You]
b/w Better To Forget Him

Donny Most (Ralph Malph on *Happy Days*) did his best to sound like his idol, Barry Manilow, on "All Roads (Lead Back to You)."

Penny Marshall and Cindy Williams of *Laverne and Shirley* had millions of fans, but only a handful bought their album. Ditto that of their TV pals, Lenny and Squiggy. The problem for both was that their approach fell somewhere between comedy and straight-faced rock'n'roll — with neither really coming off.

It all started in a five-thousand-watt radio station in Fresno, California, and went from there to TV stardom and a big-time record deal. Ted Knight wasn't the only MTM rep player to use his sitcom status to launch a singing career. In 1975, "Carlton the Doorman" of *Rhoda* asked the musical question "Who Is It?"

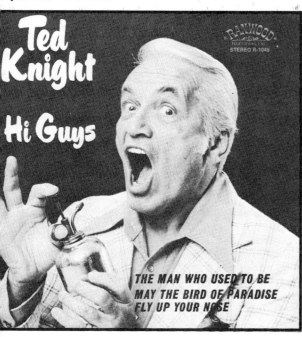

Telly Savalas stuck pretty close to the original Phil Spector arrangement on his update of "You've Lost That Lovin' Feelin'," the old Righteous Brothers hit. Telly's recording career coincided with *Kojak*'s rise to fame.

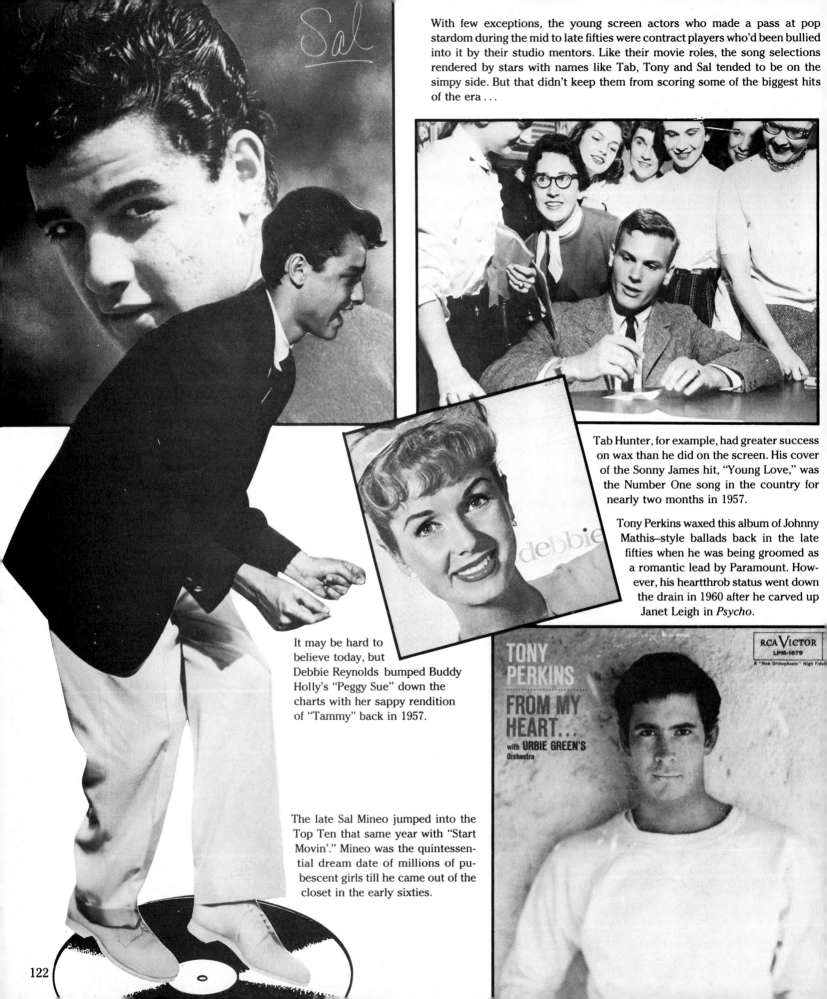

Sal

With few exceptions, the young screen actors who made a pass at pop stardom during the mid to late fifties were contract players who'd been bullied into it by their studio mentors. Like their movie roles, the song selections rendered by stars with names like Tab, Tony and Sal tended to be on the simpy side. But that didn't keep them from scoring some of the biggest hits of the era . . .

Tab Hunter, for example, had greater success on wax than he did on the screen. His cover of the Sonny James hit, "Young Love," was the Number One song in the country for nearly two months in 1957.

Tony Perkins waxed this album of Johnny Mathis–style ballads back in the late fifties when he was being groomed as a romantic lead by Paramount. However, his heartthrob status went down the drain in 1960 after he carved up Janet Leigh in *Psycho*.

It may be hard to believe today, but Debbie Reynolds bumped Buddy Holly's "Peggy Sue" down the charts with her sappy rendition of "Tammy" back in 1957.

The late Sal Mineo jumped into the Top Ten that same year with "Start Movin'." Mineo was the quintessential dream date of millions of pubescent girls till he came out of the closet in the early sixties.

debbie

RCA VICTOR
LPM-1679
A "New Orthophonic" High Fidel

TONY PERKINS

FROM MY HEART...
with URBIE GREEN'S Orchestra

122

The stars who follow here weren't necessarily out to achieve Teen Idol status when they launched their recording careers, but they weren't exactly trying to avoid it either.

Goldie made the move to reggae on her first single release. But "Pitta Patta" didn't cause Bob Marley to lose any sleep.

Peter Fonda has made not one, but two, stabs at launching a recording career; first in the late sixties during his Roger Corman period when he waxed songs by Donovan and Gram Parsons and then again in 1977 when he recorded under the guise of a fictional Country singer named Bobby Ogden. Fonda's vocal was mixed down real low on "Outlaw Blues," but it didn't help. You could still hear him.

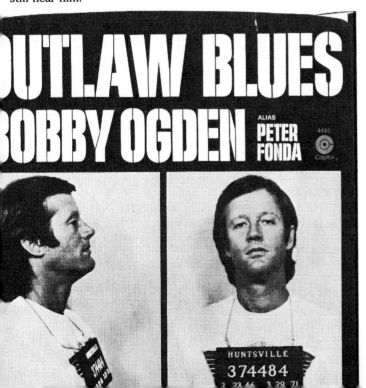

Robert Mitchum gargled his way through "The Ballad of Thunder Road" in 1958. You can laugh, but it made the charts twice (in 1958 and 1962), thereby inspiring the King of Cool to branch out in several other pop music directions. A brief flirtation with Latin music produced *Calypso . . . Is Like So*, which contains the never-to-be-forgotten classic, "Mama Looka Boo Boo."

On *Lyrics for Lovers*, Dirk Bogarde sounded like a cross between Queen Elizabeth and Johnny Ray.

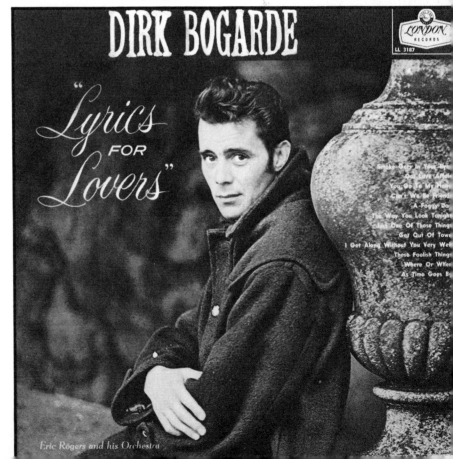

Who says that rock belongs only to the young? Over the years, the pop record industry has opened its arms to an extraordinarily diverse array of talent — including the Polygrip set. (Of course, there are those who would say that this has less to do with largesse on the industry's part than on its tendency to exploit anything that can still move.)

Mae West was well into her seventies when she made her stunning rock debut in 1966 with *Way Out West*. Backed by a teenaged rock band in the Mersey mold, Mae put on her rock'n'roll shoes, delivering songs by Dylan and Lennon and McCartney in a style that was something of a cross between Marlene Dietrich and Buffy Sainte-Marie. Although critical response was decidedly mixed, Mae kept up the momentum by turning out an electrified Christmas album featuring the single "Put the Loot in the Boot, Santa." However, like many rock artists, she suffered a dry spell following her initial burst of creativity. It was 1973 before she reappeared with a new album entitled *Great Balls of* (get it?) *Fire*, which boasted her highly individual interpretations of "Light My Fire" and "Rock Around the Clock." No question about it, the kid had soul.

Walter Brennan's chart-busting style involved reciting syrupy yarns, about old prospectors and faithful mules, over mushy strings and a heavenly choir — a formula created for him by the rock producer Jerry Capeheart (who also co-authored "Summertime Blues"). The Academy Award–winning actor's first hit, "Dutchman's Gold," was written off as a fluke by the industry, but he showed them when he came back even stronger with "Old Rivers" in 1962. In all, he scored three Top Forty hits in as many years. Later, in an ending fit for one of his records, he died while watching himself in an old movie on TV.

In 1979, the late Ethel Merman released an album on which she bellowed a dozen of her old Broadway hits over a mechanical disco beat. Listening to it now, you get the impression that the whole thing was strictly intended for yuks. But really, shouldn't somebody have told Ethel?

And then there were the guys at Buddah Records who got the bright idea of having octogenarian George Burns stammer his way through the Stones' "(I Can't Get No) Satisfaction" in 1971. Close, but no cigar. George fared a little better when he made the switch to Country with "I Wish I Was Eighteen Again."

In 1969, comedienne Moms Mabley got into the act with her moving rendition of the Dion hit "Abraham, Martin and John," a cut from her album of the same name. Although Moms had made many comedy records in the past, she performed the songs on this, her most successful album, in a straightforward emotional manner. The only problem was that most of the words were unintelligible owing to the fact that Moms didn't have any teeth.

Figuring that their listeners couldn't tell the difference, record companies in the fifties often put a rock'n'roll label on records that weren't even in the neighborhood — like this one, for example, by the old jazzbo Scatman Crothers, which boasts such favorite rave-ups as "Baby, Won't You Please Come Home" and "Ghost Riders in the Sky."

Don Cornell

It was bad enough when whitebread singers like Eddie Fisher tried to palm off dippy tunes like "Dungaree Doll" as rock'n'roll, but it was downright insulting when a smarmy crooner like Don Cornell made the Hit Parade with hokum like "Teenage Meeting" and "The Bible Tells Me So." A former Big Band singer with Sammy Kaye, Cornell must have been well into his forties when his fading fortunes forced him to court the Clearasil set.

Perry Como might have intended to be taken seriously when he covered the R&B hit "Ko Ko Mo" in 1958, but when Bing Crosby ba-ba-ba-booed his way through "Hey Jude," it was mostly for laughs. Former Big Band singer Kay Starr had survival on her mind when she slid off the "Wheel of Fortune" onto the "Rock and Roll Waltz"; but poor Muddy Waters switched from the blues to the twist and psychedelic-style rock only under pressure from his boss, Leonard Chess. It figured that Cab Calloway would try for a disco update of "Minnie the Moocher," but it was a surprise when Frank Sinatra, once one of rock's most outspoken foes, let down his toupee for a ring-a-ding rendition of "Ev'rybody's Twistin'" in 1962.

The winner, hands down.

We've gotten used to the idea of movie stars in the White House, tap dancers in the Senate and Shirley Temple at the UN, but have you ever noticed how many high-ranking pols have tried to reverse that trend by breaking into the Top Ten . . .

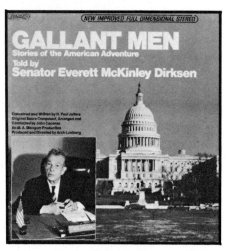

It all started back in the mid-sixties when Senator Everett Dirksen, the last of the golden-throated orators, wrapped his dulcet tones around "The Gallant Men," a flag-waving narrative dedicated to all the boys who had lost their lives fighting to "Keep America Free." Although this platter was intended to be patriotic rather than political — coming, as it did, at the beginning of the counterculture movement, its message took on a distinct Love-It-or-Leave-It tone. Surprisingly, however, it landed smack on the Top Forty, nestling comfortably between the Beatles and the Stones. Its success led to a string of concert dates for Dirksen, as well as three additional LPs — on Capitol, naturally.

In 1969, the year of the Woodstock Festival and Moratorium Day, comedian Red Skelton came very close to scoring a Top Forty hit with his unique rendition of "The Pledge of Allegiance." Some months later after the "Pledge's" sales had waned, Burger King pressed it on paper and gave it out gratis with a burger and an order of fries. God bless.

The first record to address the issue of America's military involvement in Vietnam head-on came shortly after "The Gallant Men," with Staff Sgt. Barry Sadler's "The Ballad of the Green Berets." Originally commissioned by the U.S. Army as a morale booster for the troops, "Beret" was later recorded again by Sadler for RCA. Released in 1966, a year of staggering military losses in Southeast Asia and burgeoning social problems here at home, the record nonetheless became one of the biggest-selling singles in the history of pop.

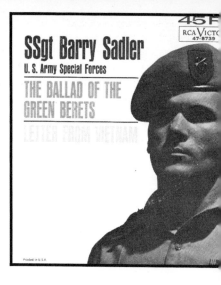

While Lieutenant William Calley awaited the outcome of his trial for the My Lai massacre, a group called the C Company put out a single called "The Battle Hymn of Lt. Calley," which interspersed the story of a soldier who "tried to do his duty and to get the upper hand" with actual passages from Calley's trial.

In 1967, a few months after the Summer of Love, Victor Lundberg hit the Top Ten with a moving recitation called "An Open Letter to My Teenage Son." While a chorus hummed "The Battle Hymn of the Republic," "Letter's" narrator sermonized on long hair, beards and whether God was dead. Eventually, Pops got around to the subject of war and draft-card burners, saying, "Son, your mother will always love you . . . because she's a woman. But if you ever decide to burn your draft card then burn your birth certificate too. I have no son."

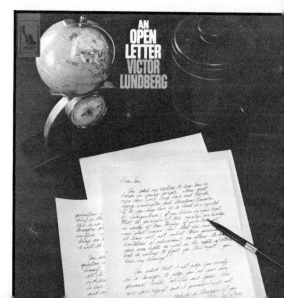

The success of these oddball hits didn't go un-noticed within the record industry. It wasn't long before more right-wing celebs got into the act.

As the generation gap grew wider in 1967, Art Linkletter's actress-daughter, eighteen-year-old Diane, joined him to record a plea for parent-child understanding, "We Love You, Call Collect." Diane played the part of a runaway teen writing a letter to her folks about all the strange experiences and "weirdos — pot smokers and speed freaks" — she'd encountered since leaving home. Even so, she goes on to tell them, they must trust her to make her own decisions about her life. Diane's soliloquy is followed by one from her father, begging her to come home. At the end, Art actually breaks down as he beseeches, "We love you, call collect." Ironically, this record got the publicity boost that sent it up the charts when Diane leaped to her death from a sixth-floor window two years later while under the influence of LSD.

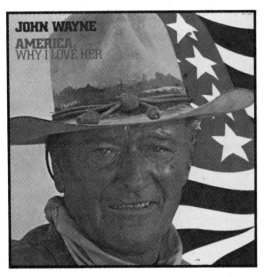

In the midst of the Watergate mess, John Wayne, the Sweetheart of the Right, released an LP entitled *America, Why I Love Her*, containing such classics as "The Hyphen," on which he berates all those ungrateful immigrants like the "Mexican hyphen Americans" and the "Afro hyphen Americans" who don't have the guts to stand up and be counted as plain old unmitigated Americans. The Duke reminded us that we all came from other places, "different creeds and different races," but that no little line, be it the swastika or the Russian Hammer and Sickle, could "flame the flames of hatred faster than The Hyphen."

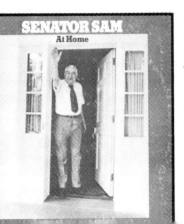

Politics and pop mixed it up once again in 1973 when the folks at Columbia decided to turn Sam Ervin, Jr., into a recording star. On his album, *Senator Sam at Home*, the former chairman of the House investigation of Watergate stuttered his way through such favorites as "Bridge Over Troubled Waters" and "If I Had a Hammer" in his inimitable Foghorn Leghorn style. He pontificated on religion, matrimony, the law, drunken driving and more, wrapping the whole thing up with a red, white and blue chorus from "The Star-Spangled Banner."

Lest you think that only blowhards and right-wingers have been immortalized on wax, let the record show that the sentiments of the flamboyant left-wing congressman from Harlem, Adam Clayton Powell, also ended up between the grooves. He cut his first (and only) album in order to answer his critics after being bounced from the House of Representatives.

127

In February of 1974, Sister Janet Mead's finger-poppin' rendition of "The Lord's Prayer" soared to the Number Five chart position and sold 50,000 copies within ten days of its initial release. The problem for Sister Mead, as for any other pop artist, was in coming up with new material. Ultimately, she decided to play it safe by covering a Donovan song called "Brother Sun and Sister Moon" her next time at bat. But the thirty-six-year-old Australian nun ended up back at her old job when her follow-up fell flat.

In the beginning, Alfred E. Newman's first records like "Nose Job" and "It's a Gas" (two minutes of belching and other whoopee-cushion wit) were just paper pressings that came as a bonus in *Mad* magazine, but they proved so popular that Bigtop Records ended up signing the What Me Worry? Kid to a three-record deal.

"Look! It's your favorite mouse all grown up and gone disco. Now you and your children can catch Mickey Mouse Fever!" So begins the TV commercial for Columbia House's *Mickey Mouse Disco*, an album that bills itself as the rock debut of Walt Disney's cartoon mouse. In point of fact, however, the only real Disney star to put in an appearance on the album is Donald Duck — who quacks out a few words of encouragement on "Macho Duck." The rest of the album consists of cheerless renditions of such Disney classics as "Zip a Dee Doo Dah" and "Chim Chim Cheree," performed by a group of anonymous Nashville studio musicians. Yet, such is the prestige of the Mickey Mouse name that the album went platinum within months of the inauguration of the TV campaign. It was quickly followed by several other Mouska-offerings, including the Jane Fonda–inspired *Mousercize*.

Mickey's stunning success in the rock market (over three million copies sold) sent industry scouts scurrying in search of other children's stars with comparable clout. The first to be signed to a major label was TV's Ronald McDonald, who was snapped up by Casablanca Records. Lewis Merenstein, who signed McDonald, told *Rolling Stone*, "Rather than struggle to break in a new name, I want an established artist." But just in case, McDonald's first album also featured numbers by such well-known guest stars as the Muppets, Strawberry Shortcake, and Shamu the Whale.

Mrs. Elva Miller was an unassuming Los Angeles matron who had always wanted to be an opera star. The only problem was that her singing voice sounded something like Tiny Tim's. Discouraged from pursuing a professional career by her family, she began making private recordings for her own pleasure. Somehow, her tapes, which happened to be screamingly funny, came to the attention of Capitol Records, who signed her to do an album of popular tunes entitled *Mrs. Miller's Greatest Hits*. To everyone's surprise, two of the cuts — "Downtown" and "A Lover's Concerto" — ended up making the charts. Her subsequent appearances on Mike and Merv and Johnny left everyone wondering whether or not she was for real.

Throughout Mrs. Millermania, Elva remained completely oblivious to the fact that she was a joke to the media, not to mention her own fans. However, it wasn't long before the joke grew stale — to everyone but Elva. When Capitol gave her the boot, she formed her own record company (Mrs. Miller Records) and released her next single on her own. But this turned out to be an expensive conceit, and eventually Elva was forced to face the fact that her singing career was kaput. Sadder, but perhaps wiser, she retired to civilian life.

With so many records bearing Pope John Paul John Paul's name in the wake of his visit to America in 1979, you'd have thought that the Pontiff was trying to come on like the Singing Nun. But JPJP wasn't attempting to parlay his ecclesiastical clout into a recording career. Actually, he — or rather, the Vatican — had a piece of only one of the many "Pope" albums that glutted the market at that time. The rest were chintzy rip-offs that consisted of the Pope's speeches re-recorded over stock musical cuts. On one such offering, his famous whoop was synchronized to a mechanical disco beat. The unauthorized Pope platters nevertheless put a heavy crimp in the official album's sales and helped to usher in his record company's eventual decline. The label? Infinity, of course.

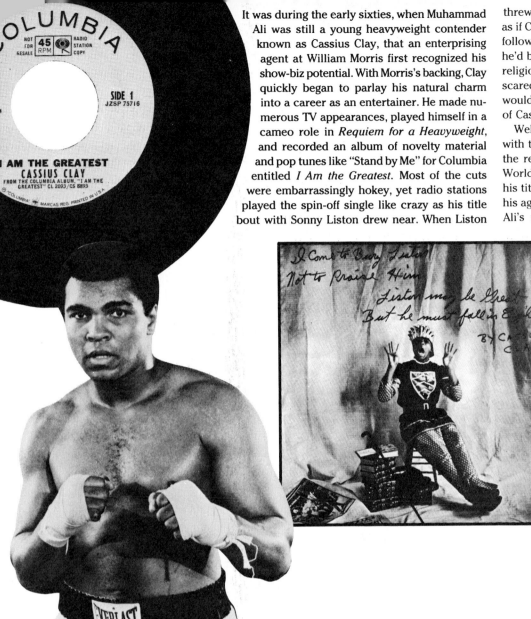

It was during the early sixties, when Muhammad Ali was still a young heavyweight contender known as Cassius Clay, that an enterprising agent at William Morris first recognized his show-biz potential. With Morris's backing, Clay quickly began to parlay his natural charm into a career as an entertainer. He made numerous TV appearances, played himself in a cameo role in *Requiem for a Heavyweight*, and recorded an album of novelty material and pop tunes like "Stand by Me" for Columbia entitled *I Am the Greatest*. Most of the cuts were embarrassingly hokey, yet radio stations played the spin-off single like crazy as his title bout with Sonny Liston drew near. When Liston threw in the towel in the seventh round, it looked as if Cassius had it made. But at a press conference following the fight, the new champ announced that he'd become a member of the Nation of Islam — a religious group with a black supremacy credo that scared most white folks to death — and that he would henceforth be known by his Muslim name of Cassius X (later Muhammad Ali).

Well, you can imagine how this news went over with the guys at William Morris — not to mention the rest of the entertainment community. As the World Boxing Commission moved to strip him of his title, citing his violation of some technicalities, his agent was deluged with abrupt cancellations of Ali's upcoming personal appearance dates. Radio stations pulled "I Am the Greatest" from their play lists, and record stores packed up the album and sent it back whence it came. Within three years, Ali had created an even bigger ruckus by using his status as a Muslim minister to challenge the draft. Ali would eventually return to television to peddle everything from pizza to roach powder, and to the movies to play himself in a feature-length film a decade later, but for a while there, it appeared that not only his crown, but his show-biz career, was down for the count.

Argentinian wrestler Antonino Rocca claimed to have gotten his musical education from Arturo Toscanini, but you couldn't prove it by this album. Its cuts included things like "Liebestraum Cha Cha Cha."

In the liner notes of his 1964 album, he said he wanted to be known as "a musician who happened to throw balls," but pitcher Denny McLain couldn't get to first base with his career as a pop organist.

In 1976, the Globetrotters did it right on "The Duke of Earl," and a year later, Meadowlark Lemon spun off with a nifty version of "Personality," the old Lloyd Price hit.

129

In the fifties and sixties, you could count the women rock'n'roll stars on both hands (and still have a few fingers to spare), but with the advent of disco in the seventies and the media's growing preoccupation with sex, the distaff side soon began popping up all over the charts. For a while there, it seemed as if any cute young thing with a talent for wearing spandex was likely to get the nod.

From Europe came supermodels Madleen Kane and Amanda Lear. Madleen's rock credentials included the cover of *Vogue* and a certain jet-set cachet, while Amanda's derived from being a former Roxy Music cover girl and David Bowie's Ex.

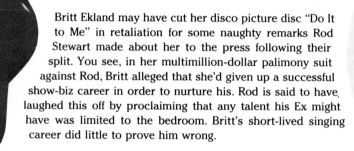

From Jamaica via the gay hangouts of Fire Island and lower Manhattan came the astonishingly beautiful Grace Jones — five and a half feet of carved ebony with the face of a jungle cat. However, though Grace had moderate success in 1977 with "I Need a Man," she remains primarily a New York phenomenon to this day. Which isn't to suggest that Grace is any less talented than her compatriots on the multitrack scene, but rather that she's failed, as yet, to hook up with a producer who knows how to deploy her special charms. In any case, she is still capable of inspiring her fans to fits of passion, like the masked marauder who handcuffed himself to her leg during one of her recent performances.

Britt Ekland may have cut her disco picture disc "Do It to Me" in retaliation for some naughty remarks Rod Stewart made about her to the press following their split. You see, in her multimillion-dollar palimony suit against Rod, Britt alleged that she'd given up a successful show-biz career in order to nurture his. Rod is said to have laughed this off by proclaiming that any talent his Ex might have was limited to the bedroom. Britt's short-lived singing career did little to prove him wrong.

"You" was an update of "Je t'aime," the heavy-breather made famous by Jane Birkin and Serge Gainsbourg (France's answer to Sonny and Cher). On it, a young actress named Farrah Fawcett Majors provided a few sighs and whispers over a lackluster musical track. But "You" lacked the élan of the original, and went largely unnoticed when first released in 1971. It was dug up and reissued as a disco single shortly after Farrah got her Angel's wings.

Cheryl Ladd, the blond starlet who took Farrah's place on *Charlie's Angels*, was determined to replace her predecessor not only on the show, but in the nation's libidos as well. Tough and ambitious, Cheryl hustled like crazy to sell herself as the next prime-time sex star. She did the poster, the talk shows, the Rona Barrett interviews. She even cut a disco album and pushed it on everything from *Don Kirschner's Rock Concert* to local L.A. club dates. Even so, it barely crawled onto the charts. Apparently, what Cheryl failed to realize was that being a pop star required an audience entirely different from the grade-school girls and middle-aged men who watched her on TV. (After she became a reborn Christian in 1981, Cheryl reportedly tried to buy back all those naughty posters and album covers.)

Thanks to the stunning success of her disco hit, "More More More," Andrea (*Deep Throat II*) True became the first porno star ever to break into the Top Ten. Never one to pass up an opportunity, Andrea pursued her new career with a vengeance — plunging into endless rounds of publicity appearances with an unbridled zeal. During the months that "More" lolled around the charts, Andrea began to think of herself as a full-fledged superstar — so much so that when Elvis died, she took out a full-page ad in *Variety* mourning the loss of her beloved colleague. But although Andrea continued her collaboration with Gregg Diamond, her next few releases fell flat. So nowadays, she's back in the skin game again.

Andrea's moment of triumph may have been heartbreakingly brief, but before it was over, it inspired several other porn stars to take the disco plunge. In 1978, Marilyn Chambers, former Ivory Snow cover girl and feature attraction of *Behind the Green Door*, made her recording debut with the theme from her latest, *Insatiable* (a film that had the distinction of being released simultaneously as a movie and a videotape cassette). Marilyn even made an abbreviated publicity tour (usually wearing little more than high heels and a fur coat) to plug her new career, but aside from providing local jocks with a little thrill, it didn't accomplish much. "Insatiable" was a bust.

The story of Barbi Benton's recording career is straight out of *Citizen Kane*, i.e., aging publishing baron tries unsuccessfully to make a star out of his comely but profoundly untalented girlfriend by shoving her down the nation's throat. Only in Barbi's version, the girlfriend was hardly a pawn in her lover's power game; in fact, it just may have been the other way around.

Barbi was a college student at UCLA in 1968 when she met Hugh Hefner while moonlighting as an extra on the old *Playboy After Dark*. Soon the two fell in love and Barbi gave up her ambition of becoming a veterinary surgeon to act as the official hostess of Hefner's West Coast manse. (That's probably just as well; formaldehyde is murder on the nails.)

Once Barbi started hanging around with all the star types who hang around with Hef, she began to get ideas about becoming a star herself. After lots of soul-searching, she finally concluded that she was meant to be a singer — even though, as she has since conceded, she was tone deaf "in the beginning." Initially Hef was against the idea; he told her she'd have to pay people to listen to her sing. But once he gave in, he backed Barbi all the way — getting her the finest producers, songwriters, backup singers and sidemen (thirty-one in all according to the jacket credits) money could buy for her album debut, *Something New*. Then, when the time was right, he introduced her to the world in a lavish *Playboy* pictorial.

But even with all the coaching and the Tender Loving Care, Barbi's singing still sounded like she was yelling at the top of her well-padded lungs. Her first release ("Staying Power" by Neil Sedaka) didn't do so well on the charts, but it did get her lots of media play. She ended up as the toast of the second-echelon talk show circuit (Griffin, Douglas, et al.) and later the star of her own extravagant Las Vegas act. One of her coaches sagely summed up her appeal when he said, "I guess Barbi's singing voice is a little weak, but you've got to admit, that girl's got a pair of tits that won't quit."

Ann-Margret and Elvis Presley in *Viva Las Vegas*

When it comes to packaging rock'n'roll for the big screen, Hollywood has been nothing if not consistent, it always gets it wrong. But try as we may, we . . .

The fifties were lean years at the once-great Hollywood film factories. For three decades prior, Hollywood had been the Mecca of disposable pop. Hit tunes, dance crazes, fashion, slang and stars — all were born at the movies. But things were different after the war. For one thing, the ticket-buying public was younger; their values and aesthetics at odds with those of past generations. To them, the flicks were little more than an excuse to drink beer and neck at the drive-in; they looked to TV and AM radio to find their newest fads and Fave Raves.

In an attempt to lure audiences away from their small screens and back into the theaters, the major studios mounted expensive epics with Technicolor, Cinemascope, and a plethora of special effects. But still the public stayed away in droves. It took pragmatic independent producers with no discernible artistic pretensions to understand that the film industry would have to tap the youth market if it expected to become viable again. "We realized that the older people were sitting at home watching TV instead of going to the movies," says Samuel Arkoff, cofounder of American International, the premier teen-exploitation movie mill of all time, "and the kids were staying away because they couldn't identify with a Clark Gable or a Gary Cooper at age 59."

So Hollywood gave the kids something they could identify with — rock'n'roll. B-movie vets like Arkoff, Sam Katzman (who started it all with *Rock Around the Clock*) and Albert Zugsmith (the world's foremost purveyor of Untamed Youth) rushed to exploit this new craze, thinking that it would soon go the way of raccoon coats and goldfish-swallowing. What they couldn't know was the rock'n'roll would not be just another flash-in-the-pan; that rock music and the people who played it would create a whole subculture of manners and morals for millions of children born during the postwar baby boom. In that sense, the film industry was as unprepared for the youth explosion of the fifties and sixties as the rest of the world. Still, it caught on faster than other segments of the entertainment biz, and it wasn't long before the drive-in circuit was inundated with teen-oriented novelty films.

As far as the actual packaging of rock'n'roll for the screen was concerned, Hollywood was nothing if not consistent — they always got it wrong. We gave them a hunk of burning funk named Presley and they gave us back a mascaraed crooner singing "Do the Clam." We gave them hot licks and the Big Beat and they gave us *Bop Girl*, *Cha-Cha-Cha Boom!* and *Beach Blanket Bingo*. And yet, the teenrock concoctions that Hollywood cranked out during the fifties and early sixties do have a special kind of charm, a clumsy exuberance that's ingratiating in its own dippy way.

Despite an uninterested record industry and a cynical Hollywood, the rock'n'roll revolution erupted from the screen and into the streets. Neither rock nor the movies would ever be the same.

CAN'T STOP THE MOVIES

The storylines of the early juke-box musicals were gossamer thin, consisting mostly of recycled "Hey kids, let's put on a show" formulas of the forties variety with abbreviated appearances by recording stars sandwiched in between. The action was contemporized by having earnest teenagers attempt to enlighten wary grown-ups as to the merits of rock'n'roll. Approximately seventy minutes and four or five musical numbers later, the adults inevitably exclaimed, "You know, this stuff isn't so bad after all!" But that too was really nothing new; movie parents had reacted exactly the same way to jazz and swing in earlier decades only to be won over in the last reel. In the case of forties collegiate musicals, however, there seemed to be at least a trace of affection on the part of the filmmakers for bobby-soxers and the Big Band sound. Not so with the middle-aged moguls who exploited rock on screen during its early years. Their idea was to cash in quickly on the latest music fad before the little pip-squeaks who dug-it-the-most came to their senses. And quickly it was. In the

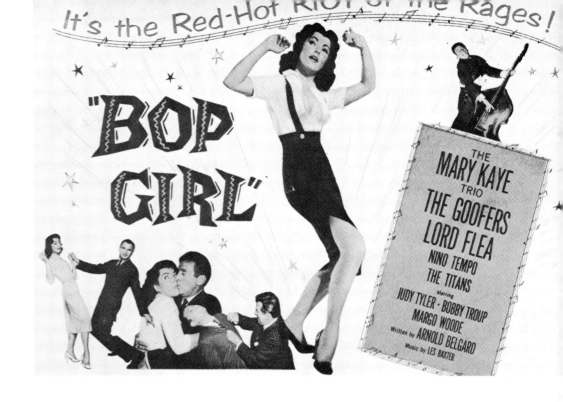

newspaper review of *The Girl Can't Help It* in 1956, for example, described Little Richard as a "diminutive South Sea Islander who plays the piano standing up.")

Ironically, many of these movies contain the only extant footage of some of the greatest talents rock'n'roll has ever known. Were it not for the speed and greed of quickie kings like Arkoff and Katzman, we would have no filmed record today of such stars as Eddie Cochran, Ritchie Valens and Frankie Lymon — just to name a few. Of course, these magic moments are not without their price. If you want to get a look at these real-life rock legends, you'd better expect to sit through an hour or so of yahoos like Julius La Rosa and Alan Dale masquerading as the real thing.

summer of 1960, for example, Sam Katzman signed Chubby Checker to a film contract just as his version of "The Twist" hit number one. The record was still riding high on the charts twenty-eight days later when Chubby made his screen debut as the star of the Katzman-produced *Twist Around the Clock*. (The critics were no less condescending to rock on screen; one

Bottom left: Conway Twitty and Mamie Van Doren in College Confidential

Mamie Van Doren and Paul Anka in *Girls Town*

Mamie Van Doren in *Untamed Youth*

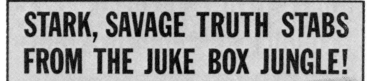

STARK, SAVAGE TRUTH STABS FROM THE JUKE BOX JUNGLE!

THE FIRST JOLTING STORY OF ORGANIZED TEEN-AGE GANGS!

RUNNING WILD

Hear the hit parade tune that's sweeping the country BILL HALEY AND HIS COMETS' "RAZZLE-DAZZLE"

STARRING
WILLIAM CAMPBELL · MAMIE Van DOREN
KEENAN WYNN · KATHLEEN CASE

SILVER... who wanted a thrill a night... every night!

SERAFINA... who knew the torments of love!

MARYLEE... who couldn't run from her secret!

GLORIA... who learned too much—too soon!

WHAT KIND OF GIRLS ARE THESE...?

Youthful rebe who don't wa to know rig from wrong

Metro-Goldwyn-Mayer Presents AN ALBERT ZUGSMITH PRODUCTION

GIRLS TOWN

LAST STOP ON THE ROAD TO NOWHERE!

AND INTRODUCING
PAUL ANKA HEAR HIM SING
"Lonely Boy" "A Time To Cry"
and the rocking title song

M · DICK CONTINO · HAROLD LLOYD, JR. CHARLES CHAPLIN,

ASSOCIATE FEATURE   THEATRE

See for yourself—the ravaged lives in the adolescent jungles of America today!

"The Delinquents"
Released thru UNITED ARTISTS

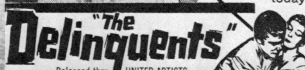

PUT THE TEENAGERS TO WORK WITH YOU WITH THIS SENSATIONAL CAMPAIGN!

TEENAGE GIRL AND BOY STREET BALLYHOO

Employ a good-looking teenage girl and a good-looking teenage boy to carry signs such as those illustrated through the busy intersections of your town. They could start from your theater each day, make their rounds and return to your theater where they should walk in opposite directions much as pickets do. It is important to note that both these teenagers should be dressed very conservatively and in good taste. Try to arrange with local newspaper photographers to follow them for any crowd display or other special interest.

NEWSPAPERS — TV AND RADIO — LOCAL GROUPS CO-OPERATION:
SET UP A TEENAGE CLINIC

Arrange with your local TV or radio public service forum to stage a round-table debate, using teenagers from public and private schools as panel members. Have a mature psychology or sociology local person act as moderator.

Use a choice of the following questions:
a.—Do the boys and girls in your school belong to groups that are likely to go wrong?
b.—If so, what do you think is the main reason?
c.—Is parental guidance the most important factor in molding character in teenagers?

LOCALIZE THE STORY THEME
Newspapers carry stories daily of juvenile delinqency. Add sock and shock to your campaign by making use of such stories, especially the headlines. Make a composite of such headlines and stories, tied in with your picture title or with a picture ad. Set it up in your lobby on an easel or near your box office.

INTERVIEW DELINQUENTS
Work with police department, local correction agencies and other interested groups for names of former juvenile delinquents (who have now been rehabilitated) with a view to having them give their own version of how their fall and rehabilitation came out.

The pressbooks that accompanied such teen
explo films as *The Delinquents* did everything but instruct
exhibitors in how to instigate youth riots as publicity stunts.

Hollywood did occasionally manage to deal intelligently with the emotional Sturm und Drang of adolescence as in *Rebel Without a Cause.* But once *Blackboard Jungle** hit the streets, the war between the generations was in full swing and screen teens were made to seem as menacing as the Creature from the Black Lagoon. This Trouble in River City theme was driven home in one quickie after another. Rock'n'roll was portrayed as a corrupter of youth, an aphrodisiac and worse — a malevolent force that gave Junior an itch to stick up the corner gas station and turned nice girls into Mamie Van Doren. Although juvenile crime, unlike the youthful obsession with rock music, wasn't exactly rampant in Averageville, USA, when

these films first began perambulating the nabes, by the time Katzman and Zugsmith had milked the subject dry, parents were convinced that it existed in epidemic proportions — with rock'n'roll as the cause. Naturally, it wasn't long before life was imitating schlock and kids actually began acting the way Hollywood said they did. Soon, teenaged audiences all over the country were merrily slashing theater seats and "rioting" at local get-togethers just like the Neanderthals they saw on the screen.

* A melodramtic film about slum school crime, considered by many to be the first rock film because of the Bill Haley songs on its soundtrack.

Vic Morrow in *Blackboard Jungle*   Jerry Lee Lewis in *College Confidential*   Frankie Vaughan in *Dangerous Youth*

In 1956, the same year that *Rock Around the Clock* bowed at the box office, Elvis Presley made his movie debut in *Love Me Tender* — a routine Western that had been refurbished to capitalize on his phenomenal popularity. Unlike most of the thirty-two Presley features that would follow in rapid succession, *Tender* boasted a healthy budget, crisp direction and a part expressly tailored to fit its down-home star. The one thing it didn't bother to provide, however, was an opportunity for Elvis, the then-and-always King of Rock'n'Roll, to do his thing. Instead, he crooned a couple of syrupy ballads — one of which furnished the film's title. Naturally, this left his fans a little disappointed, but that didn't keep them from jamming the theaters by the millions to get a long loving look at their idol. The demand for the celluloid Elvis was so great that *Love Me Tender* earned back its million-dollar production cost just three days after its premiere — something no film had ever done before. However, it was here with the astonishing success of his first film that many of Elvis's biggest problems began.

Elvis wanted desperately to be taken seriously as an actor, to become the new James Dean. (He could recite Dean's part from *Rebel Without a Cause* by heart when he first came to Hollywood, and often expressed a desire to play the dead screen idol in a film bio.) And in fact, while the critical reaction to his film debut was mixed, most reviewers grudgingly agreed that Elvis had shown real talent. But instead of upgrading his material Colonel Parker and his mouthpiece, Abe Lastfogel, the then-head of William Morris, proceeded to stick Elvis in a series of fluff musicals, most of which (with the notable exception of *Jailhouse Rock* and *King Creole*) required him to do little more than take off his shirt and sing enough cornball songs to fill a soundtrack album.

Elvis's standard film deal as designed by Parker and Lastfogel gave him 50 percent of a film's budget (later a million flat) up front plus 50 percent of its net earnings. (Parker himself took 25 percent of Presley's salary plus whatever he could squeeze out of the budget as "Technical Adviser.") Thus it was to the advantage of all concerned for Elvis to do lower quality films since they had less overhead to recoup from the profits — in other words, the cheaper the film, the bigger Elvis's (and the Colonel's) take. No offer, no matter how attractive, could induce Parker — or his client — to alter this formula. In 1975, for example, Barbra Streisand approached Presley to co-star with her as the burned-out rock singer of *A Star Is Born*. Elvis's bodyguard, Red West, who was there at the time, recalls, "She wanted him bad and I tell you it was a damn tragedy that he didn't take it because he would've been great in the part. Elvis was very keen to do it too. You could see the interest in his face. It was going to be a real challenge." But despite the obvious prestige of the project, the Colonel nixed the deal when Streisand declined to come up with Elvis's standard million-dollar advance.*

As the quality of his pictures plummeted, Elvis's audience began to dwindle — prompting Parker to compensate for the loss by upping his quota of film assignments. From 1961 through 1968, Presley starred in twenty-one of these low-budget quickies — an average of three a year. With each dismal release, Elvis's personal take skyrocketed, until he was averaging five to six million dollars annually — an income that made him the highest-paid performer in movies at the time.

As the years wore on, Elvis became so depressed about the junk he was cranking out ("my travelogues" he called them) that his unhappiness began to show on the screen. His despondency was exacerbated by the large quantities of speed he used on the set to keep his weight down and his spirits up. He could have demanded better material, but he clearly wanted no part of what he considered to be the business end of his profession. In a state-

ment made in 1963, he dutifully parroted the Colonel's company line with regard to his movie roles: "I've had intellectuals tell me that I've got to progress as an actor, explore new horizons, take on new challenges, all that routine. I'd like to progress, but I'm smart enough to realize that you can't bite off more than you can chew in this racket. You can't go beyond your limitations. They want me to try an artistic picture. That's fine. Maybe I can pull it off some day. But not now. I've done eleven pictures and they've all made money. A certain kind of audience likes me. I'd be a fool to tamper with that kind of success."

Parker's management made Elvis very rich and very comfortable — so much so that he never questioned the way his film career was handled — a fact that would contribute mightily to his personal and artistic decline. Even more than his switch-over from rock to schmaltz, and more than his plastic Vegas persona, it was Presley's schlocky cavalcade of films that was responsible for transforming him from a raging rockabilly bull into a national laughingstock.

* Legend has it that when Parker turned down a part for Elvis opposite Jayne Mansfield in *The Girl Can't Help It* for similar reasons in 1956, Mansfield flew to Memphis to plead her case to the King himself. Once there, negotiations between the two sex symbols went so well that Jayne ended up staying over at Graceland for a prolonged visit. Several days later, she flew back to Hollywood convinced that she had Elvis in the bag. Upon her return, however, Parker informed her that his boy's asking price remained the same.

February 15, 1957: the unveiling of a story-high painting of Elvis Presley atop the Paramount Theatre in New York kicks off the festivities for the opening of *Love Me Tender*.

Presley's early screen success gave rise to a rash of features that attempted to exploit the same formula used so effectively for him. Instead of wheeling rockers out for a few minutes of song as in the past, entire films — everything from Westerns to West Point romances — were mounted around the latest Teen Singing Sensation. Thus were we presented with (among others) Roy Orbison in *The Fastest Guitar Alive*, Connie Francis in *Looking for Love* and Fabian in *Hound Dog Man* — "personality" showcases that were often oblivious to a performer's talents or lack thereof. Despite their popularity, these pictures represent a low point of sorts for rock on screen. Not only were they badly made, but in many cases (Elvis's in particular) they stripped their young stars of their dignity and made it hard for fans ever to take them seriously again. Even so, their success paved the way for what is arguably the greatest rock movie ever made — *A Hard Day's Night*.

The time was 1964 and United Artists, the company that commissioned the film from British director Richard Lester, wanted something—anything — starring the Beatles before the year was out. Because UA believed that any picture featuring the group was bound to be a box-office bonanza, Lester felt free to use this vehicle as a proving ground for his experimental ideas without fear of injuring its commercial appeal. To that end, he and screenwriter Alan Owun came up with the idea of mounting a pop pastiche of a "typical" forty-eight hours in the life of the real-life Beatles. By allowing the Fab Four to play more or less their funny, fast, irreverent selves and providing them with plenty of on-screen time to do what they did best — perform their songs — Lester and Owun fused everything that was right about rock films into their own inventive amalgam of cinematic styles, thereby giving the fans what they wanted (home movies *cum* music) and at the same time knocking the critics for a loop.

The success of *A Hard Day's Night* ultimately sounded the death knell for the Arkoff-Katzman brand of rock exploitation pics — but not before inspiring dozens of low-budget spin-offs, starring mop-topped rock stars (Gerry and the Pacemakers in *Ferry Cross the Mersey*, Herman's Hermits in *Hold On*, the Dave Clark Five in *Catch Us If You Can*, etc.) running, jumping and frolicking in imitation of the originals.

Many other rock films would attempt to utilize variations on Lester's technique to display assorted Top Ten attractions of the day, but only *Head*, a zany romp directed by Bob Rafelson and starring the Monkees, would have anything fresh to say about this particular format. Nevertheless, *A Hard Day's Night* opened up a whole new world of artistic possibilities for rock on screen by demonstrating to the American and European film industries that these kinds of pop personality showcases didn't necessarily have to be awful to sell.

MILLION-SELLER RECORD CONTEST

Every teenager in the country is hep to one or more dances known as the Frug, Hully Gully, Rhino Romp, the Monkey, etc. In *Looking for Love*, Connie Francis does one of the best versions of the Chicken seen anywhere.

Contact a local dance studio and ask the proprietor to conduct a "Connie Francis Chicken Contest" using the *Looking for Love* record album. Ask the studio to give $200 worth of dance lessons to the winner. Use record albums for runners-up. Suggest that your theater ticket stubs be used for a free Chicken lesson. Most dance studios eagerly offer "free dance lessons" to attract paying prospects.

A promo idea from the press book for the 1959 picture *Looking for Love* starring that new teen singing sensation, Connie Francis

THE MOST SHOCKING FILM OF OUR GENERATION!

Meet the Hippies...the Teenyboppers...the Pot-Partygoers...out for a new thrill...a new KICK!

RIOT ON SUNSET STRIP

Untamed Youth–style flicks would eventually be updated to "expose" the violence and debauchery that supposedly lay hidden behind the good vibes of the flower power scene in grade Z thrillers like *Riot on Sunset Strip*, *Psych Out* and *I Am a Groupie*. But not for several years. In the meantime, the drive-in set switched it's allegiance from teenage riots and chickie runs to Annette Funicello's two-piece bathing suit. The countless Beach Party epics that flooded the second-run circuit through the mid-sixties — starting (technically) with *Gidget* in 1958 and commencing for real with *Beach Party* in 1963 — created a teenaged Never Never Land where body builders and balloon-chested starlets frolicked endlessly in the sand, and juvenile delinquents provided comic relief. Masterminded once again by the indefatigable Arkoff, these low-budget quickies were bi-zarre concoctions that combined rock music with Andy Hardy–style morality, surreal plots and dialogue that made you embarrassed to be alive. Nevertheless, they were practically the only thing around at the time that gave teenagers a look at their "peers," not to mention the top recording stars of the day. In 1965 alone, for example, the average *Beach*-goer could see the teen-aged Diana Ross singing about her "Surfer Boy" in *Beach Ball*, the eleven-year-old Stevie Wonder doing "Fingertips" in *Bikini Beach* and a group of fresh-scrubbed surf rockers who called themselves the Beach Boys providing musical backup for Annette in *The Monkey's Uncle*.

But, as a rule, such musical bits of business usually appeared to have been thrown in as an afterthought. So, aside from three or four hurried numbers by this group or that, what audiences mostly got from the various Beach extravaganzas were recycled Doris Day movies starring Frankie and Annette and a bunch of pituitary cases pretending to surf.

Below left: Frankie and Annette in the original *Beach Party*

1964 marked a turning point for celluloid rock. With it came not only *A Hard Day's Night*, but also what is considered by many to be the greatest rock concert film ever made — *The T.A.M.I. Show*. Filmed through the "magic of Electronovision" and directed by Steven Binder (who would go on to fashion Elvis's triumphant TV special a few years later), *The T.A.M.I. Show* featured, among others, Chuck Berry, the original Supremes, Leslie Gore, Jan and Dean, the Miracles, the Beach Boys, Gerry and the Pacemakers, the Rolling Stones and the Barbarians in concert at the Santa Monica Civic Auditorium. There, amidst the frantic frugging of the David Winters dancers (a dozen or so showgirls dressed in shimmy dresses and two-piece bathing suits), such immortals as Diana Ross and Smokey Robinson are preserved in the first blush of fame. Young Marvin Gaye, sleek and beautiful, does a few seconds of the Hitchhike — the dance born from his hit record of the same name—and James Brown twitches across the stage on one foot, dancing himself into a ten-minute-long frenzy of sweat and soul. This *tour de force* is followed by the Rolling Stones, the act everybody gathered at the Santa Monica Civic that day had come to see. And while the group that performs in *The T.A.M.I. Show* is a far cry from the mean machine it would later become, the style and personality quirks of its three brightest stars — Jagger's command as he works the crowd and the camera, Richards's scuffy elegance, and Brian Jones's studied perversity — are fully evolved and very much on display.

The success of *The T.A.M.I. Show* firmly established the concert film as a cinematic genre unto itself, a format that's still alive and well today. In the twenty years since *T.A.M.I.*, there have been the greats (*Monterey Pop, Woodstock*), the near-greats (*The Concert for Bangladesh, Rust Never Sleeps, Wattstax*), as well as the inevitable clinkers — Emerson, Lake and Palmer's *Rock and Roll Your Eyes* (which appears to have been shot almost entirely from behind the stage), *Yessongs* and Led Zeppelin's interminable and aptly titled *The Song Remains the Same*.

Along with the concert film, the documentary also became a popular approach for rock moviemakers in the sixties. Strictly speaking, the first docupic was the little-known and little-shown *Lonely Boy* (1962) in which Teen Scream Paul Anka explains in detail how he combs his hair. But it was D. A. Pennebaker's *Don't Look Back*, a grainy, dispassionate look at folk deity Bob Dylan, which set the standard for the rock documentaries that would follow. (A standard which few could equal, including Dylan himself.)

Don't Look Back followed Dylan and an entourage which at various times included Joan Baez, Bob Neuwirth, Alan Price, Donovan and Albert Grossman through his 1968 spring tour of England. Pennebaker shot some twenty hours of film and edited it chronologically to obtain a ninety-minute portrait of the artist as a young man that is consistently fascinating, though not always flattering. There is the testy Dylan jousting with the press, for example: "I could sit here and tell you why I'm not a folk singer for hours," he sneers at a hapless reporter from *Time*, "but it wouldn't do any good. All I have to do is look at you and I know everything there is to know." And there is the surly Dylan bringing the festivities at a post-concert bash to an awkward standstill as he upbraids a drunken guest for hurling a glass to the street below.

In one especially revealing moment, Pennebaker cuts from Dylan onstage singing "The Times They Are a-Changing" to Dylan riding in the back of a limousine while the same song is being played on the car radio. As the deejay gives its Top Twenty listing, all conversation ceases as the business-conscious bard checks out his chart standing in the U.K. All in all, *Don't Look Back* was a landmark achievement — not just because of the influence it had on rock movie-

Photos clockwise from bottom left: Smokey Robinson and the Miracles in The T.A.M.I. Show, Bob Dylan in *Don't Look Back*, Country Joe McDonald performs in *Monterey Pop*, just one big happy family — George, Ringo, John, Yoko and Paul in *Let It Be*, John-Luc Godard with the Stones during a break in the filming of *Sympathy for the Devil* (also known as *One Plus One*).

making, but because like *Blow Up, Morgan* and *A Hard Day's Night*, it succeeds so well in capturing the spirit of an era.

Occasionally rock docupics succeeded a little too well in capturing the essence of the behind-the-scenes world of the music biz. When that happened, reality was usually left on the cutting room floor. The Rolling Stones thought Beat photographer Robert Frank a perfect choice to fashion a documentary of their 1972 American tour, but Mick Jagger changed his mind once he got a look at the final results in *Cocksucker Blues*. Apparently Mick was unhappy with sequences showing a (staged) airborne groupie gangbang, Keith Richards inhaling a white substance off the tip of a knife blade, and Jagger himself cursing a woman with a particularly unpleasant four-letter word — so much so that he put a lid on the picture that remains there to this day. Nevertheless, the head Stone now claims that he would like to see the film released, that it's not him and the Stones but a crowd of other well-known personalities who appear in compromising scenes — including celebrated camp follower Truman Capote — who will probably keep the film out of circulation indefinitely.

The Band didn't commission *The Last Waltz*, but by the time director Martin Scorsese had finished the film, he was so enamored of his subjects that he tactfully opted to excise a sequence in which a Band member appears in close-up with globs of white powder caked around his nose. The makers of *No Nukes* also took pains to keep their rock star subjects looking like demigods so as not to diminish the film's impact as a piece of antinuke propaganda. No drugs or alcohol were allowed in the backstage areas where the cameramen were filming, and an off-key rehearsal with Crosby, Stills and Nash was spruced up after the fact.

But even with cosmetic work, some rock documentaries have inadvertently revealed an unsettling glimpse at the sadness that so often lies beneath the glittering pop facade. *Let It Be* let us eavesdrop on the Beatles during the final stages of their painful split, and Godard's *One Plus One* provided a sidelong glance at the faltering Brian Jones. No amount of editing could disguise the psychic fog that surrounded Joe Cocker as he hit the road with *Mad Dogs and Englishmen*.

When the Maysles brothers came away with the footage of the murder of a concert-goer at the 1969 Stones Altamont Festival, they made no attempt whatever to clean up the segment. On the contrary, they milked the gruesome passage for all it was worth in *Gimme Shelter*. During the film's ninety-one minutes, those few seconds capturing the shadowy scuffle between the ill-fated Meredith Hunter and a Fresno Hell's Angel are shown backwards, forwards, in slow-motion and freeze frame. Jagger himself admits, "It would've have been a pretty dull film if it hadn't been for that crazy concert at Altamont. None of us knew [the murder] was going to happen but it gave the Maysles brothers their *cinema verité* coup."

Several critics have noted that the murder sequence appears to have been mounted in such a way as to shift the blame for the tragedy away from the Stones and onto everyone from the concert's unctuous organizers to the victim himself. What it does instead, though, is to illustrate graphically the powerful bond between violence, greed and rock'n'roll. By giving audiences a look at real-life blood and gore it also provided the film with a very marketable cachet. *Gimme Shelter* is currently the second highest grossing rock film (*Woodstock* being the first) thus far released.

◆◇◆

Photos clockwise from left: Joe Cocker and entourage on tour in Mad Dogs and Englishmen, Woodstock, *Tina Turner performs in* Gimme Shelter, *George Harrison, Bob Dylan and Leon Russell in* The Concert for Bangladesh, *and the Dramatics in* Wattstax.

Budgets and ambitions for rock films grew larger and more lavish in the early seventies, and still they managed to miss the mark. Even long-running hits that had attracted youthful audiences by the millions on Broadway fizzled once they'd been overhauled for the screen. *Hair*, for example, was gray with age by the time the film industry got around to it — its peace and love shtick a distant and embarrassing memory. And what can you say about a rock remake of *The Wizard of Oz* that asked us to buy the thirty-four-year-old Diana Ross as "little" Dorothy? (Judy Garland was considered too old for the role at sixteen.)

The staggering success of *Saturday Night Fever* and *Grease* convinced the industry for a time that music-biz moguls like Robert Stigwood had the key to the rock movie — that is until Stigwood cooked up two of the biggest turkeys in the history of the genre: *Sgt. Pepper*, so lame it waylaid Peter Frampton's career, and *Times Square*, a pathetic attempt to senti- mentalize punk rock ethos into an updated *42nd Street*. And then there was talent czar Irving Azoff's comedy *cum* rock, *FM*, which was bounced from the theaters practically before its title was mounted on the marquee. But *FM*, like *Thank God It's Friday* and *Xanadu*, was basically just an excuse for a soundtrack album — in this case a top-selling two-record set that easily offset the film's losses in the end. The same should have held true for *Can't Stop the Music*, Alan Carr's paean to men's locker rooms and the Village People, and probably would have if the bottom hadn't dropped out of the group's popularity just months before the film's release. And though nobody could accuse them of trying to cash in on rock as a fad or of pandering to middlebrow tastes, pop stars turned filmmakers

like Dylan and Paul Simon didn't fare much better than the magnates in the rock movie sweepstakes.

By the seventies, rock had been around long enough to have its very own artistic pretensions (see *Performance* and *Two Lane Blacktop*) as well as a history of its own that could be tapped for screenplay source material. *The Buddy Holly Story* and *American Hot Wax* were simply variations on that old Hollywood standby — the screen biography. Like most movies of that genre, these films were extremely nonchalant with regard to historical accuracy. Their distortions usually resulted from a filmmaker's desire to liven up an otherwise uneventful story or from limitations imposed by a character's real-life counterpart — in *The Buddy Holly Story*, for example, Jerry Allison and Joe Mauldin of the Crickets show up to seek a reconciliation with Holly at his New York apartment on the night of his death, when in fact they were back home in Texas at the time. And in a misleading epilogue, *American Hot Wax* portrays Alan Freed as a victim of tightass convention who gave up the ghost along with old-time rock'n'roll — never bothering to mention the charges of fraud and corruption that brought about his downfall. The liberties taken in these otherwise admirable efforts, while not exactly crucial, have a way of spoiling the fun for reality freaks and hardcore fans who can recite early rock history by heart.

Still, the rock film did make some progress during the seventies. Young directors like Martin Scorsese and George Lucas helped to bring the rock soundtrack of age by using golden oldies to create period atmosphere in films like *Mean Streets* and *American Graffiti*. And *Tommy* had its mo-

ments — specifically standout performances by Eric Clapton, Tina Turner and Elton John — if you didn't mind sitting through several interminable Ann-Margret numbers and the standard Ken Russell bombast. *The Rocky Horror Picture Show* survived a disastrous debut and went on to become a cult classic — thanks to an ingenious midnight marketing strategy and a fanatical audience that was far more entertaining than the film. (Four years later Roger Corman's unutterably dumb *Rock'n'Roll High School* would attain similar cult status by being marketed as a midnight feature from the outset.)

Also of interest were a handful of tough little films from Britain — *Stardust, That'll Be the Day, O Lucky Man!* and the Who's *Quadrophenia*. The only problem with these efforts was that despite resounding critical praise, nobody turned out to see them — in this country anyway. They, like other "small" rock films of the period — *I Want to Hold Your Hand, The Idolmaker*, etc. — evoked little more than a sigh at the box office. Most were lucky to recoup their initial investment. In that, they were not alone — with the exception of rock soundtrack movies (*Easy Rider, Saturday Night Fever*) only three full-fledged rock films, *Grease, Flashdance* and *Footloose*, have earned the megabucks necessary to qualify as "blockbusters." In fact, the grosses for rock films are considerably lower than for those of comparable genre films. Such seemingly successful ventures as *A Hard Day's Night* and the forty or so Elvis epics were hits only in terms of their return versus their limited overhead and the modest expectations of their creators. Their initial grosses (around five million each)

would barely cover the catering budget for today's multimillion-dollar extravaganzas.

Just about everyone agrees that on the whole rock movies are a colossal drag. And after the disappointing performances of such Sure Things as *Sgt. Pepper, Grease II* and *Eddie and the Cruisers*, even Hollywood is starting to get cold feet. For now, the film industry is relying on horror and sci-fi and action fantasies to attract the blue jean and parka set.

So what of the future of the rock film? Well, for starters we can probably expect a concert film from the Rolling Stones every three or four years along with the usual round of docupics and personality films. Artsy-fartsy cinematic visions of rock will continue to be mounted by voguish directors and pop stars, and soundtracks will provide rock musicians with an escape route from their dead-end careers. And finally, as more and more filmmakers begin to borrow from the promo-clip school of cinematic imagery used so successfully in films like *Flashdance* and *Footloose*, rock movies will eventually come to look just like rock TV.

Photos clockwise from left: Valerie Perrine and the Village People in *Can't Stop the Music;* David Essex and Keith Moon in *Stardust;* the Ramones in *Rock'n'Roll High School;* John Belushi and Dan Aykroyd in *The Blues Brothers;* Oliver Reed, Roger Daltrey and Ann-Margret in *Tommy;* John Travolta in *Saturday Night Fever;* Gary Busey in *The Buddy Holly Story;* Tim Curry in *The Rocky Horror Picture Show;* Tim McIntire as Alan Freed in *American Hot Wax;* Diana Ross in *The Wiz;* Frankie Avalon in *Grease;* the Brothers Gibb in *Sgt. Pepper*

Up until just a few years ago, it would have been fair to say that when it came to rock'n'roll, TV — like the movies — almost always got it wrong. From *Bandstand* to *Solid Gold*, rock has been misrepresented, mishandled, insulted and underrated. And then came MTV. As far as rock is concerned, the effect of MTV and the whole video revolution has been nothing less than earth-shaking. It's no longer necessary to speculate about whether the ongoing vidblitz will pull the record biz out of its late seventies slump: it already has. Where once the small screen was alien territory to rock music and culture, today the future of rock'n'roll *is* TV.

Naturally, not everyone is thrilled with this turn of events. Of the many criticisms leveled at the rock-around-the-clock station, the one most often heard is that it is hopelessly whitebread. (Read racist.) But if MTV is white-bread (and it is), that's only because its impeccable research has shown that America is a whitebread country. Even so, MTV has seen fit to respond to the mounting media and industry outcry by playing lots more Michael Jackson (which we all know doesn't count) as well as a smattering of Prince and other black crossover acts. In the long run, though, black music will probably continue to be slighted by it and other mainstream rock TV formats. However, that's really nothing new. AM radio hasn't been exactly colorblind over the years either.

MTV's detractors also decry the artsy pretension and, simultaneously, the biker mentality with its glorification of sex, speed and violence which characterizes so many of the station's video selections. But they're missing the point. Rock has been pretentious since the late sixties. And as for sex and violence, everybody knows that adolescent rebellion and sexual titillation are the very stuff of rock. The real problem is that when those pretensions and preoccupations are paraded through your living room over and over and *over* again, they begin to look formulaic. Constant repetition deflates these standard rock motifs and converts them, along with various other performance rituals — windmill guitar strokes, stage strutting, etc. — into clichés. As Chrissie Hynde has observed, "To me [rock video] is the Establishment. It's everything I tried to get away from by getting into a rock and roll band, and that's the irony of it. It's like taking speed with your mom and dad." As it stands, the video revolution may be responsible for making rock respectable at last. But one way or the other, some very significant changes in teen music and culture are bound to result.

For one thing, the MTV boom is already changing the face of rock. Because the video visual is fast becoming as important as the music it evokes, new artists are being selected as much for the way they look and move on camera as for their musical talent. As a result, rock may end up populated with comely looking actors playing the part of teen idols. Cyndi Lauper, a seasoned pro who's been around forever, finally got the nod last year because the powers-that-be at CBS thought she'd come across well on film. Cyndi, admittedly a major talent, also happens to be white, blond and trendily disheveled — Central Casting's idea of a female rocker. This strategy is already beginning to pay off — as demonstrated by the success of Adam Ant, Billy Idol and Duran Duran — mediocre talents whose promo clip moves have catapulted them into the big money arena. Which is not to say that looks and poise haven't always been central to rock mystique, but at least in the old days an aspiring rocker could ingratiate himself with the public by way of his music before they got a good look at him.

Further, the importance of rock video may eventually relegate pop music itself to the role of glorified soundtrack for a stunning visual — one greatly influenced by the fact that it's broadcast primarily into white, middle-class homes with parents and young children as well as the eighteen-to-thirty-four target audience. If so, the entire essence of rock music may change drastically (if it hasn't already). Some pop auteurs are already "writing" the accompanying video scenarios right along with or *before* the music itself.

The onslaught of rock TV could also signal the end of the live concert (for supergroups anyway). Notwithstanding those roadshow outfits that earn the bulk of their income from the stadium circuit (Motorhead, Judas Priest, etc.), the monetary rewards of touring have traditionally come more from sparked album sales than box-office returns. But why bother with what has become a costly and grueling exercise when you can expose two or three cuts from your latest to millions on MTV?

Indeed, we may have seen the last of live rock altogether now that giant screens, cable and closed circuit hookups in bowling alleys, beauty shops, nightclubs, and restaurants are turning the world into one big rocking global village. It makes sense, doesn't it? Small combos with amplified instruments took the place of big bands when the cost of hiring and touring a busload full of musicians became prohibitive after the Second World War. Substituting a large screen projection of pop stars performing their latest hits for expensive, temperamental rock musicians would seem a logical next step. Besides, nothing's more natural to the generations who've grown up watching TV than having an electronic image constantly flickering in the background of their lives.

All in all, the success of MTV and various other video venues means that rock is now bigger business than ever. So, you can count on rock video being around for a long long time to come. Sure, the caliber of rock'n'roll you get there is a far cry from the primitive and joyful thing it was in its youth. But then again, what isn't?

America tunes in Elvis Presley in his first appearance on *The Ed Sullivan Show.*

These days it's impossible to convey the excitement that built from one week to the next back in the fifties and sixties when you knew that Elvis, the Beatles — or even Pat Boone — were going to appear live on *The Ed Sullivan Show.* Of course, you had to sit through Topo Gigio and an elephant act to see them, but somehow that only heightened the fun. Although it took Sullivan a while to get around to Presley (contrary to legend, El had made several network appearances prior to his *Sullivan* debut), from that point on he took special pains to book up-and-coming rock acts just as they broke in this country. In so doing, this unlikely champion provided American youngsters, as he called them, with what was often their first look at the biggest names in pop.

Teen music attractions were responsible for keeping Sullivan's show viable well over a decade, creating a Sunday night fever unparalleled since the show's demise in 1971. And in turn, an appearance on Sullivan conferred a special kind of status on a rock'n'roller. True, the circuslike atmosphere was hardly an ideal showcase for this new antisocial art form, but at the time it was either that or stars lip-syncing their hit records on *American Bandstand* or Snookey Lanson doing "Hound Dog" on *Your Hit Parade.*

The Beatles with Ed Sullivan during a rehearsal break

From the mid-fifties to the early sixties, local dee-jay heroes, like Lloyd Thaxton and Sam Riddley in the West and Clay Cole and Jerry Blavat in the East, hosted local rock shows of the kind originated by Alan Freed and his *Big Beat Dance Party* — where kids gathered after school to do the latest steps and hog the camera. While all maintained a loyal following and some even went into syndication, Dick Clark's *American Bandstand* emerged as the big winner, the MTV of its day.

Alan Freed in a publicity shot for his local New York dance party show, *The Big Beat*

James Brown with the inimitable Lloyd Thaxton

A *Bandstand* record reviewer gives it a 65.

Like their *Beach Party* screen counterparts, *Hullabaloo* and *Shindig* used the lure of big-name rockers to attract their young audiences, but it was improbable guest stars like Hedy Lamarr, Mickey Rooney and Ed Wynn, along with the show's own second-string regulars, who dominated the action. At right, Hedy frugs up a storm with host Jimmy O'Neill. (You may remember Jimmy from those famous Stridex Medicated Pad commercials: "Okay, Sally, go wash your face with plenty of soap and water." After Sally lathers up at a sink in the middle of the studio, she rubs a Stridex pad across her face and presents it to the camera. Yuk. The pad looks like it's been used to swab down a rubber tire. "Look at that dirt, Sally," says Jimmy sternly; "soap and water can't get you Stridex clean.")

Anne Murray on *The Midnight Special*

Tackiness aside, the very abundance of shows featuring rock as a regular part of their formats made the mid to late sixties something of a golden era for rock TV. Unfortunately, network attempts to attract the Woodstock generation with late-night rock programming during the early part of the following decade weren't nearly so successful. NBC came up with *Midnight Special*, a Vegas-y variety show that, like *Shindig* and *Hullabaloo* before it, thought nothing of sticking George Burns between Elton John and Stevie Wonder. ABC offered *In Concert*, a respectfully rendered, but basically boring, no-frills rock concert. After two and a half years in competitive time slots, *Midnight Special* finally won out, moving into an impressive eight-year run and proving once again that rock fans are no more discerning than the average TV viewer.

Hedy Lamarr with *Hullabaloo* host Jimmy O'Neil

Below: Sarah Dash of Labelle explains the meaning of "Voulez-vous coucher avec moi" to Dick Cavett.

As opposed to the sixties when rock cheerfully ran amok on both local and national TV, the early seventies were a particularly bleak period for small screen rock. It wasn't until 1975 and the inauguration of *Saturday Night Live* that pop music got anything resembling a fair shake from TV.

It was also during the late seventies that rock personalities suddenly began showing up on pedestrian talk shows. While less intrepid interviewers like Dinah and Merv tended to restrict their invitations to well-behaved rockers, Mike Douglas and Tom Snyder opened their doors not only to Blasts from the Past like Dion and Chubby Checker, but also to various punks and New Wavers in a last-ditch attempt to boost their ratings. But aside from David Letterman, who actually seems to know who people like Sly Stone and Ted Nugent are, talk show hosts have traditionally treated rock musicians like they were visitors from another planet — making it tough

for rockers torn between minding their manners and being true to their badass selves. Still, thanks to the spontaneity endemic to such low-budget offerings, talk shows have provided rock with some truly transcendent moments — such as Johnny Rotten making mincemeat out of Tom Snyder on the *Tomorrow Show* and, best of all, Little Richard breaking up a heated philosophical debate between *Love Story* author Erich Segal and critic John Simon on the old *Dick Cavett Show* by ordering them to Shut Up and then rushing off the stage and into the audience screaming, "I am the greatest: OOH MAH SOUL!"

Patti Smith tells talk show host Mike Douglas how happy her mother will be that the family's "bad girl" is on TV with "TV's Mr. Nice Guy."

You Can't Do That!

It all began back in 1966 when the Beatles released *Revolver*, an album that featured the psychedelic artwork of bassist Klaus Voorman on its cover. *Revolver* was the first pop album to integrate jacket art, conceived and commissioned by the musicians themselves, with the overall conceptual aesthetics of the album. Its release marked the beginning of a new era in which pop stars would demand artistic control not only over their music but over its packaging as well. Until then, cover graphics for rock'n'roll records had usually consisted of airbrushed portrait photos, posed theme shots (i.e., teenagers standing around a juke box), or hep cartoon caricatures. The Beatles were the first "teen" act to treat their albums as a total artistic statement. With the release of *Yesterday and Today* in 1967, they also became the first to use that power to dream up a cover concept so offensive (for its time) that their record company felt compelled to repackage 750,000 copies, thereby creating an instant collectible.

Within a couple of years, the Rolling Stones had become embroiled in one cover dispute after another. In fact, they still hold the record for banned and bowdlerized sleeves. The publicity fallout precipitated by their many censorship battles eventually made it stylish, not to mention profitable, to have an album cover vetoed, expurgated, or sold under the counter in a plain brown wrapper — or, best of all, confiscated by the local vice squad. By the seventies, promotional wizards like Terry Knight and Alice Cooper were purposely packaging their releases in such a way as to guarantee public censure.

A few of the covers that kicked up a ruckus during the sixties and seventies exploited violence or "sick" humor, but most of the offending items challenged prevailing sexual taboos. Of course, rock'n'roll didn't exactly invent the idea of using sex to sell records; record companies had been using female flesh to dress up their products from the forties on. Jazz covers, for example, were notoriously sexy affairs featuring an array of gams, spike heels and fishnet stockings. Most looked like they'd been designed by horny sailors on a weekend pass.

While jazz appealed to an older, more sophisticated audience, early rock'n'roll fed off the teen and preteen market. Given the rampant parental prejudice against the stuff, record companies did their best to minimize the obvious sexual allure of rock'n'roll performers in the early days. Colonel Parker laid down the parameters of taste that would prevail on rock album covers throughout the fifties and early sixties when he nixed gritty live-action photos of Elvis (like the one that appeared on his first RCA EP) in favor of the Hollywood-style glamour shots used on his subsequent releases. For a long time thereafter, rock'n'roll records would sport the kind of airbrushed pinups found in dimestore picture frames. If the artist happened to be black, these shots were often omitted altogether or rendered in a particularly innocuous fashion (*Hi! We're the Miracles*). After all, kids had to get these platters home past Mom and Dad.

Today album cover art is heavily influenced by an art direction aesthetic found mainly in glossy skin magazines — the only purveyors of print with the bucks and the inclination to subsidize the high-priced trendsetters of the commercial art world. As a result, contemporary record packaging abounds with the kind of airbrushed, high-gloss sleaze that you used to see only in the pages of *Penthouse*, *Playboy* and *Oui*. (That's not really so surprising since skin mags and rock'n'roll share the same target audience — thirty-five-year-old-and-under males.) In addition to the obvious appeal this kind of thing has for the customer, a sexy cover has traditionally shown itself to be one of the surest ways to a rack jobber's heart, solid insurance that a new release will be prominently displayed in record stores. And yet, despite the encroachment of soft-core porn into all areas of the arts and entertainment biz, there's still the occasional case of a record distributor or retailer in the Midwest or Bible Belt who'll refuse to carry a certain record because he considers its cover to be obscene.

The line between good and bad taste is strictly arbitrary: There's no way of knowing where the ax will fall. The Ohio Players, a group that has always flaunted a campy pimp chic, never gets flack for putting shorn Amazons, clad only in chains and sticky stuff, on their album sleeves. But let a folksinger like Buffy Sainte-Marie expose one of her breasts in a cover photo, as she did in 1974 (the same year the Players put out an album graced by a naked temptress stabbing her lover in the back), and major department store retailers like Sears and Penney's go into shock.

More than likely, the protest over Buffy's self-revelation stemmed from the public's resistance to her change in image — just as it did when the Beatles made the switch from Mop Top insouciance to dead baby humor on the cover of *Yesterday and Today*. . . .

IT ALL STARTED OUT AS A HARMLESS JOKE BUT IT ENDED UP WITH DAVID BOWIE IN A DRESS!

When Capitol Records commissioned EMI to package a new LP that would combine leftover cuts from the Beatles' 1965 album *Rubber Soul* with some of their early British releases, they expected to receive an album cover adorned with the four smiling Mop Tops in a characteristically happy-go-lucky pose. What they got instead was the Fab Four decked out in butcher smocks and draped with raw meat and headless baby dolls. Neither the album title nor its contents gave any clue to the message this bizarre scene was intended to convey (although some Beatleologists later theorized that it was the group's comment on having their songs dismembered and patched together in tatty compilations of this kind). Capitol execs were thoroughly appalled by the shot; but, afraid to second-guess the boy geniuses, they went ahead and released it as it was. They came to regret their decision, however, when their switchboards were flooded with hundreds of protest calls from outraged media people. The uproar over the prerelease publicity resulted in a decision to repackage the album. Capitol employees slaved through the weekend stripping the offending cover from 750,000 records and redressing them in a hastily improvised jacket bearing an innocuous shot of the boys perched around a steamer trunk. By the time the various pieces of coordinating promotional paraphernalia were also junked, Capitol had taken a $200,000 bath on *Yesterday and Today*.

Back in Britain, where the Beatles could do no wrong, the press chastised the boys for their naughty little joke, blaming their temporary lapse in taste on their recent sojourn in the wilds of America. John Lennon responded to the criticism by asserting that the cover was no joke, but rather the Beatles' comment on Vietnam. This explanation stretched the credulity of even the most devoted Beatle fans, but at least it threw some light on whose idea the cover shot had been.

Yesterday and Today turned out to be the only Beatle album ever to lose money for Capitol Records during its initial release period — this despite the fact that it topped the charts for much of the summer of 1966. To add insult to Capitol's injury, it turned out that some of their staff had gotten lazy and simply pasted the new paper slick over the rejected cover. As a result, hundreds of unsuspecting fans purchased these makeshift affairs little knowing that behind their bland exteriors lay a genuine cultural artifact. The alert went out through the teen press to peel back your cover to see if you'd gotten hold of the original. From that moment on, the Beatles' "Butcher Block" cover became a bona fide collectible — today it fetches as much as three hundred dollars on the rare occasions when it can be found.

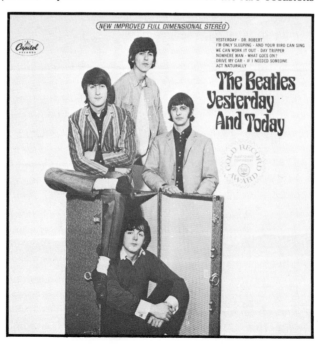

It took five months for John Lennon to get the other Beatles to approve the cover photo for *Two Virgins*, his first album without George, Paul and Ringo. Their OK came only after he had agreed to postpone its release until after that of the "White Album." But then, EMI, the Beatles' distributor, turned thumbs down on the picture — prompting John and Yoko to make a personal plea on its behalf to Sir Joseph Lockwood, captain of the monolithic organization. During their meeting, Sir Joe asked the couple why they felt obliged to expose their privates to the world. Yoko, whose idea the photo had been, patiently explained that this was their Art. Lockwood suggested that if they wanted art, they should photograph a statue in the park.

In the end, two small independent labels were persuaded to distribute the record in the U.S. and U.K. (with EMI pressing). But despite the fact that it was shipped in a paper envelope (with a peek-a-boo shot of the couple on each side), a number of its local distributors were arrested on charges of selling pornography. One raid in New Jersey netted the local vice squad 30,000 albums. Because of the cover, the record itself, a makeshift potpourri of riffs, electronic bird calls and other avant-garde flourishes, was banned from the airwaves in almost every market. As a result, *Two Virgins* sold only a few thousand copies.

Until this point, the British establishment had taken a boys-will-be-boys attitude toward the Beatles' various pranks, primarily because of the enormous wealth the group had pumped into the national economy, but the *Two Virgins* cover was the last straw. The Beatles were no longer viewed as mischievous jokers, but as subversives intent on using their awesome power to corrupt the morals of the young. By the time John and Yoko's album made its official debut in November of 1968, Scotland Yard had begun to harass the group with drug raids on their London homes, just as they had their less lovable rivals, the Rolling Stones, for two years prior.

In October of 1968, Lennon was arrested for possession of a tiny amount of cannabis. A month later (on the day *Two Virgins* was released), he pled guilty to the charges. However, he subsequently maintained that he'd taken the rap to spare further anguish to Yoko, who was several months pregnant at the time. (She later miscarried.) His guilty plea would return to haunt him in four years, when the Nixon regime used it as a basis for denying him American citizenship.

In an interview given shortly before his death, Lennon good-naturedly mimicked the public outcry provoked by the cover at the time: "What are they doing? That Japanese witch has made him crazy and he's gone bananas! [But] all Yoko did was to take the bananas part of me out of the closet. Actually, it was a complete relief to meet someone who was as far out there as I was."

Beatles fans and establishment types weren't the only ones who saw the *Two Virgins* cover as proof that Yoko had finally lured Lennon over the edge. In 1982, Paul McCartney recalled, "... when [John] and Yoko were madly in love, the rest of us Beatles didn't handle it very well. We got very uptight about stuff that wasn't offensive. If they want to pose in the nude, who cares? But at the time, it was, 'Oh bloody hell, look at 'em, they've gone off their rockers, those two.' It wasn't easy to cope with all that. We knew good old Johnny. But he'd changed. Our friend was suddenly on an album cover nude, and it was just weird. I think a lot of people felt that way: 'Hey, why didn't he just stay like he was in the Beatles, why'd he go freaky?'"

But for Lennon, the *Two Virgins* cover was a "statement of awakening." He said later, "[It was] my way of saying 'this Beatle thing you've heard about — well, this is how I am really. This is me naked with the woman I love. You want to share it?' And some did. And some didn't. But now, of course, you can't buy the cover for two hundred bucks."

Had the Rolling Stones managed to pull off their original plan for the cover of their 1968 album release, it would have borne the title *Cosmic Christmas* along with a shot of Mick Jagger ensconced in a Brixton prison cell while doing time for a drug bust. The scheme would've worked too, if guards hadn't discovered the film stashed in photographer Michael Cooper's jacket as he departed Jagger's prison digs.

So instead, the album was adorned with a 3-D op art photo showing the boys dressed in sorcerer's drag floating cross-legged in the cosmos and was subsequently rechristened *Their Satanic Majesties Request*. But the record's fancy wrapping couldn't save it from a dire fate. Not only was it deemed by many to be an artistic disaster, drawing uncomplimentary comparisons with both the look and sound of *Sgt. Pepper*, which had come out earlier that year, but the hefty price tag for the 3-D paste-on made a major dent in its profits. Later pressings carried a color photo in its place.

The Stones had originally planned to launch the promotion of their 1969 album, *Beggars Banquet*, with a lavish world tour ending triumphantly at London's Royal Albert Hall. However, the tour was derailed when Decca, the group's British label, refused to release the album with Barry Feinstein's photograph of a graffitoed bathroom wall on the double cover. Jagger stood firm on the issue, declaring, "I don't find [the photograph] at all offensive. Decca has put out a sleeve showing an atom bomb exploding [on *The Atomic Tom Jones*]. I find that infinitely more distasteful." An additional snag developed when a couple of British radio stations accused the album's intended spin-off single, "Street Fighting Man," of being a manifesto to incite would-be urban guerrillas to storm establishment barricades. During negotiations with Jagger, Decca execs implied that if the group would sacrifice the graffiti cover, they might be convinced to release "Street Fighting Man" as planned. But Jagger refused to back down. A week later, he proposed a compromise whereby the album sleeve could be shipped in a plain paper covering stamped with the caveat "Unfit for Children" on the outside. This time it was Decca's turn to demur. In response, Jagger once again vented his spleen to the press, saying, "The job of the record company is to distribute records. All they've got to do is put them in the shops, not dictate how they should and should not look." After a three-month standoff, Jagger gave in, eventually conceding that the whole affair had been "a total waste of time."

The simple type sleeve thrown together to take the place of the original was meant to look like a formal invitation. However, its spare design once again got the Stones accused of copying the Beatles (who'd just released their minimalist art cover for what would come to be known as the "White Album"). Keith Richards later said of the episode, "We copped out — it's true. But we did it for the money, so that makes it all right."

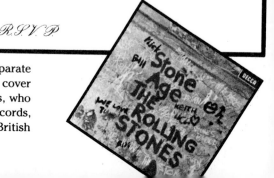

In 1971, Decca released *Stone Age*, a compilation of wildly disparate cuts from the Stones' back catalogue adorned with schlocky cover art that mimicked the suppressed graffiti sleeve. The Stones, who had by then left Decca for the greener pastures of Atlantic Records, did their best to sabotage the LP's sales by taking ads in the British music papers disavowing the whole graffiti campaign.

Once the Rolling Stones made the move from Decca to Atlantic in 1971, their promotional and album cover graphics began to show the influence of the American avant-garde. With unerring taste, Jagger sampled the work of the best and the brightest New York and L.A. commercial artists and designers along with an occasional European star. Though Atlantic indulged the group's artistic experimentation, the Stones had not seen their last controversy over packaging and design. By this point, however, Jagger had come to realize just how valuable such noisy conflicts could be in generating dollars and cents.

"Black and Blue." The Rolling Stones

ON ROLLING STONES RECORDS & TAPES

Fashion slicks were all ablaze with elegant Helmut Newton–style S&M in the summer of 1976 when the Stones mounted a billboard on Sunset Strip with a bound beauty proclaiming, "I'm black and blue from the Rolling Stones and I love it!" But within days of its erection, the sign was covered with angry spray paint editorials by the L.A. chapter of the Women Against Violence Against Women. The group picketed the billboard and then held a press conference to decry "this perpetuation of the myth that women like to brutalized," and to announce a feminist boycott of all Warner Communications (Atlantic's parent company) recordings. Warners eventually succumbed to the burgeoning protest and scrapped the entire campaign while Mick Jagger, ever the diplomat, allegedly tried to smooth things over by saying, "Fuck them if they can't take a joke."

Andy Warhol's cover design for *Sticky Fingers*, the Stones' first for Atlantic, is generally considered a landmark in commercial design. Its life-sized photo and zipper insert made it enormously eye catching, but more than that, it managed to zero in on the alpha and omega of rock'n'roll mystique — the male erogenous zone. All in all it added up to the perfect packaging job — a happy marriage of come-on and design.

Yet as celebrated as *Sticky Fingers* was in its day, it did have its drawbacks — specifically the cover die-cut and zipper insert, which made it an extremely expensive conceit. Still, Atlantic might've overlooked this drawback if the metal zipper hadn't damaged thousands of records in shipping. On later pressings the pop art construction had to be sacrificed and a photo substituted in its place.

Incidentally, a lot of people assumed that the *Sticky* crotch bulge belonged to Mick Jagger (and Mick never went out of his way to persuade them otherwise). But there's a rumor that the cover crotch actually belonged to none other than Joe Dallesandro, Warhol superstar and part-time pizza chef.

The cover for the Stones' 1978 LP, *Some Girls*, sported a takeoff on the type of ads usually found in romance magazines and featured such notables as Raquel Welch, Jayne Mansfield and Diana Dors modeling bouffant-style wigs. It was all in good fun, of course, but some of the girls didn't see the humor. Lucille Ball, for one, wasn't thrilled with the idea of having her picture displayed on a record that boasted such song selections as "When the Whip Comes Down." And Raquel Welch advised the group's legal reps that her face was her fortune and she was accustomed to being remunerated for its commercial use.

The Stones smoothed the girls' ruffled feathers by agreeing to print new jackets for the album post-haste. However, rather than substitute new faces for the old, they chose instead to play up the rhubarb by spotlighting the deletions with Day-Glo patches stamped "Under Construction."

Jagger also saw to it that the album's die-cut jacket was printed in four different color combinations, so that hard-core Stones fans would have to buy all four editions plus the before and after versions to complete their collections.

153

Photographer Bob Seidemann went to a great deal of trouble to assemble the proper components for the cover photo for Blind Faith's premiere album, spending weeks in search of the perfect hillside location and conducting numerous experiments with lighting effects and composition to give the landscape a unique surreal effect. And then, just for good measure, he planted a naked twelve-year-old holding a phallic-shaped doodad in the midst of this bucolic scene. He later explained that the shot was his conceptual homage to man's recent landing on the moon: "The virgin with no responsibility is the fruit of the tree of knowledge," he said. "As man steps into the galaxy, I want innocence to carry my spaceship." Right.

Using an unclad nymphet as an album cover come-on nonetheless struck many people as obscene. Despite Seidemann's highfalutin cop-out, the indignation elicited by the cover was so great that a new one (actually the back of the original minus the listing of album cuts) showing Faith's personnel had to be released in its place. However, Atco, the group's distributors, soon realized that the attendant hubbub had made the record a very hot item and eventually reissued the original "collectors' edition" with a gold seal strategically affixed to the child's budding chest. (Ironically, although the Seidemann cover photo is now considered a classic example of design and commercial hype, it's the second edition substitution that's the more collectible today.)

The cover of Jimi Hendrix's *Electric Ladyland*, which boasted a bevy of almost-beautiful girls lounging provocatively in their birthday suits, scandalized not only Britain's association of record dealers, but Hendrix himself — albeit for a somewhat different reason: "Man, I don't blame them," he exclaimed. "I wouldn't have put this picture on the sleeve myself, but it wasn't my decision. Actually, the girls were pretty, but they messed around with the picture so much that they all came out disfigured."

A spokesman for Hendrix's label defended the photo by saying, "In view of the title, we thought it appropriate to have nude women on the sleeve. The cover should be looked at from an artistic point of view." No matter how they were looking at it, 35,000 Britons bought the album within four days of its release. Still, the protest generated sufficient controversy to convince *Ladyland*'s American distributors to release it with a slightly more subtle photo on its cover.

On the British edition of Jimi Hendrix's *Band of Gypsys*, the last album released in his lifetime, Hendrix was pictured as a marionette. Surrounding him were various friends and idols — Brian Jones, Bob Dylan and British deejay John Peel — who were also carved out of wood.

There was some speculation at the time that the cover was meant to suggest that pop stars are puppets who jump at the public's command. Others believed that it had been inspired by Hendrix's lament that he was tired of being a clown. In any case, the message behind this curious scene was enigmatic enough to convince Capitol Records to reject it as unsuitable for the American market. Or so the story goes. In reality, however, Capitol may have been less concerned with the hidden message than with the fact that one member of the marionette band — Brian Jones — had died just several months earlier in a "drowning accident."

Remember how there was always someone in the science club or mimeograph squad who managed to get away with surreptitiously giving the "finger" in the group picture for the high-school yearbook? Well, in 1967, one of the guys in Moby Grape pulled that old stunt in the cover photo for the group's first album. A minor sensation at the time, the offending finger was later discovered by the group's record company and lopped off on subsequent releases.

Hype artist Terry Knight's involvement with Mom's Apple Pie came about as a result of his split with Grand Funk Railroad, a nasty piece of business that culminated in a flurry of public recriminations and multimillion-dollar lawsuits. As Knight set out to crank up the hyperbole for his new group, it began to appear that he intended to use them to show the world that Grand Funk's success had been largely his doing and that he could take any anonymous group off the street and do it again.

The key to Knight's campaign lay in the cover art for Mom's debut LP, which showed a wholesome-looking young woman holding out what looked, at first glance, to be a steaming dish of pie, but was instead an oozing vagina. Both the art and the concept were extravagantly crude, but that, apparently, was the intention. Knight seemed to be under the impression that he could sell Mom's records, no matter how amateurish their music, so long as the group's album cover was controversial enough. In another innovative stroke, Knight — too impatient to wait for the outraged reaction of record distributors and retailers — chose instead to censor the album cover himself and ship it directly from the pressing plant in a conspicuously plain brown wrapper. (Thus his new company name, Brown Bag records.)

The jacket illustration got plenty of attention all right, but the notoriety didn't create the sales Knight had anticipated. On the contrary, there was no particular demand for the album — obscene cover or not. Even so, Knight reissued it with an alternative cover on which the offending orifice was graphically bricked up — as if in response to an overwhelming public demand. Come to think of it, Knight may have intended to release the "censored" cover all along — it's not inconceivable that the second was commissioned at the same time as the first.

Lynyrd Skynyrd's *Street Survivors* was issued just three days prior to the fiery plane crash that took the lives of lead singer Ronnie Van Zant, guitarist Steve Gaines and his sister, backup singer Cassie Gaines. As is often the case, tragedy made the group's last record together a hot item. MCA, which had already shipped approximately 200,000 copies of the album, was besieged with new orders from all over the world. While rushing to meet the demand, the company suddenly remembered to its horror that the *Steet Survivors* cover showed the group standing in the midst of a blazing inferno. The real-life parallel was too eerie to ignore. Although a new cover (actually the photo on the back of the original) was quickly improvised for subsequent pressings, it was obviously too late to do anything about the albums that had already been shipped. Today, of course, the original jacket sleeve has become a collector's item. Some people believe that its cover was prophetic — that the flames touch only those who were doomed by fate.

When Alice Cooper went into the studio to record his second Warner Brothers LP, *School's Out*, he used the occasion to announce that this, his latest disc, would have the distinction of coming encased in a pair of women's bikini panties. On the release date, however, the album was quarantined by the Federal Trade Commission because the paper fabric from which the panties were made didn't meet the government's antiflammability requirements.

Alice responded to the embargo with a two-page press release pointing out that other types of wearing apparel, such as surgical caps, were made from the same material and were not subject to such a ban. Therefore, he proposed a compromise wherein record buyers would sign an agreement that they would wear the panties only on their heads. Naturally, the story made all the papers and Alice milked the publicity for everything it was worth. By the time the furor had died down, *School's Out* — minus the panties — had gone gold and Alice was a bigger name than ever. But the best part of the story is that Alice and his management had known about the FTC regulations from the beginning. That's right: the federal panty raid was a setup and the government had unwittingly played along.

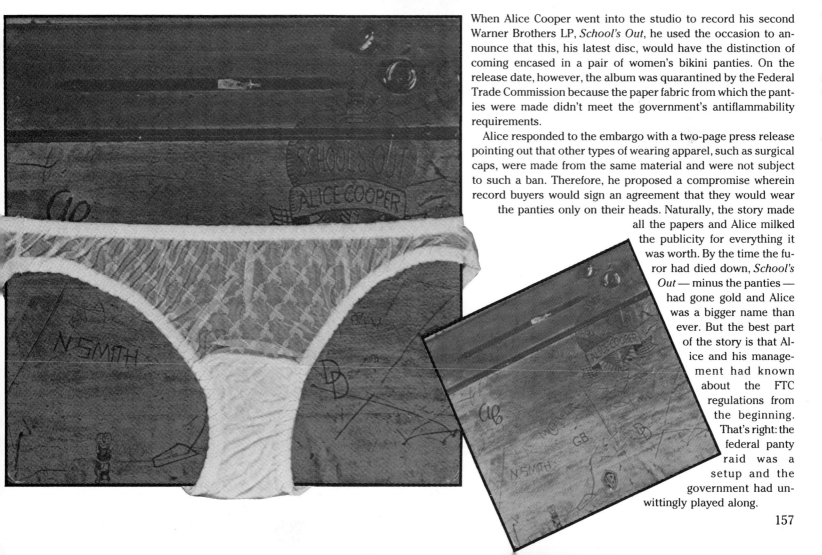

It's pretty obvious why the folks at Mercury Records felt compelled to replace the European cover of David Bowie's *The Man Who Sold the World* for American audiences. It *was* 1971, after all. But what could they possibly have been thinking when they substituted this peculiar cartoon creation in its place?

In the original artwork for David Bowie's *Diamond Dogs*, artist Guy Peelaert showed Bowie decked out as an uptown gaucho guarded by a snarling mastiff. Though striking, the piece was not quite sensational enough to suit Bowie's flamboyant tastes. In its stead, Peelaert rendered Bowie as a sideshow freak — an anatomically correct man-dog. The finished art had the desired effect: fans gawked, the trades tittered, and kids in Manhattan tore the first posters off the sides of buses and subway walls. RCA, however, fearing a possible backlash from retailers and distributors, considered withdrawing the jacket art altogether. But of course, that would have meant warfare with Bowie — who had gone to a great deal of trouble both to conjure up the image and to beat the Rolling Stones to the punch with a Peelaert cover. (Bowie first got the idea from Mick Jagger, who had been foolish enough to tell him that he had engaged the *Rock Dreams* artist to do the cover of the Stones' upcoming *It's Only Rock'n'Roll*.)

Eventually, RCA decided it had too much time and money invested in the original to junk it outright. As an alternative, they announced that the album would be shipped with a sticker covering Bowie's doggie genitals. But by the time the record hit the streets, the offending parts had been eliminated completely through the magic of airbrushing.

The cover shot of the two stunners on the cover of Roxy Music's third album wasn't a great deal more revealing than the average lingerie ad, but despite the models' strategically placed hands, American distributors demanded that they use more than their fingers to conceal their shame. Bryan Ferry, who designed the jacket, didn't attempt to dress the girls up to suit stodgy American tastes; he just plucked them from the cover altogether and left a bigger bush in their place.

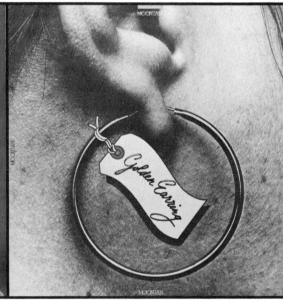

When asked why he shed his clothes for the back jacket of *Moontan*, Golden Earring vocalist Barry Hay jokingly replied that he'd done it to avoid paying the overtime fees demanded by the scantily clad beauty who graced the original British cover. Though the model's front and Barry's rear went over big in foreign markets, the group's Stateside distributor opted to focus on a less controversial part of the anatomy for the album's American release.

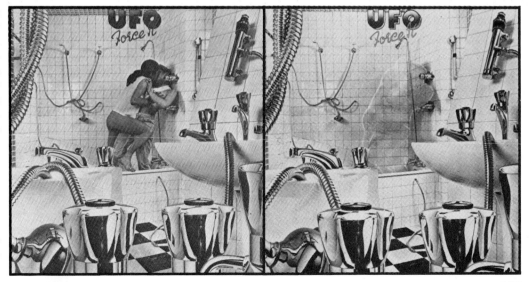

The two androgynous lovers who graced the cover of UFO's British album debut became a ghostly memory on the group's American release.

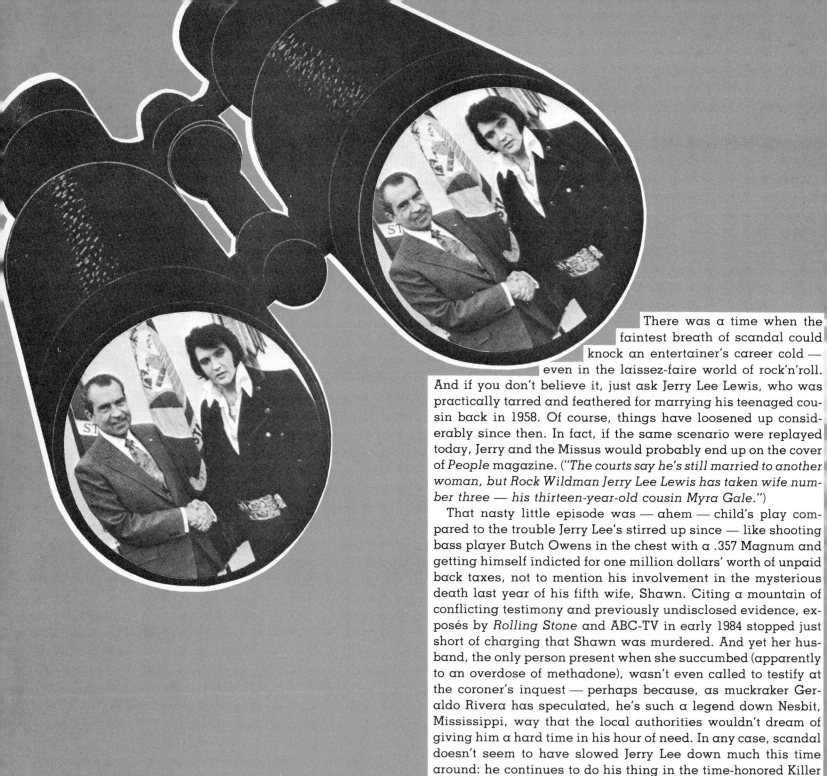

There was a time when the faintest breath of scandal could knock an entertainer's career cold — even in the laissez-faire world of rock'n'roll. And if you don't believe it, just ask Jerry Lee Lewis, who was practically tarred and feathered for marrying his teenaged cousin back in 1958. Of course, things have loosened up considerably since then. In fact, if the same scenario were replayed today, Jerry and the Missus would probably end up on the cover of *People* magazine. (*"The courts say he's still married to another woman, but Rock Wildman Jerry Lee Lewis has taken wife number three — his thirteen-year-old cousin Myra Gale."*)

That nasty little episode was — ahem — child's play compared to the trouble Jerry Lee's stirred up since — like shooting bass player Butch Owens in the chest with a .357 Magnum and getting himself indicted for one million dollars' worth of unpaid back taxes, not to mention his involvement in the mysterious death last year of his fifth wife, Shawn. Citing a mountain of conflicting testimony and previously undisclosed evidence, exposés by *Rolling Stone* and ABC-TV in early 1984 stopped just short of charging that Shawn was murdered. And yet her husband, the only person present when she succumbed (apparently to an overdose of methadone), wasn't even called to testify at the coroner's inquest — perhaps because, as muckraker Geraldo Rivera has speculated, he's such a legend down Nesbit, Mississippi, way that the local authorities wouldn't dream of giving him a hard time in his hour of need. In any case, scandal doesn't seem to have slowed Jerry Lee down much this time around: he continues to do his thing in the time-honored Killer tradition and has married again. If anything, his fans seem

The Great

more devoted than ever before. But then, the public has learned to expect bad manners from the people who play rock music and that's usually what they get. Rumor and scandal and scrapes with the law might demolish Marie Osmond or finish the Fonz, but they're part of the game for rock'n'roll stars.

Nobody understands all this better than the Rolling Stones. They're veritable masters at the fine art of parlaying mischief and mayhem into renown and record sales. Or as Keith Richards once put it, "There's no such thing as bad publicity. Not for the Stones, anyway." And he should know. In the years since he stepped into the spotlight, he's been busted for heroin and cannabis possession practically all over the globe. Mick Jagger, no slouch in that department either, has sustained a few drug busts of his own — one of which landed him behind bars. A legendary ladykiller, Mick is also said to have been responsible for two suicide attempts by ex-lovers and two illegitimate children. Speaking of which, Brian Jones could've started a baseball team with all his misbegotten spawn. (You remember Brian. He's the late lamented Stone whom Jagger and Richards are rumored to have driven insane or had bumped off, depending on which nasty rumor turns you on.) And let us not forget that little episode that occurred a while back involving a seventeen-year-old boy found shot to death in the Westchester home of Keith Richards and Anita Pallenberg, Richards's consort of many years and the mother of his two children. Now *that* was a doozy, even for the Stones — especially coming so soon after the publication of *Up and Down with the Rolling Stones*, a tawdry exposé that focused primarily on Keith and Anita's junkie escapades. And yet, you could hardly say that either event damaged Richards's rep, let alone that of the group. On the contrary, the resultant notoriety turned out to be just what the doctor ordered to perk up Their Satanic Majesties' deadly charm. The boys were back on the

top of the charts within less than a year. By the time they toured the country in the fall of '81, they'd practically become the grand old men of show business. The next thing you know, Jagger will show up with the Pope.

Until recently, inside stories about the Stones' decadent lifestyle and herculean abuse have been circulated largely through the underground press or word-of-mouth; like most rock stars, they have never deigned to discuss their private lives with the mainstream media. In the long run, their inaccessibility has made them even more fascinating and the rumors that surround them more potent. And that's exactly the way it should be — for myth and rumor are essential to rock star allure. There's nothing worse than getting to know your Fave Raves too well. Just ask Sonny and Cher.

Be forewarned, however. There are disturbing signs on the horizon, signs that all this may be changing. And not for the better either. Developments like the rapidly expanding coverage of the rock social scene in *Rolling Stone*'s Random Notes column and *People*'s weekly profiles of rock personalities may seem insignificant if considered individually, but together they spell doom and destruction for rock's fragile mystique. Once the mainstream media and the sensationalist press fully comprehend how many millions of now-grown-up fans dote on rock gossip and begin to package it accordingly, rock idols will be made to seem like regular human beings, instead of the wayward gods they are. In the end, they'll become garden-variety celebrities like hockey players and soap opera stars . . . and the next thing you know you'll turn on your TV and find Bob Dylan doing leg lifts with Richard Simmons.

So, while there's still time, let us pause to pay homage to the top-of-the-pops in rock apocrypha, the fact and fable upon which rock mystique is built — the Great Rock'n'Roll Rumors.

ROCK 'N' ROLL RUMORS

★ No record has ever gotten to the top of the charts without drugs, flesh or cash having exchanged hands between record company and disc jockey or program director.

★ Alan Freed acted as the front for a Communist plot to corrupt the nation's youth.

★ Alan Freed passed for white.

★ Johnny Otis passed for black.

★ Elvis Presley's stint in the army was actually a publicity stunt dreamed up by his mentor, Colonel Tom Parker. All those photos supposedly taken on his tour of duty in Germany were faked on a Hollywood soundstage.

★ Elvis wore his hair long to hide his horns.

★ Contrary to popular myth, Elvis's twin brother Jesse did *not* die at birth; in fact, it was Jesse who made all those idiotic movies while Elvis laid low and cranked out the record hits. Moreover, it was Elvis's brother whose body, all bloated from drug abuse and Fudgsicles, was found in the bathroom at Graceland. The real Elvis is alive and well and living somewhere south of the border.

★ In 1968 Elvis Presley paid ten million dollars to a California genetics institute to have himself cloned. The year after Presley's death, the clone escaped and is now on the loose somewhere in Los Angeles.

★ When the body of Elvis Presley was exhumed for autopsy (at the request of Geraldo Rivera and the ABC News Team), it was revealed that the casket purportedly bearing Presley's remains actually contained the body of suspected presidential assassin Lee Harvey Oswald.

★ Just before he died, Vernon Presley signed a contract to do a national tour singing a medley of his son's favorite religious songs.

★ Elvis wore custom-made diapers during the last few years of his life.

★ As an undercover agent for the FBI, Elvis Presley was responsible for the drug busts of several prominent entertainers while he himself was severely addicted to drugs.

★ Elvis Presley was actually a homosexual; the members of his Memphis Mafia weren't really his bodyguards, but his personal stash of down-home fun-buns.

★ Elvis was a degenerate who got his kicks peeking at his female party guests through two-way mirrors and watching pubescent girls wrestling on his bedroom floor.

★ When Elvis Presley discovered that his wife, Priscilla, was having an affair with her karate teacher, Mike Stone, he investigated the possiblity of obtaining an underworld "contract" to have Stone rubbed out.

★ Elvis's idea of a good time was cruising the local Memphis funeral parlors after-hours with friends and sneaking peeks at the recently departed.

★ Elvis was a God-fearing, mother-loving country boy and a pillar of the community.

★ Elvis was the Walrus.

★ Tommy Sands was banished from show business by Frank Sinatra after his five-year marriage to Nancy Sinatra ended in divorce. He laid low in Hawaii for ten years to escape Ol' Blue Eyes' wrath.

★ Behind Phil Spector's mania for personal safety (which necessitates round-the-clock bodyguards) lies an incident that took place in a Detroit men's room while he was touring with the Teddy Bears in 1958: it was there that four of the local gentry decided to deliver a particularly graphic critique of the group's performance in person by relieving themselves on Phil's pantlegs. He's been undercover ever since.

- Phil Spector kept his former wife, Veronica (Ronnie of the Ronettes), a virtual prisoner during the years they were married, monitoring her calls and refusing her to allow to leave the grounds of his Hollywood mansion — until she finally escaped with her mother after Spector threatened to kill her and keep her preserved in a glass coffin.

- Phil Spector hides behind oversized shades and the smoke-tinted windows of his numerous limos in order to conceal the extensive scar tissue he bears as the result of an accident in which his automobile crashed and exploded in flames in 1974.

- Miffed that he had gotten second billing to Chuck Berry at a 1957 Alan Freed concert, Jerry Lee Lewis finished up his act by setting fire to the piano. "Follow *that*, nigger," he told the flabbergasted Berry as he strolled off the stage.

- Chuck Berry owns land in Canada and has devised elaborate methods of escape to take him there should racial unrest, or nuclear attack, destroy standard transportation routes.

- Both Sam Cooke and Otis Redding were murdered because they refused to cut the mob in for a piece of their action — which in Cooke's case included production, management and publishing operations as well as his own singing career.

- Mitch Ryder was crippled for life from doing one too many flying knee-drops.

- Bob Dylan's inscrutable way with a lyric is the result of the fact that he's been a spaced-out heroin addict for years.

- Dylan's voice changed and his songwriting ability became significantly impaired after he sustained severe brain damage in a motorcycle accident in 1966.

- Bob Dylan was killed in a motorcycle accident in 1966; the person who tours and makes records under his name is an untalented lookalike recruited by certain record company interests to salvage their investment.

- Bob Dylan didn't really suffer a motorcycle accident in 1966; the story was cooked up by an astute publicity agent to bolster his sagging career.

- The motivating factor behind Bob Dylan's decision to come out of retirement to tour with the Rolling Thunder Review in 1972 was a rekindled interest in Judaism sparked by a trip to Israel the year before. He secretly contributed the earnings from his stint on the road to the Israeli government.

- When Bob Dylan converted to Christianity a couple of years back, he was baptized in friend and fellow zealot Debby Boone's Hollywood swimming pool.

- Dylan is the Walrus.

- Some of the rock world's most successful artist/manager collaborations have been the offshoot of the repressed passion of a gay mentor for his straight protégé. Brian Epstein and John Lennon and/or Eric Burden, and Kit Lambert and Pete Townshend are but two of many.

- Brian Epstein consummated his longstanding passion for John Lennon during a 1963 holiday in Spain.

- Brian Epstein did not OD on barbiturates as is widely believed; he was murdered by a lover during a bizarre lovemaking rite.

- Linda Eastman McCartney, who comes from a comfortable upper-middle-class background, wangled her way into rock's chic set by allowing it to assume (incorrectly) that she was an heiress to the awesome Eastman-Kodak fortune.

- The idyllic love affair that John Lennon and Yoko Ono described as having just naturally evolved after their first meeting at a London art gallery was a fantasy: in fact, Yoko pursued Lennon more obsessively than any groupie (even following him into the bathroom on occasion) until she wore him — and his wife Cynthia — down.

- Yoko Ono is a sorceress who kept John Lennon under her spell for over twenty years through the use of hypnosis.

Great Rock'n'Roll Rumors   163

★ While hit records and publishing royalties have made Paul Mc-Cartney one of the richest men in show business, Ringo Starr is virtually penniless, having lost "seven or eight million dollars" in recent years through bad investments and what he himself has described as "just plain squandering my money away." (His first wife, Maureen, was denied a million-dollar settlement several years back, when the presiding judge ruled in her ex-husband's favor, noting in the decision that Ringo was dead broke.)

★ Paul McCartney is dead.

★ Paul McCartney isn't dead.

★ George Martin was the real John, Paul, George and Ringo.

★ Brian Epstein was the real John, Paul, George and Ringo.

★ Many rock groups inadvertently act as carriers for drug smugglers when their equipment is used to hide large quantities of dope so that it can be transported illegally across the country.

★ In order to sidestep various contractual restraints, Mick Jagger, Bob Dylan, John Lennon and Jim Morrison got together for a top-secret super-session recording under the name "The Masked Marauders," thus giving birth to the legendary album of the same name.

★ It was Otis Redding, not Mick and Keith, who wrote "(I Can't Get No) Satisfaction."

★ Although newspaper accounts had them hard at work in a London recording studio many miles away, Mick Jagger and Keith Richard were actually among those present on the night Brian Jones was drowned in the swimming pool of his country estate.

★ Meredith Hunter, the man stabbed to death by a Hell's Angel at the Altamont Festival, wasn't really an innocent concert-goer, but a would-be murderer who'd come to the concert to assassinate Mick Jagger.

★ The story that Meredith Hunter, the man stabbed to death by a Hell's Angel at the Altamont Festival, intended to use the gun he was carrying to kill Mick Jagger was concocted by the Angels' defense attorneys as a cop-out for his murder (and later adopted by the Stones to cover for their staff, whose slapdash preparation for the concert had helped create a scenario for the crime).

★ Mick Jagger met with members of the Hell's Angels last year to bury the hatchet after word leaked out that the bikers had taken out a "contract" on him and the band because they hadn't "backed them" when a Fresno biker was prosecuted for stabbing Meredith Hunter to death at Altamont.

★ Whenever Keith Richards is busted for drug possession and has to get his shit together quickly to face the music, he has his drug-polluted blood completely transfused with fresh at an exclusive clinic in Switzerland.

★ Keith Richards periodically has to have his polluted blood completely transfused with fresh at an exclusive clinic in Switzerland to offset the damage done his system by eating junk food on the road for twenty years.

★ Keith Richards only goes to Switzerland to ski.

★ Keith's erstwhile common-law wife, Anita Pallenberg, presides over a witches' coven from her posh Westchester home.

★ Both Bill Wyman and Charlie Watts are at least a decade older than their fellow Rolling Stones; facelifts and the rapidly disintegrating physical condition of Jagger, Richards and Woods save them from looking like the other boys' fathers.

★ After managing to look the other way following several of his young wife Margaret's escapades, former Canadian Prime Minister Pierre Trudeau finally drew the line once and for all when reporters discovered her holed up with Mick Jagger in a New York hotel.

★ Many rock stars — the Rolling Stones, Led Zeppelin and Kiss among others — have attained their wealth, prominence and hit records through the shrewd application of black magic.

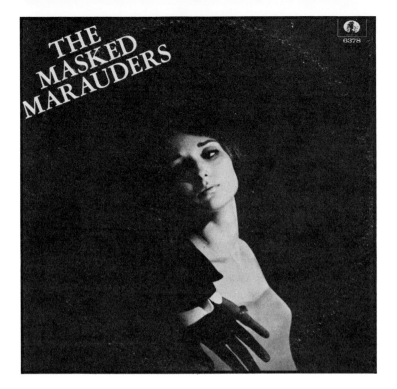

★ The Syndicate was responsible for crushing the careers of Three Dog Night and Rare Earth when they refused to cut them in on their action. (They tried to move in on Ted Nugent too, but the Motor City Madman was too scary even for the Mob.)

★ For a short time back in the early '70s, Doris Day and Sly Stone had a Family Affair.

★ Sly Stone has had to resort to plastic surgery several times over the last few years to rebuild his nose after he destroyed his nasal cartilage with heavy cocaine usage.

★ Ex-governor Jerry Brown's romances with Linda Ronstadt and Stevie Nicks were charades fabricated by him and his advisers to beef up his wimpy image.

★ It was that brazen hussy Linda Ronstadt who turned the head of ex-presidential spawn Chip Carter, causing him to abandon his wife and newborn child.

★ The casting couch is alive and well and operative for any ambitious boychik who aspires to get to first base with the many gay potentates who preside over the rock world.

★ Alice Cooper once killed a live chicken as a part of his act during a concert date in Detroit.

★ Driven into a frenzy by the music, the crowd at one of Alice Cooper's concerts pulverized a live chicken that had the misfortune of being brought onstage by Alice.

★ Alice Cooper used only rubber chickens in his act.

★ Alice Cooper used to play the part of Eddie Haskell on Leave It to Beaver.

★ Mick Jagger used to play the part of Barney Fife on The Andy Griffith Show.

★ Elvis Costello used to be Freddie of Freddie and the Dreamers.

★ Mac Rebbennac, the once and future Dr. John, was an Ivory Snow baby.

★ Grace Jones is a man.

★ David Bowie is straight.

★ Elton John is bisexual.

★ Amanda Lear is a transsexual.

★ Amanda Lear invented the rumor that she had a sex-change in order to attract publicity when she was first starting out as a disco singer.

★ The Village People were straight.

★ The illegitimate child Marilyn Monroe bore and subsequently put up for adoption in 1943 (during the period when she was selling her sexual favors to gents in San Diego bars) was taken in by a New Jersey family and eventually grew up to be singer Debbie Harry.

★ Although she looks much younger, Debbie Harry is actually a grandmother in her fifties.

★ Tom Jones and Engelbert Humperdinck are the same person.

★ Upon reaching puberty, Michael Jackson was given hormone treatments to maintain his girlish soprano and girlish good looks.

★ Michael Jackson is a case of arrested development whose sense of reality hangs suspended in that never-never land reserved for little lost boys and grown-up child stars.

★ Michael Jackson's chaste love life is the result of his unrequited love for his mentor Diana Ross.

★ Michael Jackson is Diana Ross.

★ Every rock star who has ever died is really still alive (and vice versa).

★ Geraldo Rivera has been in contact with every major rock star who has died of mysterious causes just seconds before (or after) they expired.

Only You Know and I Know—

"*Everyone who writes songs writes autobiographical songs, but [Joni's] are sometimes alarmingly specific.*"
— JAMES TAYLOR
on Joni Mitchell's
lyrical references to him
following their breakup

Ah, yes. Joni Mitchell. She's the very embodiment of the pop star as Sensitive Artist. One of those seemingly reluctant superstars who shun traditional show-biz hoopla and talk a lot about Maintaining Her Privacy and Leading a Normal Life. And yet, she's remarkably candid about her intimate relationships in her songs, harping continually on her personal angst in the lyrics, baring her soul in painfully explicit detail. She's soliloquized

about friends — mini-mogul David Geffen in "A Free Man in Paris"; lovers — Graham Nash in "Willy"; and first husband Chuck Mitchell in "I Had a King." She torched unblushingly for James Taylor in "Blond in the Bleachers," complaining that "you can't hold the hand of a rock and roll man very long," and ridiculed her former spouse again for his drab new wife and ultramodern kitchen appliances in "The Last Time I Saw Richard."

Some of Joni's subjects are flattered by her musical mentions. The late disc jockey B. Mitchell Reid was pleased as punch that he turned her on, and David Geffen rarely misses an opportunity to remind interviewers that he's the Free Man. But others — Chuck Mitchell in particular — have chafed at finding Joni's musical rendition of their romantic highs and lows pressed in wax. But Joni is at her most entertaining when she's writing

"Willy"

"The man in
the suspenders"

The late B. Mitchell Reid;
he turned Joni on.

He's so vain.

about herself and her intimate relationships. On the rare occasions when she addresses conventional topics, the results are usually remote and uninteresting. The ultimate irony is that it is shy, circumspect Joni herself who's to blame for making her life an open record; she's the Woody Allen of rock.

Of course, Joni isn't the only singer/songwriter to draw upon her private life for Top Ten inspiration. Fascinating bits of self-revelation have always been discernible in Bob Dylan's songs — for those patient enough to weed through their thick metaphorical underbrush. In many ways, Dylan's introspective lyrical ruminations transformed the popular song into a forum for public editorializing of the most personal kind, thus rendering Tin Pan Alley schmaltz and rock'n'roll jive obsolete in the process. (For a while anyway.)

Come to think of it, it was Dylan who was primarily responsible for introducing the whole Sensitive Artist routine to the music biz in the first place. He styled himself as a folk troubador while playing the part of the unwitting — sometimes unwilling — pop idol who appeared to have wandered into the limelight by accident. He courted stardom surreptitiously, making a big show of refusing to play the game by the old rules. He knew all the answers all right, but he wasn't about to list them for Gloria Stavers. Anything he had to say could be found in the words of his songs.

From Dylan on, music fans began to assume that the songs a singer recorded expressed his or her basic beliefs and true-life experiences. And sometimes, they did. Crammed with personal revelation and gossip about other ranking deities who resided atop the pop Olympus, albums began to seem like installments in an ongoing autobiography. Thus we were able to accompany the Beatles as they explored the world of acid, Krishna consciousness, romantic passion, disaffection and final disillusionment simply by listening to their latest release. Of course, these pop scenarios rarely took the form of straightforward narrative; real people were disguised or redrawn altogether. But this veil of mystery just made the songs that much more titillating, turning fans and critics alike into amateur sleuths.

In 1972, for example, the flap over the true identity of the jet-setting cad in Carly Simon's "You're So Vain" almost rivaled the controversy surrounding the identity of Deep Throat. For months following the song's release, Simon's love life, past and present, was dredged for clues. Some radio stations even conducted call-in polls to name the real So Vain. (In one such contest conducted in El Lay, Kris Kristofferson tied with Mick Jagger, you'll be interested to know.) Before the furor died down, Carly had been tentatively linked with practically every male luminary in the free world. She then went on to accelerate the controversy by declaring that Yes, the song was about one of her own unhappy love affairs, and Yes, So Vain was a celebrity, but No, she wouldn't reveal his identity because, Well, that just wouldn't be fair. In the end, Carly's coyness provided "You're So Vain" with the kind of publicity money can't buy. It became the biggest hit of her career. (As you must have heard by now, her producer, Richard Perry, just happened to let slip to a reporter a while back that So Vain was none other than Mr. Hollywood himself, Warren Beatty.)

In order for this type of guessing game to catch the public's fancy, the fans have to be familiar enough with its cast of characters to have a fair chance at recognizing them behind their fictional masks. Thousands, maybe millions (maybe all) songs are based on real people or real situations, but somehow these tributes don't pack nearly the wallop of those that sing the praises of someone with whom the public is intimately acquainted. Consequently, pop à clef can succeed only in a culture where the lives of public figures are continually on display in one form or another — a place like the good old U.S.A. where, thanks to the miracle of television and the *People* magazine school of journalism, celebrities, their families and friends are practically part of the family.

What follows is a brief survey of some of the more interesting examples of pop à clef — songs whose lyrical import springs not so much from their profundity or wit as from the gossipy light they shed on the lives of the rich and famous, most notably their creators themselves.

"You don't need me to tell you anything about Bob Dylan. Like any other artist, he stands naked in his work."

— BOB NEUWIRTH

"Sure, [my songs] are about real people. You've probably recognized all the people in them at one time or another."

— BOB DYLAN

"I know who the Sad-Eyed Lady of the Lowland really is, no matter who he says it's about."

— JOAN BAEZ

When notoriety finally shattered Bob Dylan's on-again-off-again romance with Suze Rotolo, he painted a painfully intimate picture of their domestic strife and eventual breakup in "Ballad in Plain D," blaming himself and "the changes I was going through" (presumably those brought on by his newfound fame) for causing him to lose "the could-be dream lover of my lifetime." Even though Suze was accorded the supreme honor of appearing with him on the cover of *The Freewheelin' Bob Dylan* not long after, Dylan took formal leave of his first great love in one of the album's cuts, "Don't Think Twice, It's All Right."

Dylanologists say that during the years when pop's poet laureate was pursuing Joan Baez (he reportedly asked her to marry him on at least two occasions), she was the model for no fewer than four of his most famous creations — the "Vision of Johanna," the artist who "Don't Look Back," Miss Lonely of "Like a Rolling Stone," and the little girl who makes love "Just Like a Woman." And although in "Sara," a song for his then-wife, Dylan declared that "he stayed for days in the Chelsea Hotel writing / Sad-eyed Lady of the Lowland for you," Baez has hinted that it is she who is the sad-eyed lady with "flesh like silk" and a "saintlike face." On the other hand Baez says it's not she, but Dylan crony Bob Neuwirth, who's the Rolling Stone. And just to confuse things, Neuwirth says that sixties scene-maker Edie Sedgwick was the inspiration for "Just Like a Woman" as well as "Blonde on Blonde" and "Leopard Skin Pill Box Hat."

Dylan chronicled his conversion to Christianity, chapter and verse, in his 1979 album *Slow Train Coming*. On it, he proselytized in songs like "You Gotta Serve Somebody," but more interesting was "Precious Angel," in which he sang the praises of The Woman (a black actress named Mary Alice Artes) who directed him along the road to salvation and chastised A Wife (his ex-wife with whom he'd just fought a bitter divorce and custody battle) for telling him about Buddha and Mohammed but never about "the man who died a criminal's death."

1983 found Dylan disenchanted with Christianity and involved with the Orthodox Shabbad movement of the Jewish faith. During a rare interview with a Minneapolis paper, Dylan said, "To those who care now where Bob Dylan is at, they should listen to 'Shot of Love,' off the *Shot of Love* album. It's my most perfect song. It defines where I'm at spiritually, musically, romantically and whatever else. I'm not hiding anything. It's all there."

For now, Dylan is hanging in as a born-again (and again) Jew, but if you're still confused as to his current allegiance, check out his ironic defense of Israel in "Neighborhood Bully" on 1984's *Infidel*.

Lest we forget that her husband, David Harris, was off doing time for draft evasion in a California prison, Joan Baez recorded an album named for him, and another which told us (and *told* us) that she was bearing up to her ordeal *One Day at a Time*. After the Harrises called it quits in 1971, Joan waxed nostalgic about her years with Dylan. The result was "To Bobby" and later, "Diamonds and Rust," a particularly vivid reminiscence about a boy with "eyes as blue as robin's eggs" who was "so good with words and keeping things vague."

No one is better at stirring up speculation as to the relationship between art and life than the songwriting team of Mick Jagger and Keith Richards. Ever aware of the fascination their divinely decadent life-styles hold for the public, they make it a point to toss a famous name or a tidbit of gossip into their lyrics as often as possible.

Chrissie Shrimpton, Jagger's first serious girlfriend, suspects that she was the inspiration for the Stones' 1967 hit, "19th Nervous Breakdown," since it was written following the emotional collapse she suffered due to her inability to cope with Jagger's burgeoning fame (and ego) and more specifically, his intimate friendship with Andrew Loog Oldham.

Not everyone would relish being remembered as the model for "19th Nervous Breakdown," but then it's always been terribly chic in certain circles to have a Stones song written in your honor — no matter what it is. So much so that it's not unusual to have a Stones song claimed by more than one ex-bedmate . . .

In 1964, the young British socialite Jane Ormsby-Gore confided to friends that Jagger had written the lovely "Lady Jane" for her. Still, there's no concrete evidence that the two were involved romantically, other than the fact that it was the real-life Lady Jane's patronage that had provided the Stones' entrée into London's young titled set, thereby making them the prize freaks of the '64 social season. In any case, the press didn't fail to make the connection. However, when queried as to the source of the lyric, the Stones' PR department replied that it had been inspired by a love letter supposedly written by King Henry VIII to his third wife-to-be, Jane Seymour. Despite the rumors and the official publicity line, Jagger still managed to convince Chrissie Shrimpton that *she* was, in fact, the real Lady Jane.

Remember Angela Bowie? She's the one who used to talk endlessly about how wonderful it was to be a wife, mother and lesbian. The naughty girl who regaled supermarket gazettes with the details of her expulsion from an exclusive eastern girls' school for getting a little too friendly with her fellow classmates. ("What did they expect us to do," she demanded, "fool around across the street at the Coast Guard Academy?")

These kinds of scandalous declarations were typical of David and Angela Bowie during the early seventies — a time when a major part of Bowie's act involved playing up his exotic sexual preferences and unorthodox marital life-style. It was also around this time that Angela attempted to launch her own career as a pop singer. For a while there Angie, or rather her alter ego Gyp Jones, began popping up on everything from *The Midnight Special* to *The Johnny Carson Show* (where she came across as a kind of New Wave Phyllis Newman.) Disappointment over the subsequent failure of her new career and marital problems (according to her, she and Bowie had been celibate for the last five years of their marriage) eventually prompted her to withdraw to the family manse in Geneva.

In 1979 the Bowies officially went their separate ways — Angie with a modest money settlement and David with son Zowie (who when last heard from was attempting to trade his name for a more conventional sounding moniker). For a time afterward, Angie's life seemed more chaotic than ever — with rumors of suicide attempts and an assault on her lover. For now, however, she is pursuing a quiet existence with another rock musician in L.A. But although she is more or less retired from public life, her memory is kept alive by "Angie," the classic Jagger–Richards composition written in her honor.

Marianne Faithfull says that Jagger composed "Wild Horses" during the final days of their romance in a last-ditch attempt to win her back from a wealthy Italian suitor. It seems he knew she'd be a sucker for its sentiments ("Wild Horses couldn't drag me away") since they were the first words she'd spoken to him upon waking from a coma following a suicide attempt a year earlier.

Keith Richards, on the other hand, maintains Marianne's story is baloney. He claims *he* wrote "Wild Horses" for *his* then–old lady, Anita Pallenberg, following the birth of their son, Marlon.

Confusion about the song's lyric was amplified by the rock press, which took it to be about the late Gram Parsons, onetime intimate of the band (and former shooting buddy of Keith Richards). *Crawdaddy* gushed: " 'Wild Horses' describes the paradox that fueled Parson's life and vision . . . unable to chose between devils and angels, he broke the rules and welcomed both."

Claudia Linnear didn't get around to admitting that she was the real-life "Brown Sugar" until several years after the song first broke across the country. But apparently, her reticence wasn't prompted by modesty so much as by the fact that she had played the muse for Mick while he was still a married man. Once Mick was free, however, she managed to let her little secret slip to a reporter from *Rolling Stone*. Her lack of discretion is understandable; after all, the ex–Mad Dogette just happened to be launching her own solo career at the time and that kind of publicity never hurts.

(Incidentally, the popular Claudia was also the inspiration for Leon Russell's "She Smiles Like a River.")

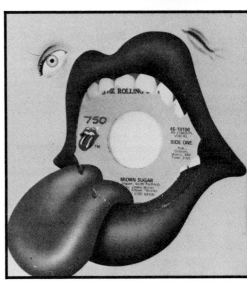

After the Jaggers' split, Studio 54's Steve Rubell made sure "Miss You" was never played when the ex–Mrs. Jagger stopped by to hold court. Why stir up painful memories? After all, everyone who was anyone knew it was Bianca Mick missed.

And one that got away . . .

Industry talk has it that the song "Claudine" was axed from the Stones' 1979 album release *Emotional Rescue* because its cryptic lyric drew upon the story of singer Claudine Longet and the 1976 shooting of her lover, professional skier Spider Sabich. Although Mick and Keith swore that any such similarity between the lyric (which Jagger delivered in his usual unintelligible drawl) and real life was purely coincidential, Atlantic Record's legal eagles got suspicious when they refused to write the words down.

"The All American Boy" tells the story of a simple country boy who gets himself a guitar (which he learns to play in "a day or two"), and sets out for Memphis to sing rock'n'roll. Once there, he meets a man with a big cigar, who says, "Come here, cat, I'm gonna make you a star." From then on, life becomes an endless stream of big money, fancy cars and adoring teenage girls until the fatal day he gets a call from Uncle Sam. The story ends with Sam himself confiscating the All American Boy's guitar and replacing it with a gun.

Released in 1958, this clever piece of pop *à clef* became a huge hit for Bobby Bare (incorrectly identified as Bill Parsons on the label). An infectious rolling tempo and a droll vocal by Bare made it fun listening but it owed most of its success to the obvious similarities between its plot line and the story of a certain Memphis Cat who'd just gone off to the army himself — Elvis Presley, the real All American Boy.

Eddie Cochran is said to have recorded "Three Steps to Heaven" in honor of his friend Buddy Holly, whose life had been snuffed out in a tragic plane crash in February of 1959. Cochran himself was killed in an auto accident fourteen months later. "Three Steps to Heaven" was his last record.

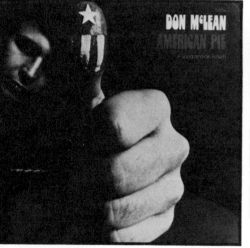

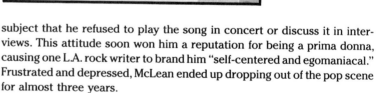

Oblique references to celebrated people or events have a way of imparting epic overtones to a popular song, but they can also end up becoming a royal pain for the artist who creates them....

Former folkie Don McLean was catapulted to national prominence in 1971 by his first hit, "American Pie," a crypto-mythic history of rock'n'roll that metaphorically catalogued pop stars like Janis Joplin ("a girl who sang the blues") and Bob Dylan ("the joker on the sidelines in a cast") and milestones such as the death of Buddy Holly ("The day the music died"). However, the press and public's continuing preoccupation with deciphering "Pie's" underlying message and enigmatic allegorical code made them unreceptive to McLean's subsequent attempts to move forward with new material. As time went on, McLean grew so fed up with the

subject that he refused to play the song in concert or discuss it in interviews. This attitude soon won him a reputation for being a prima donna, causing one L.A. rock writer to brand him "self-centered and egomaniacal." Frustrated and depressed, McLean ended up dropping out of the pop scene for almost three years.

Ironically, it was another piece of pop *à clef* that lured him out of his self-imposed exile and back into a recording studio — Fox and Gimble's "Killing Me Softly," a song inspired by one of his own past performances. He said later, "When I heard that song, I thought to myself that if my singing could affect somebody like that, I must have been doing something right. And maybe I could do it again."

In an interview given just a couple of months before his death, John Lennon berated George Harrison for paying homage to "every two-bit sax player and guitarist he'd ever met" in his autobiography, *I Me Mine*, while excluding him entirely. Characterizing their relationship as a love-hate affair, Lennon said, "I think George still bears resentment toward me for being a daddy who left home. . . . I was hurt. I was just left out, as if I didn't exist."

Harrison was probably unaware of Lennon's bitter complaints against him (since they weren't published until almost a year later) when he inadvertently answered them in "All Those Years Ago," his musical tribute to the slain Beatle leader. There, he acknowledged that he'd always looked up to Lennon, that he "was the one who had made it all clear, all those years ago." These touching sentiments were fashioned into a bouncy single that was released shortly after Lennon's murder in December of 1980.

Apparently the public found nothing exploitative in Harrison's method of mourning. On the contrary, the record jumped immediately to the Number Three spot, giving the ex-Beatle his first hit in two years. Nor did Lennon's widow take umbrage. She said, "My feeling is, if he wants to express soul like that, fine. You have to understand, we're extra-sensitive people, and we don't always express things in an orthodox way."

Proving Yoko right two years later, Paul McCartney characterized his relationship with Lennon as one of several kinds of emotional *Tug of War*. In "Here Today," he expresses the profound affection he felt for his friend while at the same time acknowledging that he never really understood him. He told a reporter from the *Times*: ". . . even though he put me down, I'm not going for it. We *were* friends, and we got it on, we got a *lot* on. . . . And I just had to be real and say, John, I love you."

Kinky Friedman, the Texas Jewboy, found himself on the wrong end of a million-dollar libel suit when lonely hearts columnist Abby van Buren decided that his song "Dear Abbie" was about her. Kinky was dumbfounded by the charges (or as he put it, "I was fuckin' blown away"). But once he regained his composure, he had a field day with the whole affair. "Obviously nobody in [Abby's] office ever listened to the song," he gloated to the press. "Its subtitle is 'Steal This Song,' for chrissakes. It's obvious to anyone with a brain the size of a LeSueur pea that it's about Abbie Hoffman."

Like the Stones and their ill-fated tribute to "Claudine," the Boomtown Rats were also foiled in an attempt to exploit a sensational crime on record. This one involved a seventeen-year-old high-school girl from San Diego named Brenda Spencer, who was found guilty of waging a sniper attack on her suburban neighborhood that left two men dead and eight children wounded. The inspiration for the Rats' lyric was provided by Spencer, who explained her actions to a reporter by saying that she was just trying to "liven up the day" because she'd always hated Mondays. The Rats single "I Don't Like Mondays" was released in Britain a few weeks later.

Not surprisingly, there were a few concerned parties who failed to see the humor in the song, namely Spencer's lawyer and the relatives of the dead and wounded. When they lobbied to protest the song's release in this country, the Rats vigorously insisted that any similarity between the song's content and the shootings was sheer coincidence.

"I Don't Like Mondays" became a Number One hit in England and throughout Europe, but it all but vanished from American airwaves soon after its release, perhaps because a number of key radio stations chose to boycott it out of sympathy for the San Diego victims and their families.

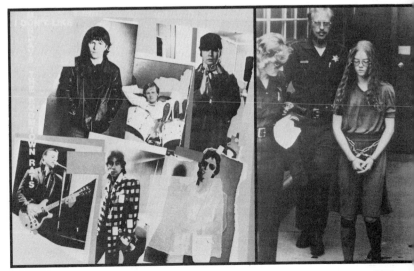

Once in a while, rock stars will use a pop format to explain why they've followed a particular course of action in their lives or to cop out for certain past transgressions — both public and private.

For years, Rick Nelson avoided going the nostalgia route taken by so many other fifties rockers during the late sixties and early seventies. For one thing, he didn't need the money; his late father Ozzie's astute management of his share of the profits from his records and the family TV show had made him a millionaire at an early age. But more importantly, Rick resented being cast as a has-been, seeing as how he'd never really stopped writing and recording during the years following his last major hit in 1962.

"I never believed in rock'n'roll revivals," he said later. "They're people trying to recapture something that can't be brought back. But I talked myself into doing [a Richard Nader revival show at Madison Square Garden] by saying that it would be good to be seen by that many people and that I could always use it as an excuse to sneak in some new material."

However, instead of being treated to the outpouring of love that usually greets old-timers at such reunions, Nelson was greeted by a resounding chorus of boos during his first few numbers — apparently in response to his new brand of country-flavored music and the Hollywood cowboy appearance of his Stone Canyon Band. The crowd's reaction became so hostile that he and his group were forced to flee the stage. "I didn't know anything about those shows and what people expected," he said later. "If I'd been to one before, I simply wouldn't have done it. I tried. I worked up a whole bunch of old songs that I hadn't performed in years. We opened with 'Be Bop Baby' figuring that that would really startle the audience. It did. They kept looking at me and my long hair as if they couldn't believe that I was the same person. But [to be what they wanted] I'd have had to cut my hair and put braces on my teeth."

Nelson ultimately ended up turning this painful experience into Top Ten gold when he wrote about it later in "Garden Party," a gentle reproof of those fans who refuse to let rock stars grow up, wherein he concludes, "If memories are all I bring — I'd rather drive a truck." "Garden Party's" upfront sentiments and cast of famous characters gave Rick his first hit in ages. However, that was a good while back — long enough that Rick must be as tired of playing it as he was of his original hits.

Like his fellow Italian heartthrobs of the fifties, Dion DiMucci's career took a nose dive following the British invasion of the mid-sixties. A has-been at the age of twenty-three, he disappeared into a mysterious self-imposed exile until 1968, the year of his smashing comeback with "Abraham, Martin and John." Then, looking for a follow-up in 1970, Dion revealed what he'd been up to all that time in "Your Own Back Yard" — a ruefully bitter account of his six-year ordeal with heroin and the disastrous effect it had had on his personal life:

> My idea of having a good time
> Was sitting with my head between my knees.
> I lost everything near and dear to me.
> Mainly my children and my wife.

Unlike the many antidrug crusaders who proselytized in song during the early seventies, Dion managed to paint a stark picture of addiction and redemption without ever sounding preachy.

> Since I've been straight
> I haven't been in my cups
> I'm not shooting downs
> I'm not using ups.
> You know I'm still crazy as a loon
> Even though I don't run out and cop a spoon.
> Thank the good lord that I've had enough.

Although largely ignored when it was released, "Your Own Back Yard" is one of the most fascinating personal statements ever made by a rock star. And you can dance to it, too.

The Grateful Dead sought to make some sense of the murder and mayhem that was visited on the Altamont Festival courtesy of the Hell's Angels in "Speedway Boogie," a cut from their 1970 album release, *Workingman's Dead*. However, instead of blaming themselves for bringing in the savage motorcycle group to act as the festival's security force, they chalked up the resultant violence and bad vibes to cosmic inevitability, noting ingenuously: "I saw things getting out of hand / But I guess they always will."

he Story Behind "This Song"

PRODUCED BY GEORGE HARRISON 1976

ive years ago, suit was filed against George Harrison and arrisongs Music, Inc. by the ate of songwriter Ronald Mack d Bright Tunes publishing. The t alleged that George Harrison's 70 composition "My Sweet rd" infringed on the copyright Mack's "He's So Fine," recorded 1963 by the Chiffons. In bruary of 1976, the case went to urt before Federal Judge Richard wen. Over three days of stimony and cross-examination, th sides attempted to prove the usical derivation of "My Sweet rd." Both plaintiff and defendant licited the opinions of usicologists and music experts om various fields. At one point in e proceedings, huge charts were troduced, on which were scribed the 3-note pattern arrison was alleged to have agiarized. In the confused

discussion which followed, differences arose as to whether or not the 3-note sequence constituted a "song." "That ain't no song," testified gospel music expert David Butler, "that's a riff." On August 31, 1976, Judge Owen ruled against Harrison, finding "My Sweet Lord" and "He's So Fine" "virtually identical," but adding that Harrison had unknowingly lifted the riff, owing to an "unconscious" familiarity with the chord pattern in question.

"The whole thing made me sort of paranoid," Harrison explained. "I got to thinking, what if every time you sat down to write a song, you had to pass your music by some expert or into a computer, to make sure you weren't copying someone else's notes. It's all a joke, really. Basically, songs are written to entertain and that's all there is to it. That's where it's at."

Occasionally a pop confession can end up being a bit *too* candid. Take the time in 1970 the *Daily Mirror*, a British tabloid, claimed that Rod Stewart had fathered an illegitimate child in 1963. At the same time that Stewart's publicity people were angrily denouncing the story as a pack of lies, Rod himself was confirming it to a Los Angeles reporter, noting that there was no use pretending it wasn't true since he'd already written about it in a song called "Jo's Lament." He cracked, "Oh yeah, everybody around me is denying it, but if they'd ever listened to *Gasoline Alley*, they'd have known it was true. But what does it matter anyway? I thought everyone in rock'n'roll had illegitimate children." Several years later, however, Rod claimed that he had made up the story to drum up some free publicity.

Sometimes Living in the Material World can be a drag for the pure of heart like George Harrison, whose 1972 "My Sweet Lord" — his first solo hit — became the target of a plagiarism suit brought by the estate of Ronald Mack, composer of the 1962 classic "He's So Fine." Although presiding judge Richard Owen acknowledged that the three-chorded refrains in the two compositions were "virtually identical," he ruled that the ex-Beatle had stolen the tune "unconsciously." Unfortunately, that little technicality didn't save Harrison from having to pay a hefty settlement. George declined public comment on the court's decision at the time, saying only that he would answer the charges on his new record release. True to his promise, George copped a not-guilty plea to his fans on "This Song," a cheerful ditty which featured the whole real-life story behind "This Song" printed on its sleeve.

As you may have noticed, Rod has never been particularly shy about exploiting his personal life on his records. In 1973, for example, he milked the public's curiosity about his romance with celebrity groupie Britt Ekland by having her contribute a few breathily prurient words of encouragement on "Tonight's the Night." And later when the couple's lovelight dimmed and Britt filed a $12.5 million palimony suit against him, he smoothed his Ex's ruffled feathers with "You're in My Heart." His strategy (along with the threat of a nasty and expensive legal battle) worked. Britt accepted his musical apology and withdrew her suit, eventually settling for a figure more than $12 million shy of her original demand.

In 1959, Paul Anka sought an "answer up above" and got a hit record after the Disney organization tried to break up his romance with their popular starlet, Annette Funicello. It seems that the folks at Disney (Uncle Walt in particular) weren't at all thrilled at the idea of having their prize cupcake paired up with a swarthy teen crooner. When Annette bravely refused to give in to their demands, they grudgingly allowed the lovebirds to continue dating — but only so long as they agreed to characterize their "friendship" as a brother-sister affair when talking to the press.

Neil Sedaka's "Oh Carol" appeared to be just another in the endless list of anonymous musical accolades like "Lucille" and "Peggy Sue" until the object of Neil's musical valentine, Carole King, became a star in her own right.

In another private tribute, Roy Orbison sang the praises of his wife, Claudette, in "Oh, Pretty Woman." He later mourned her untimely death (in a motorcycle accident) in "Too Soon to Know."

The silly love songs that Paul McCartney has written during the last several years like "My Love," "Cook of the House" and "Baby I'm Amazed" have been dedicated to his wife Linda, but there was a time back in the early sixties when Paul was getting his romantic inspiration for songs like "If I Fell" and "We Can Work It Out" from former British child star and sometime actress Jane Asher.

Jimi Hendrix nicknamed Devon Wilson "Dolly Dagger" after Mick Jagger, his rival for the title of top rock cocksman — as well as for Devon herself on occasion. A notorious junkie, groupie and maker-of-scenes, Devon was Hendrix's lover during the years he reigned as rock's wigged-out Spade King. Although he went through hundreds of women during that time, it was she who was his true soulmate — perhaps as some have said because he could never tame her.

The song Hendrix wrote for Devon paints her as a vampirish predator who will suck blood out of "burned-out supermen" like him until "she gets what she's after." Like several other close friends and associates of Hendrix, Devon Wilson died soon after he did; she jumped (or was pushed) from a window in New York's Chelsea Hotel in 1972.

Something in the way Patti Harrison moved inspired her husband George to come up with one of the biggest Beatle hits ever. "Something" has since gone on to become a standard — one that's been done by everyone from Bar Mitzvah bands to Frank Sinatra, who has dubbed it "the greatest love song of the last fifty years."

The anguished lyrics of Eric Clapton's "Layla" left millions of fans clamoring to know the identity of the "Mystery Woman" who had Clapton on his knees, but for years he refused to talk either about the song or the real-life Layla. Even insiders in the rock press were baffled, especially since Clapton hadn't been seen regularly in the company of any one particular ladyfriend with the exception of Alice Ormsby-Gore, the teenage daughter of Lord Harlech.

Having made his definitive musical statement on love and pain, Clapton disappeared from sight to struggle with a messy heroin addiction and the aftereffects of his stormy love affair. It was four years before he broke his silence, but even then, Layla's identity remained a secret. He told a reporter, "Layla was about a woman I felt really deeply about and who turned me down, and I had to pour it out in some way. I mean, her husband is a great musician. It's one of those wife-of-my-best-friend scenes and her husband has been writing great songs for years about her and she still left him.

"You see," he continued, "he grabbed one of my chicks once and so I thought I'd get even with him one day, on a petty level, and it grew from that, you know.... She was trying to attract his attention, trying to make him jealous, and so she used me."

But before Clapton knew it, things had gotten out of hand and he was madly in love. His guilt and frustration over the affair spilled over into one of the most tormented pieces of white blues ever committed to wax. When asked how the real life Layla reacted to the song, Clapton responded bitterly, "I don't think she gave a damn."

But apparently Layla couldn't turn her back on that kind of passion forever. Even so, it took six years from the time the song was written for George Harrison's wife, Patti, to get up the courage to set up housekeeping with Clapton in L.A. Clapton's fans went absolutely wild when he confirmed that she was the real Layla, and the song enjoyed an explosion of popularity all over again.

Layla's ten-year saga had a happy ending when Clapton married Patti in 1979 — happy for everyone but George Harrison, that is. When writer Mitch Glazer asked Harrison if he'd been aware of his wife's affair with his best friend during the initial storm of controversy over Layla's identity, he replied, "Well, yes — sort of. I mean, only you know the thing is with Eric that Patti and I both loved him — but there were a few funny things. I pulled his chick once. And now you'd think that he was trying to get his own back on me."

Ironically Patti and Eric had joined George for a spirited rendition of "Bye Bye Love" on *Dark Horse*, Harrison's 1975 album release. But the lyric to "So Sad," another cut on the album, probably portrayed Harrison's emotional response more accurately.

The last thing Paul Anka wanted was to have the public recognize Annette Funicello as his "Puppy Love," but nowadays pop stars understand the value of having their names romantically linked with other celebs — so much so that they sometimes feature the subject of a musical accolade in the accompanying video (as Carly Simon did with ex-boyfriend, ex–*Dynasty* star Al Corley in "You Know What to Do" and Billy Joel did with his "Uptown Girl," Christie Brinkley). Of course, things were different in the pre-video era. Back then, it could take several years and two hit records before rock fans realized that songstress Rita Coolidge was Leon Russell's "Delta Lady."

While some singer/songwriters stop short of revealing exactly who or what their songs are about, preferring instead to sit back and let the rock literati conjure up its own mythology, others have been more helpful in pinpointing the source of their inspiration. . . .

Graham Nash, for one, wasn't shy about admitting that "Our House" was the home he shared for a time with Joni Mitchell. And Stephen Stills doesn't mind naming Judy Collins as the "chestnut brown canary" of "Suite: Judy Blue Eyes." As he once told a reporter from *Rolling Stone*, "A songwriter can do three things with women — love them, suffer over them or turn them into hit records."

When word leaked out that the Knack's "My Sharona" had been written about a Los Angeles high-school girl (and part-time girlfriend of head Knacker Doug Fieger), it generated so much curiosity that the band released a new pressing of the single with the real-life Sharona's picture on the sleeve. However, the publicity backfired a few months later when the "Nuke the Knack" movement lashed out at the group with a *Sharona Sucks* bumper sticker campaign. Fieger, who'd been a good sport about the anti-Knack campaign up until then, immediately got in touch with his detractors and told them to say all the nasty things they wanted about the group, but to lay off Sharona.

sings

ASK ME
TO GO STEADY

AM I
THAT EASY TO FORGET

America was scandalized when Eddie Fisher abandoned his perky wife Debbie Reynolds for Elizabeth Taylor in 1959. But the breakup wasn't a total downer for Tammy; she scored a hit record a few months later when she asked the musical question, "Am I That Easy to Forget?"

Although the public never had an inkling of just how kinky Elvis Presley's private life really was, it was no secret that the King liked girls. Neither wedding vows nor fatherhood put a crimp in Elvis's style, since he usually had the little woman stashed back home in Memphis while he lived it up in Hollywood. By 1969, the Presleys' frequent separations had led to media speculation that the marriage was on the rocks — which made it especially compelling when Elvis sang "We can't go on together with suspicious minds" that same year.

The Presleys hung on until 1972 when Priscilla moved out of her husband's California home and into an apartment near the school of karate teacher Mike Stone, her companion of many months. Stone's wife subsequently sued him for divorce, and although Priscilla's name wasn't mentioned in court, the rumors began to fly. They were confirmed some time later when Elvis made the split legal. Following the breakup, he poured out his heartbreak on "Separate Ways," a song that rock critic Peter Guralnick has called one of the "few secular songs Elvis was able to sing with any real conviction...a painful substitute for self-expression, an artful surrogate for real life."

In 1974, shortly after it was announced that America's favorite pop couple was calling it quits, Sonny Bono sang a formal farewell to wife Cher in "Our Last Show." There he revealed how painful it had been for him to keep up the pretense of marital bliss while knowing that his marriage was on the rocks ...

> We say good-bye and the people yell
> I take my bows, but I feel like hell.
> No one knew but her and I
> We already said good-bye.

Composed during a drive to the home of John Lennon's first wife, Cynthia, the words to "Hey Jude" were Paul McCartney's way of offering encouragement to Lennon's young son Julian, who had just recently learned of his father's plans to divorce his mother and marry Yoko Ono. Ironically, John Lennon himself, upon first hearing the song, assumed that it had been written for him.

During the late seventies Kris Kristofferson largely ignored songwriting to pursue his movie career. It took the breakup of his six-year marriage to Rita Coolidge in 1981 to prod him into penning some new material. The result was *To the Bone*, an album comprised mostly of new tunes dealing with his marriage and its unhappy aftermath. "That's one of the advantages of doing this for a living," he said while out on the road to promote it. "Albums are a way to sum up your experience, make sense of things. They are a kind of cathartic. I wanted to look at that experience from as many different angles as I could. A lot of different emotions come to play at the end of a relationship — sadness, rage, humor — and I think I got them all in."

Coolidge herself had already expressed her sentiments on the subject with the single "It's Best to Leave While I'm in Love."

Carly Simon fashioned "Anticipation" out of her relationship with Cat Stevens, "Three Days" from a brief liaison with Kris Kristofferson and countless songs of married love ("You Belong to Me") and dissension ("James," "Fairweather Father") from her ten-year marriage to James Taylor. When that celebrated union broke apart, Carly made the rounds of TV music and talk shows to discuss the separation and push her new single, "Hurt," the old Timi Yuro tune.

In 1976, Fleetwood Mac's Lindsey Buckingham formally broke off his five-year romance with Stevie Nicks with the viotriolic "Go Your Own Way." Although "Dreams," Stevie's flip-side response, was a good deal more mellow, she has since compared her former lover to the Ayatollah.

The late Marvin Gaye's fourteen-year marriage to Anna Gordy Gaye (Berry's sister) ended on a bitter note when a Hollywood judge ordered him to make good on his back alimony and child support payments by recording an album and paying $600,000 of its profits to his Ex. Gaye protested the judgment saying that his wife didn't really need the money, she just wanted to make him suffer for abandoning her to marry a younger woman (Janice Hunter who left him three months after the marriage) but ultimately he abided by the decision — with the result being *Here, My Dear*, 71 minutes of musical pointed potshots aimed at his former wife.

Although scorned by the critics and largely ignored by the public, the album managed to make a dent in Gaye's debts. However, his artistic revenge backfired when Anna announced that she was considering a five-million-dollar invasion of privacy suit against him. She said, "I think he did it deliberately just to see how hurt I could become."

In "Baby, You're a Rich Man," Lennon and McCartney celebrated both their own newfound wealth and that of their mentor, Brian Epstein. Taking a vastly different tone, a somewhat jaded Bob Dylan had earlier warned an unnamed profiteer not to put a price on his soul in "Dear Landlord," a song which many people believe was addressed to his manager, Albert Grossman. Offering sarcastic sympathy for the shock that his own overwhelming success, with its attendant monetary rewards, must have been for his mentor, Dylan reminds him that he's not the first to suffer from getting "too much too fast."

John Lennon originally wrote "Sexy Sadie" about the Maharishi Mahesh Yogi after hearing of his alleged attempt to force his romantic attentions on actress Mia Farrow. When the Maharishi failed to come up with a reasonable excuse for his behavior, the boys packed their bags and headed for home. Soon afterwards, they publicly disassociated themselves from the guru. Still, Lennon couldn't bring himself to put him down in song: "I copped out," he said years later. "I just couldn't write 'Maharishi what have you done / Made a fool of everyone.' "

Although the words to such early McCartney solo efforts as "Too Many People Teaching Practices" and "Dear Boy, Betcha Never Knew How Much You Missed" came across as just so much tuneful nonsense to most people, John Lennon heard them as self-righteous sermons aimed directly at him. "There were a few little digs on *his* albums too," he said, "but he kept them so obscure that other people didn't notice them, you know, but *I* heard them. So I just thought, well, hang up being obscure; I'll just get right down to the nitty gritty." The result was "How Do You Sleep," a vitriolic attack on McCartney (on *Imagine*, an otherwise placid exercise made up mainly of love songs and utopian philosophizing) in which Lennon castigates his former writing partner for allowing domesticity to soften his creative edge. (Lennon also thought that "Get Back" was a secret message from Paul to Yoko; he said, "You know [that line] 'get back to where you once belonged'; every time he said that line in the studio, he'd look at Yoko.")

George Harrison turned a tiff with McCartney into "Wah Wah." "When I left during the *Let It Be* movie," he once recalled, "there's a scene where Paul and I are having an argument and we're trying to cover it up." ("Look, I'll play whatever you want me to play!" George says to McCartney. "Or I won't play at all. Whatever it is that'll please you, I'll do it.") "Then in the next scene I'm not there and Yoko's just screaming, doing her screeching number. Well, that's where I left and I went home and wrote 'Wah Wah.' The whole thing had given me a wah-wah, like I had such a headache with that whole argument, it was such a headache."

Even the easygoing Ringo, usually the peacemaker of the group, had a heated confrontation with McCartney (an ugly incident that he later described in a High Court affadavit following the dissolution of Apple) that ended with Paul throwing him out of his home. But as usual, Ringo was laid back in expressing his chagrin; he simply suggested that Paul "Back Off Boogaloo."

Paul McCartney had originally wanted the legal firm headed up by Linda Eastman's father and brother to take over Apple's business affairs, but John — and eventually George and Ringo — had decided on Allen Klein, the fast-talking hustler from New York City, who'd supposedly salvaged the tangled financial affairs of the Rolling Stones. Overruled but unconvinced, Paul hid his discontent between the syrupy sentiments of "The Weight" on *Abbey Road*, complaining, "You never give me your money, you only give me your funny paper" to the manager whose authority he refused to accept.

Several years later Lennon's relationship with Klein exploded in a flurry of multimillion-dollar lawsuits and numerous allegations of his financial double dealings at the Beatles' expense. In "Steel and Glass" Lennon aired his contempt for a slippery wheeler-dealer with an "L.A. tan and New York walk" who bore a striking resemblance to Allen Klein.

It was always clear that John Fogerty thought of Creedence Clearwater Revival as *his* band; he often characterized it as having one mind, one voice. And that voice was his. But during what turned out to be Creedence's last years together, two of the group's members demanded and won more creative control over its material and musical direction. The result was an album called *Mardi Gras*, which proved to be an embarrassment for all involved. Creedence continued to tour for a year afterward, but it felt to Fogerty "like we were watching the flag get dragged through the mud." Embittered over the group's ignominious downfall and the way it had been sensationalized by the rock press, Fogerty left the group to strike out on his own. He let off a little steam on "Goodbye Media Man," which was to become the first of several solo failures for Creedence's erstwhile mastermind.

Despite Creedence's striking resurgence of popularity, Fogerty refuses to reunite with the group. And the failure of a recent album effort only appears to have caused him to withdraw further. For now, he remains in seclusion on his northern California ranch. His vow of silence extends not only to the press and the other members of his band (including his brother Tom) but to his record company — which communicates with him by mail.

It's been said that David Bowie wrote "All the Young Dudes" in retaliation for the many broadsides leveled at him by his glam-rock rival, the late Marc Bolan. And while it's true that the posturing young coquette who wants to "kick it in the head when he's twenty-five" could have been Bolan, he could just as easily have been any other kid of his generation. But then again, there is that very specific reference to T. Rex . . .

Even such mild-mannered types as Adam Ant, Don Henley and Michael Jackson have used their records as a platform to air their grievances against the press, rumormongers, and assorted other mischief-makers on occasion. Ant, who made the deadly (for a rock star) mistake of admitting to a lack of vices during his first tour of America, poked fun at his critics in "Goody Two Shoes." ("Don't drink; don't smoke. What *do* you do?")

Ex-Eagle Don Henley, who'd had plenty of his own "Dirty Laundry," decried TV and tabloid sensationalism of celebrity scandal in the song of the same name, and in "Wanna Be Startin' Somethin' " (from *Thriller*), Michael Jackson painted himself as a "vegetable" being ingested by media vultures and sycophants. And millions boogied to "Billie Jean," his (fictional?) denial of paternity, during the summer of 1983.

I made the decision at sixteen or seventeen that what I did I wanted everybody to see.

There is nothing to hide. What's the secret? The secret is that there is no secret.
—JOHN LENNON

Perhaps the most candid of all contemporary songwriters, John Lennon scrupulously documented events in his life and his ever-changing state of mind in his music. From *Two Virgins* on, each of his albums narrated the latest chapter in his own real-life saga. As one writer put it, "He toyed with his celebrity, exposing its contours and parodying its extremes." Because Lennon wasn't afraid to expose his deepest feelings — no matter how lofty or vain — the body of work he leaves behind is among the most exciting and bold ever assembled by a popular musician.

With the Beatles' breakup imminent, Lennon launched his solo career with "The Ballad of John and Yoko" — a chronicle of the couple's escapades through Paris, Gibraltar and Vienna up to and including their marriage.

Unfinished Music No. 2: Life With the Lions (1969) dealt in part with Yoko's miscarriage while the *Wedding Album* released that same year celebrated the couple's honeymoon with a piece of plastic wedding cake, a reproduction of their marriage license and a souvenir booklet of their press clippings. The record itself featured such curiosities as John and Yoko cooing each other's names back and forth for twenty-two minutes over a background of amplified heartbeats and an audio *verité* rendering of the highlights of their Amsterdam Hilton bed-in, including snatches of interviews given to the Dutch press and John ordering breakfast from room service.

"Cold Turkey" (from *The Plastic Ono Band — Live Peace in Toronto 1969*) dwelt on the horrors of heroin withdrawal. Although Lennon denied that he was using hard drugs at the time this record was released, Yoko has since acknowledged that both she and her husband were using heroin during their early years together.

Composed mostly during the course of his four-month therapy at Arthur Janov's Primal Institute in Los Angeles, *The Plastic Ono Band* (also known as *The Primal Album*) is an agonizing journey through Lennon's trauma-ridden past. It opens with the pealing of funeral bells (on "Mother") to symbolize both the loss of his mother and the death of his former identity, and continues with "Well Well Well" and "Isolation," eloquent howls of frustration and despair. In "God," he sets out to renounce false faiths and false gods — magic, mantra, Christianity, Kennedy, Elvis, and finally, the Beatles.

Some Time in New York City (1972) found a beleaguered John Lennon fighting to remain in the States despite "the Man's" concentrated campaign to send him packing. Most of the songs on this effort were bogged down in hackneyed rad-lib rhetoric; critics pointed to it as further disheartening proof that Yoko had at last extinguished Lennon's creative flame. Many years later, Lennon himself said of his work from this period, "That radicalism was a phony — a combination of chip-on-the-shoulder teenage stuff and guilt for having made a fortune."

Mind Games (1973) basically reaffirmed the idealistic sentiments of *Imagine*. More interesting was *Walls and Bridges* (1974), which contained ten new songs written during what Lennon called his "lost weekend" — the eighteen lunatic months of separation from Yoko which he spent in L.A. quaffing Courvoisier with Harry Nilsson and getting thrown out of the Troubadour for heckling the Smothers Brothers and returning from the men's room wearing a Kotex on his head. Songs like "Scared" ("hatred and jealousy / gonna be the death of me"), "Going Down on Love" and "Nobody Loves You (When You're Down and Out)" mourned what seemed at the time to be the death of his marriage. Lennon later described *Walls and Bridges* as the "work of a semisick craftsman."

Written primarily during a period when Lennon was vacationing with his son in Bermuda while Yoko looked after the family fortune back in New York, *Double Fantasy* — coming as it did after the couple's separation and Lennon's subsequent five-year "retirement" from recording — was intended as a rapprochement of sorts between the Lennons themselves as well as their public. The fourteen cuts (seven his, seven hers) document the couple's positive emotional growth during Lennon's lengthy retirement from public life.

In an interview given shortly before her husband was killed, Yoko said, " 'Starting Over,' 'Woman,' 'Watching the Wheels,' those three songs — especially 'Watching the Wheels' — are songs that sum up what John was going through these past five years. For someone who's supposed to be a macho rock star to come out and say 'I'm a househusband and I still love my wife' is a very courageous thing to do."

Yoko Ono confronted her grief and anger at her husband's murder on *Season of Glass*. "Like all my records, this album has a little theme to it. First you say good-bye to sadness, and then there are flashbacks to different aspects of our relationship. After that, you *know* what happens ... and in the end a woman tries to stand up on her own. It's my diary, in fact."

"I Don't Know Why," the song which deals most directly with Lennon's death, was written shortly after the tragedy: "In the middle of the night about a week after John died, the words ... just came to me, exactly as it is on *Season of Glass*. I sang it into the tape recorder — and in the end there was a long, long curse." ("You bastards: Hate us ... / Hate me ... We had everything ..."). Here Ono says she is issuing a challenge by saying, "Look, I'm just going to be totally honest. And could you *still* love me? Not just as the cartoon called 'Widow of the Year'? But as I really am?" Some critics charged that her use of gunshot sounds and snatches of a heartrending story told by her son Sean ("I learned this from my daddy, you know") to punctuate her sentiments smacked of exploitation, but Ono was unrepentant. "There was hate coming through, but I was perfectly comfortable about it. If it had been John, he probably would have said worse things."

Ono's second solo album, *It's All Right*, found her still mourning the loss of her husband, while remaining stubbornly optimistic in the face of the tragedy. However, enthusiastic reviews did nothing to spur sales. *Milk and Honey*, a collection of roughs and rejected material from the *Double Fantasy* sessions, fared better in the marketplace — owing no doubt to Lennon's musical presence and the shocking revelations of the internal plundering of his personal effects by Lennon insiders that were cannily made public at the time of the album's release.

For a relative newcomer to the pop scene (and at well over the age of fifty, a decidedly mature one at that), Yoko Ono's musical output is remarkably prolific. And while she has finally received the public recognition as a pop artist she's said to have desired so desperately, she will probably never know whether the response reflects a genuine interest in her work, or the continuing fascination with her dead husband.

WHO'S MAKIN' LOVE WITH YOUR OLD LADY
(WHILE YOU WERE OUT MAKIN' LOVE?)

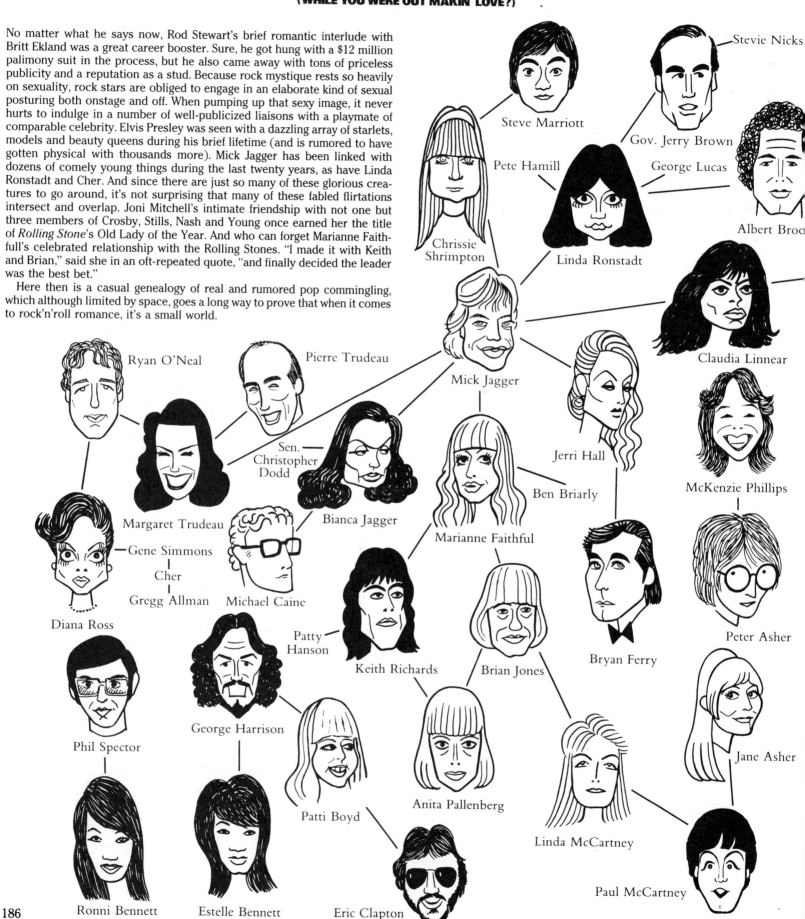

No matter what he says now, Rod Stewart's brief romantic interlude with Britt Ekland was a great career booster. Sure, he got hung with a $12 million palimony suit in the process, but he also came away with tons of priceless publicity and a reputation as a stud. Because rock mystique rests so heavily on sexuality, rock stars are obliged to engage in an elaborate kind of sexual posturing both onstage and off. When pumping up that sexy image, it never hurts to indulge in a number of well-publicized liaisons with a playmate of comparable celebrity. Elvis Presley was seen with a dazzling array of starlets, models and beauty queens during his brief lifetime (and is rumored to have gotten physical with thousands more). Mick Jagger has been linked with dozens of comely young things during the last twenty years, as have Linda Ronstadt and Cher. And since there are just so many of these glorious creatures to go around, it's not surprising that many of these fabled flirtations intersect and overlap. Joni Mitchell's intimate friendship with not one but three members of Crosby, Stills, Nash and Young once earned her the title of *Rolling Stone*'s Old Lady of the Year. And who can forget Marianne Faithfull's celebrated relationship with the Rolling Stones. "I made it with Keith and Brian," said she in an oft-repeated quote, "and finally decided the leader was the best bet."

Here then is a casual genealogy of real and rumored pop commingling, which although limited by space, goes a long way to prove that when it comes to rock'n'roll romance, it's a small world.

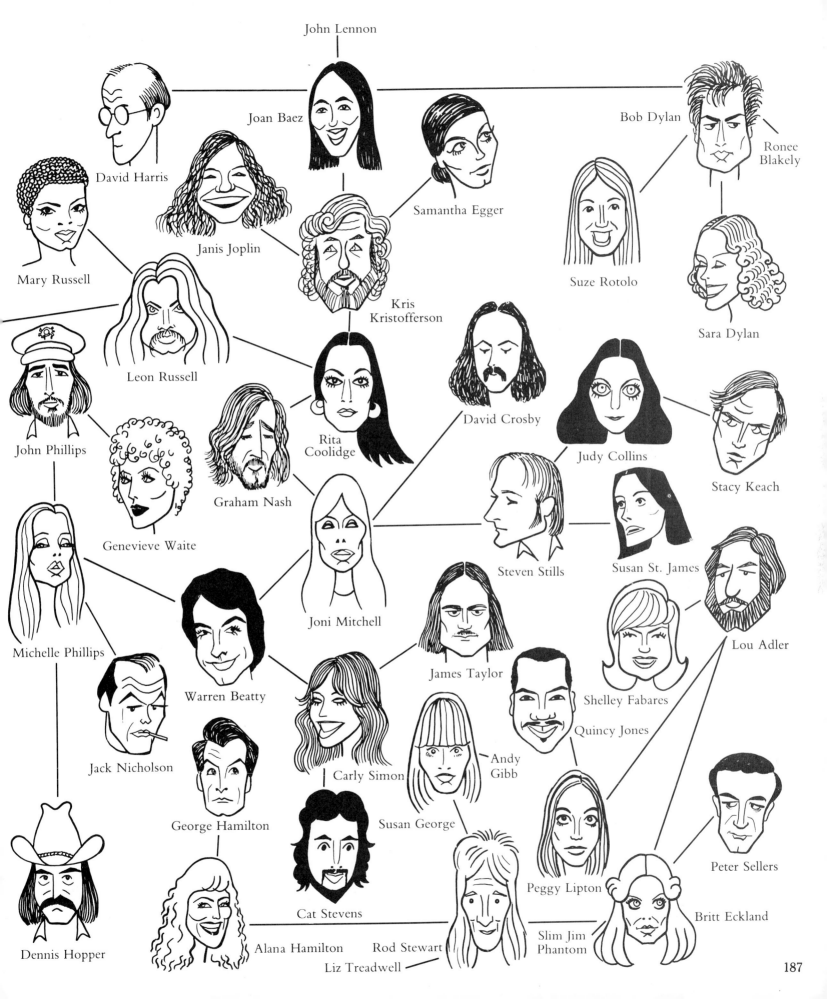

John Lennon

David Harris

Joan Baez

Samantha Egger

Bob Dylan

Ronee Blakely

Janis Joplin

Kris Kristofferson

Suze Rotolo

Mary Russell

Leon Russell

Sara Dylan

John Phillips

Genevieve Waite

Graham Nash

Rita Coolidge

David Crosby

Judy Collins

Stacy Keach

Michelle Phillips

Joni Mitchell

Steven Stills

Susan St. James

Lou Adler

Jack Nicholson

Warren Beatty

James Taylor

Shelley Fabares

George Hamilton

Carly Simon

Andy Gibb

Quincy Jones

Dennis Hopper

Cat Stevens

Susan George

Peggy Lipton

Peter Sellers

Alana Hamilton

Rod Stewart

Slim Jim Phantom

Britt Eckland

Liz Treadwell

187

Rock'N'Roll Heaven

By checking out early, rock stars spare us the embarrassment of watching them fade. And fade they must — because rock'n'roll is teenage music: crude, rebellious and hormonal. Good rock'n'roll, that is. As a rule, the people who make it best are young bucks just past the age of consent. Like Peter Pan and various other Little Lost Boys, they simply weren't meant to get old. Few things are more depressing than watching an aging Fave Rave trying to hang on to the moves that made him famous (unless it's watching him try to grow up and go straight). There's simply no room in rock mythology for someone like Bill Haley, who appeared to have grown comfortably into middle age and died of natural causes at the advanced age of fifty-six. By rock standards, Haley was a veritable fossil, an embarrassment of sorts. Pop writer Nik Cohn was only half kidding back in 1969 when he declared that if the Rolling Stones had any sense of aesthetics "they'd get themselves killed in an airplane crash — preferably two or three days before they reach 30."

Because their reign must necessarily be so brief, rock stars are allowed to live life as if there were no tomorrow. They're encouraged to wallow in full-tilt hedonism — even at the expense of their health and sanity. Boorishness of a kind that would be inexcusable in the Average Joe is tolerated, even demanded, by the faithful.

By indulging their every childish whim in full view of the public, pop idols act out the straight world's suppressed desires. In return, they're rewarded with outlandish sums of money and adoration on a grand scale. Unfortunately, all too many get in over their heads and end up drowning in a sea of self-indulgence. When this happens, their fans are saddened but not necessarily surprised. Unhappy endings are part of the bargain — the price modern heroes pay for being so rich, so lucky, so vain. While not every pop star lives up to this Faustian ideal, a surprising number have chosen death over the inevitable decline and loss of public love.

The flair with which a rock star takes his final bow can be as crucial to his legacy as the life he led and the music he played. Many an uninspired talent has made a place for himself in the annals of rock simply by making a spectacular exit. (How many people would remember Les Harvey of Stone the Crows if he hadn't been accidentally electrocuted onstage during a performance?) Death is so essential to rock mythology that it has been rated (by esteemed rock critic Greil Marcus in the *Village Voice*) according to "interest, drama, degree of violence, respect for tradition, degree of choice, etc."; catalogued by date (by *Creem* magazine in its "Let It Rot Calendar of Rock and Roll Death"); and commemorated with museum displays (by the Mudd Club, where exhibits include a plaster replica of the ham sandwich that purportedly killed Mama Cass).

If a star has the good timing to die while still at the peak of his fame and good looks, he stays forever young — a symbol of untarnished passion for countless generations to come. His face will end up being emblazoned across T-shirts, posters, cheap jewelry and commemorative decanters. His work (including some previously deemed too inferior for release) will find a newer, broader audience. Records, movies and *The 6 O'Clock News* will eulogize him. Cheap wines and newborn babies will bear his name. Friends and family (and the guy who serviced his car) will record their precious memories of him in tacky, sometimes sensational, biographies. His home and burial place will become shrines. In short, he'll become a Cult Idol — bigger in death than in life.

Any way you look at it, rock and death are inextricably linked. And just to prove it, the list of untimely Late Greats grows larger every day. Yes, given the myriad occupational hazards intrinsic to the teen idol business, the average rock star has the life expectancy of a fruitfly. But it's their very willingness to gamble with fate that makes our idols so utterly fascinating. In that respect rock stars are like tightrope walkers — the main reason they're so thrilling to watch is that every so often they fall.

In 1954 Johnny Ace became, in effect, the first rock'n'roll martyr. The first to die recklessly by his own hand, the first to be dubbed a "Late Great."

John Marshall Alexander shot himself in the head during the intermission of a Christmas Eve concert at the City Auditorium, in Houston, Texas, while engaging in an impromptu game of Russian Roulette to entertain a girlfriend. At least, that's the way the papers told it the next day. It's been rumored, however, that the twenty-five-year-old preacher's son was in fact murdered by a local black powerbroker, who was known to have been close by his dressing room at the time of the shooting.

Like many pop artists to come, Ace scored the biggest hit of his career after giving up his life. "Pledging My Love" became one of the giant records of 1955 — and one of the classic ballads of all time.

Johnny Ace

Left: Buddy Holly; *upper right:* not nearly so nerdy without his specs; *bottom right:* Ritchie Valens

Producer Norman Petty did everything in his power to dissuade Buddy Holly from marrying the Puerto Rican girl from New York he'd fallen for in 1958. It seems that Petty was concerned that Maria Elena Santiago, with her many connections in the music industry, might undermine his influence with Holly — and he was right. By that point Holly's star was very much on the rise and Petty, a small independent producer based in Clovis, New Mexico, quite naturally didn't want to lose him. But eventually, the rift between the two men had grown so deep that Holly felt compelled to pull out of their partnership. He'd hoped to take Jerry Allison and Joe Maudlin of the Crickets along with him, but Petty managed to convince them that they were the group's real attractions and Holly just another singer.

Despite his many hit records, Holly's various financial disputes left him strapped for cash, forcing him to take on a series of grueling one-nighters. Leaving his wife behind, he joined the Winter Dance Tour of 1959 to travel by bus throughout the Midwest during one of the worst winters on record. It was on that tour, of course, that the twenty-two-year-old singer lost his life when the little four-seater Beechcraft Bonanza in which he was riding crashed into a snow-covered cornfield just minutes after takeoff. According to a report filed by the FAA several months later, the pilot had become confused about his instrument reading so that in executing what he thought was a climbing turn, he was actually descending. Holly had chartered the plane to get him and his new band to their next stop ahead of the tour so they would have time to do their laundry. At the last minute, Tommy Allsup and Waylon Jennings had given up their seats to Ritchie Valens and J. P. Richardson (the Big Bopper), who were both feeling under the weather. All three musicians, as well as the plane's young pilot, were killed upon impact.

During a recent celebration of Holly's birthday, Jennings lamented, "The only reason Buddy went on that tour was because he was broke. Flat broke. He didn't want to go, but he had to make some money. I ain't saying the person's name that was the reason he was broke. But he knows who he is."

190

On February 3, 1959, Ritchie Valens talked Tommy Allsup of the Crickets into flipping a coin for his seat aboard the airplane chartered by Buddy Holly to take him and his band from Mason City, Iowa, to their next date in Moorhead, North Dakota. Exhausted and running a high fever, Valens just couldn't face another night of sleeping in his seat aboard the freezing tour bus. In fact, Valens had wanted to abandon the tour altogether. He'd even called his manager, Bob Keene, the night before to ask if he could come home. But Keene had talked him into finishing the tour.

Born Richard Valenzuela in Pacoima, California, Ritchie was raised by two sets of grandparents and various relatives after his parents split up. Something of a musical prodigy, he had mastered the guitar by the age of five. By fifteen Ritchie had dropped out of school to play in neighborhood bars for a few dollars a night. At one of those gigs he was spotted by Keene, who, struck by the effects his feverish playing had on the crowd, got him his first recording date. The result was "Come On, Let's Go," which became a mid-charting national hit. When Ritchie's second release, "Donna" (backed with "La Bamba"), busted out as a two-sided smash, Keene quickly booked Valens on a series of one-nighters and personal appearances so grueling that his weight dropped fifty pounds. The last round of dates was the Winter Dance Party with Buddy Holly and the Big Bopper through the upper Midwest. Before leaving on that fateful tour, Valens realized a longtime dream by buying his mother a new home. He'd had to borrow money from Keene for the down payment, because he'd yet to see any earnings from either "Come On" or the two-million seller, "Donna." In fact, according to a lawyer for the Valens estate, Ritchie never received a single royalty payment for a record sale.

Although the three albums he left behind have recently been reissued, Valens's musical legacy has been largely ignored. This is particularly frustrating to the Chicano community where Valens is considered something of a folk hero — the first California barrio kid to become a rock star and the first to make it in a white man's world. Only seventeen when he was killed, Ritchie Valens died before getting a chance to prove his talent. Back in 1959, they were calling him the "next Elvis," but his name might not be remembered today at all if Buddy Holly hadn't been riding with him on the night he died.

Jimmy Clanton and Ritchie Valens on the set of *Go, Johnny Go*.

Eddie Cochran

On the night before Eddie Cochran was killed in a car crash on a rain-slicked London street, his girlfriend, songwriter Sharon Sheely, is said to have found him sitting in the dark in his hotel room playing a stack of Buddy Holly records over and over. This struck her as odd since Cochran had avoided even the slightest mention of his old friend's name since his death the year before. She urged him to stop torturing himself, saying, "You'll only hurt yourself, honey," but Eddie replied that it didn't hurt him anymore because he'd be seeing Buddy again "real soon." Another version of that fateful night has Eddie running from his hotel room in terror after being visited by a vision of a swerving car and his own head cracking in two.

Eddie Cochran may not have had a Technicolor premonition of his death, but he did leave the impression with many friends that he believed that he didn't have long to live — particularly in the months following Holly's death. Actually, Cochran had originally been scheduled to make that tour through the Midwest with Holly, but had dropped out at the last minute owing to a booking mix-up. After the tragedy, Cochran, who never liked one-nighters, began to talk of retiring from performing to concentrate on songwriting and producing. He told his mother before leaving for England that this tour would be his last, saying, "After this I won't have to go out on the road anymore."

Although Dinah Washington is remembered as the Queen of the Blues, she effectively wrapped her vinegary style around everything from Big Band swing to Country & Western during her twenty-year career. Even so, her recordings were available only in ghetto record stores until 1959, when she scored an early R&B crossover with her sultry rendition of "What a Diff'rence a Day Makes." Her subsequent teamwork with Brook Benton ("You've Got What It Takes" and "A Rockin' Good Way") gave her two more hits the following year, making her one of the top female R&B artists of the postwar years.

While giving her the financial security to buy the Detroit restaurant she'd always wanted, success did little to soothe her tempestuous personal life. She made seven trips to the wedding altar — the last time with Detroit Lions football star Dick (Nighttrain) Lane, in the summer of 1963. In December of that same year, the thirty-nine-year-old singer, who had been using diet pills to get her weight down for an upcoming concert date, died after taking barbiturates and alcohol to counter the effect of the amphetamines.

Sam at home with
his baby son in 1957

Dinah Washington

In the fifties Sam Cooke was to blacks what Elvis was to white teenagers. He had everything — talent, charm, divine good looks and the smarts to make it all pay. Even whites ordinarily intimidated by black rock'n'rollers found themselves seduced by his easy grace. If ever there was a black entertainer capable of conquering the color barrier without sacrificing his ethnic roots, it was Cooke. But if he could be said to have one fatal flaw, it was his reckless sense of infallibility. Of course, a healthy ego is not exactly a hindrance in a business that involves selling oneself to millions. But the story that unfolded at the coroner's inquest into his death shows that his cockiness may have undone him in the end.

A twenty-two-year-old L.A. woman testified that Cooke had forced her to accompany him to a motel under the pretense of giving her a ride home from a party. She maintained that she had followed him into the motel office when he went to register (as "Mr. and Mrs. Cooke"), demanding to be taken to her proper destination, but had then ended up following him to his room after he assured her that he just wanted to drop off his things. Once there, however, Cooke allegedly attempted to rape her. When he went into the bathroom for a moment, she managed to escape, taking his clothes with her to prevent him from giving chase. Undaunted, Cooke ran after her clad only in a sports coat and shoes.

began pound-

While the woman called police from a pay phone in a nearby parking lot, Cooke began pounding on the door of the motel manager, Bertha Franklin, apparently under the impression that his companion was hiding within. Mrs. Franklin told the court that Cooke kicked open the door in a state of rage and proceeded to strike her. She managed to push him off and get hold of a .22 caliber pistol, which she used to shoot him three times in the chest and abdomen. Seriously wounded, the singer staggered toward her to defend himself whereupon she struck him on the head until he crumpled to the floor. He was dead when the police arrived a few minutes later. When the story of Sam Cooke's last night was related in courtroom testimony, the court ruled his shooting a justifiable homicide, but left unresolved the details that never quite jelled: Why did his companion accompany him his motel room in the first place? And why would Cooke have stopped to go to the bathroom in the midst of a "rape"? Cooke's death stunned the black community. More than just an entertainer, the twenty-nine-year-old singer had been a symbol of black power and achievement. It was especially painful that his image as a clean-cut family man, married to his high-school sweetheart, should be discredited in such an ignominious fashion.

When Cooke's body was returned to his native Chicago for burial, full-scale pandemonium broke out among the city's black population. Not since the death of Rudolph Valentino had the entertainment world witnessed such a display of grief for a performer as over 200,000 people bade farewell to a fallen idol.

Sam Cooke

Like his idol Sam Cooke, Otis Redding longed to make the transition from the R&B market to mainstream pop. After years of headlining the chitlin circuit and topping the soul charts with hits like "I've Been Loving You Too Long" and "Respect" (which he wrote), Redding finally broke through to young white audiences with his electrifying performance at the Monterey Festival in 1967. He drowned in an icy lake near Madison, Wisconsin, in December of that same year when the private twin engine Beechcraft in which he was riding hit the water in a heavy fog. The crash also claimed the lives of four members of his troupe — most of whom were in their teens. It was after his death that Redding finally achieved the crossover hit everyone expected of him with "(Sittin' on the) Dock of the Bay."

Otis Redding

Frankie Lymon

Frankie Lymon grew up fast. At ten he was hustling hookers to the white johns who came up to his Harlem neighborhood looking for a good time. By twelve, he had a giant hit record. He and his group, the Teenagers, were soon breaking attendance records all over the country and appearing on *The Ed Sullivan Show*. At thirteen, his lovemaking prowess was legendary in showbiz circles. While on the road, he was constantly accompanied by showgirl types more than twice his age who masqueraded as his mother or sister. "I had a whole stable of women," he recalled more than a decade later, "one in every city. Of course, having them pose as my mother had its disadvantages. I couldn't be seen drinking with them. And once, my little game was nearly exposed when a newpaper reporter who had been introduced to one of my 'mothers' in New York caught my act in Chicago and was introduced to another of my 'mothers.' I had a hard time convincing him that he had seen the same woman in both cities, especially since they looked nothing alike."

The Teenagers' following was completely unaware of Frankie's unsavory private life. "The public regarded me as a clean-cut, wholesome kid," he said, "and my manager and advisers wanted me to keep that image." And so he did. In the beginning anyway. With their letter sweaters and childishly saccharine sentiments, Frankie Lymon and the Teenagers seemed the spirit of youthful innocence. When they performed, they made their entrance onstage in a flurry of flying somersaults, handsprings and spins. Their choreography was as elaborate as their vocal harmonies, but it was their exhilaration that dazzled the crowds. Thousands of kids caught the fever in 1956 when the group toured the country with "Why Do Fools Fall in Love?" Within a year of their debut, the Teenagers scored two more hits, "I Want You to Be My

Girl" and "The ABC's of Love." But all too quickly, things began to go sour — beginning with the Gee label's push to groom Frankie as a "legit" solo act, something along the lines of Sammy Davis, Jr. Naturally, the idea of becoming a big-name star in his own right appealed to Lymon. He left the Teenagers without looking back.

Frankie's first release as a single was an ill-advised retread of "Goody Goody," the old Ella Fitzgerald gem, which he cut at the behest of his mentors at Gee. The record was a moderate-sized hit, but Frankie's young fans were turned off by the syrupy quality of his new grown-up sound. Although he continued to record and play endless local club dates, Frankie's career more or less died with his first solo flight. It had lasted only eighteen months.

Like many other youthful black rock'n'roll acts of the fifties, the Teenagers had little money to cushion their fall from grace. According to one of the group's surviving members, Jimmy Merchant, the group never saw any royalties from either publishing rights or record sales. Even the income from their live performances went to their managers at Gee. Jimmy Merchant told David Goldblatt of the *Village Voice* that the group had been assured that their earnings were going into a trust fund until they turned twenty-one. "We were to get X amount of dollars per week, which turned out to be exactly $11.00. Later it was $27.00. They said that was all we were legally entitled to. It was an 'allowance' they called it." As is so often the case with such arrangements, upkeep and overhead quickly depleted the "trust fund" so there was almost nothing left for the boys when they came of age.

Frankie Lymon never really adjusted to life after stardom. He slid into the sordid existence of a desperate street junkie (an addiction he's rumored to have acquired courtesy of the female lead singer of a famous fifties do-wop group). Dead broke, he returned to Harlem where he eked out a meager existence. In 1967, he underwent thirty-three days of dope detox at a New York hospital to prepare for a comeback attempt, but a year later he was found dead of a heroin overdose in the bathroom of his grandmother's Harlem apartment. He was twenty-six.

Shortly before he died, Frankie told an interviewer, "They were always careful to keep the kid happy. They bought him what he wanted. What did I want? What would any kid of thirteen want? I certainly didn't want to think about bank accounts and taxes and getting the proper receipts and that sort of thing. They would pat me on the head and tell me how great I was. I was merely a pawn in a big chess game."

Frankie Lymon's story is one of the saddest to be found in a business brimming over with tearjerkers. But Morris Levy, former head (along with the late George Goldner) of Gee Records, seems unmoved by it: "I have no apologies to make to the Teenagers, no apologies at all. Remember," he told Goldblatt for the *Voice* article, "who it was who buried Frankie."

It was Brian who came up with the name Rolling Stones from a Muddy Waters song. It was Brian with his exotically hip dress, sunlit haystack of flaxen blond hair and articulate outspokenness who epitomized the combination of pop cool and outlaw arrogance that became synonymous with the Rolling Stones. It was Brian, masterful musician and lightning-fast learner, who introduced reed instruments, sitar, dulcimer, harpsichord and steel guitar to the Stones' expanding sound vocabulary. The one thing Brian Jones didn't do was write the songs, and therein lies the beginning of his end.

At the heart of the Jagger–Richards songwriting team was a personal alliance based, at least in the beginning, on jealousy. Much to the annoyance of the band, Jones often appointed himself group leader in interviews. There is no question that when the Stones started he was the most accomplished musician. And in the early days it was Jones, not Jagger, who was the group's standout sex symbol. His position, front and center, in the cover photos for *12x5* and *December's Children* offers proof of that.

The rivalry came out in the open with the arrival of German model Anita Pallenberg into the Stones' circle. The very mirror image of Brian with her electrifying sexuality, Carnaby Street flash and golden hair, she was his pride and joy. She was also the envy of Mick and Keith. When Anita switched allegiance to Keith (supposedly after Brian demanded that she have sex with him and two prostitutes he'd brought back to London from Morocco), Brian was devastated. It was also the first sign that the balance of power was slipping away from him.

Increasingly, he relied on drugs. He wanted to go to the edge — the edge of his music, the edge of his psyche — and drugs took him there. Unfortunately, there was no return ticket. After his initial cannabis bust in May 1967, Brian took the first of two forced vacations in drug rehab homes. But the damage was already done. Whether because he couldn't pick up an instrument (as has been rumored) or simply because the Stones couldn't or wouldn't deal with him in the studio, Brian is hardly heard on his last two albums with the band, *Their Satanic Majesties Request* and *Beggars Banquet*. The final humiliation came when Jagger and Richards fired him (although the official notice had it that he had quit to pursue other musical interests).

Coming as it did less than a month after his departure from the group, Brian's death by drowning in the swimming pool of his country estate sent the London rock rumor mill into overdrive. Those supposedly in the know called his death a suicide although the circumstances made that seem doubtful. Even more unlikely was the widely held notion that Jagger and Richards had in some way been involved — although their ostracism of him had certainly helped to kill his spirit. Consequently, when Jagger's tribute to him at the Stones' Hyde Park concert went afoul, it seemed wickedly appropriate. Jagger, festooned in a ruffled tunic dress, read a selection from Shelley's *Adonais* ("Peace, peace! / He is not dead, he does not sleep / He has awakened from the dream of life") like he was bawling "Satisfaction" and then, on cue, boxes were opened to release two thousand white butterflies as a memorial gesture — but more than half the butterflies plummeted to the ground having suffocated inside the boxes. Realizing what had happened, Jagger quickly launched into a manic version of "Jumping Jack Flash."

Brian Jones still had a lot of music in him when he died. His last real recording was an album of organic psychedelia by the Pipes of Pan of Joujouka in Morocco, and he had talked enthusiastically to old friend and mentor Alexis Korner of plans for a new group during his last few months. Right to the end, Brian took everything he did — his music, his artistic visions, his work and play as a Rolling Stone — seriously. He would have been deeply offended to hear the final verdict of his passing: "death by misadventure."

Jagger may have been the front man, but it was Brian's group in the beginning.

The "Beautiful One" contemplates his visage before a concert date.

A shaky show of solidarity a few months before Brian's "withdrawal" from the Stones

He was a symbol of the black power movement, but like his predecessors in the fifties, Jimi Hendrix was a victim of white exploitation.

As a symbol of the burgeoning Black Power movement of the sixties, Jimi Hendrix seemed the embodiment of the reawakened pride of America's black population — a self-motivated rock star who not only refused to apologize for being black, but appeared to have thrown off the shackles of the white management that had so exploited black music and musicians during the postwar era. But sadly, that image turned out to be just another pretty fantasy. Hendrix might've forsaken pancake and Dixie Peach, but he was as much a slave to white powerbrokers and audiences as his hapless predecessors.

In some ways, Hendrix's violent, groin-grinding flamboyance onstage, which led him to be branded by one critic as "the flower generation's electric nigger dandy," obscured his true worth as a musician. Today it is widely acknowledged that he revolutionized rock by redefining its pivotal instrument, the electric guitar. He reached into the guts of his Stratocaster, and pulled them out with both brutality and tenderness, then put them through an ear-razing ringer of amplication, feedback, distortion and personal voodoo magic. Hendrix was the first black rock musician to play new electric blues for the new electric youth, singing alien acid poetry with the earthy magnetism of a Delta bluesman.

Born in Seattle where his father, Al, was a gardener, Hendrix hit the chitlin circuit immediately after being discharged from the army in 1963 for "medical reasons." Cheapo recordings and sloppy demos cut with Little Richard, the Isley Brothers and Curtis Knight during that period all resurfaced with Hendrix's name in bold print once his first LP, *Are You Experienced?*, and guitar-burning spectacle at the Monterey Pop Festival made him a hippie household word in 1967. It was shortly after he signed with hotshot manager Michael Jeffrey that a record producer who had worked with Hendrix during his years as a struggling musician turned up with a two-year-old agreement in which Hendrix agreed to make records for him in return for what might best be described as a modest royalty. Hendrix had recorded for the producer merely as a backup man for Curtis Knight, yet the producer was awarded not only a piece of the guitarist's first three Reprise LPs and of the rights to *Band of Gypsys* but was able to issue and reissue those Knight tracks in fourteen different permutations.

In the short three and a half years he was an international star, Jimi Hendrix attracted hustlers and con artists like moths to a flame. A quiet, reclusive man bewildered by his fans, he simply lacked the ability to say no. But if his untimely, undignified death (after choking on his own vomit following barbiturate intoxication) in a London flat came as a shock to the rock world, the extent to which his music and memory would be vandalized were equally disturbing. After his death, his father was informed by Michael Jeffrey that the estate amounted to only $21,000 in cash. The income from tours, million-selling albums and publishing royalties that had supposedly been banked in a Bahamian holding company were nowhere to be found.

In the meantime, posthumous albums began popping up all over the place. Producer Alan Douglas created two "new" Hendrix LPs by overdubbing new rhythm tracks on incomplete demos and, like most things Hendrix at the time, both became big sellers. A Jimi Hendrix Memorial Fund set up by some Seattle lawyers and two California porno-moviehouse kingpins staged four benefit concerts in Seattle and sold memberships and memorabilia, but none of the proceeds was ever recovered. Further, bassist Noel Redding and drummer Mitch Mitchell of the original Experience were forced to sue for royalties on the posthumous records and payment for their appearances in two Hendrix documentaries.

It has been speculated that the rape of Jimi Hendrix was a professional job, that the Mob had a piece of his creative action. But more likely, it was accomplished by a handful of cunning but unrelated vultures who tore Hendrix apart bit by bit both during his lifetime and after until there was simply nothing left.

Janis at home in Mill Valley

Myra Friedman described Janis in performance as "a headlong assault, a hysterical discharge, an act of total extermination."

When Janis Joplin's body was found in October of 1970 jammed between her hotel bed and the wall, rumors circulated to the effect that some junkie friend or lover had murdered her with a massive injection of heroin. But although some of these stories found their way into the press, none was given much credence. Ultimately, conjecture focused on whether Janis had purposely taken her own life. In the endless postmortems that followed, friends acknowledged that she was chronically depressed and had spoken of suicide on more than one occasion. Prone to hysterical bouts of self-pity, Janis had apparently lived in fear that her career was slipping, that other musicians didn't take her seriously, and that men were interested in her only for her money. Lending credibility to the suicide theory was the fact that she had signed her will just several days before her death.

But on the flip side of this sad song were Janis's happiness over her marriage to a wealthy young student at Berkeley and her satisfaction with the band she'd assembled to record what turned out to be her last album, *Pearl*. These factors convinced the L.A. coroner, and later a team of behavioral scientists, that her death was an accident. However, the issue was still being debated in the courts four years later after an insurance company, which had issued a $200,000 policy on the singer, challenged the coroner's verdict. Janis's kosmic blues were rehashed yet again in the

ensuing courtroom battle when Albert Grossman, whose management concern was the beneficiary of the policy, took the insurance company to court. Grossman testified that Janis "was going through a happy time, relative to Janis," prior to her death, citing her wedding plans and ongoing recording sessions, while the defense pointed to Joplin's heavy alcohol and drug use as a sign of chronic depression. In the end, both sides tacitly acknowledged that there was no way to assess what was in Janis's mind the night she died. The case was ultimately settled out of court (for less than half the amount originally contested).

Myra Friedman, Joplin's friend, addressed the suicide issue in her brilliant book, *Buried Alive*, by saying "the term accidental as applied to Joplin's death was only a legal technicality, meaning that Janis did not know that it would be precisely this shot which would end her suffering. But rather that Janis was fully aware of the end rewards of doping, having seen a number of her friends die. In fact, she was a little in love with the idea of the never, never land of dreams." Friedman concluded, "I myself find it almost impossible to believe that a conscious thought of suicide never entered her mind. The sheer omnipotence of the possibilities — the vision of the power in it all. To create herself as so memorable. The thought of it must have been irresistible."

With his horn-rimmed glasses and frumpy clothes, Canned Heat's Al Wilson came across as the class nerd as compared to the feathered freaks who ruled the rock scene during the sixties. Nevertheless, in rock circles Wilson was revered for his perfect pitch and proficiency on the blues harp. He had both co-founded the group (with Bob Hite) and authored two of its best-known hits, "Goin' Up the Country" — for which he did the vocal — and "On the Road Again." Nearly blind and subject to severe depressions, Wilson was an enigmatic figure who tended to remain aloof even from his friends. That remoteness, along with his love of nature, helps to account for the fact that he was camping out in Hite's back yard the night he died from an apparent overdose of sleeping pills. (Hite's wife was the only one at home at the time, the rest of the band having left for a tour of Europe.)

Eleven years later, Hite himself would die prematurely of a heart attack at the age of thirty-eight. The 300-pound singer, who was known for his high-powered vocals and extensive knowledge of R&B and blues, became ill shortly before a scheduled performance at a North Hollywood club.

Al Wilson

Bob Hite

Tammi and Marvin

At one time Tammi Terrell was the most precious jewel in the star-studded Motown crown, and yet today she is accorded only marginal mentions in most pop histories. In fact, she might not be remembered at all were it not for the controversy surrounding her death and the devastating effect it had on the career of her friend and singing partner, Marvin Gaye.

Though still in her teens when she caught the eye of Motown kingpin Berry Gordy in 1965, Tammi was already a seasoned professional who had performed on record for several minor labels and in nightclubs since the age of eleven. In some ways, her singing style was still unformed, but she was blessed with a rich satiny voice and a presence that oozed a kittenish sex appeal.

Gordy wooed the luscious nineteen-year-old away from Scepter, her record company, with the promise of a full-star treatment. Within a few months of her arrival, she'd been transformed from a ripe girl-next-door type into an uptown vamp — Motown style. Having achieved some success with two of her first three Motown releases, Tammi was given the opportunity of recording with Motown's biggest solo star, Marvelous Marvin Gaye. Together the duo scored four smash hits within a period of two years. The two became so intimate during their collaboration that many people assumed they were lovers, despite the fact that Gaye was married to the boss's sister. Their combined fortunes were soaring when tragedy struck: Terrell collapsed in Gaye's arms during a performance, apparently having suffered a severe cerebral spasm.

Rumors linking Terrell's maladies with injuries supposedly inflicted by one or another friend or lover began to spread like wildfire through De-

troit's black-music circles, eventually finding their way into the papers. Among those implicated were a married member of one of Motown's most popular groups and a famous athlete known to have a penchant for pummeling his ladyfriends. (Naturally Motown refused to comment on these stories, and none of the allegations was ever substantiated.)

For the next year and a half, Terrell underwent six rounds of exploratory surgery. If the operations shed any light on her rapidly deteriorating physical condition, the results were never made public. During this agonizing period, she made several courageous attempts at a comeback, but was continually thwarted by physical and emotional breakdowns. Finally in March of 1970, at the age of twenty-four, she succumbed to her illness.

Tammi Terrell's death robbed pop music of one of it freshest talents and was almost responsible for taking a second — the late Marvin Gaye. For four years following Terrell's death, Gaye virtually stopped performing. On the rare occasions when he did venture onstage, he suffered severe mental anguish, often becoming physically ill. Soon he began spending almost all his time at home, eventually becoming a virtual recluse.

Gaye stayed underground for some ten years in all, recording primarily in his home studio. It took marital problems and a hefty alimony settlement to push him out in front of the public again. It was then that he first spoke publicly about Terrell's death: "Tammi's death hurt so much," he said. "Not because she and I were lovers; I wish we had been, but the relationship was platonic. I was hurt because such a talented and beautiful human being died so young."

We tend to forget it now that he's ascended to the hallowed hall of Rock'n'Roll Heaven — but Jim Morrison's career was on a major slide when he died in 1971. Hounded by headline-hunting do-gooders on the one hand and hard-nosed rock critics on the other, Morrison had taken a brutal drubbing in the press from friend and foe alike during the last years of his life. At the time of his death, he and the Doors had been banned from practically every major municipal arena in the country and dropped from the playlists of several important stations, owing to the public outcry over his feigned acts of masturbation and fellatio during a 1969 concert in Miami. Before the furor abated, the group had forfeited over a million dollars in revenues and Morrison himself faced up to ten years in prison terms. His beauty fading and his spirit nearly extinguished, Morrison was fast becoming an embarrassment to all but his most devoted fans. In fact, if he hadn't bought the farm when he did, there's every chance that he would've ended up a pathetic has-been in the seventies, a broken-down Blast from the Past.

Actually, a heavy malaise had descended over Jim Morrison practically from the moment the Doors first started to make it big. In 1968, a scant two years after their first hit, he tried to quit, but was persuaded to give it a few months more. Although he continued to write and perform with the group, in some ways this attempted break was the beginning of the end. As his star grew brighter, he became progressively more withdrawn and neurotic. Terrorizing groupies and drinking beer at topless bars on the Strip became his primary pastimes. Soon his alcoholic stupors — so numbing that on occasion his friends feared him to be dead — became debilitating in the extreme, causing him to miss rehearsals, recording sessions and even concerts with alarming frequency. Likewise, his onstage behavior grew more and more frenzied. He baited his audiences with insults and obscenities, rewarding those who rushed the stage for a closer look by spitting on their heads. By 1969, it was clear that Morrison was

completely out of control. Angrier and more desperate than ever before, he seemed constantly on the verge of collapse. Fans turned out by the hundreds of thousands to watch the spectacle; it was as if they wanted to be present when Morrison finally stepped over the edge.

And then on a sultry March evening in 1969, a besotted Jim Morrison asked several thousand Miami teenagers, "Do you want to see my cock?" He was subsequently charged in absentia with drunkenness, obscenity and indecent exposure and ordered to stand trial. He surrendered to FBI agents in Phoenix several weeks later.

In the months following the Miami incident, Morrison went into a major funk. His depression began to manifest itself externally as well. He let himself go to seed, hiding his Adonis-like beauty behind a scruffy beard, dark glasses and a whiskey paunch. It was as if he was purposely trying, once and for all, to desecrate his Lizard King image.

With a dispirited Morrison still at the helm, the Doors continued to tour those remaining cities that would allow them to appear. During those performances, local cops would often surround Morrison onstage, in the hope that he would perform one of his illicit acts on their turf. Sick of bucking the guardians of public decency, Morrison began to lapse into pathetic self-parody on stage. Privately, he told friends that he was tired of being a pop idol — that he was too old for rock'n'roll.

As Morrison became more and more unmanageable, rumors began to spread that the other Doors were fed up with his little games — his drinking and his pranks — not to mention the additional financial burden his legal problems had generated. Early in 1971, the rock press reported that the group was working up new material that they would record without him. After finishing his final album commitment with the group, Jim took refuge in Paris. There, he was sure, he could settle down and devote himself to some serious writing, and get back to the poetry he'd abandoned for

Jim and Pamela

rock stardom. This was not the first time Morrison had tried to establish himself as a poet: in 1968 he'd published a collection of verse, but the critics had savaged it. This was one of the great disappointments of his life. Until then, he'd labored under the delusion that his success was the result of his talent for infusing elements of poetry into his music, but the failure of his book forced him to confront the fact that the public was far more interested in the spectacle of his madness and maleness than his art.

In Paris, Jim made a short-lived attempt to cut down on his boozing and do some work on a book he'd been planning about the Miami debacle, but he quickly grew bored with both pursuits. Unencumbered by the burden of being Jim Morrison, Rock Star, he devoted himself to full-time boozing, with a group of trendy friends, while his common-law wife Pamela Courson, herself a heroin addict, searched out her own brand of thrills in the Parisian netherworld of junkies, hookers and transvestites. Morrison spoke little, drank a lot and fell out of second-story windows on occasion. Even in retirement, he seemed hell-bent on destroying himself. He was to succeed in that endeavor within a mere six months.

For reasons that remain unclear, Morrison's death was not made public until six days after it occurred. His manager, Bill Siddons, explained that he and Jim's wife had delayed the announcement in the hope of avoiding the "notoriety and circus-like atmosphere that had surrounded the deaths of Janis Joplin and Jimi Hendrix." But naturally, the mysterious manner in which Morrison's death was handled has made it (after Elvis's) just about the most rumor-ridden and talked-about rock death of all time.

Siddons had first gone to Paris after receiving a panicky call from Pamela Morrison. When he arrived at the couple's flat, he found her with a sealed coffin and a death certificate bearing Morrison's name. The official cause of death was listed as a heart attack. Pamela allegedly told Siddons that she had awakened at 4 A.M. to find Morrison coughing up blood and complaining of chest pains. Inexplicably, he sought to ease his discomfort by taking a bath. A few hours later, she awakened again to find him still gone from the room. She went into the bathroom where she discovered his lifeless body sitting up in the tub.

Despite the official story, some artists and filmmakers with whom Morrison socialized in Paris contend that he died of a heroin overdose. They believe that he had probably snorted a lethal hit of smack — in the presence of either his wife or his friends — at the Circus, a Parisian nightclub known to be a major heroin emporium. It has been said that Morrison collapsed while still at the Circus, whereupon his companions helped him back to his hotel and placed him in a bathtub packed with ice in a futile attempt to revive him. Some even claim to have seen an unconscious Morrison being carried out of the club on the night of his death.

Because there is no concrete proof that the grave which bears Morrison's name actually contains his body, another theory has evolved which holds that Morrison is not really dead at all, that with the help of his wife, he created an entirely new identity and is now living out his life as someone else. A poet perhaps. This is the story his fans would most like to believe.

If those in the Doors' inner circle know what really happened to Jim Morrison, they're not talking. The one person who could have shed some light on the mystery was Pamela Courson Morrison, but she herself died three years after Jim, of a heroin overdose.

In the meantime, Jim Morrison has never been bigger. The fascination with the Morrison myth has pushed sales of Doors reissues to between 300,000 and 400,000 a year, and Morrison's exploits have been converted into a deliciously lurid biography that is soon to become a major motion picture. As *Rolling Stone* so aptly put it in a 1982 cover story come-on, "Jim Morrison: he's hot, he's sexy . . . he's dead."

Left: Gene Vincent with the Blue Caps; *middle:* with Lennon and McCartney at the Cavern; *right:* a year before his death

Legendary rockcat Gene Vincent was born in 1935 to a dirt-poor family in Norfolk, Virginia. At the age of fifteen, he left home to enlist in the navy. After putting in five years there, he suffered a mishap that would alter the course of his life: while walking across the base, he was struck by a staff car, which inflicted multiple fractures to his left leg. (When referring to his injury in later years, he often attributed it to a motorcycle crash or a bullet wound sustained in Korea.) Following a year-long hospital confinement, he was given an honorable discharge and sent home with two Distinguished Service medals, his shattered leg still in a cast. To occupy his recuperation time, he organized a band for a local radio station. While there, he cut a little ditty he'd co-authored entitled "Be-Bop-A-Lula." The song was subsequently released by Capitol and went on to sell nine million copies. More hits followed, along with a triumphant appearance on *The Ed Sullivan Show*. Fresh out of the navy, his leg only partially healed, a bewildered Gene Vincent suddenly found himself catapulted from obscurity to full-blown rock stardom. But like many early rock immortals, his success was fleeting; he achieved only a handful of hits during his moment of glory.

Bad luck and managerial blunders plagued Gene Vincent's short-lived career. To begin with, Vincent never got the hang of dealing with the media; an early tiff with Dick Clark, for example, resulted in his being banned from *Bandstand*, a fate worse than death for a rock star at the time. By 1958, he was a virtual outcast in a scene that had come to be dominated by boy-next-door rock attractions like Frankie Avalon and Pat Boone. Then, to make matters worse, the IRS began to harass him for nonpayment of back taxes, and the musicians union revoked his membership. He was eventually forced to seek work abroad.

Late in 1959, Vincent flew to England for a concert tour that was later extended upon the arrival of his pal Eddie Cochran. But several months later, an automobile carrying Gene, Eddie and Eddie's girlfriend crashed on a rainy London street, killing Eddie and further damaging Vincent's leg. Distraught over Cochran's death and his own declining fortunes, Gene used alcohol to help him forget his troubles. Because Vincent was reluctant to have his leg properly treated, it never really mended. His doctors recommended that it be amputated, but Vincent chose instead to live with the pain, even going so far as to incorporate it into his act on occasion: if things weren't going well during a performance, he was not above kneeling on the floor and pulling up his pants to exhibit his mangled limb with its cumbrous brace as a ploy to win over the crowd. Sometimes all his thrashing around during a show caused him so much agony that he would suddenly black out and crumple to the stage. There's a story that once while being carried from the stage on a stretcher after one of these bizarre displays, Vincent suddenly regained consciousness and jumped back into the spotlight to finish his song.

Although Vincent became something of a cult figure in Europe, by the mid-sixties his reputation as a misfit had caught up with him there as it had back home. Some nasty headlines in the British papers resulting from a couple of unpleasant run-ins with the law eventually sent Vincent back to the States to try for a comeback. In California he waxed albums for several different labels, but despite the support of the critics, the sales were minimal at best. His career once again in limbo, he flew back to England for a concert date only to discover that it had been canceled minutes before his arrival (owing to a disappointing advance sale). Heartbroken, he returned to America.

The last years of Vincent's life were spent in a little apartment in West Hollywood where he supported himself by playing local gigs for a few dollars a night. Despite his humbled circumstances, he remained proud — almost arrogant — boasting to his occasional visitors that he'd thrown away more money in his lifetime than most people ever earn. Then, on October 12, 1971, during a visit to his mother-in-law, Vincent sprawled over a coffee table, blood spurting from his mouth. He was rushed to a nearby hospital, but was dead within the hour. Doctors cited an ulcer, brought on by serious depression and heavy drinking, as the cause of death. He was thirty-six years old. Gene Vincent — the idol of everyone from John Lennon to Alice Cooper — was so deeply in debt at the end of his life that the only possessions he had of any real value were his guitar and the black leather jacket he wore to his grave.

Duane... *left:* in the studio with Eric Clapton for "Layla"; *right:* with brother Gregg in the Allman Brothers Band

Duane Allman first won his reputation as master of the slide guitar backing soul stars like Aretha Franklin, Otis Redding and Wilson Pickett in Muscle Shoals, Alabama. Fed up with trying to make a name for himself in L.A. playing psychedelic-style rock, Allman finally achieved the sound he was looking for by joining forces with a Florida band that included Dickey Betts and Berry Oakley. He summoned brother Gregg Allman back from the Coast and the Allman Brothers was born.

After months of fine tuning, the band journeyed to New York to record its first album. *The Allman Brothers Band* garnered superb reviews but only a smattering of sales. Nevertheless, the group's reputation continued to build with the release of a live set at the Fillmore East and Duane's electrifying duet with Eric Clapton on "Layla" in 1970. Before long, gold records followed one after another, and the group was drawing nightly audiences of 10,000, then 50,000 and finally 687,000 at a concert at Watkins Glen, New York. But in October 1971, fate stepped in to claim the life of the Allmans' leader and guiding force in a freak accident. Allman, who had just left the home of Berry Oakley, was dragged fifty feet on his motorcycle after swerving to avoid an oncoming truck. He died on the operating table three hours later. Grief-stricken but determined to carry on, the band went back into the studio to complete *Eat a Peach*, their work in progress. The inevitable notoriety that accompanied Duane's death made it the Allmans' biggest-selling album ever as well as providing them with their only Top Ten single to date ("Ramblin' Man").

Misfortune struck the Allman Brothers Band again just one year later when bassist Berry Oakley, who'd become moody and disconsolate over Duane's death, was killed after his motorcycle plowed into a city bus, three blocks from the site of Allman's crash. (Oakley died of a cerebral hemorrhage after refusing hospital treatment following the collision.) As before, tragedy catapulted the band into headlines, this time permanently cementing their legendary status. Sadly, though, it also sapped the creative energy of the surviving members — especially Gregg Allman, who by this time had already turned to hard drugs to ease the pain of his brother's death.

Keith Relf, for years the driving force behind the Yardbirds, the celebrated British R&B revival group, was electrocuted in his West London home in the spring of 1976. Relf, who had apparently been rehearsing to prepare for a new band he planned to start with his sister, was discovered by his eight-year-old son lying on the floor of his basement holding a live electric guitar. Although Relf had been associated with such supertalents as Eric Clapton, Jeff Beck and John Mayall during his career, none of their stardust ever rubbed off on him. After pushing the Yardbirds through many highs (their hits — "Over Under Sideways Down," "For Your Love," etc.) and lows (the group's perpetual personnel changes and hassles over muscial direction), Relf died in relative obscurity at the age of thirty-three.

Keith Relf

In many ways, Clyde McPhatter, more than anyone else, was the sound of R&B. It was his soaring vocals and droll delivery that created the sexy, insinuating sound of such classics as "Money Honey," and "Have Mercy, Baby." Countless soul singers have acknowledged their debt to his style. To Jackie Wilson, Ben E. King, Marv Johnson and Smokey Robinson, Clyde McPhatter was "The Man."

Like most other R&B stars, McPhatter started singing in church. His professional career began with Billy Ward and the Dominoes, whom he led to R&B chart-topping glory with innumerable hits. When Ward fired him for a minor infraction, Ahmet Ertegun bagged him for Atlantic. Once there, he formed the Drifters and scored several of his best-known hits. Then, like another well-known rock'n'roll singer, he was drafted into the army at the height of his success. "It was his dream," recalls Jerry Wexler, who produced several of McPhatter's greatest recorded performances, "to transcend the R&B category and take a place in show biz alongside Perry Como and Nat Cole." Thus did McPhatter begin to spurn the funk that had made him famous in favor of a more mainstream approach.

Although his material grew increasingly saccharine, Clyde went on to score the biggest hits of his career in the years following his return from the service, finally winning his first gold record for "A Lover's Question" in 1958. By the sixties, however, his sanitized brand of soul was no longer fashionable, despite the fact that covers of his old fifties hits were providing British rockers with a multitude of new ones. Always a loner, McPhatter began to withdraw even more from his friends and mentors in the music business. Ultimately, he found solace in the bottle. His performances (mostly small club dates and rock'n'roll revivals) grew more erratic and undependable. There was no guarantee that he could make it to the end of a set — if he bothered to show up at all. He made a few tentative attempts at recording during this period, bouncing from one label to another. Sadly, his last sessions at Mercury exhibited almost nothing of his former glory. McPhatter died in 1972 of a variety of ailments — liver, heart and kidney diseases among them — brought on by heavy alcohol consumption. He was forty-one.

Clyde McPhatter ... *top:* during his hit-making period; *middle:* schmoozing with Ahmet Ertegun; *bottom:* a year before his death.

The Temps

Paul Williams, onetime charter member of the Temptations, died from a gunshot wound in August of 1973. The thirty-four-year-old singer's body was found slumped in his car, just two blocks from the Motown studios where he and the Temps had begun their recording career ten years earlier. His hand still grasped the revolver that had administered the fatal shot.

Williams, whose booming baritone had helped to create the distinctive Temptations sound on such hits as "The Way You Do the Things You Do," had been forced to leave the group in 1971. Plagued by heavy drug and alcohol problems, he was $80,000 in debt at the time of his death. Although rumors of mob involvement circulated at the time, Williams's history of emotional disturbance and the pat look of the death scene led Detroit police to conclude that his gunshot wound was self-inflicted. Eddie Kendricks, a close friend of Williams's since childhood, has suggested that the pressure on Paul may have become unbearable in part because he — like his fellow group members — had failed to see a proper share of his earnings from the Temps' hit-making years.

Jim Croce was thirty years old when the small single-engine aircraft in which he was a passenger crashed into a tree upon takeoff just outside Natchitoches, Louisiana. On tour to promote his second hit single, "Bad, Bad Leroy Brown," Croce had only just come to national prominence after years of struggling to support his family and singing career with part-time gigs as a truck driver and substitute teacher.

The sad story of Jim Croce's death was made even sadder by the news that his wife, Ingrid, at one time his writing and singing partner, was forced to sue the publishing companies that were collecting royalties on her husband's songs for his share of their earnings. Finally, in October of 1983, a Manhattan court awarded Croce's widow, who now lives in San Diego with her young son, just under one million dollars.

Jim Croce

Rory Storme

In the fertile Liverpool music scene of 1960, the one group that seemed most likely to make it was Rory Storme and the Hurricanes.

Rory Storme was a tall blond Liverpool youth with a talent for mixing daredevil stunts with rock'n'roll. His specialty involved shimmying up pillars and hanging from balcony railings, and his occasional falls kept the crowds coming back for more. During the early sixties, Storme developed a friendly rivalry with the Beatles, sharing gigs and late-night carousings with John, Paul, George and the ill-starred Pete Best, in Liverpool and Hamburg. However, as the Beatles' following grew larger, Storme's began to fall off — so much so that when they borrowed his drummer, one Ringo Starr, he really couldn't complain.

Once Beatlemania exploded in 1964, Storme was able to parlay his Cavern credentials into some degree of notoriety. But in spite of the occasional helping hand from Brian Epstein — who'd always felt guilty about pinching Ringo Starr — stardom just wasn't in the cards for Storme. After years of odd jobs and disappointments, he finally lost heart. In June of 1972, he and his mother — both of whom had been despondent since the death of Storme's father several months earlier — were found lying together in their Liverpool flat, partners in an apparent suicide pact.

Almost to the last, Storme had fought to keep his dreams of stardom alive. The year before his death, a part-time gig playing piano with a dance band had landed him at a seaside resort in Majorca, where he chanced to save a woman swimmer from drowning. Immediately following the rescue, Storme blew his last few pennies calling the papers back home in an attempt to squeeze a little publicity out of the event. But sadly, no one recognized his name.

No matter how great his success, it was never enough for Bobby Darin. He boasted that he'd be a legend by the age of twenty-five, but in truth, Darin's notorious ego disguised massive insecurities. He spent most of his life struggling for the public's approval — only to turn his back on it once it was given. The hit records, the Grammy Awards, the Oscar nominations — all lost their value for him the second they were proffered. He always needed to reach out for something more — often for things beyond his grasp. At the time of his death in 1973, he was in the midst of radically revamping his public image for the fifth time in fifteen years.

Bobby Darin had officially become a rock'n'roll star in 1958 with his recording of "Splish Splash." Within a year, he had garnered three gold records and had been voted Grammy Newcomer of the Year. But instead of coasting on his pop success, Darin felt compelled to make the transition to the supperclub circuit. Although only in his early twenties, he was somewhat embarrassed by his teen idol status. He desperately wanted to make his way into show business's Old Guard. It wasn't long before he was firmly entrenched in the expense-account havens of New York and Las Vegas with an act so frenetic that it made Sammy Davis, Jr., look laid back.

Around this time Bobby also fast-talked himself into a co-starring role in a big-budget comedy called *Come September* starring Sandra Dee, who would later become his wife. (Before marrying Sandra, Darin had been romantically involved with her mother, Mary.) Although Darin acquitted himself reasonably well in his film debut, coming off something like a young Sinatra, his follow-up roles were silly and flat. That only made him more determined to make it on the big screen. His tenacity eventually paid off when a small role in *Capt. Newman, M.D.* won him an Academy Award nomination for Best Supporting Actor. Unfortunately, the unusually overbearing promo campaign he mounted in his own behalf alienated, rather than won over, Hollywood's Old Guard. Ultimately, Bobby ended up losing not only the Oscar, but his dreams of big-time movie stardom.

In the late sixties, Darin once again went through another major transformation — this time after becoming involved with Senator Robert Kennedy. Suddenly, he was obsessed with the subject of politics — the politics of youth and protest in particular. As the two men grew closer, Darin devoted more and more time to his friend's presidential campaign. When Kennedy was gunned down in Los Angeles, Darin was devastated. Obviously under severe emotional strain, he began to act strangely:

Above: Primming for an appearance on *The Dick Clark Saturday Night Show* with a young Connie Francis; *left:* making his final comeback in 1972

Left: Der Bobby

he threw out the toupee he'd worn since his early twenties and let what was left of his hair grow long; jeans and love beads took the place of his tuxedos and shiny suits. Although he continued to make TV and nightclub appearances, his repertoire came to consist mostly of folk and protest songs, usually of a political nature. One night in 1969 during an appearance on *The Tonight Show* he startled Johnny Carson by describing his recent religious rebirth and the ghostly visions he'd had of the late Robert Kennedy. There was no doubting his sincerity, but that just made him all the more difficult to watch. The old finger-popping hipster looked sadly out of place in his new role as an aging flower child.

Eventually, Darin's bookings began to fall off, convincing him that the time had come to drop out of the Hollywood Rat Race. In 1969 he headed for Northern California where he lived in a trailer home in Big Sur for a year, seeing few people and spending most his time in the local library trying to catch up on the education he'd missed as a kid. Darin also hoped to use his self-imposed exile to come to terms with several emotional jolts he'd suffered during the previous few years — the Kennedy assassination, the breakup of his marriage and the discovery that he was illegitimate. (Until his thirtieth birthday, Darin believed that his mother was his sister. "I wanted to spare him being illegitimate," his mother said recently. "But he was thinking about going into politics and I didn't want it to get out that way.") Instead, he ended up unhappy and in serious money trouble, most of his savings having been depleted by an unsuccessful film venture. Darin eventually returned to L.A. where he played small clubs — still singing country and folk. He formed his own record label and released *Born Robert Walden Cassotto*, an album filled with bleak, self-conscious Rod McKuen-style poetry and songs laced with political comment.

Around this time Bobby started having serious trouble with his heart. A victim of rheumatic fever as a kid, Darin had always been sickly, despite the tough exterior he liked to project. His first open heart surgery involved a complicated procedure in which two valves were replaced. That operation behind him, Bobby dusted off his tuxedo and ring-a-ding style and bounced back into high-paying club dates. His manager would later say of this period: "Bobby had reconciled in his heart that it isn't the kind of clothes you wear, it's who you are in your own heart."

As Darin's career began to pick up steam, his health worsened. Still plagued by the shortness of breath and general malaise that had led him to seek his first operation, he ultimately contracted septicemia — an inflammation of the blood vessels surrounding the heart. On December 19, 1973, he entered the hospital for his second round of surgery. After eight hours on the operating table, Bobby Darin's heart finally gave out. He was thirty-seven years old.

Two days following Gram Parsons's death from a heroin overdose in Joshua Tree, California, a coffin bearing his remains was hijacked from the Los Angeles Airport by two men claiming to be hearse drivers from a local funeral home. A short time later, one Phil Kaufman, a former roadie and fixit man for Parsons, was charged with the theft. Kaufman, a tattooed biker type who was known to be an ex-con and erstwhile associate of Charlie Manson, readily acknowledged intercepting the coffin and transporting it back to Joshua Tree where he'd burnt it on a massive slab of stone called Cap Rock. He denied rumors that the cremation had been part of an occult funeral rite, saying instead that it had been carried out at his late friend's behest. Although several of Parsons's friends corroborated Kaufman's story, the singer had left nothing in writing to indicate that these were indeed his last wishes or to designate Kaufman as his official executor.

Parsons's wife and family suspected that Kaufman and his accomplices had acted on less noble sentiments — namely their resentment at having been excluded from what was intended to be the family's private burial rites. Open warfare broke out between Kaufman and Parsons's second wife, Gretchen, who accused him of stealing what was left of her dead husband's money and personal possessions. Kaufman admitted having given two guitars to Parsons's daughter (by another woman), whom he considered to be Parsons's only legal heir. As for the missing cash, he managed to convince police that it was money owed him by Parsons at the time of his death. He later retaliated against the widow by regaling the rock press with the painful details of the couple's last unhappy months together. The whole business cast a weird and sickening pall over events that were already sufficiently grim.

Gram Parsons remains an undefined and enigmatic figure — thanks in no small part to the distance he maintained between himself and even his closest friends, and his talent for embroidering the truth. The sketchy bio of his early years includes a father who sang country music and died in a Georgia jail, a stretch at Harvard as a theology student, and a stint with his own Cambridge-based bluegrass group. Sheltered from the day-to-day demands of survival by a hefty trust fund, Parsons seems to have ambled lazily through life. After leaving Harvard, he spent some time experimenting with LSD, and then rejected all drugs completely in conjunction with a renewed interest in religion. In 1968, he gained acceptance into the high-flying Byrds only to abandon them a scant three months later on the eve of a South African tour, owing to his disapproval of apartheid. His subsequent sojourn with the Flying Burrito Brothers lasted until 1970 when he decamped to the French Riviera with Keith Richards and the Rolling Stones. There, at Richards's estate, Nellcote, Parsons schooled Richards in the subtleties of honky-tonk while Richards in turn turned him on to the Good Life.

Stories of orgiastic revels and jetset-style highs began to filter back to Parsons's friends at home.

Though Parsons was said to have a pronounced melancholy bent — a quality that permeates his work — no one close to him has shed any light on the fears or frustrations that might have led him to heroin. His friend Keith Richards said later that Parsons was "one of those guys who couldn't stand the thought of growing old — the kind who's determined to pack it in before 30." If that's true, he accomplished his goal, having beat that deadline by a good four years.

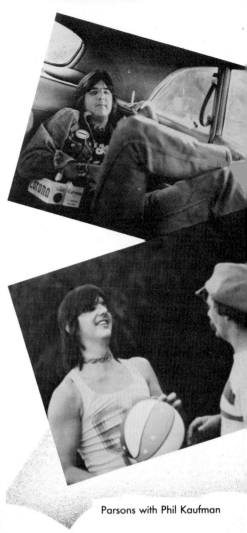

Parsons with Phil Kaufman

The Grateful Dead

In March of 1973, twenty-seven-year-old Ron (Pigpen) McKernan, the notorious hard-drinking, hard-living singer/organist of the Grateful Dead, succumbed to complications arising from cirrhosis of the liver. Or as Jerry Garcia put it later, "He was a juicer, man. It did him in."

McKernan had been one of the Dead's primary creative forces during the halcyon days when the group presided over the famous San Francisco Acid Tests. Shy and soft-spoken offstage, Pigpen's biker leathers and psychedelic grubbiness nonetheless made him a symbol of the Dead's outlaw image. His decline, and the band's struggle to compensate for it, precipitated a major shift in both the Dead's musical and philosophical direction.

Although McKernan's physical deterioration isolated him from the Dead's social and professional milieu during the last years of his life, his funeral was attended by more than two hundred cronies from the group's fabled Fillmore days, including Ken Kesey and a flock of local Hell's Angels. Despite the high hipness quotient of the mourners, the proceedings were conducted strictly by the Book — in accordance with the family's wishes. Afterwards, Garcia was succinct as ever in assessing Pigpen's last gig: "The services were a bummer, man. Strictly for the straights."

someone). He told the crowd, "Now the trick with wearing a suit like this is the same trick as living in America today, which is how to come to terms with wealth." But the audience wasn't about to be seduced by this imposter who called himself Phil Ochs. They'd come out to spend an evening with the Conscience of the Movement — the last of the genuine folk philosophers. Instead, they found an overweight poseur wearing a shitkicker's idea of a monkey suit. Ochs managed to sing a few songs despite the constant catcalls, but the concert was a disaster. When he finally fled the stage, a heckler shouted, "Phil Ochs is dead."

In many ways, Ochs was right on target in guessing that popular tastes would return to primal rock in the seventies. He was just a mite too early (which is sometimes worse than being too late). But then again, the time would never have been right for Phil Ochs to become Elvis Presley. The sensitive, neurotic kid from Queens was entirely too conscious of what it *meant* to be Elvis to get anywhere close to becoming the real thing.

People who knew Ochs during those years say that he first began to crack during the Chicago Seven conspiracy trial, where he testified for the defense. The real problem for Ochs, as for so many other activists from the sixties, came when the struggle was over, after the U.S. withdrawal from Vietnam and Nixon's downfall. Without a cause to champion, he was just another forlorn folkie singing old labor songs.

The heckler who'd yelled out that Phil Ochs was dead was very close to the truth. Phil Ochs was actually dying. His physical deterioration accelerated following the Carnegie Hall debacle. Always an enthusiastic drinker, he soon became an out-and-out lush. Tormented by paranoid delusions, he took to wandering the streets and sleeping wherever he landed. He ranted and raved and carried dangerous weapons, which he sometimes used to threaten old friends. Finally, in 1974, he ended his misery by hanging himself in his sister's Long Island home.

Not long before he died, Ochs drunkenly dictated his obituary into a friend's tape recorder: "Although [Phil Ochs] had some brilliant ideas . . . and a couple of good songs, like 'Crucifixion' and 'Changes,' he was no longer needed and useful. And he was too embarrassing at parties."

God bless the troubadour who tries to be a star.

Phil Ochs had a thing about Elvis. Although his popularity in the folk world was second only to Dylan's, deep down inside what he really wanted was to stand center stage in Elvis's famous gold lamé suit and make the girls scream. As Ochs's career began to flounder, this dream grew into an obsession. One night in 1970, he finally got to realize his fantasy. Dressed in a gold evening suit from Nudie, Elvis's favorite costumier, Ochs made his debut as a rock'n'roll singer at Carnegie Hall. But as he launched into old Holly and Presley hits, the audience began to boo and someone called out, "Where's Phil Ochs?" Phil was ready for this reaction — he had his reply all worked out. He explained to the angry crowd that the answer to the world's problems lay in merging politics with rock'n'roll. That what the counterculture needed to survive was a leader who was a combination of Ché Guevera and Elvis (just stopping short of saying that *he* was that

The Average White Band

206

Cass Elliot once jokingly told a reporter, "Pop music is just long hours, hard work and lots of drugs." But it wasn't the hours or the work or the drugs that killed Mama Cass — or was it? For years, it has been believed that she died after choking on a ham sandwich and subsequently inhaling her own vomit. But in the spring of 1981, her erstwhile colleague, Papa John Phillips, told the press that Cass had in fact died of a heroin overdose. There was speculation at the time that Phillips was only trying to divert attention away from his own ongoing *tsouris* — a possible prison term of up to fifteen years for conspiracy to distribute narcotics. Even so, this OD story had been floating around in rock circles for years.

Hard as it may be to swallow the idea of Cass Elliot as a heroin addict, she'd certainly suffered enough frustrations with her career to make her seek an escape — especially after the bitter breakup of the Mamas and the Papas. It was then, in 1968, that Cass had ill-advisedly agreed to launch her solo act in Las Vegas — for what was at the time an unprecedented amount of money, more than almost any other star in the history of that high-rolling town. The trouble for Cass came in living up to the fee. Press coverage of her debut began to accelerate when she announced that she was embarking on a serious crash diet to slim down for the engagement. Her weight dropped from 285 to 175 in a matter of months. But she also ended up with massive health problems — mononucleosis, hepatitis and tonsillitis among them. By the time opening night rolled around, she was a wreck. Her physical condition was further aggravated by a paralyzing case of nerves brought on by all the attention she'd been getting in the papers. Only twenty minutes after her opening song, she stopped the show and fled to her dressing room where she collapsed from nervous exhaustion. The rest of the run was canceled, unleashing a torrent of unflattering publicity. Cass went underground for a while.

In 1969 she accomplished a well-received comeback with a successful solo album and a TV special. However, a lackluster album duo with British rocker Dave Mason got mixed reviews from the press and an even weaker reception from her former fans. During the next few years, Cass was able to bolster her career with appearances on TV shows like *The Tonight Show* and *Hollywood Squares*; her decision to trade her hippie earth-mother image for show-biz glitz may have lost her some fans from the old days, but at least she was in demand again.

On the night she died, Cass had just completed a triumphant concert date at the London Palladium — complete with a final standing ovation. Said to be in high spirits, she returned to the borrowed flat of friend Harry Nilsson (some reports placed her at a London hotel) where she was visited by several friends who stopped by to offer their congratulations. The next morning her lifeless body was found in the bedroom. Soon afterward, a spokesman for the London coroner's office articulated the ham-sandwich theory to the press. A week later, however, the coroner revised his verdict and declared the thirty-one-year-old singer to have been a victim of a heart attack, noting that the

"heart muscle had turned to fat due to obesity." (This is the theory that Cass's former colleague Michelle Phillips insists is true — despite her ex-husband's allegations of drug abuse.) And yet, it's the ham sandwich story that's stuck.

Maybe someday the truth about what happened to Mama Cass Elliot will finally be revealed. Until then, we'll just have to wait for the movie. After many years of unfriendly negotiation with John Phillips, Lea Kunkel seems finally to have secured the rights to her late sister's story, which she will co-produce with ex-Mama Michelle Phillips.

Remember all those headlines that trumpeted the death of Average White Band drummer Robbie McIntosh, and the near-fatal overdose of guitarist Alan Gorrie? Actually, the reason that the story created such a flap had less to do with the tragedy that had befallen the two musicians than to the fact that Gorrie had been nursed back to life by none other than the ubiquitous Cher. For weeks after, the *Enquirer, Star, Globe*–type sheets breathlessly recounted the details of how the pop queen had rushed the ailing Gorrie to her Beverly Hills home, where she spent hours walking him around and packing him in ice to prevent unconsciousness. (Gorrie has since downplayed Cher's Florence Nightingale role in his recovery.)

Not so lucky was Robbie McIntosh, twenty-four, who, after becoming ill, was taken back to his Hollywood hotel room, where he died the following day. Of course, the big question on the collective mind of the media wasn't how or why the musicians had gotten hold of the lethal combination of heroin laced with strychnine, but how Cher, once an outspoken antidrug crusader, had managed to get involved in such an unsavory scene. Had the recently divorced (from Sonny Bono) TV and pop personality succumbed to a life of rock and roll debauchery now that she was out there on her own?

Cher answered some of these questions herself when she took the stand at the grand jury investigation into McIntosh's death several months later.

She explained that she had been one of a party of people who had gone to the home of up-the-establishment entrepreneur Stuart Moss (founder of the bogus Freelandia Airlines, the so-called not-for-profit airline club) to celebrate the band's sold-out gig earlier that evening at the Troubadour. During the course of the evening's festivities, the host produced a vial of white powder which his guests assumed was cocaine but was in fact heroin. When Gorrie and McIntosh became violently ill after snorting it, Cher called her physician to describe their condition. She was advised that Gorrie could be revived by traditional resuscitation methods but that McIntosh needed immediate medical care. According to her testimony, she left to take Gorrie to the Bono mansion with Moss's assurances that he would get McIntosh to a hospital promptly. But instead Moss convinced the sick man's wife to take him back to their hotel room. He died there several hours later. Upon hearing the news, Moss — who was already in hot water with the law for his Freelandia scam — fled, reportedly to South America. He eventually came forward to plead guilty to involuntary manslaughter in McIntosh's drug-induced death — a charge that can carry up to a fifteen-year prison sentence in California. However, Moss was given a greatly reduced sentence of 120 days and four years' probation after his probation officer conceded on the stand that he didn't really think he was a threat to society.

Paul Kossoff

During his sojourn with Back Street Crawler and Free, Paul Kossoff gained a reputation as one of the most innovative guitar stylists in rock. But today, unfortunately, Kossoff is remembered more for the bizarre circumstances surrounding his death — or deaths — than for his talent or technique.

In August of 1975, Kossoff went into a coma after complaining of stomach pains. He was rushed to a nearby hospital where, thanks to the determined ministrations of the emergency-room team, he was revived thirty-five minutes later. Although an official hospital statement attributed this scrape with death to a blood clot that had traveled from his leg to his heart, Kossoff later admitted that heavy heroin use was essentially to blame for his various ills. He credited his addiction to an identity crisis he'd suffered following the demise of Free.

Once out of the hospital, Kossoff assured interviewers that he was a new man. "It feels like closing the book on that whole period of my life," he said, "closing the book on drugs, and on letting people down." Seven months later, Kossoff was dead — this time for good. The twenty-five-year-old musician expired in his sleep from heart and kidney failure aboard a New York–bound plane.

The public was shocked in 1970 when a Detroit paper revealed that Florence Ballard, one of the founding members of the Supremes, had been reduced to living on welfare payments following her banishment from Motown. Her unhappy situation was made public two years after her split with the group when the *Michigan Chronicle* discovered her trying to scrape together the change to buy a head of cabbage and a box of cornmeal.

Like Diana Ross, Ballard had been a ghetto kid who'd started her career at Motown by doing errands and occasional backup work. But although she was widely acknowledged as having the best voice of the three, Ballard did not have the patronage of Berry Gordy — unlike Ross, who was to become the focus of a romantic fixation of the Motown boss. Eventually, Ballard and Mary Wilson, the third Supreme, began to realize that as far as Gordy was concerned, Diana Ross *was* the Supremes. Dissension within the group accelerated as Ross's stature increased and the other two were shunted into the background. Ballard's complaints over money and billing became more and more vocal, eventually finding their way into print, and bringing about her ouster. Motown portrayed the split as amicable, attributing Ballard's departure to her dislike of touring.

Because Motown had a policy during the sixties of paying even its biggest stars a small weekly salary along with an occasional perk, Ballard ended up with almost nothing to show for her eight years as a member of a group whose chart standing had been eclipsed only by Elvis and the Beatles, aside from her twelve gold records and a dilapidated pink Cadillac. Claiming she was owed back royalties and a million-dollar settlement for agreeing to leave the group, she filed suit against Motown for $8.7 million in 1971, but the case was dismissed for lack of evidence. Her disappointment at the judgment was compounded by the humiliation she suffered when the details of her financial situation were splashed all over the papers.

Estranged from her husband, Ballard lost her home and was forced to move back to the Detroit housing projects in which she'd lived as a child. During the next few years, she was mugged, robbed and reduced to seeking support for her three children from Aid to Dependent Children. Despite her compromised situation, 1976 found her still dreaming of a comeback. Grossly overweight from years of inactivity, she launched into a crash diet to get herself back into shape, but after a few days, her blood pressure shot up from the shock of the sudden weight loss and, reportedly, from a substantial intake of liquor. Within several weeks of that first physical trauma, the thirty-two-year-old singer was dead following a heart attack.

Although it's been widely rumored that Florence Ballard died in poverty, her sister has since claimed that she was financially secure, having received an "unexplained legal settlement" just before her death. At any rate, her story — with many embellishments (most notably a happy ending) — has since become enormously valuable to two savvy show-biz packagers, David Geffen and Michael Bennett, who used it as the basis for the Broadway hit *Dreamgirls*, the thinly disguised saga of Motown, Berry Gordy and the Supremes.

Florence Ballard (right) with Diana Ross, Mary Wilson, and Barbara Martin of the Primettes

Tim Buckley

Considered something of a musical prodigy as a youngster, Tim Buckley began his professional career while still in high school, and recorded his first album at the age of nineteen. Although he exhibited a precocious grasp of all kinds of music, Buckley, like a lot of other young hopefuls in the early sixties, devoted most of his energies to becoming Bob Dylan. For years, he traveled the coffeehouse and college circuit, gradually building a loyal, if modest, following — which included a number of big-name admirers, such as George Harrison, Eric Clapton and Paul Simon.

It was Buckley's second album, *Goodbye and Hello* (1967), a stunning showcase of his prodigious songwriting talents and three-octave vocal range, that provided his breakthrough, and with it his first moderate-sized hit record ("No Man Can Find the War"). At this point, however, Buckley broke his career's momentum by shifting from folk to experimental jazz. His new sound involved a good bit of dissonant noodling and unstructured improvisation embellished with gongs, flutes and his own ear-splitting yodels.

Baffled at first by this avant-garde posturing, Buckley's folkie fans eventually became hostile toward his new musical direction. Buckley in turn had little patience with his audience's lack of imagination. At one point when someone in a Philadelphia concert audience took advantage of a lull in the cacophony to call out, "How about 'Buzzin Fly'?" (a Buckley favorite), he testily responded, "How about horseshit?" After three unsuccessful albums and two years of unfriendly audience response, Buckley grew weary of trying to make his followers accept the fact that he was growing up. He dropped from public view during the early seventies, living reclusively with his family and writing movie scripts.

In the spring of 1975, however, Buckley's luck seemed to be changing. First he got word that he was being seriously considered by director Hal Ashby to play the part of Woodie Guthrie in *Bound for Glory*. Then, a June concert date in Dallas turned out to be an unexpected success, with Buckley playing to an enthusiastic sold-out crowd. And yet, less than twenty-four hours after that concert, Tim Buckley was dead from what the L. A. coroner diagnosed as "unspecified causes." Although he had admitted using hard drugs in the past, his friends insisted that he'd been clean for more than a year.

The L. A. police also had their suspicions about the twenty-eight-year-old singer's mysterious demise, but they chose not to pursue an investigation until a week later, when they received a tip that a UCLA graduate student had boasted to friends of being with Buckley on the day before his death. After comparing his story with that of Buckley's wife, the investigators theorized that Buckley had expired after snorting heroin, thinking it to be cocaine.

The student was subsequently convicted of committing "involuntary manslaughter" by virtue of providing the drugs that killed Buckley. However, he received a substantially reduced four-month sentence — with four years' probation — owing to the court's belief that Buckley had inhaled the heroin (which had apparently been casually spread out on a coffee table) without his knowledge.

Backstage during a 1956 tour
date in Long Beach, California

Hamming it up with a hound
dog on the *Steve Allen Show*

Rehearsing with the Jordanaires

Making a hit with
messenger girls during his
first visit to MGM

It seems only fitting that the demise of Elvis Presley, the greatest rock
star of all time, should enter the annals of rock'n'roll as perhaps the most
extreme and bizarre chapter of all. By the end of his life at the age of
forty-two, Elvis, nearly a hundred pounds overweight, had lost virtually
all powers of reasoning. No routine OD, it took eight deadly drugs and a
variety of ailments, including heart disease, hardening of the arteries,
diabetes and a perforated colon to fell the King. In a business where
reckless excess and kinky exits are a matter of course, the abuse that
finally put an end to Elvis's suffering proved that in death, as in life, he
was an impossible act to follow.

Death exposed the truth that lurked behind the Presley legend, revealing
the man to be, in the words of his onetime bodyguard Red West, a "walking pharmaceutical shop who took pills to get up, pills to go to sleep, and
pills to go out on the job," a sexual predator who had as many as fifteen
women a week, and a maniacal gun freak who used automatic rifles to
frighten his friends and lay waste to offending TV sets. Although these
disclosures came as a shock to most folks, the media had been aware of
Presley's deterioration for years, but with few (and generally scabrous)

Knocking 'em dead at the
Mississippi-Alabama Fair in 1956

With Richard Egan
on the set of
Love Me Tender

A recording session in 1972

A mess at one of his last concert dates

One of the many final "tributes" from
family and friends

exceptions, they had preferred to sweep the dirt under the carpet. After all, Presley was a Living Legend. Countless people had a stake in his success. The myth had to take precedence over the truth. Besides, no one wanted to hear that the beloved country boy who'd sung his way up from poverty to pink Cadillacs and antebellum estates was, in reality, a junkie with a strong sadistic streak. When a trio of renegade members of his Memphis Mafia finally came forward to expose the truth about their former employer posthumously, the world listened in rapt attention, but despised them for killing the dream.

As lurid revelations tarnished Elvis's image, his death was transformed into a macabre sideshow, with thousands of hucksters rushing to cash in on the publicity. Fortunes were made in commemorative schlock and dimestore Presleyana. Across the street from Graceland, emporiums sprang up overnight, hawking Presley mugs, rugs, jewelry, T-shirts and a copy of his "last will and testament." One enterprising soul even tried to sell an empty vial of pills purportedly found next to his dead body. Records bearing Presley's name in their titles went gold with dizzying speed. And anyone who'd ever spent ten minutes with Elvis — as well as many who hadn't — declared themselves his intimate friends in order to publish their reminiscences. Among the more imaginative was *Elvis Presley: King of Kings* by Ilona Panta, a psychic who claimed that God personally chatted with her about Elvis and whose book asked the question "Will you be ready when Elvis returns?" And then there was *A Presley Speaks* by Elvis's uncle Vester Presley, official gatekeeper at Graceland, priced at $10 in paperback and $25 for the deluxe boxed edition, which came with an engraved cover and a white satin scarf wrapping.

The predictable media blitz rained endless Elvis articles, editorials, TV panel discussions and tributes down upon the masses. Yet, with all the speculation and rehashing of events, no one got around to addressing the most fascinating question of all raised by Presley's death: whether the King himself was aware of the schizophrenic disjunction between his public image and his private life. A self-styled antidrug crusader, he went so far as to bully an agent's badge out of the Federal Bureau of Controlled Substances at a time when he himself was hooked on amphetamines and barbiturates. At one point he'd even turned his home into an arsenal, with the idea of meting out backwoods justice to local drug pushers whose names he'd obtained from Memphis narcs. He sometimes had to be physically restrained from carrying out his plan.

How did Elvis reconcile his own habit with his vendetta against drug abuse? Perhaps, in his confused mind, the idea of annihilating drug dealers was a symbolic attack, a way of slaying the dragon that was destroying his own life. But it's more likely that he'd worked out his own cockeyed rationale (one familiar to millions of middle-class prescription-drug abusers — like his own mother Gladys, who relied on large amounts of legally prescribed amphetamines to keep her weight down during the last years of her life). Columnist Nancy Anderson recalls several interviews with Elvis during which he spent most of his time railing against narcotic abuse. "I would never touch drugs," he assured her. "The way he figured it," Anderson says, "you got drugs off the street, not the doctor. He campaigned among his friends to get them off 'drugs.'"

Then again, maybe the King had long since given up trying to reconcile real life with the make-believe that had surrounded him since he was a boy. To wit, there's a wonderfully revealing moment in *This Is Elvis*, the elegant documentary of Presley's life, which catches a relaxed Elvis explaining his tardiness to his goon squad by saying that he'd had his "head buried in a beaver." Then appearing to notice the camera and mikes for the first time, he quickly launches into a gospel tune. Watching that scene, it's hard to believe that Elvis Presley wasn't fully aware of the hypocrisy on which his image was built.

It would be convenient to blame Elvis's decline on the bloodsuckers who surrounded him. But the sad truth is that Elvis was a tyrant who banished anyone who challenged his dictums. Indeed, his stepmother, Dee Presley, has declared that "there wasn't a person in the world who would say no to him. If there was a man or a woman strong enough, he'd be alive today." Upon discovering that his father had hired two private detectives to trace the source of his drugs after a near fatal OD, Elvis threatened to bar him from Graceland and cut off his $75,000-a-year salary. Even the loss of his beloved wife Priscilla and his longtime girlfriend Linda Thompson failed to bring about a change of heart. Joe Esposito, Presley's head honcho, once remarked, "He was the Boss. Nobody told him what to do. And anyway, how do you protect a man from himself?"

It's been observed time and time again that Presley was a prisoner of fame. And he was. But he was also a prisoner of his own vanity. In the old days, Colonel Parker had sheltered him from view as a way of titillating the public, but in later years Presley hid himself from adoring fans because he could no longer live up to the image they — and he — had of the King. As he grew older, he became increasingly depressed over the devastating change in his appearance. When he turned forty, he knew he was "gettin' up there" and it hurt. In the end, death relieved Presley of the burden of the public's fantasies. And more importantly, it put an end to the desecration of rock's foremost symbol, restoring him forever to the beautiful young punk of long ago.

Marc Bolan had a burning desire to be famous, a desire that ultimately propelled him out of the teeming streets of London's East End and into a career as a model and later as a Donovan-style rocker. In 1973, he traded his caftans and flower-power ditties for glitter and heavy metal, scoring a slew of hits in the process. His turnabout injected new life and glamour into a scene that had been suffering from a severe case of the doldrums.

Bolan's string of British hits got him and his group T. Rex touted over here as the Next Big Thing from Britain, the next sensation — the "new Beatles" yet. But aside from one hit single ("Bang a Gong"), Bolan never came close to achieving the superstar status that comes with cracking the American market. The critics in this country dismissed his music as teeny-bopper drivel

and Bolan as Donny Osmond in drag. His bitchiness under fire didn't help matters; when not blowing his own horn to reporters, he was forever taking potshots at other, bigger, names. Especially David Bowie. From the beginning Bolan's main problem was living up to his own hype. By the time he toured America in 1974, he'd already become something of a has-been and many of his dates had to be canceled to avoid the embarrassment of half-filled halls. As he struggled for recognition on these shores, his standing at home began to falter. In 1975, he fled to the Bahamas to seek relief from the British income tax and nervous exhaustion brought on by what he later described as "life lived in a twilight of drugs, booze and sex."

Attracted by the energy of the expanding punk movement, he returned to England where he attempted a comeback two years later. But Marc Bolan represented everything the punk movement detested — it was too late for him to ride the New Wave. His career permanently crippled, Bolan once again lapsed into inactivity and drink. It was at this melancholy juncture that he was killed when the car in which he was riding (his girlfriend, disco singer Gloria Jones, who was later charged with drunk driving, at the wheel) smashed into a tree. Bolan sang his swansong just several days before his twenty-ninth birthday.

Marc Bolan: too much
success and not quite enough

Ronnie Van Zant, the lead singer and guiding light behind Lynyrd Skynyrd, liked to say that he wanted to die with his boots on. And so he did — in a plane crash just outside a little town called McComb, Mississippi. Van Zant had been sleeping on the floor of the group's leased twin-engine prop plane when the passengers were instructed to return to their seats to prepare for an emergency landing. He was killed instantly by a single head injury when the pilot crash-landed in a swamp. Of the twenty-six people aboard the plane, six died — including Van Zant, guitarist Steve Gaines, his sister Cassie, the group's assistant road manager, the pilot and co-pilot. Nineteen others were seriously injured. The hardworking Southern band, which had traveled three hundred days out of the previous year, was on the first leg of an American tour that would have kept them on the road for almost five months. Ironically, Skynyrd's crew had decided to trade in the thirty-year-old plane, which had already begun to show alarming signs of wear and tear, at their next stop. The caravan was celebrating their last night on board with a farewell bash when the engine began to sputter.

The death of Ronnie Van Zant is another of those incalculable losses to rock'n'roll. Charismatic without being a pinup boy, he had both the talent

Lynyrd Skynyrd

and the instincts that make a superstar. If he laid on the shitkicker routine a little thick, it was only because he knew how important image was to rock legend. His boasts of brawls and marathon boozing may all have been true, but behind the swagger and gut bucket vocals lay a sensitive artist whose ballads are some of the most lyrical to be found in country rock. With Van Zant's death and the subsequent demise of Lynyrd Skynyrd, the creative impetus of Southern rock stumbled. Though others would flaunt the stars and bars on the concert trail, none would ever better the legacy left by Duane Allman and Ronnie Van Zant.

Donny Hathaway

Donny Hathaway's musical gifts were so dazzling that they stunned even the most seasoned music-biz pros. During his short career, he was sponsored by such luminaries as Roberta Flack, King Curtis and Ahmet Ertegun. Raised by his grandmother, gospel singer Martha Pitts, Hathaway started singing publicly at the age of three. By the time he was twenty-two, he was producing the likes of Aretha Franklin and Jerry Butler. Public acclaim came in the form of two gold records and a Grammy nomination for his vocal collaboration with Flack on "Where Is the Love" and "The Closer I Get To You."

Like everything else in his life, the end came too soon for Hathaway. The thirty-three-year-old singer was killed after falling fifteen stories from the window of his New York hotel room. His death was later ruled a suicide after it was discovered that his door had been bolted from the inside.

Photos from left: as a winsome teenager in 1964; with the group in 1968; as Uncle Ernie in *Tommy*; overweight and wasted the year he died

By all accounts — including his own — Keith Moon was one of the most beloved figures in the rock world. A mad-dog exhibitionist who would do anything for a laugh, Moon was an inspired lunatic who steadfastly refused to grow up. This made him a great favorite with the fans — especially teenage boys. Even as he grew older, richer, and more desperate for attention, he remained one of them. In many ways, Keith Moon never matured beyond that day in 1962 when, at the age of fifteen, he first sat in on the drums with the East End surf group that would later become the Who.

Stories of Moon's stunts are legion; they include the time he almost drowned after driving a Lincoln Continental to the bottom of a hotel pool, and another, when he was almost shot by a security guard while crawling along the window ledge of Mick and Bianca Jagger's eleventh-floor hotel suite. In 1972, he was arrested for holding up a post office with a water pistol, and he once had himself kidnapped at gunpoint from a busy London street as a publicity stunt. Over the years, he demolished countless drum sets, hotel rooms (thereby earning the Who a lifetime ban from the Holiday Inns of America), and one expensive car after another. After he moved to America, his Malibu neighbors grew accustomed to the sight of Moon, dressed in a Nazi uniform, passed out face down in the sand.

For all his charm and wit, Keith Moon could be as dangerous to those around him as he was to himself. In 1976, for example, he accidentally killed his chauffeur, Cornelius Boland, whom he ran over while trying to escape a mob of fans. (Moon pleaded guilty to drunk driving; the charges were dismissed.) And Peter Townshend believes that an explosive Moon had set off near him during a performance was responsible for partially deafening him in one ear. He said later, "Keith was a very positive musician, a very positive performer, but a very negative animal. He needed you for his act — on and off stage."

Not surprisingly, Moon's maniacal bent exacted a drastic toll on his health. He broke his collarbone, spine, both ankles and wrists, and lost the use of two fingers during his days on the road. By the end of his life, chronic drinking and assorted battle scars had transformed the puckishly good-looking boy into a bloated creature who looked decades older than his thirty-one years.

Ironically, Keith Moon died during a period of protracted good behavior. Plans for an upcoming winter tour, and a part in Monty Python's *Life of Brian*, had given him the incentive to spend several weeks drying out at a posh sanatorium. On the last night of Moon's life, he spent an evening of uncharacteristic calm, attending a screening (of *The Buddy Holly Story*) with Paul and Linda McCartney, and his fiancée, Swedish model Annette Walter-Lax. Thirteen hours later, he was dead from an overdose of a sedative called Heminevrin, which he'd been taking to facilitate alcohol withdrawal and put a lid on his manic behavior.

Lowell George, guitarist, singer, songwriter, soul and wit of the late lamented cult band Little Feat, was a brilliant, lovable bear of a man whom Jackson Browne once dubbed "the Orson Welles of rock." George died on June 29, 1979, at age thirty-four in an Arlington, Virginia, hotel room of either heart failure or a drug overdose, depending on whose version you believe. The party line (and official postmortem) is that George's ticker failed the morning after a particularly exhausting concert performance in Washington, D.C. It's hardly an implausible story — George was tipping the scales at a dangerous three hundred pounds at the time and had suffered a nasty bout of hepatitis the year before. But the underground vibe, bolstered by a few newspaper obits, credits an OD as the cause of death and points to reports that the drugs (mostly prescription) that were spotted in George's room when his body was first discovered were gone when police arrived. (Of course, a *third* possibility is that the *combination* of drugs, a strenuous performance and George's physical condition may have caused his heart to short circuit.)

Those who knew him called Lowell George the best. Singer Bonnie Raitt said George "was the best singer, songwriter and guitar player I have ever heard, hands down, in my life." California born, the son of a Hollywood furrier-to-the-stars, he made his show biz debut at six in a harmonica duet with his brother on *The Ted Mack Original Amateur Hour.* (The boys finished second to a Hungarian acrobat trio.) His first band lost its record contract after only one flop single. Later, he did some time with the Mothers of Invention, but when George played "Willin' " for his boss, Zappa fired him and ordered him to start his own band so he could do it right. That band, Little Feat, made three universally acclaimed albums, broke up, reformed, made a few more critical winners, and broke up again. By 1979, they had only one gold album to show for their efforts, the double live *Waiting for Columbus.* It is typical of the group's jinxed karma that George died in the middle of what was shaping up to be a triumphant tour to promote his eagerly awaited solo debut, *Thanks I'll Eat It Here.*

What little public recognition George and company achieved brought its own special problems. At one point, it was revealed that one member of the group's entourage was allegedly tied in with one of L.A.'s big-time cocaine dealers. There was also a great deal of gossip regarding George's so-called excessive behavior — although given the hefty work schedule of Feat records and tours, sessions and outside production (including LPs by Bonnie Raitt and the Grateful Dead), it's hard to believe that he had time for much else.

And finally, there are the aforementioned rumors as to the cause of his death. But perhaps George summed it up best at the end of "Crazy Captain Gunboat Willie," when he sang, "Don't believe, no don't believe / Don't believe everything you hear."

Lowell George with Little Feat

and performing as a single

Chicago

In what was later ruled an accidental death, Terry Kath, the thirty-two-year-old lead guitarist and principal soloist for Chicago, shot himself to death — reportedly while engaging in a game of Russian roulette. Distraught over conflicts within the band and the ouster of the group's producer/mentor, James William Guercio, Kath was described by his former colleagues as chronically depressed. Overweight and insecure about holding on to his stardom, Kath had taken to playing around with guns during the last several years of his life, despite the group's vociferous disapproval. Drummer Danny Seraphine (who discovered his body) said later, "[Terry] was never really happy with himself, never content. He was always searching, and at the end he didn't like what he found."

Sid Vicious

It might be stretching a point to call Sid Vicious a rock star; by his own admission he'd only just learned to play his bass guitar a few weeks before the notorious Sex Pistols tour of 1978. Yet to many people, Sid remains the quintessential Punk primarily because he didn't just spout off about murder and mayhem, he made them a way of life. Sid's rock star status derives less from mere musical accomplishments, than from the part he played in the grisly death of his girlfriend Nancy Spungen and his own flamboyant exit a few months later.

Sid and Nancy had been together since the spring of 1977 when she'd flown over to London (on money she'd earned as a topless dancer) for the express purpose of landing one of the members of the up-and-coming Sex Pistols. (She'd originally set her sights on Johnny Rotten, but settled for Sid when Johnny was otherwise engaged.) It is believed that Nancy was already caught up in a heavy heroin habit when she met Sid, and that in fact it was she who turned him on. In any case, Sid took to junk with a religious fervor, once going so far as to use a doctored ball-point pen cartridge in place of a syringe after manager Malcolm McLaren confiscated his works.

Sid and Nancy became devoted to smack and to each other despite the fact that Nancy was not particularly well received by the rest of the band. She was so unpopular, in fact, that McLaren tried — unsuccessfully — to have

her kidnapped and sent back to America. He did succeed, however, in preventing Nancy from accompanying Sid on the American tour. Nancy got her revenge by getting Sid hooked again after he'd gone through two weeks of pre-tour detox.

The Sex Pistols were touted as the Next Big Thing when they came to America. Their contrived hostility and shockingly bad manners created a landslide of publicity in the press. But the circuslike hype ended up reducing the tour to a traveling freak show. By the the time the smoke had cleared, the group had managed to incur the wrath of not only the straights but the punk community as well — which accused it of making a joke out of a serious musical movement with its posturing and cheap theatrics.

Consequently, things were far from rosy when Sid and Nancy returned to the States following a brief post-tour layoff in London. And yet, the lovebirds were talking of marriage by the time they returned from a week's visit with Nancy's parents in Main Line Philadelphia. They set up headquarters in New York's trendy Chelsea Hotel with the idea that Sid would continue to perform as a solo and Nancy would be his manager. The problem was that the star attraction was so bombed on downers at his first few club dates that he never really got around to doing a show. Furthermore, he couldn't play gigs more than a day's travel away from his local methadone clinic without getting a case of the bends. Still, the couple seemed closer than ever despite their troubles, although there was constant discussion between them of death and suicide pacts.

On the last night of Nancy Spungen's life, she and Sid paid a visit to a musician friend to present him with Sid's beloved leather jacket and collection of Sex Pistols clippings. The musician said later that they also showed him a knife with a five-inch blade. The next morning, Nancy's dead body was found propped up beneath the sink in the adjoining bathroom of the couple's hotel suite. The autopsy report showed that she had died from stab wounds made with a five-inch blade. Sid told the police that he couldn't remember anything of the previous night's events, having nodded off early in the evening. However, he was positive that Nancy must have stabbed herself, because she'd been talking about suicide for weeks. The homicide boys were slightly dubious about that one. They charged Sid with murder and carted him off to jail.

Things started looking up for Sid five days later when he was released on $50,000 bail posted by McLaren and taken on as a legal client by the amazing F. Lee Bailey. Sid was then on the loose for two months until allegedly assaulting Todd Smith (Patti's brother) — whereupon he was remanded to Rikers Island. He was set free again, this time in his mother's custody, but within a matter of hours he was dead — the victim of a heroin overdose. Word went out in underground circles that Sid had been stuck with a "hot shot," a lethally pure hit of heroin, by someone wishing to avenge Spungen's murder. But according to his mother, Anne Beverly, he had seen no one since leaving jail. No one except her, of course. The day after her son's death, she told the press: "Someone gave him enough heroin to kill himself. That's as bad as murder."

A year later, Beverly admitted to a London paper that she'd bought the drugs that killed Sid. "I suppose it was fate, really. He died because I tried to help him." Beverly, who was said to have had a close relationship with her son, went on to explain that she'd procured the dope for Sid to keep him from trying to get it himself, thereby risking another arrest. What she didn't realize, she said, was that the heroin she bought was ninety percent pure. As she herself put it, "It was just *too* good."

The L.A. police department closed the file on the death of fifties great Larry Williams just two days after he was found shot to death in the dining room of his plush, two-story home. Calling the shooting an apparent suicide, investigators speculated that Williams (the creator of such classics as "Short Fat Fanny" and "Dizzy Miss Lizzy") had probably been despondent over the recent breakup of his third marriage — or possibly over his failed recording career, which had been derailed by changing musical tastes and a nasty drug bust in 1959.

Aside from a short stint with Epic Records and some occasional freelance production gigs, Williams appeared to have been relatively inactive on the music scene during the sixties and seventies. To the casual onlooker, it would seem that he had every reason to put an end to his misery. And yet, there is considerable evidence to the contrary, leaving the manner of his untimely demise still in question. For one thing, Williams was found wearing a hat and coat as if dressed to go out — an unlikely costume for a man intent on taking his own life. And second, there is the fact that despite his apparent steady run of bad luck, he had been living in high style for years in a posh area of Los Angeles. Furthermore, his family and friends maintained that he'd been his usual upbeat self during the preceding few weeks and they refused to believe that he had taken his own life. In fact, his mother and his lawyer went so far as to suggest to reporters that Williams had been murdered. Not surprisingly, they refused to say why or by whom. Nevertheless, investigators ruled out foul play despite evidence they'd turned up linking Williams to local drug circles and a highly successful prostitution ring.

Larry Williams in 1957 and 1976

Tim Hardin

Although Tim Hardin was only thirty-nine when he died, his death came as no shock to those who'd known him well. On the contrary, most of his friends and associates voiced surprise that he'd lasted as long as he had. Despite a conventional upbringing in Oregon and a stretch in the marines, Hardin was known to have pursued a notoriously reckless life. A heroin addict since sixteen, he made no secret of his longtime romance with liquor and drugs. He unabashedly proffered his junkie credo to an interviewer from *Wet* magazine, saying: "I can watch people die. I've seen people croak and I've thrown them out of the window...out of the window because you don't want the body in the pad. You might get busted for what you're already doing."

Hardin was best remembered as an interpreter of traditional country and folk material, and yet he himself was a gifted and prolific songwriter. But throughout most of his career, even the most knowledgeable fans remained unaware that songs like "If I Were a Carpenter," "Misty Roses" and the magnificent "Reason to Believe" were his creations. His one and only hit record was a song he didn't write — Bobby Darin's "Simple Song of Freedom."

Toward the end of his life, Hardin tended to blame both his personal and professional problems on music-business politics, portraying himself as a victim of industry abuse. But those who knew him say he had only himself to blame for his hard-luck story; they speak of countless record sessions missed or aborted because the drug-blitzed Hardin had nodded out. And those who saw him perform — especially during the last few years of his life — recall an overweight, disfigured junkie stumbling through his own compositions in a stoned-out stupor.

After spending most of his adult life riding the comeback trail, Hardin finally gave up the fight on a sunny California day in 1980. His lifeless body was discovered on the floor of his Los Angeles home. An anonymous caller tipped police to his death.

Led Zeppelin

The run of persistent bad luck that had plagued Led Zeppelin since 1975 — including riots over ticket sales that got the group banned in Boston and a crippling car crash that sent Robert Plant into retirement for two years — culminated in the fall of 1980 with the death of drummer John Bonham, the driving force behind the group for more than twelve years. Bonham choked on his own vomit after downing an estimated forty shots of vodka.

At first there was talk that the group might replace Bonham with Aynsley Dunbar or even Bonham's sixteen-year-old son Jason. But in the end, the boys didn't have the heart to go out and pretend that things were the same. A short time later, they issued a statement which read: "We wish it to be known that the loss of our dear friend and the deep respect we have for his family, together with the sense of undivided harmony felt by ourselves and our manager, have led us to decide that we could not continue as we were."

There was some speculation by the rock press following the announcement that the surviving members of the close-knit group might have believed that their own bad karma — especially their much-flaunted flirtation with the occult — had doomed them to suffer the eternal wrath of the gods. However, though Jimmy Page was briefly a student of black magic and Satanist Aleister Crowley, the group's diabolical image was mostly just so much show biz; in real life the boys were devoted family men who lived quiet lives when not on the road. Although suspicious of outsiders, they were generous to those who did manage to penetrate their ranks. In all the years that Led Zeppelin traveled this country and Europe, the only serious blot on their record was a backstage fracas that occurred when Bonham and the group's three-hundred-pound manager Peter Grant administered a brutal beating to a security guard who had stopped Bonham's son from taking a souvenir placard. Bonham's subsequent conviction for assault and battery resulted in a hasty cancellation of the rest of the tour. And then, as Plant was making plans for a precipitous departure from America, he received news of his own son's death from a mysterious viral infection. It was three years before the group was in any shape to face another round of concert dates in the States. But Bonham died in his sleep on the day the tickets went on sale.

As the ambiguous wording of the group's farewell statement indicates, Led Zeppelin may live to fly another day, but for the time being, Jimmy Page, Robert Plant and John Paul Jones will have to console themselves with their awesome royalties and faded memories of better days.

Making his film debut in *Rock Around the Clock*

Haley during his heyday

Looking very much the same at a *Happy Days* publicity bash in 1978

It's commonly believed that Bill Haley suffered his popular and creative decline good-naturedly, moving gracefully into middle age with few regrets. But, sad to say, that wasn't the case. Like Elvis, Berry, Holly, et al., Bill Haley was a victim of rock'n'roll. In the two decades between the close of his hitmaking period in the fifties and his death from a heart attack in 1981, he languished lonely and embittered, drinking himself into oblivion amidst a stack of moldering summonses for unpaid taxes and alimony. By the end of his life, he had slipped into total madness, according to biographer John Swenson.

Thanks primarily to the blistering riffs of his tenor sax-man Rudy Pompilli, and being in the right place at the right time, Haley got a lot of the credit for inventing rock'n'roll. But, as writer David Hinckley put it, "he was bright enough to ride the wave . . . but not bright enough to control it." By the early sixties, he'd blown everything — his band, his money, and his first marriage. It was around that time that he moved to the border town of Harlingen, Texas, where he lived an intensely private, if not reclusive, life with his second wife. A longstanding dispute with the IRS prevented him from performing in this country, but he continued to tour Britain and Europe until 1976. It was in that year that Pompilli died of cancer, leaving Haley depressed and disconsolate. "I really went into hiding," he said later. "I wouldn't tell anybody I was Bill Haley. I lived in Mexico and fished. I had just enough money to buy frijoles." He agreed to perform again only as a last resort.

It seems strange now to think of millions of teenagers going wild over this paunchy hillbilly with the lacquered kiss curl — even in 1953. Haley himself was as bewildered by the reaction as the rest of the grown-up world. A sweet and introverted man, he often apologized for the ruckus he stirred up by saying, "I'm just a regular guy, trying to earn a living."

However embittered Haley may have become in the end, he was secure in the belief that he would go down in history as the Father of Rock'n'Roll — or so he said in one of the brief telephone interviews he granted during his twenty-year "retirement." And while the critics aren't quite so generous in their assessment of his contribution to rock music and culture, it is generally conceded that Haley was the force that provided the transition between white pop and R&B, and as such paved the way for Presley — the man who would ultimately define rock'n'roll and in so doing make Haley himself obsolete. It was Haley, in fact, who gave Elvis one of his biggest breaks when he allowed him to open a 20,000-seat concert in 1955. Francis Beecher, one of the original Comets, recalls Haley telling Colonel Parker, "Sure, he can do the show. What do I care? He can't hurt *me*."

Photos from left:
Lennon during the Beatles'
Cavern days; Beatle John;   John and Yoko during the
recording of *Some Time in New York City*;

back to black leather for the
Rock & Roll album; John and Yoko
around the time of the release of
Double Fantasy

Elvis Presley died of his own weakness. Jimi Hendrix, Janis Joplin and Brian Jones played the odds of immortality and lost. Buddy Holly simply got on the wrong plane. But John Lennon — a devoted husband and father, an uncompromising artist and, of course, a Beatle — was gunned down in front of his New York apartment building by a man for whom he had autographed an album only a few short hours before — a man police described succinctly as "a wacko with a gun."

The facts nearly defy comprehension. Shortly before 11 P.M. on the evening of December 8, 1980, Lennon and his wife Yoko Ono pulled up in a limousine in front of the Dakota, the exclusive Central Park West building where they lived. They were returning from the Record Plant, the Manhattan studio where they had recorded the album *Double Fantasy* only a few months before. That night, the two had put the finishing touches on a new Yoko single called "Walking on Thin Ice." As they walked up to the Dakota's ornate cast-iron gate, a pudgy young man stepped out from the crowd of Lennon-watchers that usually congregated outside the door, dropped into a "police crouch," and fired several times with a .38 caliber revolver. While Lennon lay bleeding to death, the assailant, a twenty-five-year-old Beatles fan named Mark David Chapman, stood quietly reading a copy of *The Catcher in the Rye*. John Lennon died on the way to the hospital. Mark David Chapman pleaded guilty and got twenty years to life.

What followed demonstrates the incredible emotional impact the Beatles and Lennon in particular had on their fans. Hundreds, sometimes thousands, stood silently behind police barricades across the street from the Dakota in the days that followed. They hung wreaths and messages of love and grief on the Dakota gates, played Lennon and Beatles music on tape recorders, and wept rivers of tears. The Sunday after the shooting, at the request of Yoko, the world held a ten-minute silent vigil in Lennon's memory. From a window in their Dakota apartment, Yoko and the couple's five-year-old son, Sean, watched over 100,000 people gather in New York's Central Park to give peace a chance, if only for those ten quiet minutes.

Amid the mourners, of course, were the money changers. Sensationalist tabloids like the *Star* and the *New York Post* hit a new low when they printed front-page pictures of Lennon's corpse taken the night before in the city morgue. Quickie Lennon paperback bios and lightweight magazine eulogies, consisting mostly of old quotes and old pictures, hit the stands even before the smoke from Chapman's gun had cleared. And when *Rolling Stone* magazine outdid itself with a poignant memorial issue featuring a stunning cover photo of John, naked, lying next to Yoko, curled up in a fetal position, memorabilia vultures outdid themselves by charging up to ten dollars for the issue. Prices for Lennon record collectibles shot up; even Yoko's critically reviled solo records began fetching as much as forty dollars each. With all due speed, EMI immediately announced plans to rerelease all of the Lennon solo works in Britain in a deluxe boxed set. Yet it should be noted that the supply, however exploitative, was only meeting the unprecedented demand

for all things Lennon.

Memorials to John Lennon ranged from the sublime to the ridiculous. The night after the shooting, avant-garde musician Captain Beefheart opened a New York concert with a spontaneous, transcendental sax solo, which, he announced, was "from John, through Don [Beefheart's real name], to Sean." And someone mysteriously pasted mimeographed posters with Lennon's picture and the lyrics to Television's "Little Johnny Jewel" throughout Greenwich Village that same evening. On the first anniversary of his death, the Cincinnati Pops Orchestra staged a hopelessly schlocky memorial concert featuring MOR thrush Roberta Flack and hammy Blood, Sweat and Tears honker David Clayton-Thomas trading choruses on the likes of "She Loves You" and "The Continuing Story of Bungalow Bill."

Subsequent "tributes" included books by an ex-lover and by a psychic who for years was the Lennons' trusted adviser, as well as one co-authored by Peter Brown, former Apple exec and Lennon's best man at his marriage to Yoko. Though told from many different points of view, these tell-all affairs did offer a disconcertingly unified view of a star who, like Elvis, was greatly at odds with his public image — a man who for all his talk of peace and love, for example, could be stunningly cruel to those around him, especially women, whom he sometimes physically abused. All three books portrayed Yoko in varying degrees as a cunning manipulator whose jealousy of her husband's enormous popularity led her to cut him off from his career.

John Lennon once said that the King is always killed by courtiers, who keep him "overfed, overindulged, and overdrunk to keep him tied to the throne." But in giving up his life as a pop star for one as a (very rich) husband and father, Lennon may simply have traded one type of elegant isolation for another — for he was never so disconnected and shielded from the world as during the five "Dakota years." "There's Nazis in the bathroom just below the stairs," he wrote in 1981's "Nobody Told Me," "always something happening and nothing going on."

Two years after Lennon's death, one renegade Dakota courtier, Fred Seaman, declared, "Screw the myth — bring in some reality." Seaman's method of setting the record straight involved stealing Lennon's unreleased recordings, love letters, and diaries which he intended to use (for a price) to establish himself as the ultimate Lennon authority. While most of the material has since been returned and Seaman convicted of second-degree grand larceny, there is still would-be Lennon biographer Albert Goldman to contend with. If he does to Lennon what he did to poor Elvis, we may end up with more reality than we can bear. But even if future revelations offer positive proof that Lennon was less than a saint, he will still rank as the most influential of all pop politicians (greater even than Elvis or Dylan) and his loss the most tragic in a profession littered with untimely passings. And, as with Elvis, tales of his sins and imperfections will recharge public curiosity and make him just that much more fascinating.

Photos from left: pre-dreadlock Marley in the Wailers; back from the dead after an assassination attempt by a gang of marauding gunmen; preaching Rastafarism to a visitor.

In his eulogy of Bob Marley, Rastafarian mystic and former Wailer Peter Tosh said, "Death is not pain because Rastas don't die." And though that might sound like the usual kind of soothing sentiment so often heard at funerals, in fact, millions of people around the world believe that Bob Marley is not dead at all, but somewhere else in another form. During his time on earth, Marley became far more than a performer to his following. He was deemed to have supernatural powers and direct contact with God, a belief which he did little to discourage.

Marley died at age thirty-six of a raging cancer that eventually consumed his lungs, liver and brain. By then, his long, tangled Samson-like dreadlocks — the knotted strands of hair Rastas wear like a badge of courage — had fallen out from the extensive chemotherapy treatments he'd undergone in New York and Germany. As a result of his deteriorating condition, Marley was also forbidden to smoke marijuana, a ban that denied him not just his pleasure, but his religious sacrament as well.

He was born in 1945 in the country parish of St. Anne's, Jamaica (birthplace of Marcus Garvey), the son of a blond, blue-eyed British army captain and a native woman. His mixed ancestry was all too ironically emblematic of the conflict between white cultural imperialism in Jamaica and the nascent African pride movement, a struggle depicted with unflinching passion in Marley classics like "Slave Driver" and "I Shot the Sheriff" (later given watered-down Top Twenty treatment by Eric Clapton). That that conflict haunted Marley throughout his life was evidenced not only in his music but in his attempts to keep his past shrouded in mystery. Until the day he died, he refused to admit that his father was white and insisted that his mother lived in Africa — when in fact she lived in Wilmington, Delaware. (Marley himself spent time in Wilmington during the late sixties working as a waiter.)

Even as a teenager, Marley and his two natty Wailer sidekicks from Kingston's notorious Trench Town ghetto, Bunny Livingston and Peter Tosh, were scoring major Jamaican hits with rebel anthems like "Rude Boy." Marley's rise to prominence outside Jamaica, although initially slow, was inevitable — aided in no small part by his overtly sexual stage presence and his image as a ganja-smoking womanizer. (His countless sexual conquests had become the stuff of rock legend long before he died.)

Marley's success was also augmented by his command of the music business. When he became disenchanted with the parasitic producers and record company sharks who preyed on the Jamaican music industry, he struck a blow for equality and black financial clout by setting up (with the considerable assistance of Chris Blackwell of Island Records) his own label and studio operation, Tuff Gong. His business acumen paid off with two rambling Kingston estates littered with German-made luxury cars, a platoon of hired help and hangers-on, and the children he'd fathered by his many "wives." (Marley's controversial politics later forced him to take up residence outside of Jamaica.)

But whatever earthly pleasures Marley partook of after hours, he nevertheless came to be viewed as a paragon of spiritual and political righteousness, not just within the narrow militant scope of the Rasta rap, but for all of his Third World brethren. While black deejays and programmers in the United States denied their own heritage by branding reggae "slave music," and refusing to play it alongside the penthouse soul of Gamble and Huff, the head Wailer's influence was spreading far beyond the jewel-blue waters of the Caribbean. In 1979, the United Nations awarded him a citation on behalf of the Third World. A year later, the Wailers were the inaugural band at the ceremony marking the birth of the black-ruled African nation of Zimbabwe, the former white-ruled Rhodesia. In pop circles, Marley could count among his most ardent admirers rock aristocrats like the Stones, Paul Simon, Paul McCartney and Stevie Wonder.

Marley's growing influence in pop and political circles brought him international celebrity. It also made him some powerful enemies: in 1976 he was nearly killed when two cars wheeled into the yard of his home bearing gunmen who jumped out and opened fire with automatic rifles. Marley, his common-law wife Rita and his manager Don Taylor all bought bullets. But miraculously, all survived. Two days later, Marley astounded a crowd of 80,000 by appearing at the Smile Jamaica Concert, where he smilingly opened his shirt to exhibit his wounds. Although never proven, it was widely believed that the assassination attempt was the work of the anti-socialist faction that opposed Prime Minister Michael Manley, whom Marley supported.

In the end, however, it wasn't Marley's party affiliations that made him a Third World figurehead, but the strong anti-authoritarian stance he took in his music. It's not for us mere mortals to say whether Marley is now or always was a deity as so many of his admirers believe, but he was a gifted and charismatic performer, one who (despite the fact that he could neither read or write) poetically articulated the sentiments of the largest segment of the world's population. He was also a shrewd self-promoter who amassed an astonishing amount of money, women and fame during his short time on earth — and that's more than enough to make him a god by pop standards.

Mike Bloomfield

On February 15, 1981, the body of Mike Bloomfield, the virtuoso blues guitarist, was found slumped behind the wheel of his car in a quiet residential area of San Francisco. An empty vial bearing a Valium prescription label was found in his jacket and death was later attributed to suicide by an overdose of that drug. Bloomfield was thirty-seven.

The papers carried the usual round of shocked and skeptical reactions to the verdict from the deceased's friends the following morning. His success with a recent one-man show and his prolific album output over the preceding five years were cited as evidence of his positive frame of mind. However, knowing that Bloomfield was a reformed junkie who occasionally fell off the wagon, an anonymous friend has offered up a different scenario for the las night of his life. he suspects that Bloomfield got involved in a social scene where heroin was casually being snorted or skin-popped and was left to die by his frightened companions after collapsing from a lethal injection.

A rich kid from Chicago, Mike Bloomfield had originally been subsidized in his musical aspirations by a 2.5-million-dollar trust fund set up for him by his father. Over the years, he became an expert ethno-musicologist, specializing in folk and blues, who spent much of his time studying esoteric music and searching out the old musicians who still made it. As a kid, he hung out in bars on Chicago's rough South Side learning his craft by playing alongside such blues pioneers as Muddy Waters and B. B. King. By 1965, Bloomfield had joined up with the Butterfield Blues Band where he recreated the electric blues of his idols, always remaining scrupulously faithful to their original version.

In 1966, Bloomfield made his most ambitious try for stardom — he broke away from Butterfield to form his own group, the Electric Flag. But internal dissension shattered the group before it found its groove. After the Flag's demise in 1968, Bloomfield began mainlining heroin, eventually cultivating a serious habit that would stick with him well into the seventies. Before long, his skills began to disintegrate and he devoted less and less energy to his work. He spent his time "watching *The Tonight Show* and shooting dope," until a group of musician friends shamed him into pulling himself together and picking up his guitar. "From then on I vowed never again. It moved me so that these people wanted to see me playing again, it affected my heart tremendously."

But even though he appears to have remained more or less straight from that time forward, Bloomfield could never really regain his momentum. The albums that followed showed little spark, and, as always, he was plagued by the barbs of certain rock critics who saw him as a poseur, diluting the authentic tradition of black music with his blue-eyed soul.

Bloomfield was always completely up-front about acknowledging his journeyman status. Sadly, however, it may have been his undeserved reputation as a dilettante that lay at the heart of both his personal and professional woes. For, to the end, Mike Bloomfield remained the ultimate session man, maker of monumental riffs, but never the star attraction.

In the past the Beach Boys have sometimes seemed to be too wholesome for their own good. Only guiding genius Brian Wilson's prodigious eccentricity saved them from becoming the Cowsills or the Carpenters in the public mind. But as has recently come to light, it turns out that drummer Dennis Wilson was as wildly out of control as his brother, or for that matter any of the all-time rock'n'roll biggies. It took his death while diving from a friend's houseboat off Marina del Rey in the chilling winter waters of the Pacific to reveal the bizarre twists and turns his life had taken in the twenty years since the Beach Boys crested their first musical wave. Always the Cute One in a group made up (practically from the beginning) of paunchy, balding musicians, Wilson was a compulsive womanizer, whose many romances and five marriages included one to the nineteen-year-old daughter of his first cousin and fellow Beach Boy Mike Love, whom he married a year after the birth of their son (his fourth child). Wilson's relations with Love had been aggravated earlier when Love accused him of supplying the beleaguered Brian with drugs. A restraining order had to be issued to keep the two from settling the matter with their fists. Continuous intragroup feuding, which had begun with their decline from popularity in the late sixties, had recently focused on Dennis's drinking problem, culminating in an ultimatum barring him from an upcoming tour if he didn't dry out. And, in fact, he had made an attempt at detox a few weeks before his death — although he was apparently hitting the bottle pretty hard on the day he died.

Dennis also had the distinction of having been involved with members of the Manson "family," who camped out in his house right up until they were pinned for the Tate–LaBianca murders. Although the Manson group drained him of as much as $100,000 and gave him the clap, friends said he found it hard to resist their sex-and-drugs life-style. However, all that stopped when they began making telephone threats on his life following Manson's arrest.

Although Dennis had had some critical success with a solo effort called *Pacific Ocean Blue* and some strong original work on the group's 1970 album, *Sunflower*, he — like his fellow Beach Boys — remained more or less at the mercy of Brian's lethargic muse throughout his career. Even so, his association with the group had made him a wealthy rock star. Concert dates and royalties from early hits regularly earned him as much as $600,000 a year, though at the end he was literally homeless, having squandered millions during his brief lifetime.

As more and more stories of Brian's drug- and booze-related troubles were made public in the seventies, media speculation had it that he would become another early rock casualty. But ultimately it would be Dennis who was sacrificed to the gods of rock'n'roll. "When all the veneer is stripped away," wrote journalist Jim Jerome following Dennis's death, "the truth about the Beach Boys is that ex–Interior Secretary James Watt was only partly wrong in [1983's] famous gaffe about the group attracting the 'wrong element.' They didn't attract it so much as conceal what lurked behind the surface of their own innocent myth."

Dennis Wilson

Millions of voting-age fans can't be wrong: a Beach Boy visit to the White House helps to make amends for Watt's boner.

It was business as usual for Jackie Wilson on a Saturday night in September of 1975, when he took to the stage for an oldies revival in Cherry Hill, New Jersey, and proceeded to wrap his honeyed tenor around a selection of his best-loved hits, which he punctuated with a dizzying display of his patented splits, spins and leaps. By this point, Wilson was something of a has-been in the sense that he hadn't had a hit record in almost ten years, and yet by the time he brought his set to a close with a soaring version of "Lonely Teardrops," he'd electrified his audience as only a handful of other performers — his admirers James Brown and Elvis among them — could. But it was during that number that a heart attack crumpled Wilson to the floor, his head banging off the stage. For several long minutes, the crowd gaped in horror as the Coasters' Cornell Gunter administered resuscitation to the lifeless singer, keeping him alive until the arrival of a paramedic unit.

Many people assumed that Jackie Wilson died following his onstage collapse (a belief fueled in no small part by several ill-informed newspaper accounts), but although Wilson survived, the oxygen starvation he suffered left him with extensive brain damage and total physical paralysis. Following his recovery from a four-month coma, his days were spent in bed or a wheelchair, staring vacantly into space. When death came to Wilson some eight years later, it was unheralded and anticlimactic.

Until that terrible night in 1975, Jackie Wilson had always lived on the edge. There were alcohol and drugs (ups, downs, heroin, LSD), a narrow scrape with death in 1961 when a bullet fired by a deranged female fan became permanently lodged in his chest, and legal woes brought on by his casual attitude toward marriage — not to mention his career's careening highs and lows. Even as he lay virtually lifeless, controversy continued to swirl around him.

There was concern over lack of money for his care as well as rumors of neglect and physical abuse, the

Jackie Wilson

strangest of which involved mysterious injuries — two black eyes and a broken nose — suffered while he was still comatose. Although authorities were quick to discount charges of abuse or negligence, the subsequent discovery of the wooden arm of his wheelchair beneath Wilson's bed led to speculation that it had been broken off and used to inflict a cruel beating to the pitifully defenseless man.

Wilson's prognosis was still uncertain as family, friends, former business associates and government agents began to wage a furious battle over his remaining assets. However, an IRS levy of $300,000 for uncollected taxes several months later revealed Wilson to be virtually bankrupt. This was particularly baffling in light of Wilson's years of constant touring and many million-selling hits, which, taken together, were estimated to have generated around $200 million in revenues. The government turned to Wilson's label, Brunswick Records, for an explanation, and Brunswick, in turn, alleged that Wilson owed them $150,000 in unrecouped advance monies. Later, however, a court-appointed guardian for Wilson challenged this claim and filed suit against the company, charging that Brunswick had failed to pay and account for over $1 million in royalties. The guardian also discovered that although Wilson appeared to have been eligible for health insurance through a union affiliation, Brunswick had failed to contribute to his pension and welfare fund (on account of his alleged indebtedness to the company), thereby leaving him without medical coverage.

As it happens, additional intimations of misconduct in the handling of Jackie Wilson's affairs had come to light even before his collapse. According to press reports in the *Bergen Record* and later in the *Village Voice* and *Rolling Stone*, Nat Tarnopol, Wilson's manager and the head of Brunswick, and six other label execs had been indicted three months earlier in a mail fraud and conspiracy scheme that involved selling records to distributors for merchandise or cash, which they then used to make payoffs to deejays and program directors. Since these record sales went unrecorded, company officials were further accused of defrauding their artists and writers of royalties. This last accusation has particular relevance to Wilson's story, since for over a decade he had been the label's biggest-selling artist.

These were not the first allegations of unorthodox business practices and mismanagement leveled at Brunswick. There is also evidence that Wilson had become disenchanted with the way his career was being handled at least as far back as 1968. (Carl Davis, Wilson's producer, has made reference to a falling-out between Wilson and Tarnopol around this time.) Still, he was never able to bring himself to make a break with Brunswick. Perhaps he felt that taking sides against the company might be hazardous to his health. (At the first mail fraud trial, Eugene Record, leader of the Chi-Lites, one of the label's biggest attractions in the seventies, testified that he had been threatened and assaulted by one of Tarnopol's men during an argument over royalties.)

Tarnopol and his associates were eventually found guilty of charges stemming from payola abuse in a jury trial; but when they appealed their case to the Third Circuit Court, the conviction was overturned and a new trial ordered. The government's second attempt to nail Brunswick ended in a mistrial in May 1978 after its case fell apart under cross examination, owing partly to the fact that no Brunswick artist was willing — or able — to come forward and testify that he'd been defrauded.

As tragic as the intimations of Brunswick's double-dealing in Wilson's financial affairs was the pathetic treatment his prodigious talents received from the label's staff musicians and arrangers. Wilson's willingness to allow his vocals to be smothered with sugary orchestrations and to perform hackneyed standards ("Danny Boy" and assorted Jolson favorites) instead of the blues-based pop that had made him a star was the most lethal in a series of career missteps that began with his split from Berry Gordy in 1958. Not that he would necessarily have fared much better financially with Gordy, but at least his music wouldn't have been undermined. When asked by an interviewer why he stayed with Brunswick, he could only answer: "My heart says go, but my soul says stay."

At the time of his death from gunshot wounds inflicted by his father in the spring of 1984, Marvin Gaye's career was in the midst of a stunning reversal. After a decade of financial and emotional turmoil, the success of "Sexual Healing" two years earlier found him waxing humble in interviews — thanking God, his family and most especially the record industry for his stunning change of luck. This all-new Marvin Gaye was part of a well-thought-out gameplan. After losing the Grammy (eight times), a fortune, and a following with canceled performances and erratic recorded work, Gaye had decided to play ball with the music business. Suddenly, he was accessible in a way he hadn't been since his early Motown days — honoring concert dates, playing benefits, and even acting as a presenter on the Dick Clark Music Awards. The strategy paid off with a Grammy, a Top Ten record and a comeback unusual for one who'd slipped so far.

In the past, Gaye had exhibited a general disdain for the record industry and sometimes even his fans. His public persona was cocky, if not hostile. His personal philosophy as it unfolded in public pronouncements was a jumble of contradictions — reflecting the great ambivalence he harbored toward himself and his celebrity. Nowhere was that ambivalence more apparent than in his spiritual beliefs. Certainly Gaye was a religious man, but one who had an uncomfortable relationship with his God — in his mind a stern and unforgiving presence. Although he spent a great deal of time pondering cosmic imponderables and writing about them in his music, he said, "I don't think I'm a Christian. A Christian is a man who follows Christ. My church is within me."

It's possible that in Gaye's mind organized religion was linked with his father — a Pentecostal minister and strict disciplinarian who, Gaye once said, kept him in line with brutal beatings. Although Gaye had supported both his parents since his early days at Motown, he'd apparently never gotten the recognition from his father he'd so desired. For twenty years, Gaye Senior had lived in his famous son's shadow — all the while withholding his approval. A Motown exec remembers that at one point during contractual negotiations with Gaye, he requested that a cash bonus of $1 million be given him in a suitcase so he could take it to his father and say, "See that, that's a million dollars. I just wanted to show you how successful I am." Gaye's relationship with his mother, on the other hand, was a devoted one. He adored her and she doted on him — no matter how outrageous his behavior. Indeed, family friends have speculated that Gaye's murder was the upshot of a long-standing rivalry for Alberta Gaye's affections.

Like Jerry Lee Lewis, Gaye seems never to have been able to reconcile his secular and spiritual selves, owing primarily to the fact that his public allure was so closely tied to his sexuality. He was at once a sexual satyr and a social commentator, a humanist and a sadist capable of inflicting physical abuse on lovers, friends and family members, and an ambitious talent who alternately sought, then fled from, the spotlight. Even his musical persona was a lie: while creating some of the most memorable juke-box soul of all time, he harbored an intense anger and frustration at not being allowed to make the crossover into mainstream pop of the kind sung by Sinatra and Nat King Cole.

Although his behavior had been noticeably peculiar almost from the time he first came to national prominence, Gaye's image as conjured up by Motown was that of an elegant soul man at ease with his talent and lot in life. Consequently, no one seemed to find it strange (or if they did Motown persuaded them otherwise) when he began training in deadly earnest to become a running back with the Detroit Lions in 1970 — despite the fact that he was over thirty and out of shape, with no history as an athlete, let alone as a pro. When he dropped from sight a few years later following the death of his singing partner, Tammi Terrell, his self-imposed exile was chalked up to artistic temperament — one that ultimately brought forth his greatest triumph, the monumental *What's Goin' On,* the first protest album from a major black star.

For years, Gaye remained a recluse, composing and recording in his home studio, intensely private and withdrawn. Ironically, he himself would be responsible for making the sordid details of his personal life

public when he chronicled his marriage and divorce to Anna Gordy Gaye in *Here, My Dear*. As a struggling musician at Motown, Gaye had been clever and ambitious enough to marry the boss's sister, a woman whose astute business instincts and patronage both pulled him out of the very talented Motown ranks and sustained him during his unproductive periods. Although it had survived years of his casual dalliances, the fourteen-year-old marriage was finally shattered by Gaye's infatuation with a young woman named Janis Hunter. However, his divorce wasn't even final before his subsequent marriage to Hunter ended after he menaced her with a knife. Disconsolate, Gaye made his way to Hawaii, where he lived alone in a van. A deepening depression resulted in a plot to kidnap his four-year-old son by Hunter and a suicide attempt. With divorce lawyers and IRS agents closing in fast, he fled to Europe in 1980, finally settling in Belgium. While there, a contract with Columbia gave him the monetary inspiration to begin work on new material. The result was "Sexual Healing" — his ticket back to the States.

Gaye's exile had gone largely unnoticed in this country: the public remained for the most part unaware of the details of his second divorce and drug troubles. While touring to promote "Sexual Healing," he referred to his rampant "smoking and snorting" in the past tense — implying that all that lay behind him. But in fact, by this point, Gaye was snowblind. As an insecure, yet arrogant artist who looked to millions for approval, Gaye had the kind of temperament cocaine loves. Although he used it to bolster his confidence, it ultimately ended up subverting it — bringing out his bad self until it dominated his tormented psyche.

Alberta Gaye looked the other way as dealers and street people came and went at all hours of the night to the house in an upper-middle-class section of L.A. she shared with her son and husband. If she had any misgivings about the course Gaye's life was taking, she kept them to herself — perhaps with the knowledge that criticism could lead to banishment. Gaye's father, on the other hand, chastised him constantly, finally banishing him with the help of the police. Gaye later returned home seeking a reconciliation, but that didn't keep him from continuing to bait his father and possibly roughing him up. (It was also during this period that one of Gaye's girlfriends pressed charges for assault and battery.)

It has been speculated that when the case is closed on the murder of Marvin Gaye, it just may be that the singer will be shown to be complicit in his own death. So fearful of death plots that he'd surrounded himself with armed bodyguards in addition to stocking his home with guns, Gaye seemed sometimes to anticipate the death he feared, talking for years about suicide and even going so far as to hold a gun to his head at a family gathering a few months before his demise. Some close to him feel that on the last day of his life, Marvin Gaye orchestrated what he could not bring himself to do — by goading his father into a killing rage.

Life in the FAST Lane

"In rock'n'roll, you're built up to be torn down. Like architecture in America, you build it up and let it stand for ten years, then call it shabby and rip it down and put up something else."
— JONI MITCHELL

Rock'n'roll giveth and rock'n'roll taketh away. To be a rock star is to enjoy the greatest and most handsomely paid celebrity in the world while at the same time knowing that your days in the sun will almost certainly be few. Del Shannon says: "I remember sitting in the back seat of a limousine in 1965, and I was the unhappiest person in the world. My driver said, 'What's wrong with you, man? How can *you* be depressed?' And I replied, 'Because I may never be on top again. There's no way this can last.' "

Shannon knew that built-in obsolescence is the flip side of rock stardom, that it rarely lasts longer than four or five years as a rule. Not only do young fans lose interest in pop idols as they grow older, but the stars themselves have a tendency to blaze brightly and burn out fast. Very few can sustain the pace it takes to stay on top.

Today, cocaine is the high-octane fuel of the music world. (Texas Jewboy Kinky Friedman says he gave up the white stuff after he blew his nose and Bob Marley came out.) In the old days, however, it was amphetamine that fired the mythic energy and creative imaginations of such pop *auteurs* as Elvis, Jerry Lee Lewis, Jackie Wilson, Little Richard, Brian Wilson and Pete Townshend. Acid provided the inspiration for the Beatles and San Francisco bands like the Dead and the Airplane back in the sixties. Champagne and brandy sharpened Grace Slick's sarcastic tongue and mercurial onstage persona. Alice Cooper kept his nightmare on the road for five years by chug-a-lugging two cases of beer a day. Lou Reed conjured up the sinister imagery of his greatest songs while Waiting for the Man. Etta James and Little Esther Phillips did some of their finest work as teenagers while hung up on junk. Ray Charles's most prolific period as a composer/arranger/orchestra leader occurred in the midst of a nineteen-year heroin addiction. And let us not forget that most famous and resilient of all rock junkies — the unsinkable Keith Richards. Of course, the list doesn't stop there. You could go on forever naming stars who carved their niche in pop history while bombed out of their skulls. The challenge lies in trying to think of someone who did it straight.

Once a recording artist has made that long hard climb to the top, the problem becomes hanging on. Sometimes the very magnitude of a star's success can torpedo his delicate psyche. Take Brian Wilson. He was doing fine until the rock press labeled him a Genius. He's never been the same since. Meat Loaf had the misfortune to sell eight million copies of his *first* album, *Bat Out of Hell*. So intimidated was he by this astounding accomplishment that he literally couldn't speak, let alone sing. "I thought I was sick and went to a doctor. After that I still couldn't sing so I didn't talk. Then I *really* started to go nuts." By the time Mr. Loaf (as the *New York Times* calls him) finally found his voice again two years later, he'd lost his audience. Where once he'd headlined at gigantic arenas, he was now canceling club dates for lack of ticket sales.

Having blown the lid off the record biz with the seven-million-selling *Frampton Comes Alive* in 1976, Peter Frampton was also faced with the impossible task of topping himself next time at bat. When his following album (*I'm in You*) sold only a paltry three million, the industry dubbed it a flop. Then, to add insult to injury, his much ballyhooed acting debut in the unintentionally hilarious *Sgt. Pepper* proved to be a disaster. The baby-

225

faced rocker's run of bad luck snowballed when a near fatal auto accident in the Bahamas left him in the hospital with serious head injuries and his longtime live-in girlfriend sued him for a million dollars in palimony. Seemingly fed up with fame, the shell-shocked singer threw out the last vestige of Peter Frampton superstar when he cut off his trademarked blond curls in 1981. His time at the top had lasted a grand total of four years.

Thanks to the frantic hyperbole employed by record companies' publicity departments, some aspiring popsters are eclipsed by their own reputations even before they sing or play a single note. Johnny Winter is one of many whose confidence was deflated by an overbearing advance hype. Even the indomitable Bruce Springsteen shows signs of having trouble living up to his billing as the "Future of Rock'n'Roll." It takes him from two to three years of obsessively hard work to squeeze out albums worthy of such grandiloquent praise.

Sometimes the bum reviews are easier to live with than the raves — although plenty of pop giants have been known to go into shock after a rap in *Rolling Stone*. Eric Clapton fell into a deep depression following the unenthusiastic response to his post-*Layla* efforts. Lou Reed once offered to teach the late Lester Bangs a lesson in music appreciation by beating him to a pulp. Billy Joel used the Madison Square Garden stage as a platform to lambaste a New York critic who'd put down his latest album release. And on a recent Jefferson Starship album, Paul Kantner sent to the group's critics this less-than-subtle message: "Fuck you, we do what we want."

Even critic's darling Randy Newman often finds himself paralyzed by the thought of the imminent media response to an ongoing work. "When I'm writing songs," he once lamented, "the minutes are like hours. I sit there with nothing — just a big picture of [rock critic] Greil Marcus in my head hanging over the piano."

Nor does a rock star's renegade status make him immune to the kind of tabloid sensationalism that plagues run-of-the-mill celebs. For some, lurid headlines and racy rumors simply mean more record sales. For others, they are a source of great personal embarrassment and pain. In 1968, Aretha Franklin made the cover of *Time*, but the accompanying article, while lavish in its praise for Aretha and her talent, touched on the tempestuous nature of her relationship with men — particularly her father, who came across as something of a gospel-spouting Sportin' Life, and then-husband, Ted White, who was described as "a street corner wheeler dealer." White, it was briefly noted, had recently "roughed her up in public at Atlanta's Regency House Hotel." Unfortunately, it was this single piece of information that most people remembered. Humiliated by the story, Aretha tearfully refuted its charges during an appearance on *The Tonight Show*. Privately, she vowed never to let the press near her personal life again. A few months following the article's publication, her marriage to White capsized, and before long,

Aretha Franklin

she was blowing recording sessions and concert dates left and right. She has since said she spent the remainder of that year sitting around crying. There was speculation that she intended to pack in her singing career and, worse, that she'd suffered an emotional breakdown. But though none of those rumors was ever substantiated, one thing was certain: Aretha Franklin never again performed with the fervor of her early years.

At least Aretha came away from her moment of glory with something to show for her trouble. She may not sell many records anymore, but she's a millionaire who lives a quiet, cushy life in Southern California. Not so lucky were the dozens of stars from the fifties and sixties who came away with nothing to show for years of million-selling hits. Martha Reeves was so broke by the time she'd permanently parted company with Motown that she had to farm her young son out to relatives while she kept herself alive with occasional gigs in little L.A. dives; Mitch Ryder (who's now making a comeback) wound up as a forklift operator in Denver after one too many acid trips; former folkie Chad Mitchell, down on his luck and low on money, got five years for smuggling 400 pounds of grass across the Mexican border in 1973; and when last heard from, Barbara ("Hello Stranger") Lewis was working in a record store in Detroit.

If a recording artist comes away broke from a successful career, it's usually safe to assume that someone got rich at his or her expense. On the other hand, plenty of stars are fully capable of blowing their own fortunes completely unassisted. In 1971, for example, Isaac Hayes used the millions he made with *Shaft* to buy a gold-plated ermine-lined Caddy and a couple of Colonial-style Memphis mansions. By 1976, however, he was six million dollars in debt. Sly Stone, at one time the highest-paid black performer in pop, is rumored to have squandered millions on high living. While Hayes eventually went on to recoup a portion of his losses as well as some of his status as a hitmaker, by the time Sly got back down to business in the seventies, his reputation as a fuck-up caused him to be branded a loser, both by the industry and the rock press — a reputation he has yet to overcome.

And then there's the flip side of the pop success syndrome wherein stars make so much money that they end up devoting practically all their time and ingenuity to dreaming up ways to unload it. They collect antique cars (Elton John), thoroughbred ponies (Olivia Newton-John) and Art Nouveau *objets d'art* (Rod Stewart). Before you know it, they're dropping $16,000 on peanut butter sandwiches — as Elvis supposedly did when he chartered a jet to fly him and his cronies round trip from Memphis to Denver to pick up an order of what he claimed were the world's finest peanut butter and jelly sandwiches from a Denver hotel.

Temptations — both material and physical — abound for millionaire rock stars. When the cops answered a call at Don Henley's L.A. home a while back, for example, they found an unclad sixteen-year-old girl passed out from a drug overdose and a stash the size of Bogotá. Henley was lucky; he walked away from that little infraction with a slap on the wrist and two years' penance in a drug rehab program. It's not uncommon, however, for law enforcement officials to make Examples of naughty rock star offenders by sticking them with stiff fines and prison sentences. The lengthy roll call of rock musicians who have spent time behind bars includes most of the biggest names in pop. Some, like Chuck Berry, were robbed of their careers by overzealous guardians of the public morality. Others, like Brian Jones, were literally hounded into immortality.

Even if a rock star does manage to survive the rip-offs, the road, the easy money, the drugs, the fans and the press, there is still the very real possibility that he or she will end up deaf. Numbered among the rockers who have ravaged their eardrums from years of standing downwind of their own high-decibel blast are Pete Townshend, Frankie Valli, Brian Wilson, Jerry Garcia, Roger Daltrey, John Entwhistle and Ted Nugent (who maintains that being deaf is a small price to pay for rock stardom). No doubt there are many others who have suffered comparable hearing loss but aren't anxious to let it get around.

Is it any wonder that when the going gets rough in rock, the tough get religion? Countless pop celebrities have found salvation not only from legal woes and drug dependence but also from brain drain, physical deterioration, career decline and the pressure of making art to order by getting next to God. Until recently, however, not just any God would do. For many years, a rocker's religious affiliation had to be esoteric to be hip. When Peter Townshend saw the light (and momentarily gave up drugs in the early sixties) it was through the teachings of Meher Baba; Seals and Crofts got the Word through the mysticism of Baha'i; Mahavishnu John McLaughlin overcame his penchant for getting stoned and falling off stages thanks to the guidance of guru Sri Chinmoy; and Cat Stevens coped with his declining impact on the pop marketplace by becoming a Muslim. (Cat, whose real name is Steven Demetri Georgiou, now answers to the name of Yusuf.)

Right: Donovan gets down with TM

A number of these exotic conversions were directly inspired by the Beatles' involvement with the Maharishi Mahesh Yogi, the most famous rock religious saga ever. As you probably remember, taking up TM was the trendy thing for beleaguered rockers to do in the sixties. Numbered among its devotees were Brian Jones, Marianne Faithfull, Ray Manzarek, the Beach Boys and Eric Burdon, all of whom, like the Beatles, used meditation as a way of contending with the rigors of fame and clearing their heads of the psychic residue from countless acid trips. Donovan turned to TM to clean up his image following a spell of bad luck that began with an "exposé" in a London paper, supposedly penned by a former girlfriend, entitled "My Dope-Crazed Weekend with Donovan," and culminated in a drug bust and subsequent run-in with U.S. Immigration.

By the close of the sixties, Eastern religions had started to lose their status in the rock community as more and more big-name popsters began turning to that ol' time religion — the Pentecostal Christianity of such patron saints of rock as Elvis Presley, Little Richard, Jerry Lee Lewis, et al. — to satisfy their souls.

Although few people know it, Pat Boone — the clean-cut teen crooner of the fifties — had degenerated into a Nehru-jacketed Vegas swinger by the mid-sixties, one whose weakness for gambling, girls and booze left him with a shaky marriage and almost $1 million in debts. But a career as a born-again proselytizer put Pat back in the black by 1968 — thanks in no small part to his lucrative tours of the Holy Land, religious self-help books and part-time gigs with Rex Humbard, Oral Roberts and TV's *700 Club*.

By the seventies, dramatic stories of spiritual redemption had become commonplace in rock. In 1970, Fleetwood Mac's Jeremy Spencer gave up his pursuit of fame and turned all his earthly possessions over to the Children of God; street-corner heartthrob Dion DiMucci fought off a longstanding heroin habit with a heavy dose of the Gospel; B. J. Thomas used speed to recover

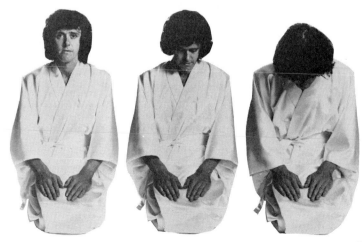

from a serious knife wound (sustained in a fight with a New York hotel clerk) and religion to recover from the speed; Al Green traded sexy songs for inspirational music and a career in the ministry following a bizarre incident in which a woman friend threw a pot of scalding-hot grits on his bare back after he refused her marriage proposal; British rocker Cliff Richard swore off sex (he claims to have been celibate since 1965) as well as his tendency to use what he calls the "F-word" in his everyday speech after becoming an ardent Baptist; and Wayne Cochran, like his idol, Little Richard, claims to have cured himself of a terminal disease by being reborn in Christ.

The most fascinating religious trip of all was Bob Dylan's much-publicized conversion to Christianity — particularly since it followed so closely a rekindled interest in his Jewish heritage. (This was not Dylan's first radical religious turnabout: in the seventies, his spiritual quest had led him from Buddhism to Hinduism to Hollywood

psychic Tamara Rand, best remembered for faking a television interview in which she "predicted" John Hinckley's attack on the President.) Dylan turned to the Bible at a time when he was floundering, not only in his personal life, but also in his recording career. His wife of twelve years had just left him, taking with her half his assets and all four of his children. In addition, his artistic reputation had been seriously eroded by several lackluster albums and a disastrous foray into movie-making with the critically reviled *Renaldo and Clara*. All of which led some Dylanologists to suspect the Tambourine Man's sudden infatuation with Christianity was actually a means of providing himself with a fresh source of artistic inspiration. (One even went so far as to suggest that we were lucky that Dylan only claimed he had found Jesus; that he wasn't above claiming he *was* Jesus.) In any case, Dylan's new obsession did provide him with a hit album and his first Grammy. But the failure of his second Christian LP (*Saved*) indicated that the novelty of Dylan as the Pop Messiah was starting to wear thin with his fans. However, by 1983 Dylan — always one step ahead of the faithful — appeared to be in the midst of yet another religious switchover; this time to Hasidism.

Just as there are no atheists in the foxholes, by 1980 there didn't seem to be any in rock'n'roll either. Arlo Guthrie had become a Roman Catholic and Van Morrison, Roger McGuinn, and Maria Muldaur had jumped on the born-again bandwagon. In 1981, Donna Summer's rekindled religious beliefs gave her the strength to mount a ten-million-dollar lawsuit against her former mentor, the late Neil Bogart, and Casablanca records. Even punk priestess Patti Smith has seemed to be leaning toward more spiritual concerns of late. For her, the turning point came when she witnessed the coronation of Pope John Paul II on TV. And despite the fact that his is one of the world's most recognized faces, Michael Jackson, a Jehovah's Witness, still pursues his own personal ministry, selling *The Watchtower* door-to-door in L.A.

When you think about it, religion — and the getting thereof —has had a radical effect on the history of rock'n'roll. There's Little Richard, for example, who (literally) threw it

Top: Little Richard during his comeback period; *left*: a typical ad for a Richard Penniman revival meeting; *right:* spreading the gospel to Tom Snyder with fellow believer Wayne Cochran

all away to preach the Gospel. Not just once but twice. In many ways, his loss was as devastating to rock as those of Cochran, Lewis and Holly. But to hear the Right Reverend Richard Penniman tell it, if he hadn't walked out on his sinful rock star existence when he did, he would've been carried out in an oblong box. Today, the legendary kink who delighted in orgies, hard drugs and lavish earthly possessions is no more. The unabashed homosexual who canvassed audiences for comely teenaged boys to act as his "personal valet" now claims that his greatest ambition is to settle down with the right girl and raise a family. Not surprisingly, this new-model Richard Penniman has become something of an embarrassment to the rock world now that he devotes all his time and talents to denouncing rock'n'roll as the "devil's music" from the pulpit to *People* magazine.

The sad truth is that rock fans have always been far less interested in a reformed rocker than in a colorful psychopath. To wit, TM may have eased the troubled minds of countless pop personalities during the Flower Power Era, but it wasn't particularly good for their careers. Once they realized that they

Santana as funky rocker... and snazzy mystic

were being used in the Maharishi's own bid for stardom, the Beatles quietly retreated from their previous public exhortations. The Beach Boys, on the other hand, remained intent on popularizing the practice of meditation in this country. They went on to blow a national tour by using the Munchkin-voiced Maharishi as an opening act. By the early seventies, Donovan seemed to be the only popster who hadn't given up on the guru. But he got the message after critics attributed the dippy (even for him) lyrics on his '72 and '73 comeback albums to a case of cosmic gas. One *Creem* writer dismissed him as a "TM junkie," saying, "I can only hope that [Donovan] gained peace of mind in his religious commitment because it has wreaked havoc on his songwriting talent." And finally, George Harrison's blissed-

out Krishna consciousness is rumored to have cost him not only his wife Patti (owing to its emphasis on spiritual purity) but also many millions of fans who eventually grew tired of hearing him harp on his mystical trip in his music.

Carlos Santana is another gung-ho convert who turned off his fans by laying on the mystical shtick a little too thick in interviews, performance and song. Ironically Santana had first embraced guru Sri Chinmoy's philosophy as a way of counteracting the harmful effect that foul language, drug use and various other passions of the flesh had had on his career. Santana's conversion was responsible for not only his stunning physical transformation from funky, long-haired rocker to white-clad ice-cream man, but a new (and unfortunate) name change to Devadip Carlos Santana. Within a few years, however, Devadip had begun to withdraw somewhat from his fervid religious stance — apparently in response to a spate of withering reviews that accused him of being a pious pain in the ass. Finally, in the fall of 1982, Santana announced that he'd sworn off Chinmoy altogether and taken up tennis.

Actually, a clean-up of any sort — religious or otherwise — is apt to have a devastating effect on a rock musician's image. For example, Alice Cooper based so much of his outlaw mystique on his reputation as a boozer that a drying-out spell in a drink tank dried up his audience as well. Similarly, the public doesn't seem to be nearly as enamored of Grace Slick now that she's got her alcohol-inspired antics under control. Both Dylan and McCartney have been taken to task by the rock press for the tranquilizing effect domestic bliss has had on their work. And Eric Clapton's post–dope addiction recordings have likewise been dismissed as dull and uninspired. Many critics were simply voicing their disdain for the safe — and therefore unfashionable — life-styles chosen by these stars. But in all fairness, you'd have to say that these charges were not totally unfounded. And so, we are left to wonder if redemption and rehabilitation numb rock creativity or whether these pop artists have simply outlived their Genius — or their Time.

Just as rock is filled with countless sad stories of young lions who succumbed at the height of their youth and fame, so is it filled with equally compelling tales of those who have come away from rock stardom with their lives, but whose manic energy and mythic productivity have, for one reason or another, been sapped before they reached their thirtieth birthday. For them, life becomes a constant repetition of the past. They spend the rest of their days attempting to recapture something of their old fire, singing their old hits and reliving the past with journalists and rock scholars. A very few may go on to do work as fine as, if not better than, that of their youth. But by then, it usually doesn't matter, since their fans will prefer to remember them as they once were.

Here then are some of the great rock'n'roll burn-outs, mythic martyrs who had had the good luck — and misfortune — to live past their prime.

Chuck Berry, before the Fall

Fats Domino was a cuddly brown bear who could show you a good time on Blueberry Hill. Little Richard was a minstrel show from Mars. But Chuck Berry — born Charles Edward Berry in Saint Louis, Missouri, on October 18, 1931 — was a brown-eyed handsome man who knew how to turn on all the sweet little sixteens. Possessed of an almost telepathic genius for translating the realities of teen life into hip juke-box lingo, he captured the imagination of America's soda-shop set, bringing black and white together under the banner of rock'n'roll. He had the cool of a jazz musician, the sensibility of a poet and the grace of a movie star. (Check him out in the old Alan Freed rock flicks. Not only was he great to look at — he could act!) For all this and more, Chuck Berry was a marked man.

Chuck Berry was not unaware of the antagonism he inspired in the grown-up white world, and kept his guard up accordingly. He let Leonard Chess take care of business, even when it meant apportioning co-writing credits on his songs to influential friends like Alan Freed and a Chicago retailer. He didn't drink and he stayed away from drugs. But the one weakness he couldn't kick was his fondness for young women.

In 1959 during a trip to New Mexico, he brought back a fourteen-year-old Spanish-speaking Apache woman to work as a hat-check girl in his Saint Louis club, Chuck Berry's Club Bandstand. When he fired her a short time later, she took revenge by informing the police that she was a minor. Berry was arrested and subsequently charged with transportation of a woman across state lines for immoral purposes.

This was not Berry's first run-in with the law; he'd done three years in reform school for a bungled robbery as a kid. Earlier in 1959, he had been arrested in Mississippi for trying to pick up a young white girl who happened to be the daughter of the local sheriff. In this instance, however, he was quite simply railroaded. The girl later confessed that she had been a prostitute before Berry met her, so it could hardly be said, as the indictment stated, that he "compelled, induced and incited" her to "give herself up to debauchery."

Unfortunately, when confronted with the Mann Act charge, the best Berry could come up with in his own defense was that he had brought the Apache girl to Saint Louis because he thought Latin music was the "coming thing" and he wanted her to teach him Spanish. To make matters worse, the presiding judge on the case insisted on referring to him as "this Negro" and "what's-his-name." The courtroom proceedings were such a travesty that the judge was eventually taken off the case and a mistrial declared. A second trial and two years of public humiliation later, Berry went up the river to the federal pen in Terre Haute, Indiana.

While he was in prison, Berry's marriage fell apart, and the Club Bandstand closed down. Worst of all, when he was released in 1964, he seemed to have lost the will to defend his kind of music against the onslaught of manufactured pretty boys and sugary schlock that had filled the void during his absence.

The hits "Nadine" and "No Particular Place to Go" announced Berry's return, but the general suspicion is that these were written before his prison stay. Following his release in 1964, Berry concentrated on assuming control of his business affairs and establishing an amusement park and music club complex called Berry Park in Wentzville, Missouri. He continued to record and even signed a lucrative deal with Mercury records in 1966, temporarily leaving Chess, the label for which he'd cut all his classics. But if Berry still had the knack, he didn't go out of his way to show it.

"I never saw a man so changed," said Carl Perkins. "I did a tour of England with him after he got out of prison in 1970. Before he'd been an easygoing guy, the kind who'd jam in the dressing room, sit and swap licks and jokes. But in England, he was distant and bitter."

Even more revealing was Berry's method of touring. He traveled with only his guitar, usually without so much as an amp, and showed up for his gig expecting a pick-up band to be provided by the promoter. His "rehearsals" were usually little more than a sound check. One musician who played with Berry at a recent show in New York says that he was instructed to go out and get a copy of *Chuck Berry's Greatest Hits* and learn the tunes off the record to prepare for the performance. The results of this haphazard approach ranged from brilliant (when the band was right and Berry was on) to merely perfunctory take-the-money-and-run disgraces.

The early '70s rock'n'roll revival created a new demand for Chuck Berry. He toured Britain to exuberant response and jammed with John Lennon on TV's *Mike Douglas Show* in 1972. That was also the year of Chuck's first (!) Number One record, the ribald singalong, "My Ding-A-Ling," which had been a part of his stage act for years. Berry must have enjoyed a rueful laugh at the idea that someone prosecuted under the Mann Act could go gold with such schoolyard smut.

However, even that triumph went sour in 1979 when the IRS nailed him for tax evasion. A corporate honcho or political fat cat would've gotten off with a fine and a slap on the wrist, but incredibly, Chuck Berry — a national treasure — pulled 100 days at Lompoc Prison Farm and a three-year suspended sentence. The judge also ordered him to donate a thousand hours of community service. Atlantic Records added insult to injury by dropping him from their roster.

Why Chuck Berry? A quarter of a century after "Maybellene," Chuck Berry's major crime still comes down to being a brown-eyed handsome man who turned on white kids with rock'n'roll. Berry has suffered terribly for that sin, but he keeps his bitterness buried deep inside. As might be expected, he is wary of the public and openly hostile to the press. When not denying that he was ever behind bars, he evades pointed questions about his past by saying that he's saving the truth for his autobiography. Berry has no known close friends or business associates aside from his daughter Ingrid, who has occasionally acted as both his stage partner and road manager. When not going through the motions for people who have no idea how good he once was, he retreats to the solitude of his home in Berry Park.

Early in 1984 the Academy of Recording Arts and Sciences did its best to set the record straight by presenting him with a Life Achievement Award calling him the "Father of Rock'n'Roll." But in doing so, it was paying homage to the man he used to be; Chuck Berry hasn't written a great rock'n'roll song in almost twenty years.

Bottom left: Jamming with John Lennon on *The Mike Douglas Show; bottom right:* Although Chuck and Keith Richards seem to be getting along pretty well during this recent night out on the town, Berry has roughed up Richards on a couple of occasions: once when he jumped up to jam with him at an L.A. concert and again several years later when a remark he made during a backstage visit ruffled Chuck's feathers.

As a winsome teenager
with the Johnny Otis Show

Blond and bountiful in 1968

Etta James is one of those curious show-business phenomena — a virtual unknown who's a "legend in her own time." To hardcore soul music buffs, she stands for everything that was once fresh and irrepressible about the R&B sound, and yet, most kids today have never even heard her name. That's not really so surprising — her official return to the public arena in 1978 marked the end of what had been a twenty-year absence. She never really went the rock revival route, or sold out to Vegas or TV, but then, she probably couldn't have if she'd wanted to. After all, a three-hundred-pound woman whose act includes getting personal with a microphone and stripper squats isn't exactly family viewing fare. Had it not been for a large gay following that supported her loyally throughout the sixties and seventies when she performed at heavy leather bars like The Stud in San Francisco, Etta might not have survived at all. The fact is she's been underground for so long that many people are surprised to hear she's still around. The good news is that Etta James is very much around, but that's not to say that her life hasn't had its ups and downs. . . .

Her story begins back in 1953 when she barged into the San Francisco hotel room of R&B kingpin Johnny Otis demanding an audition. "I was playing the Fillmore in San Francisco in the early 1950s," Otis recalls. "That was before it became a rock center; it was a ghetto theater then. We got there early and went to my hotel room to rest. My manager called the room and said, 'There's a little girl here who wants so sing for you.' I said, 'Tell her to see me at the theater.' She grabbed the phone and said, 'No! I want to sing for you now.' So I said come on up. After she sang a little, I was so impressed I called her mother and said I was taking Etta to Los Angeles with me." The exposure with Otis's traveling show as well as several major R&B hits ("At Last," "Roll with Me, Henry," "Sunday Kind of Love") catapulted the gutsy teenager to the top of the R&B pantheon with breathtaking speed.

The first signs that Etta was beginning to buckle under the burden of fame emerged when she began missing concert dates with alarming frequency. The press ignored her capricious behavior, but seized upon her subsequent arrests for shoplifting and bouncing checks as a pretext for tabloid editorializing. The implication was that the motivating factor behind Etta's escapades was an addiction to heroin. Not that she has ever been secretive about her habit then or now; "I became a drug addict . . . and it was my downfall. I got addicted at age twenty-two and everybody knew it — the industry, the public, everybody."

In 1969, she tried to kick with the aid of methadone, but it turned out to be "the most horrible thing I've ever experienced. It sets up a blockage against heroin, but creates a stomach habit. Then the blockage wears off, and you have a double craving; your stomach craves methadone and your veins crave heroin." When she could no longer obtain methadone legally, she began buying it, along with heroin, on the street. After she was arrested again for writing bad checks, an L.A. judge gave her the option of rehabilitation or prison. "Man, those were my bubble years," she recalls. "Because that's what I was in. I remember some parts of those years, and some parts I don't. The

parts I don't, I don't need to remember. But that's why I did it. I was using the stuff for exactly that reason — so I wouldn't have to deal with what was going on. Of course. I didn't find that out till later."

After eighteen frustrating years of making stabs at detox only to slide back again and again to the street life, Etta finally managed to clean up her act sufficiently to make an official comeback in 1978 as the opening act for the Rolling Stones in several major cities on their summer tour. She has since released several new albums — one under the auspices of the legendary Jerry Wexler. Obviously, there are quite a few industry bigwigs who feel that Etta James isn't done for yet. One admirer who played a valuable role in getting Etta back on her feet was Keith Richards, even though she says she couldn't tell the difference between him and what she calls "those other skinny little British fags" when he first got in touch with her. As she recalls it now, "I didn't know nothin' about nothin'. Most of the time people had to lead me up onstage to perform. But when the Stones were getting their 1975 tour together, I was in the hospital trying to detox, and I got this nice letter from Keith Richards saying he knew I was having trouble and asking me if I would open their show for them. He said they always felt like the best way to get your head together and deal with your troubles was to go out on tour. I wrote back and told him I was too sick just then and he wrote and said he understood and they wouldn't forget me. They didn't either."

In all fairness, you'd have to say that today, several years after ending her self-imposed exile from the music business, Etta James is still treading water as far as her career is concerned. Her last two comeback albums, *Deep in the Night* and *Changes*, enjoyed a modest success, but she still has to shake her ass on the club circuit to bring home the bacon for her two kids — although she no longer has to dress in the alley as she did at The Stud. Currently living in L.A., Etta is married to Artis Mills of whom she says, "He's the kind of guy who knows how to do everything. I'm a freaked out casualty and he's a cooled out country boy."

While she continues to keep plugging, she feels in some ways her troubles both then and now derive from being ahead of her time. "Now you can get away with anything, but in those days, if you made one wrong move that was it. I'm an artist, whatever mistakes I've made — I was a junkie, a spoiled brat, I missed gigs — but still, they shouldn't just erase my name from the record."

Etta . . . as she looks today

Jimmie today

Jimmie at the height of his popularity, with first wife, Colleen

At the time of the attack, Rodgers's career was already in a serious state of decline. A native of Washington state, he had come on strong during the fifties with his commercial backwoods pop sound, hitting first with "Honeycomb" and then "Kisses Sweeter Than Wine" and "Oh, Oh, I'm Falling in Love Again." His stock fell drastically in the early sixties, but press coverage of the accident gave his career a much-needed boost. "It was very dramatic and I got lots of exposure," he said later. "Before the accident my career was only in fair shape. After I got out of the hospital, I worked fancy places like Caesars Palace that I had never worked before. Things were great for a while." But apparently Rodgers's eagerness to return to performing ultimately hurt his career. "I came back too soon. I wasn't strong enough physically or vocally. A lot of times I was so weak I had to be led on stage." A collapse in New Mexico the following year proved to be a major setback, leading ultimately to a nine-year hiatus. During that time, Rodgers divorced his first wife, Colleen (by whom he had two children), and married again.

The severe beating Jimmie Rodgers suffered on a December night in 1967 could have killed him. Some people evidently thought it did; one fan magazine announced his demise a month later in a story that recounted the mysterious events of that evening. "I almost died when I saw that story," Rodgers quipped later. "I told the magazine that I would sue if they didn't print a retraction but I haven't seen one yet, so there's probably still a lot of people out there who think I'm dead."

The real story: Rodgers was found lying next to his car alongside an L.A. freeway unconscious and beaten within inches of his life. Doctors said afterwards that he had apparently been attacked with a blunt instrument in what was probably a robbery attempt. His wrists had been broken, possibly in an attempt to ward off blows, and X-rays revealed a four-inch fracture at the back of his skull.

Although reports of Jimmie Rodgers's death may have been greatly exaggerated, his career is not exactly alive and well. After making his third comeback try in 1976 he continues to play small-time gigs on the club and lounge circuit. He has admitted that he doesn't particularly like show business or the little clubs he is forced to play but he needs the money to support his family. (He's fathered two more children by his second wife.)

For now, the mystery surrounding Jimmie Rodgers's "accident" remains unsolved. No one seems to know for sure just who administered the beating to Rodgers that night in 1967. However, there were allegations at the time that police, thinking Rodgers drunk, roughed him up and exacerbated his wounds. And in fact, Rodgers fingered three L.A. cops in a multimillion-dollar lawsuit that was settled out of court for $200,000 in 1973.

Jan Berry and Dean Torrence didn't just sing the California gospel of sun, sea, cars and girls — they lived it — and in living it, they were its best salesmen. Together with their friendly rivals the Beach Boys, Jan and Dean gave Young America every good reason ("two girls for every boy") to go west.

But in April of 1966 everything shattered. Berry, who had co-written and produced the pair's biggest hits while studying to be a doctor, had just gotten bad news from his draftboard. Blind with rage, he peeled out in his Corvette, and plowed into the back of a parked truck on Whittier Boulevard in Los Angeles. The rest of the story is like "Dead Man's Curve" come true. Almost.

Although Berry miraculously survived that accident, he lay paralyzed for over a year and suffered extensive brain damage, resulting in aphasia. He knew that he was Jan Berry, that he was once famous and that he had things to say and do. He just couldn't seem to remember how.

Before the accident, Jan was known in pop circles for his arrogance. As a patient, he was no different. He stubbornly insisted on recovering his way by returning to his empty Bel-Air house to live on his own. There, he became an easy mark for the leeches who wanted a piece of what was left of Jan Berry, Rock Star.

By this point, Jan and Dean were yesterday's news. After recording a solo album to mark time until Jan's recovery, Dean Torrence quit music to open an album graphics company called Kitty Hawk. Jan, on the other hand, had no intention of giving up his stardom, despite protracted depressions so severe they reportedly led to a couple of suicide attempts. With the help of producer Lou Adler and an aspiring songwriter named Joni Jacobs, he wrote a few tunes and released one called "Mother Earth" as a single in 1970 (he couldn't sing the song all the way through; his vocal had to be spliced together).

In 1973, Jan and Dean decided to make a stab at performing as the special guests at a California Surfers Stomp reunion starring the Surfaris, the Marketts and surf guitar king Dick Dale. Owing

to Jan's impaired speech, the pair was forced to lip-sync to a pre-recorded tape of their old hits. But just seconds into their first song, something went wrong with the recording and the audience realized that they weren't actually singing. Also disconcerting were Jan's jerky onstage movements, the result of a lingering paralysis on one side of his body. The audience's initial reaction was confusion, followed by noisy indignation; the crowd, which had come together to cheer the triumphant return of Jan and Dean, wound up booing them off the stage.

Fortunately, the story does not end there. A 1978 TV movie based on the Jan and Dean story, entitled *Dead Man's Curve*, encouraged the duo to try again — first with an impromptu appearance at a concert by Beach Boy Mike Love's Celebration band, then at a Murray-the-K reunion show in New York. After that, they did a series of stadium dates with the Beach Boys. Jan didn't always remember the words to his songs, and he occasionally sang a fraction of a second behind the beat. Still, he was living proof that you can come back from Dead Man's Curve.

Jan and Dean in 1962 and at a recent surf music reunion

Left: A promo shot of Brian with wife Marilyn to launch the ill-fated group Spring
Right: At the board for *15 Big Ones* in 1976

As a lanky, doughy-faced kid growing up in suburban Hawthorne, California, Brian Wilson seemed normal enough. His interests were average: sports, cars, girls. To look at him you'd never dream that he possessed monumental musical gifts. But his father Murray knew. As the eldest of three brothers, Brian became the object of his domineering father's frustrated musical ambitions. In Murray Wilson's eyes, Brian was at once the most talented creature on the planet and the laziest and most inefficient. As a result, Brian's disposition often careened from cocky and competitive to melancholy and withdrawn. To complicate matters, he was also deaf in one ear (the result, it is believed, of a beating by his father). But these problems vanished the minute he got into a recording studio or in front of an audience to play his songs.

Unfortunately, the one thing Brian Wilson never got over was being *the* Brian Wilson, resident genius of the Beach Boys. His group had started out as a kind of Wilson family hobby in which Brian, his younger brothers Carl and Dennis, cousin Mike Love and friend Al Jardine all participated. However, by 1964, just two years after their first record, Brian had fashioned an astounding number of hits ("Surfin' Safari," "409," "Surfer Girl," "In My Room," "Fun, Fun, Fun," etc.) out of Chuck Berryesque guitar riffs and Four Freshman–style harmonies. For years, he could do no wrong; every Beach Boy ditty he dreamed up turned to Top Ten gold. He had barely entered his twenties before he was being acclaimed as one of the true geniuses in rock. That's when his world began to crumble — when the critics began referring to what he did as Art.

Additional pressure was heaped on Brian by his father, who managed the group with all the warmth of a Marine drill sergeant. During the Beach Boys' early years together, the elder Wilson imposed himself on all aspects of Brian's life and work, nagging him about everything from production technique to his fear of water (which he deemed bad for the group's image). So overbearing was Murray Wilson's presence that the boys eventually fired him.

Yet another burden for the head Beach Boy was the group's increasing dependence on him to maintain their hit-making status in the face of growing competition both here and abroad. As rock became more and more Serious in the mid-sixties, Brian began to feel that he was being left behind. And indeed, to rock's new stoned-out philosopher hipsters, the Beach Boys came off as plastic and square — too clean, too corny, too Good Vibes L.A. What Brian couldn't — or wouldn't — see was that his audience was growing up and away from his vision of the endless summer of childhood.

Touring also took its toll — doctors warned Brian that the high decibel level at Beach Boys concerts threatened to damage his good ear permanently. Finally, in 1965, after suffering a nervous breakdown on a flight en route to a Houston concert, he announced his retirement from the road. Replaced at first by Glen Campbell and then by Bruce Johnston, he became a recording studio recluse devoting virtually all his time to trying to re-create on tape the sounds he heard in his head.

In 1966, while the rest of the group was away on tour, Wilson attempted to respond to the growing sophistication of pop by creating what still stands as his masterpiece — *Pet Sounds*. Unfortunately, however, this album proved to be too avant-garde for Beach Boys fans and too sweet for the psychedelic set; it would end up becoming the group's first bomb, and the disappointing sales hurt Brian deeply. He turned to acid for cosmic enlightenment, but

drugs only increased his anxiety. That Brian was starting to unhinge became only too clear when he had a sandbox installed under his grand piano in the living room of his Beverly Hills home. There, sitting at the keyboard, the Beach Boy who hated the water sought inspiration for new beach opuses by wiggling his toes in the sand.

The aborted 1966–67 *Smile* project further deepened Brian's funk. *Smile* was to have been a monumental experiment in pop expansion, an ambitious album that would prove once and for all that Brian Wilson could beat the Beatles at their own game. The album's failure and the rift it caused within the band, combined with the Beatles' release in June of 1967 of the earth-shaking *Sgt. Pepper*, provided the one-two punch that knocked Brian out of the sandbox. He retreated into a full-blown depression.

Because his driver's license had been revoked earlier following several serious auto accidents, Brian rarely ventured out of his house. On the rare occasions when he did visit friends, he traveled by taxi, often mooching the fare. By the early seventies, music-business gossip had him aimlessly cruising L.A. till all hours of the morning huddled in the back of a limo, dressed only in a terrycloth robe. There was also talk of overprotective — if not bullying — bodyguards who kept him a virtual prisoner in his own home, refusing him access to the smallest amount of spending money. Some even went so far as to say that Brian Wilson had retreated backward into childhood, that he had gone completely and irrevocably insane.

There was some truth to these rumors, but the overall picture was slightly more complex. It seems that with Brian's somewhat vague approval, his family (more specifically, Marilyn Wilson, his patient and long-suffering wife) had hired "bodyguards" in a desperate attempt to keep him away from drugs — particularly cocaine, which he himself admitted had turned him into a "useless little vegetable" in the past. Brian's sentries were also under instruction to keep him away from another of his self-destructive habits — his love of junk food. Always fleshy, even as a kid, Brian had ballooned into a grotesquely overweight and lethargic man during his slow disintegration in the sixties, thanks to a massive intake of cheeseburgers and candy bars.

In 1982, the controversy over the power wielded by Brian's protectors went public when two of his bodyguards, Stan Love (Beach Boy Mike's brother and Brian's cousin) and Rushton Pamplin, became objects of a civil suit mounted by Brian's late brother Dennis. He accused them, among other things, of "pursuing me through three rooms of my house, breaking windows and damaging furniture" whereupon one of the men "held me down on the floor while the other severely beat me." In a countercomplaint, Love admitted to a family feud with Dennis Wilson dating back to 1975 when he was first brought in as "protector, aide and counselor to try and rehabilitate Brian Wilson." Love maintained that for the next several years, he and Pamplin had overseen what he described as Brian's "remarkable recovery," going on to say that his long-standing disagreement with Dennis "stemmed from Dennis Wilson's providing Brian Wilson with heroin and cocaine, despite the fact that these drugs were severely damaging Brian's physical, psychological and mental health." The rumors surrounding Brian became even more murky when in the spring of 1983, his onetime nurse-companion Carolyn Williams alleged in a suit against his brothers, aides and accountant that the forty-year-old singer had been abducted from his bed at Cedars Sinai Hospital in L.A. and flown against his will to Hawaii.

But despite the determined efforts of his various watchdogs and the continuing interest and reverence accorded him by the rock establishment, Brian Wilson's talent has been dormant for well over a decade. Yet he has seemingly never given up his attempt to recapture the carefree state of mind that sparked his initial creative breakthrough. Throughout the seventies and on into the eighties, he was on, then off, drugs, tried Transcendental Meditation, health foods, jogging and twenty-four-hour psychiatric care at a cost rumored to hit $50,000 a month.

In a television interview taped shortly before his brother Dennis's death, which stressed the progress he'd been making, Brian was asked if there was anything that still caused him problems. "The most difficult time [I have] is waking up in the morning and facing reality," he replied ingenuously. "... when I hear the birds singing, I think, is that me?"

Left: John during his Wolf King period following the breakup of the Mamas and the Papas. *Right:* With Mackenzie, Spanky MacFarlane and Denny Dougherty for the group's ill-fated reprise.

For some rockers, drugs are an expensive recreation. For others, they are a retreat from the pressures of creating art on demand. For John Phillips, leader of the Mamas and the Papas, they were daily bread.

Phillips's drug nightmare first made headlines on July 31, 1980, when the feds arrested him at his lavish digs in Bridgehampton, Long Island, and charged him with heading a major pill-pushing operation — specifically with buying large quantities of amphetamines, opiates and other assorted mind-benders, unloading what he didn't need for a nifty profit and keeping the rest. However, subsequent reports and Phillips's own confessions indicated that he used far more drugs than he passed around. He admitted squandering as much as a million dollars a year on his and third wife Genevieve Waite's coke and smack habits.

Drug use was certainly an implied part of the free-style hippie life Papa John had promoted in Mamas and Papas hits like "California Dreaming." In 1967, he had been instrumental in organizing the Monterey Pop Festival, the event which officially ushered in the New Acid Age. But the dream soured in the seventies when Phillips started tampering with the hard stuff in an attempt to deal with the frustration of trying to revive a faltering career and being forty years old in a young man's game. Phillips's life-style became so debauched that Roman Polanski was convinced that he and his circle were somehow involved in the murder of his wife, Sharon Tate. In his 1984 autobiography, *Roman,* Polanski recounts several months he spent tracking Phillips in an effort to prove his guilt.

Like Papa, like daughter. When John's bust became public, it was revealed that Mackenzie Phillips, his daughter from his first marriage, had fallen prey to the same bad habits as her father. As one of the stars of *American Graffiti* and the hit TV series *One Day at a Time,* Mackenzie had become a star while still in her teens. Early in 1981, unprofessional behavior forced her dismissal from the show. Shortly after her father's arrest, Mackenzie joined him at a psychiatric hospital in New Jersey for a mental and physical overhaul. "I kept trying to get her to come for drug treatment," Phillips later explained, "because she was just sitting in her apartment shooting coke." Since their clean-up, John and Mackenzie have been singing a different tune, recounting their harrowing stories in counseling sessions for other addicts and doing the talk show/lecture circuit, ostensibly to warn others away from the drug trap.

This born-again routine proved very effective for the father-daughter duo. It (along with Phillips's testimony against a former associate) convinced the presiding judge in his case to let him off with serving only thirty days of an eight-year stretch. That little nuisance out of the way, Phillips unveiled plans to reunite the Mamas and the Papas, with Spanky McFarlane taking Cass Elliot's place and Mackenzie filling in for Mama Michelle. Meanwhile, Mackenzie (who is now said by *The Star* to be suffering from anorexia nervosa) announced plans for a TV bio of her drug-drenched travails — in which she would probably star.

Speaking of Michelle, the second Mrs. Phillips, who was so appalled by John's druggie scene that she tried for several years to obtain custody of his and Waite's son Tammerlaine, recently wrote a letter to *People* following that magazine's glowing coverage of John's latest clean-up campaign, in which she tartly observed, "I only hope that John's ninth attempt at detoxification is more successful than his previous eight."

◆◆◆◆◆◆◆◆◆◆◆◆◆◆◆◆◆◆◆◆ ★ ◆◆◆◆◆◆◆◆◆◆◆◆◆◆◆◆◆◆◆◆

He wanted to take you higher and he was just the guy to do it — a raucous rock'n'soul gangleader with flashy threads, the punchiest band in the land and tunes that wouldn't let you sit down. But when he fell from grace, the seemingly invincible Sly Stone crashed harder than anyone.

For his first twenty-five years, Sly (né Sylvester Stewart) led a charmed life. Born in Texas in 1944, he was still in his teens when he became one of San Francisco's top R&B disc jockeys. Before he was twenty, he had already produced hits for the Beau Brummels, Bobby Freeman and Grace Slick's Great Society. With his own group, the interracial intersexual Sly and the Family Stone, he pioneered a robust brand of hot-wired R&B fused with jazzy chops and high party fervor, while enjoying a nonstop string of hits. Sly and the Family Stone's fire-eating performance at the Woodstock Festival certified Sly as a top-drawer star.

Maybe it was the pressure of maintaining the group's success or the heat put on him by friends in the black power movement to use his celebrity to take a political stand. Or maybe it was the abundance of cocaine and angel dust floating around the scene at the time. Whatever it was, Sly blew it just when he was at his peak. By 1972, his career was speeding toward ruin. His life-style fairly reeked of self-destruction. People began predicting an early death in the manner of Hendrix and Joplin. He canceled shows at the last minute (causing riots in several U.S. cities), made alternately hostile and incomprehensible statements to the press, and turned out increasingly spotty albums. Then in a fit of hubris, he got married in front of 10,000 people on the stage of Madison Square Garden before a 1974 Family Stone show. The wedding, a Felliniesque spectacle, featured ten towering Halston models in long black gowns carrying giant gold fans and newscaster Geraldo Rivera as ringmaster/emcee. Also in attendance was the happy couple's nine-month-old son. The nuptials lasted almost an hour, the marriage just slightly longer.

Following Sly's divorce, there was a drug bust (on charges of "possession" and "possession for sale" of cannabis, cocaine and dangerous drugs) as well as rumors that he had taken up freebasing cocaine. By the mid-seventies, Sly's record sales had plummeted and pop's top party music-maker was an official has-been. In 1976 he released an album called *Heard Ya Missed Me, Well I'm Back,* but apparently he'd heard wrong. "I didn't have to do this album for the money," he claimed at the time. "I just gotta. I feel the music the most of anybody." But a *Jet* magazine article that same year reported that in fact Sly was broke; that although he still lived in the Hollywood mansion acquired back when he was the highest paid black performer in pop, he could now barely afford to buy food or pay his telephone bill.

Sly's continued attempts to revive his career despite such setbacks as an aborted collaboration with Parliament Funkadelic mastermind George Clinton fizzled after he and Clinton were arrested in L.A. for possession of narcotics following what was apparently a four-month freebasing spree. On his next album, in 1979, Sly claimed to be *Back on the Right Track,* but you couldn't prove it by the record's performance in the marketplace.

Of late, Sly's name has appeared on the police blotter more often than on records and marquees. He's been accused of petty larceny (pocketing the ring of a female acquaintance) and robbery ("borrowing" a van and sound equipment). In the summer of '83 during a guest shot to promote a Manhattan club date, he calmly told David Letterman that those charges were all misunderstandings, that he was in fact doing business as usual. But within several months, he was back in court: this time pleading no contest to charges of possession of cocaine and drug paraphernalia in Fort Myers, Florida. Soon after, Sly showed up at a Fort Myers drug rehab center. "You know it's the eighties," observed *Rolling Stone,* "when even Sly Stone is getting off drugs."

Left: The Jefferson Airplane, ca. 1967. *Right:* Grace with daughter China (née God) in 1977.

As the regal, raven-haired siren of rock's premier hippie band, the Jefferson Airplane and its '70s pop offshoot, the Jefferson Starship, Grace Slick was the very embodiment of psychedelic immortality. A former preppie of Puritan descent, Grace turned on, tuned in and dropped out with manic glee. During her first marriage to musician Jerry Slick in the early '60s, she claims to have had two medicine chests in their San Francisco bathroom — one for prescription drugs and one for everything else. ("I was always afraid that I'd get the mescaline mixed up with the mouthwash.") She was the Acid Queen, the "voice that launched a thousand trips"; legend has it that she took acid and other adventure drugs the way other people eat three meals a day. But, as it turns out, her real love was booze. While the rest of the San Francisco hippie community tripped the light fantastic, Grace was pickled in Dom Pérignon. She also subscribed to the ongoing philosophy of free love. After separating from Slick (with whom she'd formed her first band, the Great Society), Grace lived with Airplane drummer Spencer Dryden, then with the group's guitarist-singer, Paul Kantner, with whom she had daughter China (née God) in 1971. In between, she made countless sexual conquests. While still with Kantner, she told an interviewer, "Just let somebody tell me not to go out and get drunk or not to fuck some guy and that's the first thing I want to do."

Once she joined the Jefferson Airplane in 1967, Grace had it both ways — the financial success of a million-selling album in *Surrealistic Pillow* and a public forum for her rebel spirit. She showed up at a Finch College reunion party at the White House thrown by fellow alumna Tricia Nixon with counter-culture tummler Abbie Hoffman as her "bodyguard." After being turned away at the gate, she announced to the press that she and Abbie had intended to spike the party libations with powdered LSD. As it happens, only Hoffman's presence kept Grace from gaining admission; Mrs. Nixon and Tricia had been dying to meet her. So much so that they'd dispatched the White House social secretary to fetch her from the waiting alumnae, but by then, she and Hoffman had fled.

Although she came on like the ultimate liberated woman, in reality, Slick behaved more like one of the boys. For fifteen years, she reveled in her role as the renegade goddess of rock — continually trying to outdo her male cohorts at boozing, promiscuity and madcap stunts. She was branded an incorrigible, but criticism only egged her on. "The press would call me a mean bitch," she says. "Next time I'd be even meaner." But her daredevil image carried a high price. Continuing her freewheeling ways well into the Me Decade, she had two serious booze and drug-related auto accidents. Frequent weight gains brought on primarily from her love of high-caloric libations caused *Creem* magazine to dub her the Liz Taylor of rock. Further, her growing aggressiveness and cutting sarcasm proved to be a continual source of friction within the Airplane/Starship, eventually precipitating the departure of singer Marty Balin in 1971. For years, she and Balin had been the focus of the Airplane's live performances, as they stood downstage from the group, singing and staring hard into each other's eyes. But apparently their relationship had never been what it seemed. "I hate it when she does that sexy stuff on stage," Balin said after returning to the Starship several years later, "it makes me want to puke! Fuck Grace Slick? I wouldn't even let her *blow* me!"

Slick's 1976 marriage to Starship lightman Skip Johnson (thirteen years her junior) seemed an indication that she intended to get her act together. But then, during a 1978 European tour with the group, she suffered another attack of temperament. Claiming to be ill (apparently owing to a major case of nerves and a champagne-besotted revel the night before), she refused to perform at a concert date in Lorelei, Germany. When the band canceled the show, the German audience rioted, destroying several hundred thousand dollars' worth of Starship equipment. At a concert date the following night, Slick was so smashed and out of control that the band turned off her mike. After that fiasco, she quit the band in a blaze of histrionics.

A prolonged period of serious self-examination followed. "My husband told me if I kept it up I was going to be pathetic," she recalls. "I don't mind being obnoxious. I don't mind being disgusting and I don't mind being a freak. But I *don't* want to be pathetic."

Since then, Slick has apparently managed to give up booze. In order to do so, she traded life as a rock star for that of a suburban mother. After two years of supermarkets and carpools, she decided to take a shot at a solo career. When the response — both public and critical — to her initial album efforts to proved to be little more than lukewarm, Slick made a tentative return to the Starship, doing background vocals on their 1981 album, *Modern Times.*

And for now, there she remains. Even though she continues to go it alone on occasion, her musical fortunes seem permanently linked to the old gang. They need her; she needs them. The group's male vocalist, Mickey Thomas, may indeed be able to sound like either Balin or Slick, as he once jokingly boasted, but it's Slick's fiery presence that keeps the group viable. While it's true that she now looks more like one of the ladies-who-lunch than a rock star (and why shouldn't she — she's well into her forties, after all), she still has a face the camera loves — an invaluable asset in this video age. Whether she's been drunk (often) or off-key (more often), she's always been the Airplane/Starship's main attraction — a fact she modestly acknowledges. "When you put six ducks and one rat on a stage," she explains, "the rat's gonna stand out."

Grace with
second husband
Skip Johnson

Any number of scene-makers were christened the Girl of the Moment in the sixties, but none ever worked so hard at living up to the title as Marianne Faithfull, the convent girl who became an overnight sensation with the release of the Stones' outtake "As Tears Go By." And though the current Faithfull is far removed from the winsome sixteen-year-old who made her debut in 1964, it just may be that her Moment isn't over yet.

Almost everyone who came of age during the Flower Power Era remembers the story of Marianne Faithfull's discovery: how the titled daughter of a Hungarian baroness met Mick Jagger and Andrew Loog Oldham at a party and was subsequently persuaded by them to record a Stones tune, despite the fact that she'd never sung a note in her life; and how after that record became an international hit she left her husband and young son to enter into a lengthy and celebrated affair with the "pimply lout" who'd first gotten her attention by spilling a drink down the front of her dress. During that period of myriad busts and hit records, Mick and Marianne were pop's golden couple, the king and queen of swinging London.

That fabled romance was ultimately subverted, according to Faithfull, by Jagger's obsessive devotion to his career. Then at the height of his youthful energy and productivity, Jagger continually left his young mistress to her own devices while he labored in the studio for days and nights on end. This is not to say that Marianne's life was entirely without its entertaining interludes; there were the drug busts at Cheynes Walk, the posh Chelsea townhouse she shared with Jagger, along with the notorious Redlands raid at Keith Richards's country estate which found her lolling around in nothing but a fur rug, followed by Jagger's subsequent trial and imprisonment for possession of amphetamines (which Marianne later admitted were hers). And who can forget her much publicized pregnancy, which incurred the wrath of no less a personage than the Archbishop of Canterbury. Thanks to these exploits — and others — she became a celebrity of the first order, a gossip column perennial and the tabloid's darling, and yet by this point her primary role in life was to play the part of Jagger's Old Lady, a pursuit that required her to do little more than pick out his clothes (which helps to explain his frilly costumes during this period) and oversee the maintenance of Cheynes Walk. But the life of a *Hausfrau* was hardly diverting enough for a woman of Faithfull's youth and ambition. Of course, she was a recording star in her own right, but one who was nevertheless at the mercy of her mentors — Jagger and Oldham. By then, Oldham himself was quietly being eased out of the picture and Jagger was far too busy fashioning his personal pop legacy to bother with hers. "I wasn't smoking or drinking, cigarettes or alcohol, taking drugs, I didn't even sleep around," she said later. "All I did from the minute I got up to the minute I fell down was work, from the age of seventeen, to about twenty. And then suddenly, when I found myself financially OK, living with Jagger, I thought, right, I'm now going to start doing a bit of living, and of course, I did with a vengeance."

As she and Jagger grew further apart, she began to identify with the ousted Stone, Brian Jones, whom — according to Jagger's biographer, Tony Scaduto — she viewed as a fellow victim of her lover's ambition and Machiavellian schemes. Her resentment was further inflamed by Jagger's growing involvement in film — which she considered an encroachment on her acting career, limited as it was. (Her primary acting credit at the time was *Girl on a Motorcycle,* a glorified skin flick, whose alternate title, *Naked Under Leather,* said it all.) Finally, while on location with Jagger in Australia for his second feature, *Ned Kelly,* she unsuccessfully attempted to end her life by downing 150 sleeping pills.

Following her recovery and final break with Jagger, Faithfull began to pursue acting seriously with appearances in several BBC and stage productions as well as the abortive underground film *Lucifer Rising.* She also played Ophelia to Nicol Williamson's Hamlet in the Tony Richardson stage production and film. "I am Ophelia," she remarked at the time, "I know what it's like to be mad."

Just as it seemed that she'd finally gotten her life under control, she was rushed to the hospital after an apparent drug overdose. A year after that episode, she was found wandering a London street in a state of drugged (or drunken) confusion. She formally registered as a heroin addict in the government's drug maintenance program and was later hospitalized in a National Health hospital. "If you're rich you can go to Switzerland and have your blood changed," she said, "but this is the ground root level, the street addict level." Eventually her drug problem began to affect her acting career. Fired from one play for not being able to remember her lines, she then lost a featured role in a Roman Polanski film after showing up stoned for an audition. Her addiction also caused her to lose custody of her son, Nicholas, to her first husband. Throughout this unhappy time, the tabloids reveled in her downfall; one story even had her slinging hash at a London beanery. Of course, Marianne Faithfull was the perfect fall guy for the rock world's double standard. While Jagger and the Stones went their merry way, free to pursue all manner of decadent thrills with the public's blessing, she was painted the sadder-but-wiser Fallen Woman, the tramp who must now pay the awful dues for her wicked wicked ways.

With the exception of an occasional what-ever-happened-to story, she remained an elusive figure throughout most of the seventies. But beneath Marianne Faithfull's aura of vulnerability and pathos lay a more resilient woman than anyone had imagined. (In a telling moment during an interview several years later she told a reporter, "You *don't* know how poor my mother and I were and you *don't* know how ambitious I was.") The failure of a 1975 album, *Faithless,* made her consider abandoning singing more or less for good until she met and married rock musician Ben Briarly. With her young husband's help, she created *Broken English* (1980), a collection of tough autobiographical songs and a few well-chosen covers ("Sister Morphine") that bowed to unqualified critical raves. But even in the midst of triumph, Marianne once again proved herself to be the Heartbreak Kid: in New York to promote the album, her voice was a little more than a parched rasp during an appearance on *Saturday Night Live.* By the time she took the stage at a New York rock club later that evening she could barely be heard at all, yet she finished the set much to the fascination and discomfort of the audience. Faithfull later attributed the debacle to a case of laryngitis and a surprise visit from former Stones' consort Anita Pallenberg. "That was the last thing I needed," she said ruefully. To make matters worse, there was another bust following her return to England — this time for a small amount of heroin which she claimed she was holding for a friend.

By 1982, a second solo album (*Dangerous Acquaintances*) had shattered once and for all Faithfull's professional waif image. Her subsequent performance dates in the States drew all manner of fans — teenagers, jetsetters, movie stars and grown-up sixties grads — curious to see how the eighties were treating the once-and-future Girl of the Moment. What they found was a kind of pop Marlene Dietrich, a glamorous figure with a husky, talky vocal delivery, who wasn't the least bit shy about trading on her world-weary image. And though more than a few writers clucked over her faded beauty (and there were plenty of unflattering photographs to prove their point), she looked remarkably good for someone who'd packed so much living into the last twenty years.

1983 found her marriage to Briarly kaput (the announcement of the impending divorce in *Rolling Stone* was accompanied by a very sexy photo in which Marianne appeared to have forgotten her shirt) and critics beginning to tire of her seemingly boundless remorse. But although it had become obvious that she was not necessarily going to prove herself a major musical talent (as it had seemed for a moment in the beginning), it was clear that Marianne Faithfull's life and exploits would always make news.

The many sides of Marianne: from virginal schoolgirl to world-weary vamp

In the years since he first came to this country, Joe Cocker has lurched in and out of the spotlight so many times that even his most devoted fans don't know whether to regard him as a has-been or an extremely low-profile superstar.

In 1967, Cocker was a pipefitter's apprentice making eighteen shillings a week. A year later, hard-sell manager Dee Anthony (Tony Bennett, J Geils, Peter Frampton, etc.) brought him to America and got him on *The Ed Sullivan Show*. From there, he went on to spend nine grueling months on the road. Next came his historic appearance at Woodstock and suddenly he was a legend. He became one of rock's top attractions, a heavyweight capable of commanding staggering sums of money for only a few hours' work.

After Woodstock, Cocker was ready for a rest. He dissolved his band and made plans to hole up in L.A. for a while. Then, the Immigration Department stepped in and decreed that he had to tour if he wanted to keep his working papers. Thus was born Mag Dogs and Englishmen — a ragtag circus of roadies, groupies, musicians, their wives, dogs and children and various other hangers-on. The Mad Dogs tour was a tremendous success not only for Cocker, but for Leon Russell, whom it established as a major star. After the smoke cleared, Russell and and most of the gang went on to ply their trades elsewhere, leaving Cocker to his own devices. He was also left to pay the bills — which included such expenses as $12,000 to fly the entire troupe from Seattle to Tulsa (Leon Russell's hometown) for a picnic and then back for its next date in San Francisco. Although the tour left Cocker financially humbled, it nevertheless made him an even more valuable commodity — everybody seemed to want a piece of the action. Being a passive sort, Cocker didn't seem capable of saying no to either of the major factions that were then battling for his allegiance (Denny Cordell of Shelter Records and Dee Anthony). So instead, he chose to ignore the entire situation and retire. Later, he would settle with Anthony for a substantial sum of money.

The strain of facing up to his own success seemed more than Cocker could bear. He was busted twice — once in America for possession of drugs in 1968 and again in Australia on similar charges. Following that last infraction, Cocker — who'd been ordered to leave the country — got roaring drunk and collapsed on stage at one of his final dates. Later that same evening, he was thrown out of his Melbourne hotel following a fracas involving his girlfriend, the hotel staff and the cops. So began a long string of public embarrassments and career setbacks. As the details of his sad story were aired by the press, Cocker's image gradually deteriorated from that of sixties hero to shell-shocked victim. Soon his dependence on alcohol and drugs (grass and cocaine, not heroin, as was widely believed), alre... y well developed in his early touring days, began to impair his performing abilities, and before long, he'd added throwing up and falling down to his onstage repertoire. His 1972 comeback tour was an inevitable failure. By 1974, he'd reached the absolute nadir of his career when a celebrity-packed (Cher, Marc Bolan, Diana Ross, John Sebastian) house at the Roxy, which

had gathered to see him make yet another comeback, saw instead a poor drunken sod stumble and mumble his way through a performance. One witness later described the spectacle as "one of the most embarrassing displays of a dead body I've ever seen." After that, people began coming to his shows just to see if he could sink any lower.

The seventies held more than their share of humiliation for Cocker, and yet, he managed to score several new hits ("Cry Me a River," "High Time We Went," "You Are So Beautiful") during its first few years. In 1977, he left A&M, his label of almost ten years, reportedly owing them — as well as various managers and other personnel — hundreds of thousands of dollars. It was hoped that a new contract with Elektra would help to ease that financial burden, but an album produced from that union proved to be only moderately successful. After another lengthy layoff, Cocker returned to the States in 1981 to proclaim that he had gotten his daily liquor intake down to a few beers a day. As circumspect and soft-spoken as ever, Cocker even made a few appearances on TV talk shows to reassure his fans that he had his life under control. He looked slightly the worse for wear, but sounded as good as ever. However, pop audiences seemed to have little interest in this scarred veteran of the Flower Power Era, and his only record sales of note occurred in the gospel field. And then, in the summer of 1982, Cocker's career registered a sudden rally with his duet with Jennifer Warnes, "Up Where We Belong," his first Number One song.

The fans who turn out to see him today are greeted by a somewhat spaced, but decidedly well-behaved, Joe Cocker. Always something of a freak, especially during his heyday, Cocker's manic stage presence is now considerably subdued. There are no more (or fewer anyway) spastic jerks, no more grappling with an imaginary guitar. While his face still contorts occasionally, he usually manages to keep his body under control and his arms decorously at his sides. What remains of the old manic Joe Cocker stage persona is a kind of benign Judy Garland quality that creates an interesting tension throughout his performances — one that makes audiences, who are fully aware of his past history, pull for him to make it through a set and explode in gratitude and relief when he does. All in all, it makes for quite a show.

When everyone calls you God, what do you do for an encore? Back in 1966 a record company promotion proclaimed "Clapton is God" in mock graffiti all over London. Soon, Clapton fans, apparently believing the slogan to be authentic, began speading the Word themselves, scrawling it on subway walls and tenement halls. So pervasive was Clapton's image as a sainted rock martyr that *Rolling Stone* even did a cover showing him as Jesus on the cross.

Clapton may not have been God, but he was certainly a godsend to rock guitar. With the Yardbirds, John Mayall's Bluesbreakers and the archetypal power trio, Cream, he pioneered a fiery, technically dazzling fusion of blues emotion, rock grit and flights of jazzy improvisational fancy that became the model for countless white rock guitarists to come.

But the recognition that came with greatness very nearly cost Clapton everything. After the quick demise of Blind Faith (Clapton, Cream drummer Ginger Baker, Traffic singer-organist Steve Winwood and bassist Rick Grech), his own 1969 supergroup venture, Clapton seemed determined to stay out of the spotlight: he retreated into backup spots for dixie soul duo Delaney and Bonnie, Leon Russell and Beatle buddy George Harrison. His first "solo" album featured a cast of near thousands from the Delaney and Bonnie aggregation, and for his next band, he adopted the guise of Derek and the Dominoes. At around the same time, he also retreated into a psychological fog as the result of an addiction to heroin.

There were any number of factors that might have led Eric Clapton to addiction at the height of his career: the burden of living up to a reputation he felt was undeserved, the deaths of his friends Jimi Hendrix and Duane Allman, and a clandestine affair with Patti Harrison, his best friend's wife. On a more practical level, Clapton hoped junk would lend a little character to his somewhat shallow baritone — as he'd been told it had done for his idol, Ray Charles. (And in fact, his voice has grown huskier over the years —thanks in all likelihood to chain-smoking more than anything else.)

By 1971, Clapton had become a walking disaster zone; people who saw him were amazed that he could even stand up, let alone continue to work. For a while, it looked as if the Living Legend were well on his way to being dead. That Clapton had intentionally cultivated his desperate condition only made him a more romantic figure.

Clapton's various troubles caused him to drop almost entirely from public view — with his famous Clapton and Friends concert at London's Rainbow Theatre in 1973 being virtually the sole exception. (And he very nearly didn't show up for that. Strolling in at practically the last minute, he casually attributed his tardiness to the fact that his trousers had to be let out to accommodate a recent weight gain.) For three years he holed up in his Surrey home, eventually converting all his money and possessions into the deadly white powder. In the necromaniac frenzy that followed the deaths of Joplin, Jones and Hendrix, his self-imposed exile generated a bumper crop of rumors — first that he was an addict, second that he was dying and, finally, that he was dead. Clapton himself had contributed to the ghoulish speculation by telling interviewers that he didn't expect to live past the age of thirty, that, in fact, he relished the idea of dying young.

But Clapton came back — thanks to the help of friends like Peter Townshend and a Chinese electro-acupuncture drug withdrawal method — and when he did, he seemed a changed man. Certainly a changed musician. Most of his albums from 1974's *461 Ocean Boulevard* on have consisted mainly of easygoing commercial blues, ballads and shuffling rockers — material conspicuously lacking the transcendent glory of his vintage work.

Clapton himself seemed to have mixed feelings about having cleaned up his act, saying, "I still feel that to be a junkie is to be part of a very elite club. I've also got this death wish. I don't like life. That's another reason for taking heroin, because it's like surrounding yourself in pink cotton wool. Nothing bothers you whatsoever. Nothing will faze you in any way."

Clapton's marriage to Patti Harrison in 1979 suggested that he did intend to hang around for a while. However, this newfound peace of mind was jarred by the death of longtime Clapton bassist Carl Radle, who — like Clapton — had been a heroin addict for many years. Although Radle was reportedly felled by a kidney infection, there was speculation that despondency resulting from having been fired by Clapton had more than likely contributed to his death. Then in 1981, at the start of a nationwide tour, a perforated ulcer landed Clapton in a Midwestern hospital, leading to stories that his abstinence was a charade; that in fact, he had traded drug abuse for alcoholism. It was almost two years before he again ventured out on the road and into the grooves (with *Money and Cigarettes*). By early 1984, Clapton was feeling well enough to organize a series of fund-raising concerts to help out multiple sclerosis victim Ronnie Lane, much as Townshend had done for him a decade earlier. There, in what *Rolling Stone* hailed as the "concert of the year," Clapton — the spiffy ex-junkie — electrified fans with an inspired rendition of his old hit "Cocaine."

Clapton . . . with the Yardbirds, Cream, Blind Faith, and finally as a venerated sixties survivor

Ronnie Campagna

There was every reason to think of Gregg Allman as a villain back in 1976. Forsaking the memory of his late guitar hero brother Duane and the hard-playing Southern rock'n'roll tradition of the Allman Brothers Band, he turned out solo albums that leaned toward commercial FM fare, even going so far as to incorporate a slushy string section into one of his tours. And then there were the tales of Allman's excessive alcohol and drug abuse. Now this in and of itself shouldn't have gotten him into hot water; after all, such stuff is standard behavior for a rock star. The problem was that he also developed a reputation for being surly and arrogant as well as being a drunk and a druggie. This led many people to conclude that Gregg had let stardom go to his head. As if to prove them right, Allman up and married Cher — all wrong for a hard-rocking country boy's image. Allman must have known that his fancy new wife wouldn't go over well with the good ol' boy contingent, but apparently Cher had been his dream date ever since he was in high school: "I bought all Cher's records," he confessed after they married. "She was my idol." He'd first seen her in the flesh while he and Duane were playing in the house band at the Whiskey à Go-Go. "Isn't that the most beautiful woman you ever saw?" he remembers asking his brother.

Together Cher and her hulking, flaxen-haired rocker became the darlings of the supermarket gossip sheets. As Allman and Woman, the pair even made an inauspicious attempt at becoming the backwoods Sonny and Cher. Their union produced an embarrassing album of Vegas pop prophetically titled *Two the Hard Way*, and a son named Elijah Blue.

And those were the good times. Things went downhill from there starting in January of 1975, when Allman took the stand before a Georgia grand jury to give evidence against his road manager and personal valet, John "Scooter" Herring, who was charged with five counts of conspiracy to distribute narcotics, including cocaine. By the time Allman was called to testify at Herring's trial six months later, public sentiment against him was so strong that he had to be escorted into the courtroom by a phalanx of U.S. marshals. "I was scared to go in there and have them ask me those things," he said later, "but it was either that or go to jail." In return for his testimony, Allman — a former heroin addict, admitted cocaine user, and for many years Herring's best customer — was granted total immunity. Herring got seventy-five years. In true Southern tradition, justice was swift; the entire proceedings — trial, conviction and sentencing — were carried out in less than three days. In fact, the whole affair swept by so quickly that most observers completely forgot Allman's offhand recollection that Herring had saved his life after a near-fatal overdose in 1974.

The Scooter incident was the climax but not the end of Allman's travails. He licked drugs via methadone maintenance a short time later, but that didn't remove the taint of having ratted on a friend. He was still rock star *non grata* in most music circles — especially that of the Allman Brothers Band. The bad feelings generated by the trial had simply been too great. The band exploded in a blaze of recriminations and bad blood, most of it directed at Gregg from singer/guitarist Dickey Betts. "There's no way we can work with Gregg ever again," he said at the time. "I mean what can you do when a man who's worked with you personally for two years and saved your life twice is sitting there with his life on the line and you walk into court and tap on the mike and say, 'Testing, one two three,' like Gregg did."

For months after the trial, the story of Allman's troubles was splashed across the scandal mags; one cover illustration even showed Gregg and manager Phil Walden offering a blow of coke to then-President Carter (who owed a good part of his election victory to the Allman's fund-raising concerts and the youth vote that had come with their endorsement). Finally, Allman's marriage to Cher, which had faltered earlier, dissolved once and for all when a combination of downs and booze caused him to fall face forward into a plate of spaghetti during a night out at a Hollywood bistro.

Still smarting from his split with Cher and the Allman and Woman fiasco, Gregg went back to Macon to ask forgiveness from his old band — most specifically from Betts and drummer Butch Trucks. To everyone's amazement, they seemed open to the idea of a reconciliation. But by then, of course, both these musicians had tried and failed to get their own bands going and were beginning to feel some financial strain. As luck would have it, Scooter Herring, out on bail at the time, saw fit to bestow his blessing on the proposed reunion. That was all it took. In 1979, the reborn Allman Brothers Band produced a moderately successful album. But just as it did, their label, Capricorn, capsized.

Today, Gregg Allman is no longer the villain he seemed back in 1976. In fact, apart from an occasional public dig from Cher or the announcement of yet another Allman Brothers split, reconciliation or solo venture, you hardly ever hear his name. On the rare occasions when he has consented to talk about the past, it's as if he's recalling a dream. In his memory Hollywood remains a vile place that makes normal people go insane.

Allman and what's-her-name

Long before Lou Reed started conducting tours through an urban inferno populated by junkies, transvestites, sexual deviants and other social outcasts in songs like "Heroin," "Waiting for the Man," and his freak serenade to the Warhol crowd, "Walk on the Wild Side," it was obvious that he was not your average Joe. As a high-school student on Long Island, he underwent electro-shock therapy for depression. At Syracuse University, where he was an English major, he ran with a hip crowd and studied with the late poet Delmore Schwartz. While there, he is said to have pointed a gun (unloaded) at the commanding officer's head in order to get himself excused from ROTC.

Reed's roller-coaster ride to fame officially begins with the Velvet Underground, a quartet of inspired New York art scene amateurs who took their name from a porno novel. In the sixties while the Frisco acid-rock clique monopolized the airwaves with its psychedelic peace-and-love shtick, the Velvets were cranking out savage, primitive rock'n'roll that glorified drugs, sado-masochism and death. (Reed once told a *Daily News* reporter that the difference between the Velvets and the Grateful Dead was that the Dead took little kids backstage and turned them on while the Velvets shot them up.)

In recent years, Reed has denied that he ever took heroin, saying in one interview that "nobody could be here now having done all the things I'm supposed to have done." But in at least one mid-seventies story, he admitted to shooting speed, and when he mimed mainlining during "Heroin" and "Waiting for the Man," audiences weren't sure whether he was kidding or not. His sexual predilection was another much-discussed mystery. After a brief marriage to a pretty blond waitress named Betty in 1972, he took up for a while with a hulking male transvestite alternately referred to as Rachel and "Thing." It was also around this time that Reed was rumored to have had a torrid romance with David Bowie. Then late in 1980 during a performance at a New York club (where his selections included "White Christmas" and "The Star-Spangled Banner"), Reed announced that he was getting hitched again — this time to a woman named Sylvia Morales. Shortly thereafter, he and the Missus settled down to a cozy existence in suburban New Jersey.

A 1982 album (*The Blue Mask*) born of that pairing exhibited a calmer, more introspective Lou Reed — one who quite obviously relished his comfortable new life-style, not to mention his new wife. There the erstwhile celebrant of bisexuality proclaimed that "only a woman can love a man." And the self-styled degenerate druggie who once wrote, "I saw my head laughing, rolling on the ground" asked us to believe that he was "just your average guy." Both admirers and detractors alike were left to wonder if this pose wasn't just another Lou Reed mind game, the kind he'd been playing on the public for years.

As fascinating as they are, Lou Reed's mercurial personality and special brand of daring have never been particularly salable. Despite the Velvet's legendary status, the group's influence was restricted primarily to other musicians; their public reception was limited — so limited that Reed ended up working for his father's Long Island accounting firm following the group's demise. To date Reed's one and only record to go gold is 1972's *Transformer* — produced by David Bowie, then a nascent rock hero and Reed's longtime admirer. The success of that album prompted Reed to lay on his own androgynous burlesque extra thick in imitation of Bowie and, of course, himself. "I mimic me probably better than anybody," he said at the time, "so if everybody else is making money ripping me off, I figured maybe I better get in on it. Why not? I created Lou Reed. I have nothing faintly in common with that guy, but I can play him well. Really well."

Following *Transformer*, Reed tripped up even his most ardent fans with a morbid operatic LP entitled *Berlin*. He hit again with the wild live *Rock and Roll Animal*, then turned right around and issued *Sally Can't Dance*, which he himself said "sucked." Next in 1975 came the disastrous *Metal Machine Music*, a songless two-record set of electronic beeping and farting. After that, Reed took stock of his accelerating decline and vowed to the press that there would be "no more bullshit, no more dyed-hair-faggot-junkie trip." He went on to say that he was as proud of his newest work, *Coney Island Baby*, as of anything he'd done with the Velvets. Unfortunately, the critics did not agree; they dismissed it as mere self-parody. Then in the late seventies, just as his career took a turn for the better with *Street Hassle*, Reed put out a double live LP called *Take No Prisoners*, in which he spiced up his greatest hits with long, twisted Lenny Bruce–like raps, including one where he directly insulted two prominent rock critics. No doubt it was the pressure of being famous, yet flat-out broke that caused him to blow up at his record company president, Clive Davis, during a New York show in 1979, angrily demanding, "Where's the money?"

Lou Reed's influence on rock is incalculable and his knack for career miscalculation greater still. After returning to his former label, RCA, in 1981, Reed is reported to have turned right around and sued them. Yet, whatever problems Reed may have had with RCA appeared to have been ironed out by the summer of 1982 and the release of *The Blue Mask*. Both that album and 1983's *Legendary Hearts* found him rhapsodizing about married love (not counting the obligatory songs about drugs and suicide, of course) in much the same manner as John Lennon on *Double Fantasy*. Together those LPs earned him the greatest plaudits of his career. Some critics even ranked *Hearts* over Bruce Springsteen's epic *Nebraska*, released earlier that same year. But while that album scored big on the charts and in the marketplace, *Hearts'* sales were predictably pallid. The contrasting fates of these two works provide a clue as to what is at the core of Lou Reed's failure to break through to widespread public acceptance: he may be more prolific than Springsteen and his lyrics more inspired, but the Boss is young and cute (two things Reed seems never to have been) and when it comes to rock'n'roll, young and cute are where it's at.

Lou Reed ... just a regular guy

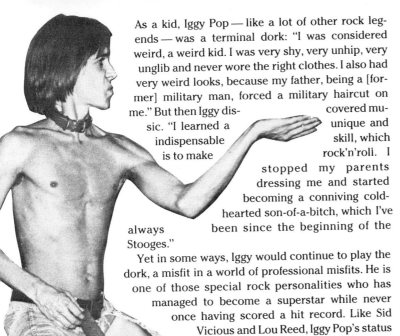

As a kid, Iggy Pop — like a lot of other rock legends — was a terminal dork: "I was considered weird, a weird kid. I was very shy, very unhip, very unglib and never wore the right clothes. I also had very weird looks, because my father, being a [former] military man, forced a military haircut on me." But then Iggy discovered music. "I learned a unique and indispensable skill, which is to make rock'n'roll. I stopped my parents dressing me and started becoming a conniving coldhearted son-of-a-bitch, which I've always been since the beginning of the Stooges."

Yet in some ways, Iggy would continue to play the dork, a misfit in a world of professional misfits. He is one of those special rock personalities who has managed to become a superstar while never once having scored a hit record. Like Sid Vicious and Lou Reed, Iggy Pop's status as a rock legend rests more on his demented sensibility than on his hit-making ability. A product of the Detroit garage-punk scene of the sixties, Iggy (the former James Newell Osterberg) started out as a drummer for a local band called the Iguanas but he eventually discovered that his kamikaze pyrotechnics worked best up front at the mike. His next group, the slambang white-noise Stooges, provided the perfect vehicle for the Ig's unique theatrical depravity. He turned on the anticharm against their heavy-metal blast, cursing at his audience, puking onstage and diving into broken glass. (You can hear the bottles smashing on the live Stooges LP *Metallic K.O.*) During his stage gambits, he incurred countless injuries — often cutting himself with his microphone, burning himself by swirling its long cord around his body or subjecting himself to violent physical contact with his audience. Taking audience participation to a new high, Iggy often encouraged spectators to perform fellatio on him and beat him up. Offstage, Iggy embellished his outlaw image by letting it be known that he'd cultivated a "vicious drug habit." The Stooges became known as a bad-ass druggie band and Iggy himself as a perverted junkie who surrounded himself with hoods and lowlife JDs.

After two albums and a degree of cult success, the Stooges ultimately shattered under the pressure of various legal, financial, chemical and personality problems. In the interim, Iggy did yard work and lived with his parents in their mobile home. Virtually penniless, he went to New York City where he survived mostly on a diet of drugs and slept on the floor of the men's room at Elektra Records. Then a friend introduced him to David Bowie and his manager, Tony DeFries. "I approached Tony about managing me and he agreed. That's the day I signed away my soul." DeFries's first move was to take Iggy up to Clive Davis at Columbia where his special rendition of "The Shadow of Your Smile" won him a contract and a six-figure advance. Next, Bowie and DeFries took Pop to London to groom him for the big time. To get things rolling, Bowie, who was then putting together his own stable of rock acts, called a press conference to introduce Iggy. However, the usually well-behaved Bowie showed up drunk for the affair, and during the course of the proceedings, grabbed his new protégé and planted a big juicy kiss on his lips. Iggy responded to this display of affection by punching his mentor in the face. Things went steadily downhill from there. According to Iggy, he and his band (the reassembled Stooges) were forced to submit to a demeaning publicity hype that included "riding in limousines just to go to the drugstore." He also claimed that the money for such contrived ostentation was coming directly out of his own advance. Other sources of irritation between Mainman (DeFreis's management firm) and Pop arose from the company's tough position on drugs. DeFries also nixed some of Pop's more explicit compositions like "Gimme Some Skin," "I'm Sick of You," "Penetration," "Tight Pants," etc. after the wife of a Columbia exec happened to overhear him singing a little number called "Fresh Rag." (Sample: "I can smell you walkin' down the street with your fresh rag on.") Moreover, the group was extremely displeased with the way Bowie mixed the album's surviving cuts. "Half the time the good parts were mixed out by that fucking carrot top — sabotaged, I think." Whether or not his complaints were justified, Iggy took the rap for his eventual break with DeFries. Once again, he was branded a loser.

After the Stooges split (for the second time), Iggy headed for L.A. where he took on the role of the pop scene's court jester. There was talk for a time of his teaming up with the three surviving Doors (poetic if ironic justice, given his fixation on rock's other destructo king, Jim Morrison), but nothing ever came of the proposed union. Finally, in a fit of depression, Iggy overdosed on a huge quantity of Quaaludes, Valium and Seconal at an L.A. beanery. The cops picked him up and gave him the choice of jail or a padded cell. He chose the latter. However, twenty-four hours later, he'd busted out of the mental hospital and downed what was left of his stash. The aftereffects of this rampage frightened Iggy to such an extent that he finally committed himself to the hospital voluntarily. After many months of psychiatric therapy, he finally graduated from a city-run drug withdrawal program.

Still an ardent admirer of Pop's unique talents, David Bowie visited him often in the hospital and eventually ended up carting him off to Berlin where he managed to keep him busy, off drugs and solvent. Bowie then produced and co-wrote two albums for Iggy, and, in a show of support, even picked up the tab for a promotional tour of America. Unfortunately, most of the people who turned out for this event expected the old Iggy and at times, Pop was forced to fall back on bad habits (like taking amphetamines and cocaine) to get up the energy to keep the fans happy.

The onset of the eighties found Iggy toning down his old manic persona and attempting a more commercial approach. His manners were considerably improved, and his body still as classically chiseled as ever despite years of flamboyant abuse. He seemed comfortable — almost happy — with himself. But naturally now that Iggy Pop has finally tamed his self-destructive urges, the fans don't seem to be nearly as interested.

Top left: Iggy as punk progenitor

Still Iggy after all these years: his manic days are over, but he still drops trow for the faithful at infrequent club dates.

So you want to be a Rock'n'Roll Star

Rock stardom doesn't derive solely from the ability to crank out hit records. Sure, talent helps. But it isn't everything....

There is no future in rock'n'roll. It's only recycled past.... Basically, rock'n'roll isn't protest, and never was. It's only — it promotes interfamily tension. Or it used to anyway. Now it can't even do that, because fathers don't ever get outraged with the music. Either they like it, or it sounds similar to what they liked as kids. So rock'n'roll's gone, that's all gone.

— MICK JAGGER, quoted in *Rolling Stone*

You've heard it a thousand times before. Rock'n'roll is dead — mortally wounded by enemies from within and without. Its old audience is grown-up and exhausted, its current one too small or too spacey to keep its rebel spirit alive. And admittedly, there is evidence to support the charge. Record sales are down, concert attendance is off. The Top Ten suffers from an overabundance of freeze-dried pop formulas and a glossy, flossy overproduced sound. Many of the bands that dominate the LP and singles charts are little more than traveling circus troupes — anonymous ciphers with interchangeable faces and riffs. Their members die or are discarded and no one seems to notice, let alone care. Only a few of the old-fashioned brand-name stars remain. Those that do are obliged to come up with at least one

album masterpiece a year, to tour six months of that same year to promote it, and to give interviews in the time that's left over. As a result, their lives are an endless blur of recording studios, airports, bars and groupies. And think of the professional hazards they face. The odds are that the average rock Fave Rave will be deaf by the time he's thirty, or a has-been — or both. If he lives that long, that is. And yet, even with all this, there probably isn't a kid anywhere who wouldn't walk over his grandmother to become a rock'n'roll star.

The funny thing is that it's not really all that hard to do. There's a formula for achieving rock stardom, a method to the madness. Pop appeal doesn't derive solely from the ability to crank out hit records. Sure, talent is helpful. But it isn't everything. Indeed, rock renown often has less to do with musical skills than with tenacity, personal style and a willingness to play the game. You may have noticed certain pertinent rules and regulations of the rock trade in the preceding pages, but just in case you missed them, here's a brief recap:

START EARLY. Even if you're Little Richard incarnate, you've got to put in at least five or six years of local bar gigs, botched auditions and contractual rip-offs before you get a chance to strut your stuff in front of the masses for real. Once you've broken through the public consciousness, follow Rick James's example and knock a few years off your age. (Rick used to be the same age as his former bandmate in the Mynah Birds, Neil Young, who is now pushing forty while the irrepressible Rick hangs tough at twenty-nine.)

YOU GOTTA HAVE A GIMMICK. As any number of rock legends from Screamin' Jay Hawkins to David Bowie have proved, it never hurts to have that special little something extra that sets you apart from the hoi polloi — be it a bone in your nose or billing yourself as a bisexual alien from outer space. (This shtick can be discarded once you've gotten the public's attention.)

ATTITUDE. Whether you're a tough kid from the ghetto or a mild-mannered child of suburbia, put on the Funk. Come on like you've been to hell and back and enjoyed the trip. (See Tom Waits.) Cultivate an air of misanthropy. Make racist remarks about beloved soul stars and label all older generation rockers boring old farts (even if they're only a few years your senior). Wax dangerous, brooding, or better yet, insane. And remember, a wasted look — jaded, sated and world weary — is irresistible in a rock'n'roll star.

DRESS RIGHT. Speaking of looks, note that your clothes, physical adornments and such can be as important to your overall impact as your amps. From Presley to Boy George, the greatest pop heroes have exhibited a natural propensity toward sartorial extravagance. They sport finery that makes Liberace look like a delivery boy. And not just onstage either. You'll find that there's no better way to make civilians sit up and take notice than to walk into a room wearing dreadlocks, a Hasidic hat and billowing muumuu. Besides, people expect this sort of thing from a rock star, and the mere fact that you do it will help to convince them that that's what you are.

TAKIN' CARE OF BUSINESS. After you've been around for a while, you're bound to be approached by one or another self-styled rock tycoon who wants to look after your money and make you a star. As you will soon discover, the kind of people who are attracted to this game tend to play rough. Consequently, rating them is usually a matter of deciding who's bad and who's worse. But if — like most rock musicians — you're the sensitive type, you'll probably want the lowest animal you can find to mind the store. After all, it's a jungle out there. And anyway, you can always think up some excuse to bounce your mentor once you've made it big. But until you do, just make sure he's not doing unto you what you pay him to do unto everyone else.

CONTROVERSY. Never underestimate the power of hype — be it the kind displayed in the trades or the kind that comes packaged in *Rolling Stone*. In the former, you must be accessible — playing the part of the gracious, business-conscious star. This will mean schmoozing with Kal Rudman and stopping by record company conventions and radio stations to have your picture taken with deejays and industry types. Interviews in rock fanzines, on the other hand, should stress your outlaw image, touching on the various unsavory rumors that surround your decadent life-style. (If there are no such rumors, get some into circulation fast.) You will, of course, be required to spend some time dissecting your music — drum solos and all — in pieces of this sort, but those ho-hum interludes can be livened up with a few non sequiturs and an outrageous statement here and there. Ideally, the photographs that accompany such an article should show you in the nude or brandishing a gun. Or both. And remember, there's no such thing as bad publicity as far as a rock star is concerned — unless it's the revelation that he's traded the chaos of life on the road for home, family and domestic bliss.

FAN CLUBS. Groupies, like stretch limos and cocaine, are a standard part of the trappings of rock stardom. You'll know you're on your way once you start to find a sampling of the local talent waiting for you after a show. Even though you're dead tired and have a 7 A.M. plane to catch, pick out a few and take them back to your hotel. (It's bad for your image if you don't. Word gets around fast.) Once there, prove to them that your sexy image is no mere pose — even though it may mean contracting strains of venereal disease even the army hasn't heard of yet.

SIN AND EXCESS. Carousing with the local groupie brigade is just one of the many temptations that will entice you as you climb the ladder of rock success. Go right ahead and enjoy them. Don't worry if your self-indulgent habits start to interfere with your work and your private life. Your fans will stick with you — for a while anyway. In fact, they'll probably enjoy watching the fireworks as you blaze brightly and burn out. You, on the other hand, may find that the legal hassles, breakdowns, police harassment and financial drain that inevitably result from this kind of excessive behavior can get to be a nuisance after a while.

BAILING OUT. When this happens, you have two choices of action. You can either clean up your act or go with the flow and gear up for immortality. For those rock stars who opt to hang around a little while longer, a clean-up usually necessitates some sort of spiritual rebirth. If you're lucky, you might get enough material out of your conversion for an LP.

IF NOT GOD THEN THE MOVIES. If religion isn't the answer to your problems, you may find salvation from overindulgence, sagging record sales and too many one-nighters by becoming a movie star. Kris Kristofferson, David Bowie, Roger Daltrey, Bette Midler and Ringo Starr are only a few of many pop darlings who have successfully made the transition from music to the silver screen. (And we all know where movie stardom can lead, don't we? Straight to the White House, that's where.) If not the movies, try the soaps. Ten years ago, Rick Springfield was an out-of-work pre-teen idol; today he's a full-fledged rock star. As you no doubt know, Rick has *General Hospital* to thank for resuscitating his career.

PLAN AHEAD. The lifespan of a juke-box hero is nothing it not brief. If you're smart, you'll start planning for the future while you're still on top. Collect some real estate like Don Henley, Donna Summer and Rod Stewart. Acquire a soccer team like Peter Frampton and Elton John. Invest in oil wells like Bob Dylan or shrimp farms like Pink Floyd. Become a mink rancher like Ted Nugent. Buy yourself a small California town as did Barry Manilow. Or endorse designer jeans like Debbie Harry, Willie Nelson and Roy Orbison. At least that way you won't have to resort to rock'n'roll revivals and endless comebacks to keep yourself solvent when the rock merry-go-round finally comes to a halt. But remember, no matter how you decide to spend the rest of your life — be it as a business tycoon, born-again convert, screen idol or President of the United States — it's bound to be anticlimactic once you've been a rock'n'roll star.

Get yourself . . .

a gimmick

Screamin' Jay Hawkins   The Turbans   Tiny Tim

Jobriath

Sam the Sham   Leo Sayer   The Brains   Root Boy Slim   The Brides of Funkenstein

Orion   The Hello People   The Dream Express   The Bus Boys   Devo

(Or copy a sure thing)

Liverpool   The Monkees   The Knack   Kiss

some fancy threads

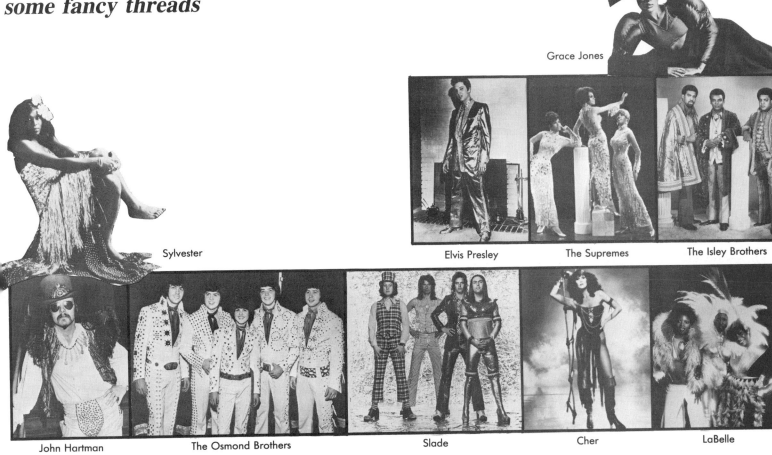

Grace Jones

Sylvester

Elvis Presley

The Supremes

The Isley Brothers

John Hartman

The Osmond Brothers

Slade

Cher

LaBelle

Graham Central Station

Roxy Music

Rick James

The Split Enz

The B-52's

an industry bigwig to chart your career

Ruth Brown with Ahmet Ertegun and Jerry Wexler

Phil Spector and the Ronettes

Berry Gordy with Paul Williams of the Temps

Don Kirshner with Carole King and Gerry Goffin

Master the basics of rock'n'roll showmanship

take off your shirt . . .

Cher

Mark Farner   Iggy Pop   Alice Cooper

Jim Dandy   David Lee Roth   Freddy Mercury

show off your assets

Ian Anderson

make it look hard

Jimi Hendrix   Duane Allman   Carlos Santana   Keith Moon   Larry Graham   Robin Trower

Elton John   Todd Rundgren   Pat Simmons   Bob Marley   Rick Neilson   Willy DeVille

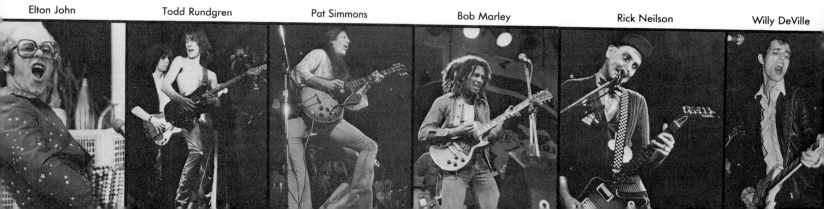

And don't be afraid to look like an idiot

Ozzy Osbourne

Todd Rundgren   The Village People   Roy Wood

Elephant's Memory   Alice Cooper   Parliament Funkadelics   The Surf Punks   Bootsy Collins

Keep telling everyone you're a genius   or a stud

Frank Zappa

Rod Stewart

and pretty soon they'll believe it

And if at first you don't succeed

try,   *try*   *again*

David Johansen

Come on funky . . .

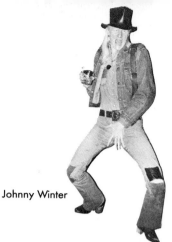

Johnny Winter

Roxy Music

but play the game

A young Paul Anka
autographs a baby

Jack Scott accepts a gold
record for "My True Love"
from Dick Clark

Roger Daltrey with columnist Earl Wilson

Michael Jackson with Jane Fonda
and Quincy Jones

Patti Smith and Lenny Kaye

Make sure to be seen with the right crowd

Rudy Vallee and Tiny Tim

Alice Cooper and Salvador Dali

David Bowie, Art Garfunkel, Paul Simon, Yoko Ono,
John Lennon and Roberta Flack at the Grammy Awards

Andy Warhol, Sylvia Miles
and Olivia Newton-John

Rod Stewart, Britt
Ekland and soccer star Pele

Rick Derringer, Edgar Winter,
Andy Warhol, Ted Nugent,
Johnny Winter and Truman
Capote

John Denver and the Muppets

Michael Jackson and E.T.

Stay forever young

Menudo

Invest your money in furs

Diana Ross

jewelry

The bejeweled fingers of Fats Domino

fancy cars

Janis Joplin

Rod Stewart

Elton John

and the house of your dreams

Elvis Presley at Graceland

When life on the road gets to be a grind,

find a nice, old-fashioned girl to help you pass the time

Alice Cooper and friend

Bored with stardom?

get busted

Mick Jagger under arrest for
drug possession in 1966

Wendy O. Williams in a skirmish
with the Milwaukee police force

get crazy

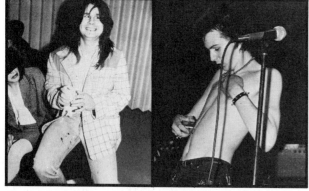

Ozzy Osbourne bites the head
off a live pigeon to enliven the
festivities at a record company
shindig

Sid Vicious cuts himself with a
broken glass during a
performance

get religion

Little Richard in 1959

The Beatles with Maharishi
Mahesh Yogi

John McLaughlin with a pinup of
Sri Chinmoy

get into the movies

Elvis Presley with Richard Egan and
Debra Paget in *Love Me Tender*

Mick Jagger in *Performance*

David Bowie in *The Man Who
Fell to Earth*

Diana Ross in *Lady
Sings the Blues*

Bob Dylan in *Pat Garrett and
Billy the Kid*

Rita Coolidge and Kris Kristofferson in
Pat Garrett and Billy the Kid

Curtis Mayfield in *Short Eyes*

or the Country & Western scene

Sonny James   Conway Twitty   Jerry Lee Lewis   Brenda Lee

retire. (You can always change your mind.)

Elton John

But if you really want to ensure your place in the Rock Hall of Fame,

Johnny Ace   Buddy Holly   Ritchie Valens   Big Bopper   Eddie Cochran   Sam Cooke

Jimi Hendrix   Janis Joplin   Jim Morrison   Keith Relf   Duane Allman   Bobby Darin

Robbie McIntosh   Al Wilson   Mama Cass Elliot   Brian Cole   Paul Kossoff   Pigpen McKernan

Phil Ochs   Rory Storme   Jim Croce   Marc Bolan   Ronnie Van Zant   Minnie Riperton

Dinah Washington   Frankie Lymon   Clyde McPhatter   Tammi Terrell   Otis Redding   Brian Jones

Florence Ballard   Tim Buckley   Chuck Willis   Gram Parsons   Gene Vincent   Elvis Presley

Keith Moon   Carl Radle   Donny Hathaway   Sid Vicious   Lowell George   Tim Hardin

Bob Hite   John Lennon   Bob Marley   Karen Carpenter   Jackie Wilson   Dennis Wilson

cash in your chips while you're still ahead of the game.

THE END

INDEX

Aerosmith, 104–105
Allman, Duane, 15, 20, 201, 238
Allman, Gregg, 15, 20, 100, 201, 239
Anderson, Ian, 61
Anka, Paul, 11, 58, 59, 88, 142, 176, 179
Ant, Adam, 58, 79, 146, 183
Avalon, Frankie, 45, 63, 72, 80, 88, 89

Baez, Joan, 11, 49, 92–93, 168–169
Balin, Marty, 8, 15
Ballard, Florence, 142, 208
Beach Boys, 140, 142, 221, 225, 227, 233
Beatles, 47, 54, 55, 65, 74, 76, 80, 94, 96–98, 104, 184, 227, 229; *Hard Day's Night*, 139; album covers, 149–151, 152. *See also individual members*
Benton, Barbi, 131
Berry, Chuck, 10, 19, 20, 44, 54, 72, 142, 163, 227, 230
Big Bopper (J. P. Richardson), 190–191
Black Sabbath, 57
Bloomfield, Mike, 220
Bolan, Mark, 212
Bono, Sonny, 100, 180
Bowie, David, 19, 42, 48, 49, 54, 57, 66–67, 170, 240, 241, 243; album covers, 158; songs, 183
Boy George, 50, 79
Brown, James, 24, 56, 142
Buckley, Tim, 209
Byrnes, Edd ("Kookie"), 108, 110–111, 114

Cassidy, David, 16, 103
Cassidy, Shawn, 16
Checker, Chubby, 20, 135
Cher, 19, 42, 47, 55, 56, 59, 100, 180, 207, 239
Chess, Leonard, 69, 230
Clapton, Eric, 8, 55, 178, 226, 229, 238
Clark, Dick, 71–72, 89
Clark, Petula, 55
Cochran, Eddie, 82, 135, 172, 191, 200
Cocker, Joe, 237
Cooke, Sam, 192
Cooper, Alice, 8, 17, 107, 157, 225, 229
Costello, Elvis, 20
Cowsills, 102–103
Creedence Clearwater Revival, 183
Croce, Jim, 203
Curry, Tim, 105

Daltrey, Roger, 16, 61, 77, 227, 243
Darin, Bobby, 88, 89, 204
Dash, Sarah, 28
Dave Clark Five, 94, 139
DeFrancos, 102
Denver, John, 14
Dion (DiMucci), 174, 227
Doors, 198–199
Donner, Ral, 82, 87
Donovan, 13, 227, 229
Dylan, Bob, 11, 42, 46, 48, 51, 55, 60, 73, 82, 92–93, 163, 228, 243; movies, 142–143, 144; songs, 167–169, 182

Eden, Barbara, 114
Elliot, Cass, 207

Epstein, Brian, 74, 76, 94, 163–164, 182, 203
Esquerita, 91
Eurythmics, 50

Fabares, Shelley, 113
Fabian, 80, 88–89, 139
Faithfull, Marianne, 21, 55, 77, 236
Field, Sally, 114
Fifth Dimension, 29, 101
Fleetwood, Mick, 58
Fogerty, John, 183
Frampton, Peter, 16, 225–226
Francis, Connie, 45, 55, 59, 139
Franklin, Aretha, 226
Freed, Alan, 71, 90, 144, 162
Funicello, Annette, 45, 55, 59, 108, 112, 140, 176, 179

Gaye, Marvin, 54, 75, 181, 197, 223
Geldof, Bob, 104, 105
George, Lowell, 16, 214
Gordy, Berry, 46, 75, 103, 197, 208, 222
Graham, Bill, 78
Grateful Dead, 175, 225
Grossman, Albert, 73, 80, 182, 196

Haley, Bill, 217
Hardin, Tim, 216
Harrison, George, 13, 60, 74, 173, 175, 178, 182–183, 203, 229
Harry, Debbie, 8, 21, 41, 50, 51
Hathaway, Donny, 213
Hendrix, Jimi, 8, 14, 29, 56, 58, 155, 177, 195, 218
Hendryx, Nona, 12, 28
Hickman, Dwayne, 114
Holly, Buddy, 10, 23, 51, 82, 144, 172, 190–191
Humperdinck, Engelbert, 101

Jackson 5, 102–103
Jackson, Michael, 17, 58, 59, 102, 103, 183, 228
Jan and Dean, 232
Jagger, Mick, 13, 42, 57, 61, 77, 78, 104, 105, 142, 152–153, 158, 236; publicity, 161; songs, 170–171, 194. *See also* Rolling Stones
James, Etta, 61, 69, 80, 225, 231
Jobriath, 107
Joel, Billy, 19, 40, 179, 226
Johansen, David, 104
John, Elton, 14, 51, 57, 58, 145, 227
Jones, Brian, 13, 194, 218. *See also* Rolling Stones
Jones, Grace, 49
Jones, Tom, 59
Joplin, Janis, 14, 56, 73, 80, 196, 218

Kath, Terry, 214
Khan, Chaka, 19
Klein, Allen, 74, 76, 77, 183
Kossoff, Paul, 208
Kristofferson, Kris, 15, 19, 181, 243

Labelle, Patti, 28, 49

Lambert, Christopher ("Kit"), 77
Led Zeppelin, 217
Lee, Brenda, 8, 10, 45, 55
Lennon, John, 13, 51, 76, 82, 151, 163–164, 173, 203; death, 218; songs, 180, 182–185
Lewis, Jerry Lee, 19, 45, 54, 71, 72, 85, 160, 225, 227
Little Anthony and the Imperials, 90
Little Richard, 19, 44, 56, 90, 91, 135, 147, 225, 227–229, 230
Lydon, John, 50, 79
Lymon, Frankie, 90, 135, 193
Lynyrd Skynyrd, 157, 212

McCartney, Paul, 13, 173, 177, 180, 182–183, 203
McIntosh, Robbie, 207
McKernan, Ron, 205
McLaren, Malcolm, 79
McPhatter, Clyde, 207
Mamas and Papas, 101
Mansfield, Jayne, 138
Manilow, Barry, 16, 61
Marley, Bob, 56, 219, 225
Midler, Bette, 19, 243
Mineo, Sal, 122
Mitchell, Joni, 166–167, 179
Monkees, 96, 139
Moon, Keith, 213. *See also* Who
Morrison, Jim, 198–199, 241

Nelson, Rick, 10, 80, 84, 108, 174
Nelson, Willie, 19
New York Dolls, 104–105
Nugent, Ted, 57, 61

Ochs, Phil, 59, 206
Oldham, Andrew Loog, 77, 170, 236
Ono, Yoko, 17, 151, 173, 180, 184–185
Orbison, Roy, 51, 59, 82, 139, 176, 243
Osmond Brothers, 102–103
Osmond, Donny, 100
Osmond, Marie, 100

Parker, Graham, 51
Parker, Colonel Tom, 70, 76, 83, 84, 86, 138, 149, 162, 211, 217
Parsons, Gram, 205
Pendergrass, Teddy, 29
Perkins, Carl, 58, 80, 86
Peter, Paul and Mary, 80
Phillips, John, 234
Pop, Iggy, 241
Presley, Elvis, 10, 19, 42, 45, 51, 54, 55, 59, 61–63, 66, 70, 78, 162, 172, 180, 225, 227; album covers, 149; death, 210–211, 218; imitators/successors, 81–87; movies, 138–139; TV, 142

Redding, Otis, 193
Reed, Lou, 240
Relf, Keith, 201
Richards, Keith, 13, 60, 161, 170–171, 194, 205, 225, 231
Riperton, Minnie, 28
Robinson, Smokey, 29

Rodgers, Jimmie, 232
Rolling Stones, 48, 60, 74, 77, 78, 80, 94, 104, 142, 151, 161, 194; album covers, 149, 152–153, 158; movies, 143, 145. *See also individual members*
Ronettes, 46, 55
Ronstadt, Linda, 15, 19, 67, 80, 81
Ross, Diana, 14, 75, 140, 142, 208
Rotten, Johnny, 50, 51, 79, 109, 215
Russell, Leon, 179
Rydell, Bobby, 88, 89

Sainte-Marie, Buffy, 49, 81, 93, 149
Sands, Tommy, 83, 88, 162
Sedaka, Neil, 45, 176
Sex Pistols, 21, 42, 50, 79, 215
Shangri-Las, 46
Simon, Carly, 56, 167, 179, 181
Sinatra, Frank, 88
Slick, Grace, 8, 14, 56, 235
Smith, Patti, 8, 17
Spanky and Our Gang, 101
Spector, Phil, 162–163
Springsteen, Bruce, 8, 16, 41
Starr, Ringo, 13, 19, 59, 182, 203, 243
Stevens, Connie, 55, 110–111
Stewart, Rod, 15, 20, 57, 58, 59, 61, 175, 227, 243
Stone, Sly, 234
Storme, Rory, 203
Strange, Steve, 50
Stray Cats, 50, 58
Supremes, 46, 75, 142, 208

Terrell, Tammi, 197
Tillotson, Johnny, 45
Tiny Tim, 108
Tosh, Peter, 56, 219
Townshend, Peter, 16, 57, 77, 163, 213, 225, 227
Travolta, John, 49, 120
Turner, Ike, 54
Turner, Tina, 54, 145
Twitty, Conway, 85

Valens, Ritchie, 190–191
Van Halen, 57
Van Zant, Ronnie, 212
Vicious, Sid, 215
Vincent, Gene, 82, 83, 200

Washington, Dinah, 192
West, Adam, 114
Who, 77, 94. *See also individual members*
Williams, Larry, 90, 216
Williams, Paul, 202
Williams, Wendy O., 21, 58
Wilson, Al, 197
Wilson, Brian, 12, 221, 225, 227, 233
Wilson, Dennis, 221, 233
Wilson, Jackie, 222, 225
Wonder, Stevie, 12, 51, 56, 75, 140

Zappa, Frank, 14, 20, 21, 107, 214

Penny Stallings' first job after leaving college was as one of the site coordinators for the Woodstock festival. She also produced the RSO roadshow company tour of *Jesus Christ Superstar*. She is the author of *Flesh and Fantasy* and was the managing editor of *Titters: The First Collection of Humor by Women*. She writes for several magazines and newspapers and is currently planning a record duet with Julio Iglesias.

Photo by Marjory Dressler

Art Direction and Design: Penny Stallings
Art Production, Coordination, Tromp l'oeil
    and Layout: Peggy Goddard
Research: Minda Novek, Alan Betrock
Edited by: Beth Rashbaum, Barry Secunda
Copyedited: Mike Mattil
Additional Material by: David Fricke
Illustrations: Bat Lash and Harold Monteil
Lettering: Stan Levy
Airbrushing: Dennis Critchlow
Typesetting: Crane Typesetting Service
Camera work and film: Jay's Publishers Services Inc.
Special Thanks to Those People Who Made This Book Possible: Gary Kenton; Pat Baird; Barbara Burns; Carol Green; Alfred Secunda; Beth Rashbaum; Barry Secunda; Peter Kanze; Peggy Goddard; Peter Carr; Mike Mattil; Connie Kramer; and Jeannie Abboud.

Additional Thanks To: Faye Rosen; Jo Bergman; Bob Furmenak; Howard Mandelbaum; Carlos Clarens; Paula Klaw; Ira Kramer; Doug Stump; Mary Evans; Ginger Barber; Harold Monteil; Bat Lash; Malka Moskowits; Kenny Kneitel; Jerry Wexler; Barry Taylor; Adrian Goddard; Frank Rose; Skye Gibson; Claude Lee; Marty at Ad-link; Golden Oldies; Nancy Lewis; Vicki Wickham; Nona Hendryx; Bob Pook; Helena Bruno; Peter Bochan; David Cherichetti; Connie Kaplan; Rick Mitz; Gilda Radner; Mary Moore; Bibi Green; Tisha Feinman; House of Oldies; Judy Hart; David Fricke; Mark del Costello; Barbara Hohol; Ken Viola; Josephine Mangiaracinia; Lynne Kellerman; Ray D'Ariano; Michael Marks; Charles Auringer; Mrs. Daisy Thomas; Al Stekler; Ruth Kolbert; Ellen Pelissaro; Ann Marie; Bob Rigere; Bob Merlis; Dusty Springfield; Eric Bergerson; Joan Hyler; Joan Bullard; Nancy LaViska; David Levine; Anne Beatts; Barry Brennan; Joe Orlando; Frank Driggs; Vicki Gold Levi; Linda Mitchell Kemp; Helen Roberts; Jerry Brandt; Carol Shookhoff; Stan Levy; Janie James; Steve Humphrey; Judy Kennedy; Gene Winik; Ike Williams; Louise Gikow; Marilise Flusser; Suzanne de Paas; Miss Pamela; Susan Blonde; Mitchell Glazer; Bill Smart; Village Oldies; Rod Swenson; Paul Chevannes; Dr. Mark Rowe; Terry Baker; Jess Brallier; David Goehring; Jay Levy; Dr. Demento; Ellen LeBrun; Joe Crowley, Jay Crowley, Bob Hillis, Al Baxter, and Lynda Warren of Jay's; Dennis Loren; Ralph Newman; Peter Hay; Keith Sluchansky; Al Merz; Megan Griffith; Betsy Round; Debbie Roth; Bill German; Sandy Charon; Steven Kelly; Myra Friedman; Lewis Cason; Virginia Lohly; Billy Wolfe; and Michael O'Donoghue for help with the last line of Rock'n'Roll Heaven.

PHOTO CREDITS

MCA — 10, ll, 14, 16, 45, 52, 53, 59, 60, 61, 157, 172, 190, 212, 217, 244, 246, 248, 249, 251, 252; Warner Bros. Records — 10, 11, 12, 13, 14, 15, 16, 17, 20, 23, 26, 28, 29, 30, 32, 35, 36, 41, 46, 47, 48, 49, 50, 53, 55, 56, 57, 58, 59, 60, 61, 63, 66, 88, 89, 92, 93, 106, 111, 122, 123, 130, 174, 175, 180, 181, 182, 205, 206, 207, 209, 212, 214, 216, 220, 228, 233, 236, 239, 244, 245, 246, 247, 248, 249, 252, 253; Capitol Records — 11, 20, 35, 41, 47, 53, 91, 94, 96, 98, 99, 123, 128, 179, 218, 244, 246, 252, 253; CAM INT. — 16, 39; David Cherichetti Collection — 134; 135; *Creem* magazine — 13, 17, 38, 49, 54, 58, 61, 66, 182, 183, 194, 195, 197, 198, 199, 200, 203, 217, 218, 227, 233, 236, 237, 238, 245, 246, 247, 250, 252, 253; *Crawdaddy* magazine — 15, 17; ABC Paramount — 103; Gary Kenton Collection — 11, 17, 34, 38, 46, 51, 55, 92, 93, 104, 230, 233, 246, 248, 252; Epic Records — 6, 7, 94, 183, 247, 248; Alan Betrock Collection — 31, 33, 36, 38, 46, 55, 65, 92, 96, 97, 106, 112, 121, 138, 139, 150, 151, 152, 153, 156, 164, 170, 172, 182, 244; Bob Furmenak — 114, 115, 118, 119, 120, 124, 125, 126, 127, 129; CMA — 56; Phototeque — 13, 17, 25, 32, 44, 58, 124, 136, 137, 138, 141, 147, 173, 210, 228, 245, 254; Movie Star News — 11, 13, 30, 45, 51, 52, 55, 59, 60, 62, 65, 71, 78, 83, 84, 86, 87, 88, 90, 91, 100, 101, 122, 125, 132, 134, 135, 136, 137, 141, 142, 162, 163, 169, 171, 172, 174, 177, 178, 210, 218, 244, 249, 251; Peter Kanze Collection — 23, 24, 26, 28, 34, 44, 47, 63, 64, 65, 68, 71, 89, 145, 146, 155, 176, 180, 200, 206, 231, 232, 233, 238, 244, 245, 252; Gary Theroux Collection — 63, 87, 103, 106, 110, 111, 120, 121, 125, 126, 128, 168, 169, 172, 174, 176, 177, 179, 183, 210; MGM Records — 12; *New York Rocker* — 66, 67, 105, 241; *Record World* — 18, 21, 26, 28, 29, 30, 32, 33, 34, 35, 39, 44, 48, 49, 51, 53, 54, 55, 56, 60, 63, 64, 90, 91, 92, 93, 97, 98, 102, 103, 104, 105, 107, 168, 170, 171, 172, 173, 174, 176, 177, 179, 180, 181, 183, 190, 192, 193, 196, 200, 202, 203, 207, 210, 214, 216, 220, 226, 229, 232, 235, 244, 245, 247, 248, 252, 253; Columbia; CBS Records — 12, 14, 26, 28, 36, 41, 50, 52, 56, 59, 75, 92, 93, 114, 127, 169, 229, 233, 247, 248, 253; RCA — 10, 11, 17, 22, 23, 45, 48, 50, 51, 52, 53, 54, 57, 66, 67, 68, 94, 100, 107, 122, 127, 180, 240, 248, 249, 252; Atlantic—48, 93, 104; Motown Records — 12, 14, 17, 46, 49, 51, 54, 59, 64, 68, 75, 102, 181, 197, 204, 208, 245, 249, 253; NBC — 93, 95, 115, 120, 146, 210, 228, 244; Chrysallis Records — 50, 61; Schomberg Library — 90, 91, 193, 250, 253; Island Records — 56, 79, 130, 208, 219, 236, 244; MOMA Still Collection — 85, 136, 137, 141, 191, 204, 210, 251, 253; Polydor — 24, 56, 57; Mercury Records — 53, 105; United Artists — 114; CBS-TV — 147; Wide World — 70, 230; UPI — 175; Peter Bochan Collection — 191, 200; ABC-TV — 10, 52, 68, 72, 100, 101, 102, 110, 114, 121, 147, 173, 244; A&M Records — 16, 253; Mark Del Costello — 61; Golden Oldies — 25, 30, 112, 114, 116, 122, 124, 125, 128, 148; ABKCO — 53; Faye Rosen — 15, 39; Lincoln Center Library For The Performing Arts — 71, 88; Aaron Neville/Linda Lee Yoshimura — 12; Nona Hendryx/Vicki Wickham — 12; Ode Records — 18; Dick Dale — 21; Acuff-Rose — 22; Don Larson — 23; Disc and That — 25; *Goldmine* magazine — 26; Pat Baird — 31; John Fisher — 72; Trinifold — 76; Ronnie Campagna — 237, 238; Walt Disney Productions — 128; ATI Agency — 107; Michael O'Donoghue — 125; Lee Blumer — 128; Peggy Goddard — 154; Baron Wolman — 177; Geffen Records — 185, 218; Memory Shop — 190; *Sepia* magazine — 192; Jerry Ohlinger — 204, 252; Mary Wilson—208; New York Public Library — 212, 247, 248, 251, 252, 253; Richard Nader — 217; Soul Publications — 231; Kitty Hawk Graphics — 232; Magna Artists — 233; Arista Records — 241, 244; Sun Records — 244; Casablanca Records — 246; Starfile — 247; XYZ Productions — 248; Rex Features — 76; Leee Black Childers — 241; Universal Pictures — 14.

Cover Photos: Dr. Mark Rowe; Movie Star News; Casablanca Records; Epic Records